John Griffiths

Enactments in Parliament, specially concerning the universities of Oxford and Cambridge

John Griffiths

Enactments in Parliament, specially concerning the universities of Oxford and Cambridge

ISBN/EAN: 9783337152024

Printed in Europe, USA, Canada, Australia, Japan

Cover: Foto ©Paul-Georg Meister /pixelio.de

More available books at **www.hansebooks.com**

ENACTMENTS IN PARLIAMENT

SPECIALLY CONCERNING

THE UNIVERSITIES OF

OXFORD AND CAMBRIDGE

COLLECTED AND ARRANGED

BY THE

REV. JOHN GRIFFITHS, M.A.

KEEPER OF THE ARCHIVES OF THE
UNIVERSITY OF OXFORD

OXFORD

AT THE CLARENDON PRESS

M.DCCC.LXIX.

PREFACE.

This volume is intended to contain such Acts of Parliament, or portions of Acts, now in force, as concern in some especial way the two Universities of Oxford and Cambridge, or either of those bodies, or any of their Colleges.

In compiling it, the rule of selection has been to print those enactments only which have their application clearly shewn by the term "College" or "University" or some other academical word occurring in them.

An exception to this rule, apparent rather than real, may be found, whenever any Act extending or modifying some previous enactment, which was couched in precise language, is itself expressed in general terms. But two real exceptions to it have been admitted, 39 Geo. 3, c. 73, and 3 & 4 Will. 4, c. 31; because these

Acts, though applying to all bodies corporate, appear to have a peculiar interest for Oxford and Cambridge. The former exempts from legacy duty all bequests of books, pictures, or other specific articles, given in order to be kept and preserved: the other forbids the holding of elections, the admission of officers, and the performance of similar duties on Sunday.

On the other hand, no attempt has been made to gather together the numerous private Acts which have been obtained for the sale or exchange of lands or other estates.

The first two Acts in the collection are printed from the original Rolls of Parliament. Then to the end of the reign of Queen Anne the text follows the authentic edition of the Statutes of the Realm in nine volumes folio, which was prepared under the direction of the Commissioners on Public Records. The remainder, that is, all the volume after the first 64 pages, is given from the authorised copies issued by the King's or Queen's Printers. Wherever the note *So in orig.* occurs in the margin, indicating a belief that there is some error in the text, these are the originals intended by the note.

Pains have been taken to make the Index full, and yet to keep it free from repetition. For this purpose a classification of subjects has been adopted, which use will soon make familiar.

Circumstances, which need not be related, have made the passage of the volume through the press very slow; and several enactments in it have been superseded or virtually repealed by the legislation of the last Session of Parliament. The subjects of these are printed in Italic type in the following list.

In pages 24, 42, and 64, reference is made to 21 & 22 Vict. c. 48, the Act 30 & 31 Vict. c. 75 not having been passed when those pages were printed.

OXFORD,
December 14, 1868.

CORRECTIONS.

PAGE.
- **21.** Omit the Act 37 Hen. 8, c. 17; which was repealed by 26 & 27 Vict. c. 125.
- **51.** Omit the Act 12 & 13 Gul. 3, c. 11; which was repealed by 30 & 31 Vict. c. 59.
- **59.** Dele the whole of s. 2, and read instead,
  [Section 2, requiring Bishops to tender the Declaration against Transubstantiation in certain cases, is repealed by 10 Geo. 4, c. 7, s. 1.]
- **63.** Add, as a foot note on s. 5,
  So much of section 5 as relates to the Declaration against Transubstantiation is repealed by 10 Geo. 4, c. 7, s. 1.
- **73.** Add, as a foot note on 32 Geo. 2, c. 33. s. 13,
  This exemption is continued in 49 Geo. 3, c. 32, by which the duty of one shilling in the pound, first imposed on offices and employments of profit by 31 Geo. 2, c. 22, was made perpetual.
- **98.** Dele the whole of ss. 95 and 96, and read instead,
  [Sections 95 and 96 contain provisions respecting a new Market, in case one should be made by the Corporation.
- **111.** Read, as *note* a,
  The Land Tax, properly so called, was made perpetual and redeemable by 38 Geo. 3, c. 60; the continuance of the duty of four shillings in the pound, previously imposed on offices and employments of profit and other personal estate by the annual Land Tax Acts, being left to future Acts of Parliament.

  Also add, at the end of *note* c,
  The Acts of Parliament, which since 38 Geo. 3, c. 60, have continued the duty of four shillings in the pound upon offices and employments of profit, have likewise continued this exemption: see s. 21 of 6 Geo. 4, c. 9, the latest Act in which the exempting clauses have been repeated in full. The duty was made perpetual by 6 & 7 Will. 4, c. 97.
- **183.** Add, as a foot note on s. 69,
  The "arrangements" contemplated in ss. 69-71 may be made "by the authority" of the Ecclesiastical Commissioners for England. See 23 & 24 Vict. c. 59, s. 10.
- **197.** Add, as a foot note on s. 31,
  A different Local Board for the Oxford District is appointed by 21 & 22 Vict. c. 98, s. 82.
- **238.** Dele the whole of s. 48, and read instead,
  [Section 48, enabling Colleges to sell or exchange estates with the consent of the Church Estates Commissioners, is repealed by 21 & 22 Vict. c. 44, s. 5.]
- **284.** Insert at the top of the page,
  [Section 8 directs that the Members of the General Council shall be chosen for a term not exceeding five years, and shall be capable of re-appointment.
- **298.** Add, as a foot note on "eighty-four" in line 5 of s. 11,
  The Act 17 & 18 Vict. c. 84 is intituled An Act to extend the provisions of the Acts for the Augmentation of Benefices.
- **305.** Add, as a foot note on "declaration" in line 4 from the foot of the page,
  The Declaration appointed in s. 2 is superseded by another in 31 & 32 Vict. c. 65, s. 1.

SUBJECTS OF THE ENACTMENTS.

The letter *C.* or *O.* after a Subject signifies that the Enactment relates solely to Cambridge or solely to Oxford. The Enactments which have their Subjects printed in Italic type have been superseded or virtually repealed by 31 & 32 Vict. c. 72.

		PAGE
13 H. 4.	Archbishop of Canterbury's right of Visitation	1
12 & 13 E. 4. . . .	Remission of a Fee Farm Rent . . *O.*	8
14 & 15 H. 8, c. 5, s. 3. .	Privilege of Graduates in Medicine . .	10
27 H. 8, c. 42. . . .	Discharge from First Fruits and Tenths	10
33 H. 8, c. 27. . . .	Leases	19
2 & 3 E. 6, c. 1, s. 6. .	Prayers in Latin, Greek, or Hebrew . .	23
1 El. c. 1, s. 12. . .	*Oath of Supremacy*	24
1 El. c. 4, s. 7. . . .	Discharge from First Fruits and Tenths	25
13 El. c. 10.	Leases	25
13 El. c. 12, s. 5. . .	Privilege of Bachelors of Divinity . . .	27
13 El. c. 29.	Incorporation of the Universities . . .	27
14 El. c. 11, ss. 5, 7. .	Leases	32
18 El. c. 6.	Corn Rents	33
18 El. c. 11.	Leases	35
31 El. c. 6.	Elections of Fellows &c.	37
43 El. c. 4, s. 2. . .	Exemption from Charity Commissions .	40
3 J. 1, c. 5, s. 13. . .	Patronage belonging to Papists . . .	40
7 J. 1, c. 6.	*Oath of Allegiance*	42
12 C. 2, c. 34, s. 4. . .	Privilege for planting Tobacco . . .	43
14 C. 2, c. 4. . . .	Uniformity of Common Prayer . . .	43
1 W. & M. c. 8, s. 12.	*Oaths of Allegiance and Supremacy*	47
1 W. & M. c. 26, s. 2.	Patronage belonging to Papists .	48
7 & 8 W. 3, c. 37. . .	Licence of Mortmain	50

SUBJECTS OF THE ENACTMENTS.

		PAGE
10 Anne, c. 45.	Grants of Canonries &c. to Professorships of Divinity	52
13 Anne, c. 6.	Grants of Prebends to Heads of certain Colleges	55
13 Anne, c. 13.	Patronage belonging to Papists	58
1 G. 1, st. 2, c. 13.	Oaths of Allegiance, Supremacy, and Abjuration	64
9 G. 2, c. 36, s. 4.	Exemption from certain restrictions in Mortmain	67
11 G. 2, c. 17, s. 5.	Patronage belonging to Papists	68
17 G. 2, c. 40, ss. 11, 12.	Wine Licences	70
18 G. 2, c. 20, s. 15.	Qualification of Justices of the Peace	72
32 G. 2, c. 33, s. 13.	Exemption of Academical Offices from Tax	73
5 G. 3, c. 17.	Leases of Incorporeal Hereditaments	73
7 G. 3, c. 99.	Addenbrooke's Hospital . . . . C.	76
11 G. 3, c. 19, ss. 77 &c.	Oxford Market . . . . . . O.	78
12 G. 3, c. 90.	Trustees of a Turnpike Road . . . C.	83
15 G. 3, c. 53.	Copy Right in perpetuity.	84
17 G. 3, c. 53, s. 13	Loans for Residence Houses	88
21 G. 3, c. 47, ss. 25 &c.	Oxford Market . . . . . . O.	89
21 G. 3, c. 56, s. 10.	Allowance in lieu of the privilege of printing Almanacs	92
28 G. 3, c. 64.	Cambridge Improvement Act . . C.	94
31 G. 3, c. 32, s. 14.	Disabilities of Roman Catholics	350
34 G. 3, c. 104.	Cambridge Improvement Act . . C.	103
35 G. 3, c. 77.	Commissioners for Navigation of the Ouse . . . . C.	109
37 G. 3, c. 170.	Trustees of a Turnpike Road . . O.	110
37 G. 3, c. 179.	Trustees of a Turnpike Road . . C.	110
38 G. 3, c. 5, s. 25.	Exemption from Land Tax	111
39 G. 3, c. 73.	Exemption from Legacy Duty	112
39 G. 3, c. 79, ss. 22, 24.	Academical Lectures: University Presses	113
39 & 40 G. 3, c. 41.	Leases	113
42 G. 3, c. 90, s. 43.	Exemption from serving in the Militia	119
42 G. 3, c. 116, ss. 17, 78.	Redemption of Land Tax	119
46 G. 3, c. cxlvii.	Warden of Wadham College may be married . . . . O.	121
47 G. 3, sess. 2, c. lx.	Protection of Watercourse . . . C.	122
52 G. 3, c. 102, s. 11.	Exemption from Registration of Charitable Donations	124
52 G. 3, c. lxxii.	Oxford Mileways . . . . . O.	125

SUBJECTS OF THE ENACTMENTS. xi

		PAGE
52 G. 3, c. cxli, ss. 43, 44.	Protection of Hobson's Conduit . . *C.*	125
55 G. 3, c. 147, s. 9. . .	Loans for purchasing Glebe Land . .	129
55 G. 3, c. 184. . . .	Stamp Duty on Certificates of Degrees .	130
55 G. 3, c. 194, s. 29. .	Privilege in respect of Apothecaries . .	130
55 G. 3, c. xlix. . . .	Trustees of a Turnpike Road . . . *C.*	131
56 G. 3, c. 136. . . .	Removal of Magdalen Hall to site of Hertford College . . . . . *O.*	132
58 G. 3, c. lxiv, ss. 11 &c.	Oxford Gas Company . . . . . *O.*	135
5 G. 4, c. 36, ss. 4, 5. . .	Loans of public money for enlarging Colleges	140
6 G. 4, c. 97.	Constables: Prostitutes at Oxford . .	142
7 & 8 G. 4, c. 75. . . .	Commissioners of Land Tax	144
7 & 8 G. 4, c. xlvii. . .	Navigation Commissioners of Rivers in the Bedford Level . . . . . *C.*	144
7 & 8 G. 4, c. cxi, s. 56. .	Saving of Privileges . . . . . *C.*	145
9 G. 4, c. 61, s. 36. . .	Privilege in respect of licensing Alehouses	145
10 G. 4, c. 7, s. 16. . .	Disabilities of Roman Catholics . . .	146
11 G. 4 & 1 W. 4, c. 64, s. 29.	Privilege in respect of licensing Alehouses	146
1 W. 4, c. 5.	Removal of Botanic Garden at Cambridge to a better site . . . . *C.*	147
1 & 2 W. 4, c. 45. . . .	Augmentation of Vicarages &c. . . .	148
2 & 3 W. 4, c. 45, s. 78. .	Exemption from the Reform Act . .	158
2 & 3 W. 4, c. 80. . . .	Identification of Lands	159
3 & 4 W. 4, c. 31. . . .	Prohibition of Elections &c. on Sunday	163
5 & 6 W. 4, c. 62, ss. 6, 8. .	*Substitution of Declarations for Oaths* .	165
5 & 6 W. 4, c. 63, s. 44. .	Privilege in respect of Weights and Measures	166
5 & 6 W. 4, c. 65, s. 5. . .	Publication of Lectures without leave .	167
5 & 6 W. 4, c. 76, s. 137. .	Exemption from Municipal Reform Act .	167
5 & 6 W. 4, c. lxix, ss. 11 &c.	Oxford Market . . . . . . *O.*	169
6 & 7 W. 4, c. 105, s. 12. .	Power to appoint the Vice-Chancellor of Cambridge a Justice of the Peace for the Town . . . . *C.*	173
1 & 2 V. c. 23. s. 5. . .	Loans for Residence Houses	174
1 & 2 V. c. 106, ss. 37 &c.	Exemptions from Residence on Benefices	175
2 & 3 V. c. 12.	Printing	177
2 & 3 V. c. ix, s. 11. . .	Saving of Privileges . . . . . *C.*	179
3 & 4 V. c. 77. s. 24. .	Exemption from Grammar Schools Act	179

		PAGE
3 & 4 V. c. 113, ss. 5 &c.	Cathedral Dignities and Patronage, &c.	180
5 & 6 V. c. 14, ss. 14 &c.	Inspectors of Corn Returns	183
5 & 6 V. c. 35.	Allowances in respect of Property Tax	186
5 & 6 V. c. 45, ss. 8 &c.	Delivery of Books for certain Libraries	187
6 & 7 V. c. 68, ss. 10 &c.	Theatres	189
6 & 7 V. c. x, ss. 304 &c.	Great Western Railway . . . . O.	190
7 & 8 V. c. lxii, ss. 184 &c.	Eastern Counties Railway . . . C.	193
9 & 10 V. c. 95, s. 140.	Exemption from County Court Act .	196
9 & 10 V. c. clxxii, ss. 33 &c.	Eastern Counties Railway . . . C.	196
11 & 12 V. c. 63, ss. 31 &c.	Local Boards of Health.	196
13 & 14 V. c. 98, ss. 5, 6.	Restriction of Preferments tenable by Heads of Colleges	199
13 & 14 V. c. xxxvii, s. 51.	Saving of Privileges . . . . C.	200
14 & 15 V. c. 36.	House Tax on College Rooms.	201
14 & 15 V. c. xcii, ss. 14 &c.	Navigation of the Cam . . . . C.	201
16 & 17 V. c. 68.	Elections to Parliament	205
16 & 17 V. c. 137, s. 62.	Exemption from Charitable Trusts Act	206
16 & 17 V. c. xxiii, ss. 14, 50.	Cambridge Waterworks Company . C.	207
17 & 18 V. c. 81.	Oxford University Reform . . . O.	208
17 & 18 V. c. ccxix.	Oxford Poor Rates . . . . . O.	217
18 & 19 V. c. 36.	Remission of Stamp Duties . . O.	227
19 & 20 V. c. 31.	Oxford University Reform . . . O.	228
19 & 20 V. c. 88.	Cambridge University Reform . C.	229
19 & 20 V. c. xvii.	Cambridge Award Act . . . C.	241
20 & 21 V. c. 25.	Oxford University Reform . . . O.	253
21 & 22 V. c. 11.	Remission of Stamp Duties . . C.	255
21 & 22 V. c. 44.	Universities and College Estates Act, 1858	256
21 & 22 V. c. 90, ss. 3 &c.	General Council of Medical Education	283
21 & 22 V. c. 98, s. 82.	Local Boards for Oxford and Cambridge Districts	285
22 & 23 V. c. 19.	Abolition of the Mayor's Oath at Oxford . . . . O.	286
22 & 23 V. c. 56, s. 11	Privilege in respect of Weights and Measures	290
23 & 24 V. c. 23.	Ordinance for St. John's College, Oxford . . . . O.	290
23 & 24 V. c. 27.	Privilege in respect of Wine Licences	291
23 & 24 V. c. 59.	Universities and College Estates Act, 1860 .	291

SUBJECTS OF THE ENACTMENTS. xiii

		PAGE
23 & 24 V. c. 91.	Craven Scholarships: Testamentary Documents . . . . . . O.	300
23 & 24 V. c. 127, ss. 2, 5.	Admission of Graduates as Attorneys or Solicitors	302
24 & 25 V. c. 9, s. 6.	Exemption from certain restrictions in Mortmain	304
24 & 25 V. c. 53.	Voting Papers	304
25 & 26 V. c. 26.	Power to make Statutes concerning certain Professorships &c. . . O.	308
27 & 28 V. c. 68, s. 3.	Qualification of University Members of the Oxford Local Board . O.	312
28 & 29 V. c. 55.	Power to make Statutes concerning the Vinerian Foundation . . O.	313
28 & 29 V. c. 108.	Local Government for the District of Oxford . . . . . O.	314
29 & 30 V. c. 59.	Commissioners of Land Tax . . O.	327
29 & 30 V. c. 89.	Electors of four Conservators of the Thames . . . . . . O.	327
30 & 31 V. c. 75, ss. 5, 6.	*Oath substituted for Oaths of Allegiance, Supremacy, and Abjuration*	328
30 & 31 V. c. 76.	Ordinance for Christ Church . . O.	329
30 & 31 V. c. 102, s. 2.	Exemption from the Reform Act .	331
30 & 31 V. c. lxxvii, ss. 39 &c.	Cambridge Gas Company . . . C.	331
31 & 32 V. c. 65.	Voting Papers	333
31 & 32 V. c. 72, ss. 8 &c.	Substitution of Declarations for Oaths	335
31 & 32 V. c. 89, s. 2.	Valuations under the Universities and College Estates Acts to be stamped	337
31 & 32 V. c. 114, s. 14.	Exemption of Christ Church from the Ecclesiastical Commission Act. O.	337
31 & 32 V. c. 118, ss. 6 &c.	Scholarships &c. connected with Public Schools	338
31 & 32 V. c. lix.	Oxford Police . . . . . O.	340

ENACTMENTS

ENACTMENTS IN PARLIAMENT.

13 HEN. IV, ROT. PARL. nu. 15.

[*Confirmatio Decreti de Visitatione Universitatis Oxoniensis ad Archiepiscopum Cantuariensem pertinenti.*]^a

PUR LERCEVESQUE DE CANTERBIRS. OXOÑ.

MEMORANDUM quod venerabilis in Christo pater Thomas Archiepiscopus Cantuariensis in presenti parliamento nostro exhibuit quandam peticionem una cum quadam cedula eidem annexa in hec verba.

A tressouereign seignor nostre seignor le Roy, Supplie humblement vostre humble Chapellein Thomas Ercevesque de Canterbirs, Que pleise a vous, tressouerein seignor, par assent des seignors espirituelx et temporelx et les Communes en cest present parlement, de grauntier, approver, ratifier, et confermer tout cco q'est compris en une cedule a iceste bille annexe; et que mesme ceste cedule puisse estre enrollee

Petitio.

---

^a This record has never before been printed accurately. As given by Prynne in "The University of Oxford's Plea refuted," pp. 20–26, from a transcript in Archbishop Parker's Register, it is full of blunders; and even in Rotuli Parliamentorum, III, 651, there are many errors. It is here printed from the original Roll of Parliament, with which, by the kindness of Thomas Duffus Hardy, Esq., Keeper of the Records, these pages have been collated while passing through the press.

et enact en cest present parlement solonc la fourme et effect de mesme la cedule; et que mesme la cedule et tout ceo q'est compris en icelle soient de ataunt de force, effect, et auctorite, et mesmes les force, effect, et auctorite eient et teignent, come ils ussent este faitz en cest parlement et par auctoritee de mesme le parlement.

Cedula. MEMORANDUM quod cum Ricardus Secundus nuper Rex Anglie, propter diversas dissensiones, lites, et discordias quondam habitas in Universitate Oxoniensi super jure et *Bulla exemptionis pretensa.* titulo visitacionis dicte Universitatis, ac de quadam bulla exempcionis pretensa ad excludendum Archiepiscopum Cantuariensem tunc existentem et successores suos, ac quoscumque alios ordinarios infra Universitatem predictam, ac quoscumque fundatores dicte Universitatis ac Collegiorum ejusdem Universitatis, a visitacione dicte Universitatis et ab omni jurisdiccione ordinaria per eosdem Archiepiscopum Ordinarios ac fundatores et suos successores ac Commissarios suos in eadem Universitate faciendis et exercendis, per breve suum venire fecerit in Cancellaria sua apud Westmonasterium bullam predictam, et Cancellarium et Procuratores dicte Universitatis adtunc existentes, sufficiens warentum sigillo communi Universitatis predicte sigillatum pro se et Universitate predicta habentes et secum in Cancellaria predicta deferentes, ad exhibendam, publicandam, ostendendam, et presentandam coram dicto nuper Rege in Cancellaria predicta bullam predictam, necnon ad respondendum ibidem et ulterius faciendum et recipiendum quod per eundem nuper Regem et consilium suum ordinatum fuisset et diffinitum; prout de recordo in eadem Cancellaria plenius liquet; ac postmodum iidem Cancellarius et Procuratores pro se et tota Universitate predicta submiserint se de materiis predictis ordinacioni et diffinicioni dicti nuper Regis:

Rex Ric. II bullae predictae Univ. Oxon. renunciare jussit: Qui quidem nuper Rex, habita inde matura et pleniori deliberacione cum consilio suo, ac clare considerans bullam predictam fore impetratam in prejudicium corone sue, ac legum et consuetudinum regni sui enervacionem, et in hereticorum et Lollardorum ac homicidarum et aliorum *Sic in MS.* malefaccorum* favorem et audaciam, dicteque Universitatis verisimilem destruccionem, ordinavit et per breve suum precepit et inhibuit dicto Cancellario, Magistris, Doctoribus, et Scolaribus Universitatis predicte, in fide, ligeancia, et dileccione quibus sibi tenebantur, ac sub pena amissionis privilegiorum Universitatis predicte, et sub forisfactura omnium aliorum que sibi forisfacere poterant, ne dictam bullam in aliqua sui parte exequi seu excercere, seu beneficium aliquod exempcionis per bullam illam aliqualiter reportare seu recipere presumerent, set omnibus exempcionibus et privilegiis in ea parte contentis coram tunc dilecto clerico suo Magistro Ricardo Ronhale (quem ad eos ex causa predicta destinavit) palam et publice pro imperpetuo renunciarent, ac super renunciatione hujusmodi quandam certificacionem sibi sub sigillo dicte Universitatis ac publica instrumenta fieri et sibi per eundem clericum suum transmitti facerent sub penis supradictis:

Postmodum allegantibus prefato Cancellario et aliis sibi adherentibus nomine Universitatis predicte visitacionem predictam ad dictum Ricardum nuper Regem solum et insolidum pertinere, consideransque quod visitacio Universitatis predicte ad prefatum Archiepiscopum et successores suos ac ad ecclesiam suam Cantuariensem pertinuit et pertinere debuit, quodque ipse aut progenitores sui Cancellarium ac Universitatem predictam retroactis temporibus minime visitare consueverant, voluit et ex certa scientia sua declaravit,* quod visitatio Cancellarii ac Procuratorum dicte Universitatis qui pro tempore forent, necnon omnium Doctorum, Magistrorum, regentium et non regentium, ac Scolarium ejusdem Universitatis quorumcumque, eorumque servientium, aliarumque personarum cujuscumque status vel condicionis extiterint libertatibus aut privilegiis dicte Universitatis utencium seu illis gaudere volentium, necnon Universitatis predicte etiam ut Universitatis, ad prefatum Archiepiscopum et successores suos ac ecclesiam suam predictam pertinuit et pertinere debuit ac futuris temporibus pertineret:

et declaravit quod visitatio Univ. Oxon. ad Archiep. Cantuar. pertinuit.

* Pat. 20 Ric. II, m. 9; dat. 1 Junii.

Postmodumque predictus nuper Rex per diversa brevia sua Cancellario, Procuratoribus, Magistris, Doctoribus, et Scolaribus Universitatis predicte preceperat, quod ipsi Archiepiscopo predicto et successoribus suis in visitacione sua predicta in eadem Universitate facienda in omnibus sub penis predictis parerent et obedirent.

Postmodumque sicut datum fuit intelligi domino nostro Regi Henrico Quarto post conquestum, quod visitante Thoma Archiepiscopo Cantuariensi jure suo metropolitico diocesim Lincolniensem, anno regni dicti Henrici Regis duodecimo, venit ad predictam Universitatem Oxoniensem ad exequendam in forma juris ecclesiastici ibidem visitacionem suam, Ricardus Courtenay adtunc Cancellarius Universitatis predicte, ac Benedictus Brent et Johannes Byrch adtunc Procuratores dicte Universitatis, ac quamplures alii eis adherentes in eadem Universitate, dictum Archiepiscopum de visitacione sua predicta et jurisdiccione ejusdem Archiepiscopi manu forti injuste impedierunt, et ei absque causa racionabili resistebant; super quo diverse lites, dissensiones, et discordie inter prefatum Thomam Archiepiscopum et eosdem Cancellarium et Procuratores ac alios scolares Universitatis predicte eorumque fautores de et super jure et impedimento visitacionis et jurisdiccionis predictarum mote fuerint et exorte in Universitate predicta:

Et super hoc, presente Thoma Comite Arundell et aliis personis honorabilibus secum existentibus in Universitate predicta, tam prefatus Archiepiscopus pro se et ecclesia sua predicta, quam prefatus Ricardus Courtenay Cancellarius Universitatis predicte et Benedictus Brent et Johannes Byrch Procuratores ejusdem Universitatis pro se et eorum adherentibus in materiis predictis ac pro Universitate predicta per assensum eorumdem adherentium, se submiserunt et concesserunt stare arbitrio, judicio, et ordinacioni ac decreto illustrissimi principis et domini, dicti domini nostri Regis Henrici, de et super jure et impedimento visitacionis et jurisdiccionis predictarum per dictos Magistrum Ricardum Cancellarium et sibi adherentes prestito, ac de dissensionibus, litibus, et discordiis predictis et earum dependenciis:

Et super hoc dictus dominus noster Rex Henricus dictum Magistrum Ricardum Courtenay Cancellarium ac dictos Benedictum Brent et Johannem Byrch Procuratores venire fecit coram eo in propria persona sua apud Lambhith in crastino Nativitatis beate Marie dicto anno regni sui duodecimo ad faciendum et recipiendum quod per eundem dominum Regem de avisamento consilii sui foret consideratum in materiis predictis; et predictus Archiepiscopus ibidem coram prefato domino Rege comparuit; et tam prefatus Archiepiscopus quam iidem Cancellarius et Procuratores adtunc ibidem coram dicto domino nostro Rege submissionem predictam in omnibus ut predictum est fore factam in forma predicta recognoverunt, et ibidem concesserunt stare arbitrio, judicio, et ordinacioni ejusdem domini nostri Regis de et super jure et impedimento visitacionis et jurisdiccionis predictarum ac aliis materiis predictis et omnibus dependenciis earumdem:

Qui quidem dominus Rex postea xvii die mensis Septembris dicto anno duodecimo apud Lambhith predictum, auditis et intellectis tam allegacionibus quam responsionibus parcium predictarum, et etiam habens consideracionem ad dictam submissionem factam tempore dicti Regis Ricardi ac ordinacionem, judicium, et determinacionem super eandem submissionem tangentia visitacionem et jurisdiccionem predictas, ac clare considerans quod visitacio Universitatis predicte etiam ut Universitatis et omnium in Universitate predicta commorantium ad dictum Archiepiscopum et successores suos ut de jure ecclesie sue predicte pertinet et de jure pertinere deberet, et quod iidem Cancellarius et Procuratores ac alii eis in hac parte adherentes eundem Archiepiscopum de visitacione et jurisdiccione predictis injuste et absque titulo seu racionabili causa manu forti impedierunt, dicta judicium, ordinacionem, et determinacionem predicti Ricardi nuper Regis ratificavit, approbavit, et confirmavit pro imperpetuo duratura: *Causa audita.*

Et ulterius, tam auctoritate sua regia quam virtute submissionis predicte sibi facte, adtunc ibidem arbitratus fuit, ordinavit, consideravit, decrevit, et adjudicavit, quod predictus Archiepiscopus et successores sui imperpetuum habeant visitacionem et jurisdiccionem in Universitate predicta tam Cancellarii Commissarii quam Procuratorum ejusdem Universitatis qui pro tempore fuerint, necnon omnium Doctorum, Magistrorum, regentium et non regentium, ac Scolarium ejusdem Universitatis quorumcumque, eorumque servientium, aliarumque personarum cujuscumque status vel condicionis extiterint, et etiam ejusdem Universitatis ut Universitatis; et quod Cancellarius, Commissarius, et Procuratores Universitatis predicte qui pro tempore fuerint, eorumque successores, *et judicata. Archiep. habet visitationem et jurisdictionem Univ. Oxon.*

et omnes alii in dicta Universitate pro tempore commorantes, futuris temporibus eidem Archiepiscopo et successoribus suis in visitacione et jurisdiccione Universitatis predicte etiam ut Universitatis in omnibus pareant et obediant; et quod nec dicti Cancellarius, Commissarius, nec Procuratores Universitatis predicte, nec eorum successores, nec aliquis alius in Universitate predicta, aliquod privilegium seu beneficium exempcionis ad excludendum prefatum Archiepiscopum seu successores suos de visitacione et jurisdiccione predictis in Universitate antedicta colore alicujus bulle seu alterius tituli cujuscumque erga predictum Archiepiscopum aut successores suos clament, habeant, seu vendicent ullo modo in futurum; et quod quociens Cancellarius, Commissarius, vel locumtenens ipsorum vel alicujus ipsorum, vel Procuratores dicte Universitatis qui pro tempore fuerint, vel eorum successores, sive aliquis eorum, impedierint vel impedierit prefatum Archiepiscopum vel successores suos aut ecclesiam suam predictam aut ipsorum vel alicujus ipsorum Commissarium vel Commissarios de hujusmodi visitacione seu jurisdiccione dicte Universitatis, vel in aliquo contravenerint vel aliquis eorum contravenerit dictis arbitrio, ordinacioni, sive judicio, per prefatum Ricardum nuper Regem factis, sive arbitrio, judicio, decreto, consideracioni, vel ordinacioni ipsius domini nostri Regis Henrici in hoc casu; vel si aliquis dicte Universitatis in futurum impedierit dictum Archiepiscopum vel successores suos aut ecclesiam suam predictam aut ipsorum vel alicujus ipsorum Commissarium vel Commissarios de visitacione sua aut jurisdiccione antedictis, vel in aliquo contravenerit dictis arbitrio, ordinacioni, sive judicio, per prefatum Ricardum nuper Regem in forma predicta factis, vel arbitrio, judicio, decreto, consideracioni, seu ordinacioni ipsius domini nostri Regis Henrici, et quod Cancellarius, Commissarius, et Procuratores Universitatis predicte tunc non fecerint diligentiam et posse eorum ad adjuvandum dictum Archiepiscopum vel successores suos aut ecclesiam suam predictam seu Commissarium vel Commissarios suos in hujusmodi casu ac etiam ad puniendum

Poenae. hujusmodi impedientes et resistentes; quod tociens omnes franchesie, libertates, et omnia privilegia ejusdem Universitatis in manus domini Regis vel heredum suorum scisiantur, in eisdem manibus ipsorum domini Regis vel heredum suorum remansura, quousque predictus Archiepiscopus vel successores sui pacificam visitacionem et jurisdiccionem in forma predicta in dicta Universitate habuerit vel habuerint; et etiam tociens Cancellarius, Commissarius, et Procuratores ejusdem Universitatis, qui pro tempore fuerint, et eorum successores, ac Universitas predicta, solvant et teneantur solvere ipsi domino nostro Regi Henrico et heredibus suis mille libras legalis monete Anglie.

Qua quidem cedula visa, ac cum matura et diligenti deliberacione examinata et intellecta, dictus dominus Rex in pleno parliamento asseruit et declaravit omnia et singula in eadem cedula contenta per ipsum secundum quod in eadem continetur facta, arbitrata, ordinata, considerata, decreta, et adjudicata in omnibus esse et extitisse; et sic de assensu dominorum spiritualium et temporalium necnon communitatis in eodem parliamento existentium, qui super eisdem pleniorem deliberacionem similiter habuerunt, et eisdem decreto et judicio plenarie consenserunt et aggreaverunt, eandem cedulam et omnia et singula in eadem contenta concessit, approbavit, ratificavit, et confirmavit; quodque eadem cedula in rotulo parliamenti secundum formam et effectum ejusdem irrotularetur et inactaretur; ac etiam quod eadem cedula et omnia in ea contenta sint tanti et talis valoris, effectus, et auctoritatis, et eosdem valorem, effectum, et auctoritatem habeant et teneant, ac si in presenti parliamento et per auctoritatem ejusdem parliamenti facta extitissent.[b]

Cedulae confirmatio.

---

[b] Of the fourteen next successors to Archbishop Arundel it is believed that none except Cardinal Pole, who in virtue of his legatine authority visited both Oxford and Cambridge by commission, attempted to exercise any power of visitation here. But the fifteenth, Archbishop Laud, claimed the "right to visit both the Universities jure metropolitico." Both resisted his claim, relying mainly on the plea that the power of visiting them was in the King alone as their founder. The arguments were heard before the King himself in Council at Hampton Court, and the case was decided in the Archbishop's favour. See Abp. Laud's Diary, 21 June 1636; Twyne's MSS. Collections in Arch. Univ. Oxon., vol. 7, De Visitatione Universitatis; Rushworth's Historical Collections, II, 324-332; Wilkins, Concilia, IV, 525, 528, from Reg. Laud, ff. 246 b, 252 a.

Et puis apres, sur diverses matires moevez parentre le dit Ercevesque et l'Ercevesque d'Everwyk sur certeines privileges pretenses par le dit Ercevesque d'Everwyk pur le College appellee la Quenhalle en la Universitee d'Oxenford, le dit Ercevesque de Canterbirs, en presence du Roy et des seignors en le dit parlement, promyst que si le dit Ercevesque d'Everwyk purroit sufficientment monstrer ascun privilege ou especialtee de record parount le dit Ercevesque de Canterbirs ne deust user n'excercer sa visitacion du dite College il se vorroit ent abstinier; sauvant a luy toutefoitz la visitacion de les escolers demurrantz en le dit College solone les juggementz et decrees faitz et donez par le dit Roy Richard et par nostre seignor le Roy Henry q'or est, come en le record ent fait plius pleinement est declarez.

12 & 13 Edw. IV, Rot. Parl. nn. 36.

[*Confirmation of Charter, 3 July 1 Edw. IV, releasing to the University of Oxford a yearly rent of 100s. due to the Crown for the assise of bread, wine, and ale.*]

Pro Cancellario et Scolaribus Universitatis Oxoniensis.

ITEM quedam alia peticio exhibita fuit eidem domino Regi in parliamento predicto per Cancellarium et Scolares universitatis in villa Oxoniensi in hec verba.

To the Kyng oure aller soueraigne liege lord. Mekely besechen unto your highnes your humble Oratours and subgiettes the channceler and Scolers of the universite in your Toune of Oxonford, that where ye by your lettres patentes beryng date the third day of Juyl in the first yere of your moost noble reigne, recityng by the same among other that where, among certeyn liberties and privileges by charters of your moost noble progenitours sumtyme Kynges of Englond graunted unto the Chaunceller and Scolers of the said universite, it hath be graunted

<small>Recital of grants of the assise of bread.</small>

unto theym that the same Chaunceller shuld have for ever-more the kepyng of assise of brede, wyne, and ale, and correction and punicion therof, within the said Toune of Oxonford and the subarbes of the same, with fynes amerciamentes and other profites growyng in that behalf, yeldyng to your said progenitours and their heires C*s.* yerely, of your grace especiall yave graunted, remitted, and released for you and your heires to the said Chaunceller and Scolers and their successours the said C*s.* yerely to you and to your heires to be payed, to be had and perceyved unto the same Chaunceller and Scolers and their successours to the commen profite of the said universite for evermore, so that they and their successours shuld pay unto your highnes and to your heires at thescheker for the said kepyng and punicion i.*d.* oonly withoute more at the fest of Seynt Michell for evermore, as in the said your lettres patentes therof is conteyned more at large; the whiche graunte, remyssion, and relese been resumed and voide for lak of certeyn provisions uppon certeyn Actes of Resumpcion hereafore made: *wine, and ale, within Oxford and the suburbs, at a fee farm rent of 100s.; and of the remission of the said rent; which remission is void under Acts of Resumption.*

Pleas it your said highnes of your moost noble and habundaunt grace, for the especiall wele and relief of the said Scolers, by the assent of the lordes spirituell and temporell and of the Commens of this your Reame in this your present parlement assembled, and by auctorite of the same, to ordeyne and establissh, that the said graunte, remission, and relese, and your said lettres patentes beryng date the said third day of Juyl as to the same graunte, remyssion, and relese in theym especified, be goode, available, and effectuell, and auctorised by auctorite of this your present parlement, any Acte of Resumpcion or other Acte made or to be made in this parlement or any other parlement afore this tyme holden whatsoever notwithstondyng. And the said Scolers shall pray contynuelly for the preservacion of your moost noble and Roiall estate. *Prayer, that the said remission may stand good.*

Qua quidem peticione in eodem parliamento lecta, audita, et mature intellecta, de assensu dominorum spiritualium et temporalium ac communitatis regni Anglie in dicto parliamento existentium ac auctoritate ejusdem, respondebatur eidem in forma que sequitur: Soit fait come il est desire. *The King's assent.*

14 & 15 Hen. VIII, Cap. V.

An Acte concerning Phisicions.

Incorporation of College of Physicians in London.

[This Act confirms and enlarges the King's letters patent, dated 23 Dec. 10 Hen. VIII, for the incorporation of the College of Physicians in London.]

Examination of Physicians out of London:

3. And where that in Diocesys of Englond oute of London it is not light to fynde alwey men hable to sufficiauntly examyn after the Statute[c] such as shalbe admytted to excersyse Physyk in them, that it may be enacted in this present parliament, that noo person fromhensforth be suffred to excercyse or practyse in Physyk through Englond untill such tyme that he be examined at London by the said President and three of the said Electys; and to have frome the said President or Electys lettres testimonialx of their approvyng and examinacion;

except Graduates of Oxford or Cambridge.

except he be a Graduat of Oxforde or Cantebrygge which hath accomplisshed all thyng for his fourme without any grace.

27 Hen. VIII, Cap. XLII.

An Acte concernyng the exoneracyon of Oxford & Cambrydg from payment of there fyrst frutes & tenthe.

Recital of 26 Hen. 8, c. 3, for payment

WHERE by an Acte made sithen the begynnyng of this parliament holden apon prorogacion at Westmynster the thirde day of November the xxvj yere of the

---

[c] The Statute here intended is 3 Hen. 8, c. 11, "An Act concerning Phesicions and Surgeons," enacting 1. that no person shall practise as a Physician or Surgeon in the City of London or within seven miles thereof, except he be first examined, approved, and admitted by the Bishop of London or by the Dean of St. Paul's for the time being with the aid of four Doctors of Physic or persons expert in surgery, as the case may be; and 2. that, beyond those limits, no person, except he have been so approved, shall practise in any diocese within the realm, unless he be first examined and approved by the Bishop of the diocese or his vicar general with the aid of persons expert in those faculties; with a proviso "that thys Acte nor any thyng therin conteyned be prejudiciall to the Universities of Oxford and Cantebrigge or either of them or to any privilegys graunted to them."

Kynges mooste noble Realme*, it is ordeyned and establisshid of First Fruits and Tenths. that the Kynges Majestie shulde have to hym his heires and successours, unyted and knytte to the Imperiall Crowne *So in orig. of this Realme, aswell the firste fructes as one yerely pension of the tenthe of all and singuler dignyties benefices and other preferrementes and promocions commonly called spiritual of what nature so ever they be within this his Realme unto the Clergie in any wyse belongyng or apperteynyng, as by the tenour of the said Acte amongest other thynges more at large it apperith; the Kynges mooste Riall Magestic hath mooste graciously and of his mooste excellent goodnes and dyvyne charitie, with the fervent zele whiche his Majestie hath conceyvyd and bearith aswell pryncipallye to the advauncement of the syncere and pure doctrine of Goddes worde and Holy Testament, as to thincrease of the knowlege in the seven liberall sciences and the thre tonges of laten greeke and hebrewe to be by his people applied and larned, considerid that if his Highnes shulde use his right in his Unyversities of Oxforde and Cambridge or in the College of our Ladye in Eton besydes Wyndesore or Saynt Marie College of Wynchestre besides Wynchestre, where yowth and good wyttes be educate and norysshed in vertue and larnyng, and of the studentes or ministers whiche be or shalbe in the same or any of the same receiave suche first frutes and tenthes as his Majestie by the said Acte is laufully intytelyd unto, the same shuld percaas discorage mannye of his subjectes whiche be both apte and wyllyng to applye theym selfes to larnyng, and cause theym by reason of the tenuytie of lyvyng to withdrawe and gyve their myndes to suche other thynges and fantacies as shulde neyther be acceptable to God ne profittable for his publique welthe. His Majestye of his mooste aboundaunt and speciall grace, havyng conceyved suche hartie love and tender affeccion to the contynuance and augmentacion of all honeste and vertuouse larnyng artes and sciences, wherewith it hath pleased Almyghtye God so aboundauntely to endowe his Hignes as in knowlege and wysdam he farre excellith any of his mooste noble progenytours, as his Grace cannot in enny wyse compare the same to annye lawe acte constitucion or statute, ne tollerate or suffer any suche ordy-

Reasons for exempting the Universities of Oxford and Cambridge and the Colleges of Eton and Winchester from such payment.

naunce, thowgh the commoditie and benefice therof shulde never so highely redounde to his profute or pleasure, as myght by annye meane hynder thadvauncement and settyng fourth of the lyvely Worde of God, wherewith his people muste be fedd noureshid and instructed, or impeache the knowlege of suche other good letters as in christoned realmes be expedyent to be lerned for the conservacion of their good pollices and the breadyng of discrete and prudent personnages to serve and administre in his comen welth, hath, aswell for avoydyng of thoccasion of these inconveniences as for the revyvyng and quickennyng of the courage of studentes, to thentent they shulde the more joyously and gladlye bende theire wittis and holye gyve theym selfes to thattaynyng of larnyng and knowledge, pryncipallye and before all other thynges in and of the holsome doctrine of Almyghtye God, and after of the vij artes liberall, and the said thre tonges, whiche be requisite and necessarie not onely for the understandyng of Scripture, but also for the conservacion and mayntenaunce of pollicie and comen justice, thought convenient for ever by the auctoritie of this his Highe Courte of Parliament to discharge acquyte and exonerate aswell the said Universities of Oxforde and Cambridge as the said Colleges of oure Ladye in Eaton besides Wyndesore and Saynt Marie College of Wynchestre besydes Wynchester and everye of theym frome the payment of ennye suche firste frutes and tenth aforesaid. And for the parfett and cleare releaxe of the said firste frutes and tenthe His Majestye is contented that it be enacted by His Highnes and the Lordes spirituall and temporall and the Comens in this present parliament assembled and by the auctoritie of the same, that the said Universities of Oxford and Cambridge, and the said Colleges of oure Ladye in Eaton besydes Wyndesore and of Saynt Marye College of Wynchester besydes Wynchester, and eyther of the said Universities of Oxford and Cambridge, and the Deanes Wardeynes Provostes Maisters Presidentes Rectours Principalles Prebendaries Personnes Vicars Chauntrie Preestes Felawes Scolers Dymyes Brotherodes Chapleines Clerkes Corusters Scolers and Studentes nowe beyng or whiche herafter shalbe within the said Universities or within eyther of theym, or within

<small>The said Universities and Colleges, and all Officers and Students, and all Offices, Promotions, &c. within them, and all Manors, Lands, &c.</small>

the said Colleges of oure Ladie in Eaton besides Wyndesore
and of Seynt Marye College of Wynchester besides Wynchester or within either of theym, by what soever name or
names they or enny of theym be founded incorporate named
or called, and their successours and the successours of every
of theym for the tyme beyng, and the said Offices Deaneries
Colleges Houses Howses Collegiate Rectories Provostshippz
Maistershippz Halles Hostelles Hospitalles Prebendes Per-
sonages Vicarages Chauntries free Chapelles Felowshippes
Scolershippes Dimishippees Brotherodes Chaplenshippes
Clerkeshippes Corustershippes and other promocions spirituall within the said Universities and within eyther of
theym and within the said Colleges of oure Ladye in Eaton
besydes Wyndesore and of Saynt Marie Collage of Wynchester besides Wynchester and every of theym, and all
and singuler other manours landes tenementes and other
possessions offices benefices and other what somever profites
and emolumentes as well spirituall as temporall, of what
soever nature or qualitie somever they be and wheresomever
they be within the Realme of England Wales Cales or
Marches of the same or within any of theym, whiche nowe
be apperteynyng or belongyng unto the said Deaneries
Colleges Houses Collegiate Rectours* Hostelles Hospitalles
Halles Prebendes Parsonages Vicarages Chauntreis free
Chappels Provostshippes Maistershippes Felawshippes Scolershippes Dimishippes Brothershippes Chapleyneshippes
Clerkeshippes Corustershippes and other promocions spirituall, frome the said thirde daye of November the foresaid
xxvj yere of the reigne of oure said Soveraigne Lorde Kyng
Henry the viijth, shall be clerelie acquieted released and
discharged, agaynste our said Soveraigne Lorde his heires
and successours for ever, of and for the payment or pay-
mentes aswell of the firste frutes of the revenueis and
profites of the said Offices Deaneries Wardeynshippes Provostshippes Mastershippes Presidentshippes Rectories Prin-
cipallshippes Prebendes Parsonages Vicaragies Chauntries
free Chapelles Felawshippes Scolershippes Dymyshippes
Brotherodes Chapleyneshippes Clerkeshippes Corustershippes
and other promocions spirituall within the said Universities
of Oxford and Cambrigge and every of theym or in the

belonging thereto, acquitted from the payment of First Fruits and Tenths.

* *So in orig.*

said Colleges of oure Ladye in Eaton besydes Wyndesore and of Saynt Marie College of Wynchester besides Wynchester, as also of and for the said yerely pension of the tenth parte of all the revenues rentes fermes tithes offerynges emolumentes and of all other profites aswell called spirituall as temporall apperteynyng or belongyng to any of the said Offices Deaneries Collegis Howses Collegiate Rectories Hostelles Hospitalles Halles Prebendes Personnagies Vicarages free Chapelles Chauntreis Felawshippes Scolershippes Dimishippes Brotherodes Chapleineshippes Clerkishippes Corustershippes or other benefice or promocion spirituallye* within the said Universities of Oxford and Cambridge or cyther of theym or within the said Colleges of oure Lady of Eton besides Wyndesore and of Saynt Mary Collage of Wynchester besides Wynchester, of what name nature or qualitie so ever they be, the said Acte of Parliament made the said thirde daye of November the foresaid xxvj yere, or any article ordynaunce provision clawse or matter in the same specified or conteyned to the contrary therof notwithstondyng.

So in orig.

Collectors shall be discharged in respect of the said Tenth remitted.

2. AND be it further enacted by the auctorite above said that all and everye persone and personnes whiche have or shall have the charge of collection of the said tenth, and their successours and the successours of every of theym, shalbe discharged and acquyted ageynste the Kynges Highness his heires and successours of and for the collection of the said tenth remytted and relexid as is aforesaid;

The Act 26 Hen. 8, c. 3, shall not prejudice the said Universities or the said Colleges.

And that the said Acte of Parliament made the xxvj yere abovesaid or ennye thyng therin conteyned concernyng the said firste frutes and tenthe parte of the said revenues profites and emolumentes aswell spirituall as temporall in eny wise be not hurtfull or prejudiciall unto the said Universities nor unto cyther of theym, nor unto the said Colleges of oure Ladye in Eaton besides Wyndesore and Saynt Mary College of Wynchester besides Wynchester nor to cyther of theym, nor unto the said Deanes Wardeynes Provostes Maisters Presidentes Rectours Principalles Prebendaries Personnes Vicars Chauntrie Preestes Felawes Scolers Dimies Brotherne Chapleynes Clerkes Corusters Scolers and Studentes within the said Universities or within

eyther of theym, nor unto their successours, or within the
said College of our Ladye in Eaton besides Wyndesore or
of Saynt Marye College of Wynchester besydes Wynchester
or within eyther of theym, nor unto the successours of eny
of theym, by whatsomever name or names they or any of
theym be founded named knowen or called, nor unto the
said Deaneries Colleges Houses Collegiate Rectours* Halles *So in orig.
Hostelles Hospitallis Prebendes Personnages Vicarages
Chauntereys fre Chapellis Scolershippes Dymyshippes Pro-
vestshippes Mastershippes Felawshippes Brotherodes Chapleyneshippes Clerkeshippes Corustershippes or other promocion spirituall within the said Universities or within
eyther of theym, or within the said Colleges of oure Ladye
in Eaton besydes Wyndesore and of Saynt Marye College
of Wynchester besides Wynchester, nor unto their or any
of their manours landes tenementes rentes possessions
benefices or other what somever profites and emolumentes
aswell spirituall as temporall of what so ever nature or qualitie
they or any of theym be within this Realme of England
Wales Cales and Marches of the same or within any of
theym, apperteynyng or belongyng unto the said Deaneries
Colleges Howses Collegiate Rectories Halles Hostelles Hospitalles Prebendes Personnages Vicareges Chauntreis free
Chapelles Felawshippes Scolershippes Dymyshippes Brotherodes Chaplenshippes Clerkeshippes or other promocions
spirituall within the said Universities or within either of
theym or within the said Colleges of oure Ladye in Eaton
besides Wyndesore, and of Saynt Marye College of Wynchester besydes Wynchester or within either of theym;
but that the said Deanes Wardeyns Provosties Maisters
Presidentes Rectours Principalles Prebendaries Personnes
Vicars Chauntrye Prestes Felawes Scolers Dymyes Brothern
Chapleyns Clerkes Corusters and other Scolers and Studentis
and their successours and every of theym for the tyme beyng
within the said Universitis or within either of theym, or
within the said Colleges of oure Ladye in Eaton besides
Wyndesore and of Saynt Marie College of Wynchester
besides Winchester or within eyther of the said Colleges,
shall have holde possede and enjoye, accordyng to their
severall interest and titles, as in the right of their said

Deaneries Colleges Howses Collegiate Rectories Hostelles Hospitalles Halles Prebendes Personnages Vicarages Chauntries free Chapelles Provostshippes Maistershippes Felawshippes Brotherodes Chapleineshippes Clerkeshippes Corustershippes and other promocions spirituall, all and singuler their manours landes tenementes rentes possessions offices benefices tithes and other what soever profites and emolumentes aswell spirituall as temporall, of what somever nature or qualitie they or enny of theym be, as quietely and freelye without payeng or payment of the said first frutes and yerely rent of the tenth or either of theym, in lyke maner fourme and condicion as thoughe the said Acte made the forsaid xxvj yere of oure said Soveraigne Lorde the Kyng for the payment of the said firste frutes and tenthe had never ben made ne ordeyned.

<small>No writs or other process shall issue out of the King's Courts for payment of the said First Fruits or Tenths remitted.</small>

3. And be it further enacted by the auctorite above said that no manner of writte or writtes precepte or preceptes or other processe, at any tyme after makyng of this present Acte, be made or written out of enny of oure said Soverayne Lorde the Kynges Courtes within this his Realme, comenlye called the Chauncerye, the Kynges Benche, Comune Place, or of his Eschequier, or oute of any other Courte place within this his Realme, for payment of the said firste frutes or tenthe remytted and releaxid as is afore rehersed, whereby any of the said Wardeynes Deanes Provostes Maisters Rectours Presidentes Principalles Personnes Vicars Chauntrie Preestes Felaws Scolers Dymyes Brotherne Chapleyns Clerkes Corusters or other Studentes and Scolers whiche nowe be or hereafter shalbe within the said Universities of Oxford and Cambrigge or within either of theym, or any of them, or their successours or the successours of ennye of them, or within the Colleges of our Ladye in Eaton besides Wyndesore and of Saynt Marie College of Wynchester besides Wynchester or eyther of theym, or their successours or the successours of enny of theym, or the Ordynaries or Collectours theirunto by the said Acte lymytted and appoynted, shalbe in any wyse sommoned distrayned attached or otherwise vexid trowbiled or greved in their bodies landes tenementes possessions aswell spirituall as temporall or other promocion spirituall, or other whatso-

ever revenues commodities and emolumentes of what nature or qualitie soever they be, or in their goodes and catalles, or in any of them, for or because of the said firste frutes and tenth parte of* eyther of theym; but that they and every of them and their successours of the said firste frutes and tenth parte and of every of theym be by this present Acte clerelie releaxid pardonned acquictid and discharged ageynst our said Soveraigne Lorde his heires and successours for ever.

<small>* So in orig. Read or.</small>

4. In consideracion of whiche his mooste gracious pardonne and releaxe of the said firste frutes and tenthe, and for encrease of larnyng in the saide Universities, His Graces pleasure is that it be enacted by auctoritie of this present Parliament, that all the Colleges Houses and Halles corporate in eyther of the said Universities shall perpetuallye fromhensforth, at theire owne propre costes and charges, fynde in everye of the said Universities one discrete and larned personnage to reade one opyn and publique lectour in every of the said Universities in any suche science or tonge as the Kynges Majestie shall assigne or appoynte to be mooste profitable for the studentes in either of the said Universities; every whiche lecture shalbe called perpetually Kyng Henry the Eight his lecture.^d

<small>Each University shall find a person to read a public lecture, which shall be called King Henry the Eighth's Lecture.</small>

[Section 5 enacted that the University of Oxford, the University of Cambridge, Eton College, and Winchester College, should each keep two masses yearly on May 8 and October 8 for the preservation of the King, Queen Anne, and the Princess Elizabeth, during their lives; and after the decease of the King should keep two solemn anniversaries on the same days yearly for ever.]

6. Provyded also that this present Acte in any wyse extende not to the Monasteries of Osneye or Rewley within the Universitie of Oxford, ne unto Barnewell within the

<small>Osney and Rewley Monasteries in</small>

<small>^d On the 12th of December 1536 the University of Oxford in Congregation assessed the Colleges severally, according to their estimated revenues, to make up a yearly stipend of twenty marks (13*l.* 6*s.* 8*d.*) for the Lecturer required by this Act. Reg. FF, fol. 130 a; a record printed by Gutch in Collectanea Curiosa, I, 188. The arrangement continued until the King superseded it ten years afterwards by founding the five Regius Professorships of Divinity, Hebrew, Greek, Civil Law, and Medicine. There is reason to believe that a similar arrangement was made at Cambridge.</small>

27 HEN. VIII, c. 42.

Oxford, and Barnwell in Cambridge, excepted from this Act; as also Benefices in the gift of Colleges &c.

subburbes of Cambrigge; ne be in anny wyse extended to eny personne or personnes whiche at this present tyme hath or hereafter shall have any Parsonnage Vicarage Chauntrie free Chapell or any other promocion spirituall, of what nature or name soever they be of, being of the patronage or gyfte of eny of the said Colleges Howses Collegiate Halles Hostelles Hospitalles or other places of Studentes within the said Universities or either of theym, or of the collacion or patronage of the said Colleges of our Ladye of Eaton besides Wyndesore or of Saynt Maries College of Wynchester besides Wynchester or eyther of theym, beyng no percell nor in any wise apperteynyng or belongyng of or unto any of the lyvinges of the said Deanes Wardeynes Provostes Maisters Presidentes Rectours Principalles Prebendaries Persones Vicars Chauntrie Preestes Felawes Scolers Dymyes Brotherne Chapleynes Clerkes Corusters and Studentes within the said Universities and eyther of theym, and within the said Collegies of our Ladye of Eton besides Wyndesore and of Sainte Marie College of Wynchester besides Wynchester and eyther of theym, by the ordynaunce or fundacion of the said Colleges and Howses or enny of them.

Durham College in Oxford may take the benefit of this Act.

7. Provyded also and be it enacted that the profutes yerely goyng to and for the exhibicion of the Wardeyne Felawes and Scollers of Durham College in Oxforde be in no wyse chargeable to the said former Acte made in the said xxvj yere concernyng the graunte of the said tenthes and firste frutes, but that the said Wardeyne Felawes and Scolers and their successours shall and may take benefite of this Acte as other Colleges in Oxford maye and shall by vertue of this present Acte.

None shall be acquitted in respect of Offices, Promotions, &c., not within the said Universities or Colleges.

8. Provyded also that this Acte nor any thyng theirin conteyned enny wise extende to acquyte and discharge any person or personnes, what soever he or they be, nowe beyng or whiche herafter shalbe within the said Universities or either of theym, or within the said Colleges of Eaton besides Wyndesore and Seynt Marie College of Wynchestre beside Wynchester or within either of theym, of and for the said firste fructes and tenth parte or either of theym, whiche nowe hathe or hereafter shalhave any Deanerie

Wardeynshippe Maistershippe Presidentshippe Rectorshippe Principallshippe Prebende Parsonnage Vicarage Chauntrie free Chapell Felawshippe Scolershippe Dymyshippe Brotherhode Chaplenshippe Clerkeshippe Cornstershippe Hospitall or other promocion spirituall, of what name nature or qualite soever it be, out of the said Universities or out of eyther of theym, beyng no parcell nor in any wise apperteynyng or belongyng of or unto the said Deaneries Colleges Howses Collegiate Rectories Hostelles Hospitalles Halles Prebendes Parsonnages Vicarages Chauntreis free Chapelles Felawshippes Scolershippes Dimishippes Brotherhodes Chapleyneshippes Clerkeshippes Cornstershippes and other promocions spirituall within the said Universities or either of theym, nor beyng enny parcell or eny wise appertaynyng or belongyng of or unto the said Colleges of our Ladye in Eaton besides Wyndesore and of Saynt Marie College of Wynchester besides Wynchester or to either of theym; any thyng conteyned in this presente Acte to the contrary therof notwithstondyng.

33 Hen. VIII, Cap. XXVII.

An Acte for Leases of Hospitales Colledges and other Corporacions to be good and effectuall withe the consent of the more partie.

ALBEIT that, by the common lawes of this Realme of Englande, all assentes eleccions grauntes and leases had made and graunted by the Deane Warden Provost Maister President or other Governor of any Cathedrall Churche Hospitall College or other Corporacion, by whatsoever name they be incorporate or founded, with thassent & consent of the more or greater parte of their Chapiter Fellowes or Bretherne of suche Corporacion, havinge voyces of assent therunto, be as good & effectuall in the lawe to the grauntees and leassees of the same, as if the residue or the whole nomber of suche Chapiter Fellowes and Bretherne of suche Corporacion havinge voices of assent had therunto

Assent by the majority of a Corporation to Leases &c. sufficient at Common Law.

Rules made by some Founders of Colleges &c. that the dissent of one member shall prevent any Grant &c.

consented and agreed; yet, the saide common lawes notwithstandinge, diverse founders of suche Deaneries Hospytals Colleges and Corporacions within this saide Realme have, upon the foundacion and establishment of the same Deaneries Hospitals Colleges and other Corporacions, established and made, amonges other their peculier actes locall statutes and ordinaunces, that yf any one of suche Corporacion havinge power or auctoritie to assent or dissassent shoulde and woulde denye anye suche graunte or grauntes, that then noe suche

Oath for the observance of such Rules.

scale eleccion or graunte shoulde be had graunted or leassed; and for the performance of the same everie person havinge power of assent to the same have bene and be daylie thereunto sworne, and so the residue may not proceede to the perfection of suche eleccions grauntes and leases accordinge to the course of the common lawes of this Realme, unlesse they shoulde incurre the daunger of perjurie:

All Rules, wherby the effect of the assent of the majority is hindered by a minority of negative voices, declared void.

For the avoydinge whereof, and for the due execucion of the common lawe universally within this Realme and everie place in one conformytie of reason to be used, be it ordeyned established and enacted by thauctoritie of this present Parliament, that all and everie peculiar acte order rule and estatute, heretofore made or hereafter to be made by any Founder or Founders of any Hospitall College Deanerie or other Corporacion at and upon the foundacion of any suche Hospitall College Deanerie or Corporacion, wherby the graunte lease gyfte or eleccion of the Governor or Ruler of suche Hospitall College Deanerie or other Corporacion, with thassent of the more parte of suche of the same Hospitall College Deanerie or Corporacion as have or shall have voice of assent to the same at the tyme of suche graunte lease gyfte or eleccion hereafter to be made, sholde be in anywise hindred or lett by any one or moe beinge the lesser number of suche Corporacion, contrarie to the fourme order and course of the common lawe of this Realme of Englande, shalbe from hensforth clerely frustrate voide and of none effecte; and that

Oaths for their observance annulled.

all othes heretofore taken by any person or persons of suche Hospitall College Deanerie and other Corporation shalbe for and concerning the observaunce of any suche order estatute or rule demed voyde and of none effecte; and that from hensforth noe manner person or persons of any such Hospitall College Deanrie or other Corporacion shalbe in anywise compelled to take anye othe for the observinge of anye suche order estatute or rule, upon the peyne of everie person soe givinge suche othe to forfeyte for everie tyme soe offendinge five poundes, the one moytie thereof to be to the use of our Soveraigne Lorde the Kinge, and thother moytie thereof to any of the Kinges subjectes which will sue for the same in any of the Kinges Courtes of Recorde by accion of debte bill playnt informacion or otherwise, wherein the defendaunt shall not be admytted to wage his lawe nor any proteccion nor essoyne or any other delatorie plea admytted or allowed. *Penalty on giving such Oath, £5*

37 Hen. VIII, Cap. XVII.

An Acte that the Doctors of the Civill Lawe may exercise Ecclesiastical Jurisdiccion.

IN most humble wise shewe and declare unto your Highnes your most faithfull humble and obedient subjectes the Lordes spirituall and temporall and the Commons of this present Parliament assembled, that where your most Royall Majestie is and hath alwayes justly bene by the worde of God supreame held in earth of the Churche of Englande, and hath full power and auctoritie to correcte punyshe & represse all manner of heresies errors vices synnes abuses idolatrie ipocrisies and supersticions sprongen and growing within the same, and to exercise all other manner of jurisdiccions commonly called ecclesiasticall jurisdiccion; neverthelcs the Bishopp of Rome and his adherentes, myndinge utterly as muche as in him* lay to abolishe obscure and delete suche power given by God to the princes of the earth, wherby they myght gather and gett to themselfes the governement and rule of the worlde, have in their counsailes & synodes provinciall made ordeyned and established and decreed diverse ordynaunces and constitucions, that noe lay or married man shulde or myght exercise or *The King supreme Head of the Church.*

Ordinances of the Bishop of Rome against any Lay or Married men exercising any Ecclesiastical Jurisdiction.

* So in orig.

occupy any jurisdiccion ecclesiasticall, nor shuld be any judge or registre in any courte commenly called ecclesiasticall courte, lest their false and usurped power which they pretended and went aboute to have in Christes Churche should decaye waxe vile and of no reputacion, as by the saide counsailes & constitucions provinciall appereth: which standinge & remaining in their effecte, not abolished by your Graces lawes, did sounde to appere to make greatly for the saide usurped power of the saide Bisshopp of Rome and to be directly repugnaunte to your Majestie of supreame hed of the Churche and prerogatyve royall, your Grace beinge a lay man. And albeit the said decrees ordynaunces and constitucions, by a Statute made in the xxv yere of your most noble Raigne, be utterly abolished frustrate and of none effecte, yet, because the contrary therunto is not used nor put in practise by the Archebisshopps Bisshopps Archedeacons and other ecclesiasticall persons, who have noe manner of jurisdiccion ecclesiasticall but by under and from your Royall Majestie, it addeth or at the lest may give occasion to some evill disposed persons to thinck and litle to regarde the procedinges and censures ecclesiasticall made by your Highnes and your vicegerent officialls commissaries and judges and visitators, beinge also lay & married men, to be of little or of none effecte or force; wherby the people gathereth harte and presumpcion to doe evill, and not to have such reverence to your most godly injunctions and proceadinges as becommeth them. But for asmuche as your Majestie is thonly and undoubtly supreame hed of the Churche of Englande and also of Irelande, to whom by holy Scripture all auctoritie and power is holy geven to heare and determyne all manner cause ecclesiasticall and to correct vice and synne whatsoever, and to all such persons as your Majestie shall appointe therunto; that in consideracion therof, aswell for the instruccion of ignorant persons, as also to avoyde the occasion of the opynion aforesaide, and setting forth of your prerogatyve royall and supremacy, it may therfore please your Highnes that it may be ordeyned and enacted by aucthoritie of this present Parliament, that all and singuler persons, aswell laye as those that nowe be married or hereafter shalbe married, being Doctors of the

Repeal therof by 25 Hen. 8, c. 19, not sufficiently explicit.

Lay or Married men, being Doctors of Civil Law,

Civill Lawe laufully create and made in any Unyversitie, which shall be made ordeyned constituted and deputed to be any Chauncelor Vicar Generall Commissarie Officiall Scribe or Registre by your Majestie or any of your heires or successors, or by any Archebisshopp Bisshopp Archdeacon or other person whatsoever having auctoritie under your Majestie your heires & successours to make any Chauncelor Vicar Generall Commissarie Officiall or Registre, may laufully execute and exercise all manner of jurisdiccion commonly called ecclesiasticall jurisdiccion, and all censures and coertions apperteyninge or in any wise belonginge unto the same, albeit suche person or persons be laye married or unmaried, soe that they be Doctors of the Civill Lawe as is aforesaide; any lawe constitucion or ordynaunce to the contrarie notwithstanding.ᵉ

may exercise Ecclesiastical Jurisdiction.

2 & 3 Edw. VI, Cap. I.

An Acte for the Unyformytie of Service and Admynistracion of the Sacramentes throughout the Realme.

[The Act enjoins on all Ministers the uniform use of "The Booke of the Common Prayer and Admynistracion of the Sacramentes and other rightes and ceremonyes of the Churche after the Use of the Churche of Englande."]

The Book of Common Prayer to be used by all Ministers.

6. Provided alwaies that it shalbe laufull to anye man that understandeth the Greke Latten and Hebrewe tongue, or other straunge tongue, to saye and have the saide prayers heretofore specified of Mattens and Evensonge in Latten or anye suche other tongue, sayinge the same privatlie, as they doe understande; and, for the further encouraging of learnynge in the tongues in the Universities of Cambridge and Oxforde, to use and exercise in their commen and open prayer in their Chappells, beinge noe Parishe Churches or other places of prayer, the Mattens Evensonge Letanye and all

Prayers in Latin &c. may be said privately, and in College Chapels; but not the Service for Holy Communion.

ᵉ This Act was repealed by 1 & 2 P. & M. c. 8, s. 6, but revived by 1 Eliz. c. 1, s. 3.

other prayers, the holie Communyon commenlye called the Masse excepted, prescribed in the saide booke prescribed, in Greke Latten or Hebrewe; anye thinge in this present Acte to the contrarie notwithstandinge.[f]

1 Eliz. Cap. I.

An Acte restoring to the Crowne thauncyent Jurisdiction over the State Ecclesiasticall and Spirituall, and abolyshing all Forreine Power repugnaunt to the same.

Oath of the Supremacy of the Crown.
[The 9th section, which has been repealed by 26 & 27 Vict. c. 125, enacted that all archbishops, bishops, and other ecclesiastical persons and officers, and all judges, magistrates, mayors, and other temporal officers, should take an oath of the Supremacy of the Crown according to the form therein prescribed[g].]

Persons taking Orders or Degrees in Universities shall take the said Oath.
12. * * * * *. Also all and every person and persons taking Orders, and all and every other person and persons whiche shalbe promoted or preferred to any degree of lerning in anye Universitie within this your Realme or Dominions, before he shall receive or take any suche Orders or bee preferred to any suche degree of learning, shall make take and receive the said Othe by this Acte set foorthe and declared as ys aforesaid, before his or their Ordinarie Commissarie Chancellour or Vicechauncellour or their sufficient Deputies in the said Universitie.

[f] This Act was continued in force by 5 & 6 Edw. VI, c. 1. It was repealed by 1 Mar. st. 2, c. 2, s. 1; but was revived by 1 Eliz. c. 2, s. 1; 1 Jac. I, c. 25, s. 8.

[g] The form of the Oath of Supremacy was altered by 1 W. & M. c. 8, s. 12; and the altered form was repeated in 1 Geo. I, st. 2, c. 13. It was combined with the Oaths of Allegiance and Abjuration into one Oath by 21 & 22 Vict. c. 48.

1 ELIZ. Cap. IV.

An Acte for the Restitution of the First Fruites and Tenthes and Rentes reserved Nomine Decime, and of Parsonages Impropriate, to Thimperiall Crowne of this Realme.

7. Provided also and be yt enacted, that all grantes immunities and lybertyes given to the Universities of Cambridge and Oxforde, or to any Colledge or Hall in either of the said Universities, and to the Colledges of Eton and Winchester, and unto every or any of them, by our Souveraigne Lorde King Henrye Theight, or any other of the Quenes Highnes progenitours or predecessoures, or by Acte of Parliament[h], for or touching the Releas or Dischardge of the said First Fruites and Tenthes, or any parte therof, shalbe allwaies and remaine in their full strengthe and vertue; and that all suche lawfull conveiaunces and assurances in the lawe as were had and made before the making of this Acte to either of the said Universitees of Oxforde and Cambridge, or to any Colledge or Hall within any of them, by what name or names soever they or any of them be incorporated or named, of any of the said Parsonages or Benefices impropriate, or of any parte of the same, or of any patronages for the maintenance of studentes or lerning, shalbe as good and effectuall in the lawe to all intentes construccions and purposes, as thoughe this Acte had never bene made.

Discharge of the Universities &c. from First Fruits &c., and Grants of Parsonages &c. to them, confirmed.

13 ELIZ. Cap. X.

An Acte against Fraudes defeating Remedies for Dilapidations, &c.

2. And for that long and unreasonable Leases made by Colledges Deane and Chapters Parsons Vicars and other having spyrytuall promotions be the cheefest causes of

[h] See 27 Hen. VIII, c. 42, before.

the dilapidations and the decaye of all spyrituall lyvynges and hospitallytie and the utter impoverishing of all successors Incumbentes in the same; bee yt enacted by thauethoritie aforesaid, that from henceforth al Leases Gyftes Grauntes Feoffmentes Conveyaunces or Estates to be made had done or suffered by any Master and Fellowes of anye Colledg, Deane & Chapter of any Cathedrall or Collegiate Church, Master or Gardian of anye Hospitall, Parson, Vicar, or any other having anye spyrytuall or ecclesiasticall lyving, or * any houses landes tythes tenementes or other hereditamentes being any parcell of the possessions of any such Colledge Cathedral Church Chapter Hospital Parsonage Vycaridg or other spyrytuall promotion, or any wayes apparteyning or belonging to the same, or of any of them, to any person or persons bodyes politike or corporate, (other then for the tearme of one and twenty yeres or three lyves from the tyme as any such Lease or Graunt shalbe made or graunted, wherupon thaccustomed yerely rent or more shalbe reserved and payable yerely during the sayd tearme,) shalbe utterly voyde and of none effect to al intentes constructions and purposes; any law custome or usage to the contrary any wayes notwithstanding.

<small>All Leases by Colleges &c. except for 21 Years or Three Lives, and at the accustomed Rent, declared void. * So in orig. Read of.</small>

<small>Proviso for Leases under College Statutes.</small>

3. Provyded neverthelesse and bee yt enacted by thauethoritye aforesaid, that this Acte nor any thing therein conteyned shalbe taken or construed to make good anye Lease or other Graunt to be made by any such Colledge or Collegiate Church within either of both the Unyversities of Oxforde and Cambridge, or els where within the Realme of England, for more yeres then are lymited by the pryvate Statutes of the same Colledge.

<small>Proviso for Leases on Surrender, or under Covenant.</small>

4. Provyded alwayes, that this Acte shall not extend to any Lease hereafter to be made upon surrender of any Lease heretofore made, or by reason of any covenaunt or condycion conteyned in any Lease heretofore made and nowe contynuing; so that the Lease to be made do not conteyne more yeres then the residue of the yeares of the former Lease nowe contynuing shalbe at the tyme of such Lease hereafter to be made, nor any lesse rent then ys reserved in the said former Lease.

13 Eliz. Cap. XII.

An Act to refourme certayne Dysorders touching Ministers of the Churche.

5. And that none hereafter shalbe admitted to any Beny- fyce with Cure of or above the value of thyrtey poundes yerely in the Queenes Bookes, unles he shall then be a Bachelour of Dyvynitie, or a Preacher lawfully alowed by some Bysshop within this Realme or by one of the Unyversities of Cambridg or Oxford. None shal have Benefice of £30 a Year, except B.D. &c.

13 Eliz. Cap. XXIX.

An Acte for Thincorporation of bothe Thunyversities.[k]

FOR the greate love and favor that the Queenes most excellent Majestie beareth towardes her Highnes Universities of Oxford and Cambridge, and for the greate zeale and care that the Lordés and Commons of this present Parliament have for the mayntenaunce of good and godly literature and the vertuouse education of youth within either of the same Universities; and to thentent that the auncient priveleges liberties and fraunchises of either of the said Universities, heretofore graunted ratified and confirmed by the Queenes Highnes and her most noble progenitors, may be had in greater estymation and be of greater force and strengthe, for the better increase of larning and the further suppressing of vice: be it therefore enacted by the auethoritye of this present Parlyament, that the Right Honorable Robert Erle of Leicester nowe The Chancellor, Masters, and

---

[k] See Blackstone's Commentaries, B. III, ch. 6, p. 84, on the special value and importance of this Act. Nevertheless it is regarded as a private Act; and the judges will not take judicial notice of it, unless it is specially pleaded and exemplified. See Grant on the Law of Corporations, p. 526.

Scholars of the University of Oxford incorporated;	Chauncellor of the said Universitie of Oxford and his successors for ever, and the Masters and Schollers of the same Universitie of Oxford for the tyme being, shalbe incorporated and have a perpetuall succession in facte dede and name by the name of the Chauncellor Masters and Schollers of the Universitie of Oxford, and that the same Chauncellor Maisters and Schollers of the same Universitie of Oxford for the tyme being, from henceforth by the name of Chauncellor Maisters and Schollers of the Universitie of Oxford, and by none other name or names, shalbe called and named for evermore; and that they
with Common Seal:	shall have a Common Seale to serve for their necessarie causes touching and concerning the said Chauncellor Maysters and Schollers of the said Universitie of Oxford and
The Chancellor, Masters, and Scholars of the University of Cambridge incorporated;	their successors: and likewyse that the Right Honorable Sir William Cicill Knight Baron of Burghley nowe Chauncellor of the said Universitie of Cambridg and his successors for ever, and the Masters and Schollers of the same Universite of Cambridg for the tyme being, shalbe incorporated and have a perpetual succession in fact deede and name by the name of the Chauncellor Maisters and Schollers of the Universitie of Cambridge, and that the same Chauncellor Masters and Schollers of the said Universitie of Cambridg for the tyme being, from henceforth by the name of Chauncellor Maisters & Schollers of the Universitie of Cambridg, and by none other name or names, shalbe called & named
with Common Seal:	for evermore; and that they shall have a Comon Seale to serve for their necessarye causes touching and concerning the said Chauncellor Maisters and Schollers of the said
Said Corporations may sue and be sued.	Universitie of Cambridg and their successors: and further that aswell the Chauncellor Maiesters and Schollers of the said Universitie of Oxford and their successors, by the name of Chauncellor Masters and Schollers of the Universitie of Oxford, as the Chauncelor Maisters and Schollers of the sayd Universitie of Cambridge and theire successors, by the name of Chauncellor Maisters and Schollers of the Universitie of Cambridg, may severally impleade and be ympleaded, and sue or be sued, for all manner of causes quarels actions realles personall and mixt, of whatsoever kynde qualitie or nature they be, and shall and maye

challeng and demaunde all manner of liberties & fraunchises, and also aunswere and defend themselves, under and by the name aforesaid, in the same causes quarels and accions, for every thinge and thinges whatsoever for the proffit and right of either of the foresaid Universities to be don, before any manner of judge either spirituall or temporall in any courtes and places within the Queenes Highnes Domynions, whatsoever they be.

2. And be it further enacted by the aucthoritie aforesaid, that the Letters Patentes of the Queenes Highnes most noble father Kinge Henry Theight made and graunted to the Chauncellor and Schollers of the Universitie of Oxford, bearing date the first daye of Aprill in the foureteine yere of his Raigne, and the Lettres Patentes of the Queenes Majestie that nowe is, made and graunted unto the Chauncellor Maisters and Schollers of the Universitie of Cambridge, bearing date the sixe and twentie daye of Aprill in the third yeare of her Highnes most gratious Raigne, and also all other Lettres Patentes by any of the progenitors or predicessors of our said Soveraigne Ladye made to either of the said corporated bodies severally or to anye of their predecessors of either of the said Universities, by whatsoever name or names the said Chauncellor Masters and Schollers of either of the saide Universities in anye of the said Lettres Patentes have ben heretofore named, shall fromhenceforth be good effectuall and avayable in the lawe, to all intentes constructions and purposes, to the foresaid nowe Chauncellor Maisters & Schollers of either of the said Universities and to their successors for evermore, after and according to the fourme wordes sentences and true meaning of every of the same Lettres Patentes, as amply fullye and largely as yf the same Lettres Patentes were recited verbatim in this present Acte of Parlyament; any thing to the contrary in any wyse notwithstandinge. *Letters Patent 1 Ap. 14 Hen. 8 to University of Oxford, and 26 Ap 3 Eliz. to University of Cambridge, and all other Letters Patents to either University, confirmed.*

3. And further more be yt enacted by thaucthoritye aforesaid, that the Chauncellor Masters and Schollers of either of the said Universities severally, and their successors forever, by the same name of Chauncellor Maisters and Schollors of either of the said Universities of Oxorde and Cambridge, shall and may severally have hold possesse *All Possessions and Privileges of the said Universities confirmed to them.*

enjoye and use, to them and to their successors for ever more, all manner of mannors lorshippes rectories parsonages landes tenementes rentes services annuyties advousons of Churches possessions pencions porcions and hereditamentes, and all manner of liberties fraunchises immunytes quietances and pryvileges view of frankpledge lawedaies and other thinges whatsoever they be, the which either of the said corporated bodies of either of the said Universities had held occupied or enjoyed, or of right ought to have had used occupied and enjoyed, at any tyme or tymes before the making of this Acte of Parlyament; according to the true intent and meaninge aswell of the said Lettres Patentes made by the said noble Prynce King Henrye Theight, made and graunted to the Chauncellor and Schollers of the Unyversitie of Oxford, bearing date as is aforesaid, as of the Lettres Patentes of the Queenes Majestie made and graunted unto the Chauncellor Masters and Schollers of the Universitie of Cambridge, bearing date as aforesaid, and as accordinge to the true intent and meaninge of all other the foresaid Lettres Patentes whatsoever; any Statute or other thinge or thinges whatsoever heretofore made or don to the contrary in anye manner of wyse notwithstandinge.

All Deeds, Obligations, &c., made to either University by any former Description, declared valid.

4. And be it further enacted by thaucthority aforesaid, that all manner of instrumentes indentures obligacions writinges obligatory and recognisaunses, made or knowledged by any person or persons or body corporate to either of the said corporated bodies of either of the said Universities, by what name or names soever the said Chauncellor Maisters and Schollers of either of the said Universities have ben heretofore called in any of the said instrumentes indentures obligacions writinges obligatori or recognizaunces, shalbe from henceforth avaylable, stand and contynue of good perfect and full force and strength, to the nowe Chauncellor Maisters and Schollers of either of the said Universities and to their successors, to all intentes construccions and purposes; althoughe they or their predecessors or any of them, in any of the said instrumentes indentures obligacions writinges obligatory or recognyzaunzes, be named by any name contrary or dyverse to

the name of the nowe Chauncellor Maisters and Schollers of either of the said Universities.

5. And bee it also enacted by thauethoritie aforesaid, that aswell the said Lettres Patentes of the Queenes Highnes said father Kinge Henry Theight, bearing date as is before expressed, made and graunted to the said corporate bodye of the said Universitie of Oxon, as the Letters Patentes of the Queenes Majestie aforesaid, graunted to the Chauncellor Maisters and Schollers of the Universitie of Cambridg, bearing date as aforesaid, and all other Lettres Patentes by any of the progenitors or predecessors of her Highnes, and all manner of liberties fraunchises immunyties quietances and previlidges letes lawedayes and other thinges whatsoever therein expressed, geven or graunted to the said Chauncellor Maisters and Schollers of either of the said Universities or to anye of their predecessors of either of the said Universities, by whatsoever name the said Chauncellor Maisters and Schollers of either of the said Universities in any of the said Letters Patentes be named, in and by vertue of this present Acte shalbe from henceforth ratyfied stablished and confirmed unto the said Chauncellor Maisters and Schollers of either of the said Universities and to their successors for ever; any Statute lawe usage custom construccion or other thing to the contrary in any wyse notwithstanding. *All Patents and Liberties graunted to either University, by any former Description, ratified and confirmed.*

6. Savinge to all and every person and persons and bodies politike and incorporate, their heyres and successors, and the heires and successors of every of them, other then to the Quenes Majestie her heires & successors, all such rightes titles interestes entrees leases conditions charges and demaundes, which they and every of them had might or should have had, of in or to any the mannors lordshippes rectories parsonages landes tenementes rentes services annuyties advousons of Churches pencions porcions hereditamentes and all other thinges in the said Lettres Patentes or in any of them mencioned or comprysed, by reason of any right title charge interest or condicion to them or any of them, or to the auncestors or predecessors of them or any of them, devolute or growne before the several dates of the same Lettres Patentes, or by reason of any gyfte *Proviso for Titles of Strangers, Lessees, &c.*

grauntc demyse or other acte or actes at any tyme made or don betwene the said Chauncelor Maisters and Schollers of either of the said Universities of Cambridge and Oxford or any of them & others, by what name or names soever the same were made or don, in like manner and fourme as they and every of them had or might have had the same before the making of this Acte; any thinge &c.

<small>Proviso for Liberties of the Mayor, Bailiffs, and Burgesses of Cambridge and Oxford.</small>
7. Provyded alwaies and be it enacted by thauethoritie aforesaid, that this Acte or anye thinge therin contayned shall not extend to the prejudice or hurt of the liberties & privileges of right belonging to the Maior Bayliffes & Burgeses of the Towne of Cambridge and Cittie of Oxford; but that they the said Maiors Bayliffes and Burgeses and every of them and their successors shalbe and contynew fre in such sort and degree, and enjoye such liberties fredomes and ymmunyties, as they or any of them lawfully may or might have don before the making of this present Acte; any thing contayned in this present Acte to the contrary notwithstandinge.

14 Eliz. Cap. XI.

An Acte for the continuacion explanacion perfiting and enlardging of divers Estatutes.

<small>13 Eliz. c. 10, s. 2, as to Leases by Colleges &c., shall not extend to Houses in Cities or Towns.</small>
5. And where in one other Acte made in the said thirteenth yeere, entituled An Acte against fraudulent Gyftes to the intent to defeate Dilapidations of Ecclesiasticall Livinges, and for Leasses to bee graunted by Collegiate Churches, there ys one braunch to avoid certeyne Leasses to bee made by Maisters and Fellowes of Colledges, Deanes and Chapiters of Cathedrall or Collegiate Churches, Maisters or Gardians of any Hospitall, or by any Parson Vicar or any other having any spirituall or ecclesiasticall living; bee yt enacted, that the said braunche nor any thing therein conteyned shall not extend to any graunt assuraunce or Leasse of any Houses belonging to any the persons or bodyes politique or corporate aforesaid, nor to any Groundes to such

Houses apperteyning, which Houses be scituate in any cytye boroughe towne corporate or market towne, or the suburbes of any of them; but that all such Houses and Groundes may bee granted dimised and assured, as by the lawes of this Realme and the severall Statutes of the said Colledges Cathedrall Churches and Hospitalles they lawfully might have been before the making of the said Statute, or lawfully might bee yf the said Statute were not; so alway that such House be not the Capitall or Dwelling House used for the habitacion of the persons abovesaid, nor have Ground to the same belonging above the quantitie of tenne acres; any thing in the said Acte to the contrary notwithstanding.

7. Provided alwaye and be yt enacted, that no Leasse shalbe permitted to bee made by force of this Acte in reversion, nor without reserving the accustomed yeerely rent at the leaste, nor without chardging the Lessee with the reparations, nor for longer tearme then fourtie yeeres at the most; nor any Houses shalbee permitted to bee aliened, unlesse that in recompence thereof there shalbe afore, with, or presently after such alienacion, good lawfull and sufficient assurance made in fee simple absolutely to such Colledges Houses Bodyes Politique or Corporate, and their successours, of landes of as good value and of as greate yerely value at the leaste as so shalbee aliened; any Statute to the contrary notwithstanding.

Leases shall not be in Reversion &c., nor for more than 40 Years: no House shall be aliened without equivalent.

18 Eliz. Cap. VI.

An Acte for the Maintenance of the Colledges in the Universityes, and of Winchester and Eaton.

FOR the better maintenance of learninge and the better relief of scollers in the Universities of Cambridge and Oxforde and the Colledges of Winchester and Eaton, be yt enacted by the Quenes Majestie the Lordes Spirituall and Temporall and the Commons in this present Parliament assembled and by thauctorytie of the same, that no Master

For the better maintenance of Colleges, &c.

Provoste Presydent Warden Deane Governor Rector or Chief Ruler of any Colledge Cathedrall Churche Halle or Howse of Learninge in any of the Universities aforesaide, nor no Provoste Warden or other Hed Officer of the saide Colledges of Winchester or Eaton, nor the corporacion of any of the same, by what tytle style or name soever they nowe be shall or may be called, after thende of this present Session of Parliament, shall make anye Lease for lief lieves or yeeres of anie ferme or anie their landes tenementes or other heredytamentes to the which anie tythes errable lande meadowe or pasture dothe or shall apperteigne, excepte that thone thirde parte at the leaste of tholde Rente be reserved and paide in Corne for the saide Colleges Cathedrall Churche Halles and Howses; that is to saye, in good Wheate after vjs. viijd. the quarter or under, and good Malte after vs. the quarter or under, to be delivered yerelie uppon dayes prefixed at the saide Colledges Cathedrall Churche Halles or Howses; and for defaulte thereof to paye to the said Colledges Cathedrall Churche Halls or Howses in readie money, at the election of the saide Lessees their executors administrators and assignes, after the rate as the beste Wheate and Malte in the markett of Cambridge for the Rentes that are to be paide to the use of the Howse or Howses there, and in the market of Oxforde for the Rentes that are to be paide to the use of the Howse or Howses there, and in the market of Winchester for the Rentes that are to be paide to the use of the Howse or Howses there, and in the market of Windesore for the Rentes that are to be paide to thuse of the Howse or Howses at Eaton, ys or shalbe solde the nexte markett daye before the saide Rente shalbe due, withowte fraude or deceipte; and that all Leases otherwise hereafter to be made, and all collaterall bondes or assuraunce to the contrarye by anye of the saide corporacions, shalbe voyde in lawe to all intentes and purposes; the same Wheat Malte or the money cominge of the same to be expended to the use of the relief of the commons and diett of the saide Colledges Cathederall Churche Halles and Howses onlie, and by no fraude nor collor lett nor solde awaye from the profitt of the saide Colledges Cathedrall Churche Halles and Howses, and the Fellowes and Scollers in the same, and the use aforesaide; upon payne of deprivacion to the Governor and Chief Rulers of the said Colleges Cathedrall Churche Halles and Howses, and all other thereto consentinge.

[Then follow two provisoes, one for a Lease of Mounken Barn at Southwick in Sussex belonging to Magdalen College, Oxford, the other for Leases of the Manor of Fyfield in Berkshire from St. John's College, Oxford, to any heir male of Sir Thomas White the Founder of the College.]

18 Eliz. Cap. XI.

An Acte for Thexplanacion of the Statutes entytuled againste the defeating of Dilapidacions and againste Leases to bee made of Spirituall Promocions in some Respectes.

WHEREAS by a Statute made in a Parliament holden at Westminster the seconde daye of Aprill in the thirtenth yere of the Raigne of our moste gracious Soveraigne Ladie, entytled An Acte against fraudulent Giftes to the intent to defeate Dilapidacions of Ecclesiasticall Lyvinges, and for Leases to be graunted by Collegiate Churches, yt was amongeste other thinges enacted by thaucthoritye of Parliament, that from thenceforth all leases gyftes grauntes feoffementes conveyaunces or estates to be made had donne or suffred by any Master and Fellowes of anye Colledge, or by anye Deane and Chapter of anye Cathedrall or Collegiate Churche, Mayster or Guardian of anye Hospitall, Parson Vicar or anye other havinge anye spirituall or ecclesiasticall lyvinge, or * anye howses landes tythes tenementes or other hereditamentes beinge any parcell of the possessions of any suche Colledge Cathedrall Churche Chapter Hospitall Parsonage Vicarage or other spirituall promocion, or any wayes apperteyninge or belonginge to the same, or of anye of them, to any person or persons bodies pollitique or corporate, other then for the terme of xxj yeres or three lyves from the tyme of * anye suche lease or graunte shalbe made or graunted whereuppon thaccustomed yerelye rente or more shalbe

Recital of 13 Eliz. c. 10, s. 2, for restraining Leases by Colleges &c.

* So in orig. Read of.

* So in orig. Read as.

reserved and payable yerelye duringe the saide tearme, shalbe utterly voyde and of none effecte to all intentes construccions and purposes, anye lawe custome or usage to the contrary notwithstandinge; as in the saide Acte more playnely appeareth: sithens the makinge of which saide Estatute dyvers of the saide ecclesiasticall and spirituall persones, and others havinge spirituall or ecclesiasticall lyvinges, have from tyme to tyme made Leases for the terme of xxj yeres or three lyves longe before the expiracion of the former yeres, contrary to the trewe meaninge and intente of the said Estatute: be yt therefore enacted by this present Parlyament, that all Leases hereafter to be made by any of the said ecclesiasticall spirituall or collegiate persons or others of any their said ecclesiasticall spirituall or collegiate landes tenementes or hereditamentes whereof any former Lease for yeres is in beinge, not to be expired surrendred or ended within three yeres nexte after the makinge of any suche newe Lease, shalbe voyde frustrate and of none effecte; any lawe usage or custome to the contrarye notwithstandinge.

Evasion thereof.

All Leases made by Colleges &c. of Lands &c. being in Lease for more than 3 Years then unexpired &c. shall be void.

2. And be yt likewise enacted by thauctoritie aforesaide, that all and everie band and covenante whatsoever hereafter to be made for renewinge or makinge of any Lease or Leases contrary to the trewe intente of this Acte, or of the saide Acte made in the said xiij yere, shalbe utterlye voyde; anye lawe Statute ordinaunce or other thinge whatsoever to the contrarye in any wise notwithstandinge.

All Bonds to the contrary shall be void.

3. Provided alwayes, that this Acte nor any thinge therein conteyned shall extende or be prejudiciall to make frustrate or voyde any Lease or Leases heretofore made by anye of the said spirituall and ecclesiasticall person or persouns or any of them; but that the same and everie of them are of the like force and effecte as they or anye of them were before the makinge of this present Statute; this Acte or any thinge therein conteyned to the contrarye notwithstandinge.

Proviso for existing Leases.

[Section 4 enables St. John's College in Oxford to grant certain Leases of the Manor of Fyfield in Berkshire to the heirs male of Sir Thomas White, the Founder of the College, any Act to the contrary notwithstanding.]

31 Eliz. Cap. VI.

An Acte against Abuses in Election of Scollers and presentacions to Benefices.

WHEREAS by the intent of the Founders of Colledges, Churches Collegiat, Churches Cathedrall, Scoles Hospitalls Halles and other like Societies within this Realme, and by the Statutes and good Orders of the same, the eleccions presentacions and nominacions of Fellowes Schollers Officers and other persons to have roome or place in the same are to be had and made of the fittest and moste meete persons, beinge capable of the same eleccions presentacions and nominacions, freelye without anye rewarde guyfte or thinge given or taken for the same; and for true performaunce whereof some ellectors presentors and nomynators in the same have or shoulde take a corporall oathe to make their eleccions presentacions and nominacions accordinglye; yet notwithstandinge it is sene and founde by experience that the saide eleccions presentacions and nominacions be manye tymes wrought and brought to passe with monye guyftes and rewardes, whereby the fyttest persons to be presented elected or nominated, wantinge money or friendes, are sildome or not at all preferred, contrarie to the good meaninge of the saide Founders and the saide good Statutes and Ordynaunces of the saide Colledges Churches Scholes Halles Hospitalls & Soeyeties, and to the great prejudice of learninge and the common wealthe and estate of the Realme: *Elections of Fellows, Scholars, &c., in Colleges &c. are often made corruptly.*

For remedye whereof, be it enacted by the Quenes most excellent Majestie the Lordes Spirituall and Temporall and the Commons in this present Parliament assembled, and by the authoritie of the same, that yf any person or persons bodyes pollitick or corporate, whiche have eleccion presentacion or nominacion, or voyce or assent in the choyse eleccion presentacion or nominacion, of anye Fellowe Scholler or any other person, to have roome or place in anye the saide Churches Colledges Scholes Hospitalls Halles or Societies, shall, at anye tyme after fortye daies next after the ende of this present Session of Parliament, have receyve or take anye *If any Member of a College &c. shall take any bribe for any election, his place in the said College &c. shall be void.*

monye fee rewarde or any other profytt, directly or indirectlie, or shall take any promyse agreament covenante bonde or other assuraunce to receyve or have any monye fee rewarde or any other profytt, directlye or indirectlye, either to him or themselves or to any other of their or anye of their freindes, for his or their voice or voices assent or assentes or consentes in electinge chosinge presentinge or nominatinge anye Officer Fellowe Scholler or other person, to have any roome or place in any the saide Churches Colledges Halles Scholes Hospitalles or Societies, that then and from thenceforthe the place roome or office whiche suche person soe offendinge shall then have in anye the saide Churches Colledges Scholles Halles Hospitalls or Societies shalbe voyde; and that then aswell the Quenes Majestie her heires and successors, and everie other person and persons their heires and successors, to whom the presentacion donacion guyfte eleccion or disposicion shall of right belonge or apperteyne of anye suche of the saide roomes or places of the saide person offendinge as aforesaide, shall or maye at their pleasure elect present nominate place or appoynte any other person or persons in the roome office or place of suche person or persons so offendinge, as yf the saide person or persons so offendinge then were naturallie deade.

Any Fellow &c. resigning his place for a bribe shall forfeit double the sum taken by him.

2. And be it further enacted by the authoritie aforesaide, that yf any Fellowe Officer or Scholler of anye the saide Churches Colledges Scholes Halles Hospitalls or Societies, or other persons havinge roome or place in anye of the same, shall at anye tyme hereafter directly or indirectlie take or receive, or by any waye devise or meanes contract or agree to have or receyve, any monye rewarde or profytt whatsoever for the levinge or resignyng upp of the same his roome or place for any other to be placed in the same, that then everie person so takinge or contractinge or agreinge to take or have any thinge for the same shall forfeyte and loose double the somme of money or value of the thinge so receyved and

Every person by or for whom a bribe shall be given shall be incapable of

taken or agreed to be receyved or taken; and everie person, by whom or for whom anye monye guyfte or rewarde as aforesaide shalbe given or agreed to be payde, shalbe uncapeable of that place or roome for that tyme or turne, and shall not be nor had nor taken to be a laufull Fellowe Scholler or

Officer of any the Churches Colledges Halles Hospitalls *the place for that time.* Scholles or Societies, or to have suche roome or place there; but that they to whome it shall apperteyne, at any tyme thereafter, shall and maye elect chose present and nominate any other person, fitt to be elected presented or nominated, into the saide roome or Felloweshippe, as yf the saide person, by or for whome anye suche money gufte or rewarde shalbe given or agreed to be payde, were dead or had resigned and leafte the same.

3. And for more syncere eleccion choyce presentacion and nominacion of Fellowes Schollers Officers and other persons to have roome or place hereafter in anye of the saide Churches Colledges Halles Scholles Hospitalls and other like Societies, be it further enacted by the authoritie aforesaide, that at the tyme of everie suche eleccion presentacion or nominacion hereafter to be had, aswell this present Acte, as Thorders and Statutes of the same Places concernynge suche eleccion presentacion or nominacion to be had, shall then and there be publiklye read, upon payne that everie person in whom defaulte thereof shalbe shall forfeyte and loose the somme of fortye poundes: all whiche forfeytures shall and maye be had & recovered in any her Majesties Courtes of Recorde by any person or persons bodies pollitique and corporate that will sue for the same by bill playnt or accion of debte, in whiche noe essoyne protection or wager of lawe shalbe allowed; thone moytie whereof shalbe to him or them that will sue for the same, thother moytie to the use of the saide Churche Colledge Hall Hospitall Schole or Societie where suche Offence shalbe commytted. *This Act shall be read at every Election of Fellows &c. Penalty, £40.* *Recovery of Penalties.*

[The Act contains six more sections, directed against corrupt practices in regard to Benefices. It is the custom at Academical Elections to read no more of it than the first three sections here printed.]

43 Eliz. Cap. IV.

An Acte to redresse the Misemployment of Landes Goodes and Stockes of Money heretofore given to Charitable Uses.

Commissions to inquire into the application of Charitable Gifts &c.

[The first section of this Act provides for the issuing of Commissions to Bishops and others, from time to time, to inquire into the application of Charitable Gifts &c.]

Not to extend to Colleges or Cathedrals.

2. Provided alwaies, that neither this Acte, nor any thinge therein conteined, shall in any wise extende to any landes tenements rents annuities profits goods chattels money or stockes of money given limitted appointe or assigned, or whiche shalbe given limitted appointed or assigned, to any Colledge Hall or Howse of Learninge within the Universities of Oxforde or Cambridge, or to the Colledges of Westmynster Eaton or Winchester, or any of them, or to any Cathedrall or Collegiate Churche within this Realme.

3 Jac. I, Cap. V.

An Acte to prevent & avoid dangers which may grow by Popish Recusantes.

Popish Recusants convict disabled from presenting to Benefices; and their rights of presentation made over to the two Universities.

13. And be it further enacted by the authority of this present Parliament, that everie person or persons that is or shall be a Popishe Recusant convict, during the tyme that he shalbe or remaine a Recusant, shall from and after the end of this present Session of Parliament be utterly disabled to present to any Benefice, with cure or without cure, Prebend or any other ecclesiasticall living, or to collate or nominate to any Freeschole Hospitall or Donative whatsoever, and from the beginning of this present Session of Parliament shall likewise be disabled to graunt any avoydance to any Benefice Prebend or other ecclesiasticall living; and that the Chauncellour and Schollers of the University of Oxforde, soe often as any of them shalbe voide, shall have the presenta-

cion nominacion collation and donacion of and to everie such Beneficc Prebend or ecclesiasticall living, Schoole Hospitall and Donative, sett lying and being in the counties of Oxford Kent Middlesex Sussex Surrey Hampshire Berkshire Buckinghamshire Gloucestershire Worcestershire Staffordshire Warwickshire Wiltshire Somersetshire Devonshire Cornewall Dorsetshire Herefordshire Northamptonshire Pembrockshire Carmarthenshire Brecknockshire Monmouthshire Cardiganshire Mountgomeryshire, the Citye of London, and in every citye and towne being a countye of it selfe lying and being within any of the limittes or precinctes of any of the counties aforesaide, or in or within any of them, as shall happen to be voide during such tyme as the patron thereof shalbe and remaine a Recusant convict as aforesaide; and that the Chancellor and Schollers of the University of Cambridge shall have the presentacion nominacion collacion and donacion of and to everie such Beneficc Prebend or ecclesiasticall living, Schoole Hospitall and Donative, set lying and being in the counties of Essex Hartfordshire Bedfordshire Cambridgeshire Huntingtonshire Suffolke Norffolke Lincolneshire Rutlandshire Leicestershire Derbishire Nottinghamshire Shropshire Cheshire Lancashire Yorkeshire the County of Durham Northumberland Cumberland Westmoreland Raduorshire Denbighshire Flintshire Carnarvonshire Angleseyshire Merionethshire Glamorganshire, and in everie city and towne being a county of itselfe lying within any of the limits or precinctes of any of the counties last before mencioned, or in or within any of them, as shall happen to be voide during such tyme as the patron thereof shall be and remaine a Recusant convict as aforesaide: Provided that neither of the saide Chauncellors and Schollers of either the saide Universities shall present or nominate to any Benefice with cure Prebend or other ecclesiasticall living any such person as shall then have any other Benefice with cure of soules; and if any such presentacion or nominacion shalbe had or made of any such person soo beneficed, the said presentacion or nominacion shalbe utterly voide, any thing in this Acte to the contrarye notwithstanding.

7 Jac. I, Cap. VI.

An Acte for administringe the Oath of Allegiance, and Reformacion of married Women Recusantes.

<small>Oath of Allegiance prescribed by 3 Jac. I, c. 4, s. 9.</small>

WHEREAS by a Statute made in the third yere of your Majesties Raigne, intituled An Act for the better discovering and repressing of Popish Recusantes, the forme of an Othe to be ministred and given to certaine persons in the same Act mencioned is lymited and prescribed[m] . . . ; to shewe howe greatly your loyall subjectes doe approve the said Oath, they prostrate themselves at your Majesties feete, beseeching your Majestie that the same Oath may be administred to all your subjectes: to which end wee doe with all humblenes beseech your Highnes that it may be enacted, and be it enacted by the authoritie of this present Parliament,

<small>To be taken by all subjects, mentioned in this Act, above the age of 18 years, viz.</small>

that all and every person and persons, aswell ecclesiasticall as temporall, of what estate dignitie preheminence sexe qualitie or degree soever hee she or they be or shalbe, above the age of eighteene yeeres, beinge hereafter in this Act mencioned and entended, shall make take and receyve a corporall Oath upon the Evangelistes, according to the tenor and effect of the said Oath sett forth in the said forementioned Statute, before such person or persons as hereafter in this Act is expressed, that is to saye; . . . .

<small>Vice-Chancellors, Heads of Houses, &c. in the Universities.</small>

the Vicechancellors of both the Universities for the tyme being, and the Presidentes Wardens Provostes Masters of Colledges and Halles and all other Heades and Principalles of Houses Proctors and Bedles of the Universities, publikelie in the Convocacion, before the Senior Masters there present; and

<small>Persons taking Degrees.</small>

all and every other persons whatsoever that is or shalbe promoted to any Degree in Schole, before the Vicechancellor of the said Universitie for the tyme being, in the Congregacion House;

<small>Fellows and Schollars in Colleges.</small>

all Fellowes of Howses and all Schollers of Halles or Colledges that nowe are or hereafter shalbe received

[m] The form of the Oath of Allegiance prescribed by 3 Jac. I, c. 4, s. 9, was altered by 1 W. & M., c. 8, s. 12; and the altered form was repeated in 1 Geo. I, st. 2, c. 13. It was combined with the Oaths of Supremacy and Abjuration into one Oath by 21 & 22 Vict. c. 48.

into the same, being under the degree of a Baron ⁿ, before the President Master Provost Warden or other head or cheif Governor of that Colledg Hall or Howse whereinto he shalbe received, and in the open Hall.

12 Car. II, Cap. XXXIV.

An Act for Prohibiting the Planting Setting or Sowing of Tobaccho in England and Ireland.

[This Act directs that no person shall after January 1, 1661, set or plant any Tobacco anywhere in England or Ireland under penalty of forty shillings per rod or pole of ground planted.] *(No person shall set or plant Tobacco.)*

4. Provided alwayes and it is hereby enacted, that this Act or * any thing therin contained shall extend to the hindering of the planting of Tobaccho in any Phisicke Garden of either University, or in any other private Garden for Phisicke or Surgery onely, soe as the quantity soe planted exceed not one halfe of one pole in any one place or garden. *(Proviso for Physic Gardens in the Universities &c. * So in orig. Read nor.)*

[This Proviso is repeated in 15 C. II, c. 7, and in 22 & 23 C. II, c. 26, by which Acts the prohibition against growing Tobacco was enforced; and it is confirmed by 1 & 2 W. IV, c. 13, which revives the prohibition in Ireland, where the growth had been allowed by 19 G. III, c. 35.]

14 Car. II, Cap. IV.

An Act for the Uniformity of Publique Prayers and Administracion of Sacraments & other Rites & Ceremonies and for establishing the Form of making ordaining and consecrating Bishops Preists and Deacons in the Church of England.

[The first section of this Act recites that the Book of Common Prayer, enjoined to be used by 1 Eliz. c. 2, has recently *(Book of Common Prayer,)*

ⁿ Persons "of or above the degree of a Baron of Parliament" are to take the Oath before four of the Privy Council, or before Commissioners appointed by the Lord Chancellor by writ of Dedimus potestatem.

revised by Commissioners and by the Convocations of both provinces, and then approved by the King.

been revised by Commissioners appointed under the Great Seal and afterwards by the Convocations of both provinces, and that the King has approved the Book so revised and has recommended to Parliament that it "be appointed to be used by all that officiate in all Cathedrall and Collegiate Churches and Chappells and in all Chappells of Colledges and Halls in both the Universities and the Colledges of Eaton and Winchester and in all Parish Churches and Chappells;" and then it enacts] That all and singuler Ministers in any Cathedrall Collegiate or Parish Church or Chappell or other place of Publique Worship within this Realme of England dominion of Wales and town of Berwick upon Tweed shall be bound to say and use the Morning Prayer Evening Prayer Celebracion and Administracion of both the Sacraments and all other the Publique and Common Prayer in such order and forme as is mencioned in the said Booke, annexed and joyned to this present Act, and entituled The Booke of Common Prayer and Administration of the Sacraments and other Rites and Ceremonies of the Church according to the use of the Church of England togeather with the Psalter or Psalmes of David pointed as they are to be sung or said in Churches and the forme or manner of making ordaining and consecrating of Bishops Preists & Deacons; and that the Morning and Evening Prayers therein contained shall upon every Lords day and upon all other dayes and occasions and att the times therein appointed be openly and solemnly read by all and every Minister or Curate in every Church Chappell or other place of Publique Worshipp within this Realme of England and places aforesaid.

To be used in all Cathedral and Parish Churches &c.

[Section 2 required every beneficed person to] declare his unfeigned assent & consent to the use of all things in the said Booke contained and prescribed in these words and no other.

Form of Assent.

I A. B. doe declare my unfaigned assent and consent to all and every thing contained and prescribed in and by the Booke intituled The Booke of Common Prayer and Administration of the Sacraments and other Rites and Ceremonies of the Church according to the use of the Church of England togeather with the Psalter or Psalmes of David pointed as they are to be sung or said in Churches and the form or

manner of making ordaining and consecrating of Bishops
Preists and Deacons.º

[The first portion of section 6, which in the ordinary editions of the Statutes is made a separate section by itself and numbered as sect. 8, is wholly repealed by the Clerical Subscription Act, 1865, 28 & 29 Vict. c. 122. It enacted that certain ecclesiastical persons, "and all Masters and other Heads, Fellowes, Chaplaines, and Tutors of or in any Colledge, Hall, House of Learning, or Hospitall, and every Publique Professor and Reader in either of the Universities," and certain other persons, shall "at or before his or theire respective admission to .... have possession" of such place or office subscribe a certain Declaration; which, after an alteration made in it by 1 Gul. & Mar. c. 8, s. 11, stands as follows.]

I A. B. do declare that I will conforme to the Liturgy of the Church of England as it is now by law established. Form of the Declaration.

Which said Declaration and Acknowledgment shall be subscribed by every of the said Masters and other Heads Fellowes Chaplaines and Tutors of or in any Colledge Hall or House of Learning and by every Publique Professor and Reader in either of the Universities before the Vice Chancellor of the respective Universities for the time being or his deputy, ... upon pain that all and every of the persons aforesaid failing in such subscription shall loose and forfeit such respective .... Mastershipp Headship Fellowship Professors place Readers place ...., and shall be utterly disabled and (ipso facto) deprived of the same, and that every such respective .... Mastership Headship Fellowship Professors place Readers place .... shall be void, as if such person so failing were naturally dead. ᵖ Before whom to be subscribed.

Persons not subscribing the same deprived.

Their places void.

13. And be it further enacted by the authority aforesaid, that no form or order of Common Prayers Administracion No other Form of Prayer to

---

º By the Clerical Subscription Act, 1865, 28 & 29 Vict. c. 122, this Form of Assent is repealed for all persons "in Holy Orders appointed to any Ecclesiastical Dignity, Benefice, or Office," and another Declaration of Assent is substituted. But the Form here printed seems to be still in force for Heads of Colleges and Halls under s. 13 of this Act.

ᵖ In the ordinary editions of the Statutes the Declaration by itself is made section 9, and the next paragraph section 10. Neither has been repealed.

be used in Colleges. of Sacraments Rites or Ceremonies shall be openly used in any Church Chappell or other publique place of or in any Colledge or Hall in either of the Universities, the Colledges of Westminster Winchester or Eaton or any of them, other then what is prescribed and appointed to be used in and by the said Booke; and that the present Governour or Head of every Colledge and Hall in the said Universities and of the said Colledges of Westminster Winchester and Eaton within one moneth after the Feast of St. Bartholomew which shall be in the yeare of our Lord one thousand six hundred sixty *Heads of Colleges &c. to subscribe the 39 Articles, and declare their assent thereunto, and to the Book of Common Prayer;* and two, and every Governour or Head of any of the said Colledges or Halls hereafter to be elected or appointed within one moneth next after his election or collation and admission into the same Government or Headshipp, shall openly and publiquely in the Church Chappell or other publique place of the same Colledge or Hall, and in the presence of the Fellowes and Scholars of the same or the greater part of them then resident, subscribe unto the nine and thirty Articles of Religion mentioned in the Statute made in the thirteenth yeare of the reigne of the late Queene Elizabeth and unto the said Booke, and declare his unfeigned assent and consent unto and approbation of the said Articles and of the same Booke and to the use of all the Prayers Rites and Ceremonies Formes and Orders in the said Booke prescribed and contained according to the form aforesaid; and *and once in every quarter of the year to read the Prayers in the College Chapel.* that all such Governours or Heads of the said Colledges and Halls or any of them as are or shall be in Holy Orders shall once (at least) in every quarter of the yeare (not having a lawfull impediment) openly and publiquely read the Morning Prayer and Service in and by the said Booke appointed to be read in the Church Chappell or other publique place of the *Penalty.* same Colledge or Hall, upon pain to loose and be suspended of and from all the benefitts and profitts belonging to the same Government or Headship by the space of six moneths by the Visitor or Visitors of the same Colledge or Hall. And if any Governour or Head of any Colledge or Hall, suspended for not subscribing unto the said Articles and Booke or for not reading of the Morning Prayer and Service as aforesaid, shall not att or before the end of six moneths next after such suspension subscribe unto the said Articles and Booke and declare his consent thereunto as aforesaid, or read the Morning Prayer and Service as aforesaid, then such Government or Headshipp shall be (ipso facto) void.

14. Provided alwaies, that it shall and may be lawfull to use the Morning and Evening Prayer and all other Prayers and Service prescribed in and by the said Booke in the Chappells or other publique places of the respective Colledges and Halls in both the Universities, in the Colledges of Westminster Winchester and Eaton, and in the Convocations of the Clergies of either province, in Latine, any thing in this Act contained to the contrary notwithstanding. *Proviso for reading the Prayers in Latin in Colleges, &c.*

[Sections 15–18 relate to Lecturers and Preachers, and provide (among other things) that, when any sermon or lecture is to be preached, the Common Prayers and Service appointed for that time of the day shall be first read.]

19. Provided neverthelesse, that this Act shall not extend to the University Churches in the Universities of this Realme, or either of them, when or att such times as any Sermon or Lecture is preached or read in the said Churches or any of them for or as the publick University Sermon or Lecture, but that the same Sermons and Lectures may be preached or read in such sort and manner as the same have been heretofore preached or read, this Act or any thing herein contained to the contrary thereof in any wise notwithstanding. *Proviso respecting University Sermons preached in the University Churches.*

25. Provided alsoe, that this Act or any thing therein contained shall not be prejudiciall or hurtfull unto the Kings Professor of the Law within the University of Oxford for or concerning the Prebend of Shipton within the Cathedrall Church of Sarum united and annexed unto the place of the same Kings Professor for the time being by the late King James of blessed memory. *Proviso for King's Professor of Law at Oxford for Prebend o Shipton.*

1 GUL. & MAR. Cap. VIII.

An Act for the Abrogating of the Oathes of Supremacy and Allegiance and Appointing other Oathes.

[This Act abrogates the Oath of Supremacy appointed by 1 Eliz. c. 1, and the Oath of Allegiance appointed by 3 Jac. I,

c. 4; and enacts that the Oaths appointed by this present Act shall be taken by such persons, in such manner, at such times, before such persons, and in such courts and places, as are prescribed by any previous Statute concerning the abrogated Oaths or either of them.]

12. And bee it enacted, that the Oathes that are intended and required to be taken by this Act are the Oathes in these expresse words hereafter following.

<small>Form of Oaths.</small>

I A B doe sincerely promise and sweare, that I will be faithfull and beare true allegiance to their Majestyes King William and Queene Mary.　　　Soe helpe me God &c.

I A B doe sweare, that I doe from my heart abhor detest and abjure, as impious and hereticall, that damnable doctrine and position, that Princes excommunicated or deprived by the Pope or any authoritie of the See of Rome may be deposed or murthered by their subjects or any other whatsoever. And I doe declare, that noe forreigne Prince Person Prelate State or Potentate hath or ought to have any jurisdiction power superiority preeminence or authoritie ecclesiasticall or spirituall within this Realme.　　　Soe helpe me God &c.

1 Gul. & Mar. Cap. XXVI.

An Act to rest in the two Universities the Presentations of Benefices belonging to Papists.

[This Act provides that every person who shall refuse or neglect to make, repeat, and subscribe the Declaration against Transubstantiation and the Invocation of Saints and the Sacrifice of the Mass prescribed by 30 Car. II, st. 2, according to the requirements of 1 Gul. & Mar. c. 15, shall be disabled to present to any Benefice as if he were a Popish Recusant convict, and that his right of presentation shall pass to the Universities according to the provisions of 3 Jac. I, c. 5, s. 13.]

<small>Trustees for Popish Recusants convict, or</small>

2. And bee it further enacted by the authoritie aforesaid, that where any person or persons are or shall be seised or possessed of any advowson right of presentation collation

or nomination to any such Ecclesiasticall Liveing Free Schoole or Hospitall as aforesaid in trust for any Papist or Popish Recusant, who shall be convicted or disabled according to the true intent and meaning of the said Statute made in the third yeare of the Raigne of the said King James the First, or by this present Act, every such person and persons soe seised and possessed in trust for any Papist or Popish Recusant convict or disabled shall be and are hereby adjudged to be disabled to present nominate or collate to any such Ecclesiasticall Liveing Free Schoole or Hospitall, or to grant any avoidance thereof; and their and every of their presentations nominations collations and grants shall be null and void to all intents and purposes whatsoever; and the Chancellors and Schollers of the said respective Universities as aforesaid upon every avoidance shall have the presentations nominations and collations to such Ecclesiasticall Liveings Free Schooles and Hospitalls in such manner as they should have the same in case such Recusant convict or disabled were seized or possessed thereof. And in case any trustee or trustees or mortgagee or grantee of any avoidance hereafter present nominate or collate, or cause to be presented nominated or collated, any person to any such Ecclesiasticall Liveing Free Schoole or Hospitall whereof the trust shall be for any Recusant convict or disabled, without giveing notice of the avoidance in writing to the Vice-Chancellor for the time being of the University to whome the presentation nomination or collation shall belong according to the true intent of this Act within three months after the avoidance shall happen, such trustee or trustees mortgagees or grantees shall forfeit and pay the summe of five hundred pounds to the said respective Chancellors and Schollers of either of the said Universities, to whome such presentation nomination or collation shall belong according to the true intent of this present Act, to be recovered in any of their Majestyes Courts of Record by action of debt bill plaint or information, wherein noe essoigne protection or wager of law shall be allowed. Provided alwayes, that the said Chancellors and Schollers of either of the said Universities shall not present or nominate to any Benefice with cure Prebend or other Ecclesiasticall Liveing any person as shall

for persons disabled by 3 Jac. I, c. 5, also disabled to present.

In such case Universities to present.

Trustees &c. presenting without giving notice of avoidance to Vice-Chancellor of the University entitled to present shall forfeit £500.

Presentation by Universities of person beneficed, void.

then have any other Benefice with cure of soules: and if any such presentation shall be had or made of any such person soe beneficed, the said presentation shall be utterly void, any thing in this Act to the contrary notwithstanding.

What absence makes living void.
Provided, that if any person soe presented or nominated to any Benefice with cure shall be absent from the same above the space of sixty dayes in any one year, that in such case the said Benefice shall become void.

7 & 8 GUL. III, Cap. XXXVII.

An Act for the Encouragement of Charitable Giftes and Dispositions.

WHEREAS it would be a great hinderance to learning and other good and charitable workes, if persons well inclined may not be permitted to found Colleges or Schools for encouragement of learning, or to augment the revenues of Colleges or Schools already founded by granting landes tenementes rentes or other hereditamentes to such Colleges or Schools, or to grant landes or other hereditamentes to other bodies politick or incorporated now in being or hereafter to be incorporated for other good and public uses; be it therefore enacted by the Kinges most Excellent Majesty by and with the advice and consent of the Lordes Spiritual and Temporal and Commons in this present Parliament assembled and by the authority of the same, that it shall and may be lawfull *The King may grant Licences to alien and to hold in Mortmain.* to and for the King our most gracious Sovereigne Lord and for his heires and successors, when and as often and in such cases as his Majesty his heires or successors shall think fitt, to grant to any person or persons bodies politick or corporate their heires and successors licence to aliene in mortmaine, and also to purchase acquire take and hold in mortmaine, in perpetuity or otherwise, any landes tenementes rentes or hereditamentes whatsoever, of whomsoever the same shall be holden.

Lands so aliened or acquired not forfeited.
2. And it is hereby declared, that landes tenementes rentes or hereditamentes so aliened or acquired and licensed shall not be subject to any forfeiture for or by reason of such alienation or acquisition.

12 & 13 Gul. III, Cap. XI.

An Act for granting to His Majesty Several Duties upon Low Wines or Spirits of the First Extraction, and continuing several additional Duties upon Coffee Tea Chocolate Spices and Pictures, and certain Impositions upon Hawkers Pedlars and Petty Chapmen, and the Duty of Fifteen per Centum upon Muslins, and for improving the Duties upon Japanned and Laquered Goods, and for continuing the Coinage Duty for the several Terms and Purposes therein mentioned.

15. And whereas by an Act made in the eleventh year of His Majesties Reign, entituled An Act for ascertaining the Measures for retailing Ale and Beer, it is enacted, that every Mayor or Chief Officer of each city town corporate borough or market town, from and after the twenty fourth day of June one thousand seven hundred, shall from time to time cause or procure all Ale Quarts and Ale Pints brought to him or them respectively to be measured compared sized and equalled with the Standard and then signed stamped and markt as in the said Act is mentioned and described; be it enacted and declared, that nothing in the said recited Act contained shall extend, or be construed or taken to extend, to deprive the two Universities of this Kingdom or either of them of their right priviledge and usage of sizing equalling signing stamping and marking of Measures for Ale and Beer within their respective limits and jurisdictions; but that they and each of them respectively shall and may have and enjoy their said right priviledge and usage, any thing in the said recited Act to the contrary thereof in any wise notwithstanding.

<small>Recital of 11 W. 3, c. 15, s. 5.</small>

<small>The said Act not to deprive the Universities of the privilege of stamping Ale and Beer Measures.</small>

10 Annæ, Cap. XLV.

An Act for confirming and rendering more effectual certain Letters Patents of King James the First for annexing a Canonry and several Rectoryes to the Regius Professor of Divinity in the University of Oxford and to the Regius Professor and Lady Margarett's Reader of Divinity in the University of Cambridge.

<small>Recital of Letters Patent of 26th Aug. 3 James I.</small>

WHEREAS our most gracious Soveraign King James the First of blessed memory, for the support and maintenance of the Regius Professor or Reader of Divinity in the University of Oxford, did by his Letters Patent, bearing date the twenty sixth day of August in the third year of his Reign, grant to the Chancellor Masters and Schollars of the said University of Oxford and their successors all that his advowson donation free disposition and right of patronage of the Rectory of Newelme alias Ewelme in the county of Oxford, and the said late King James the First by the said Letters Patent did for himself his heires and successors grant to the said Chancellor Masters and Schollars of the said University and their successors, that the said Regius Professor for the time being for ever should have and enjoy one Prebend or Canonry within the Cathedral Church of Christ in Oxford of the foundation of King Henry the Eighth, so long as he should be Regius Professor of Divinity in that University: and whereas the said King James the First, for the encrease of the stipend of the Regius Professor or Reader of Divinity in the University of Cambridge, did by other his Letters Patent of the same date grant to the Chancellor Masters and Schollars of the said University of Cambridge and their successors all that his advowson donation free disposition and right of patronage of the Rectory of Somersham (together with Colne and Pidley and other Chappelryes rights members and appurtenances) in the county of Huntington; and whereas the said King James the First (for the encrease of the stipend of the Reader of the Lecture of Divinity appointed by Margaret Countess of Richmond mother of King Henry the Seventh in the said University of Cambridge) did also by the said Letters Patent grant to the Chancellor Masters and Schollars of the said University of Cambridge and their successors all that his advowson donation free disposition and right of patronage of the Rectory of Terington in the County of Norfolk with all it's rights members and appurtenances: and whereas the said King James the First in and by the said several Letters Patent did signify and declare it to be his royal will and pleasure, that the said Canonry and several Rectoryes should for ever thereafter be held and enjoyed by the said several Professors and Reader of the Lecture aforesaid for so long time as they respectively should continue in the said respective offices or places, and did thereby further signify and declare his royal will and intention to be that one or more Act or Acts of Parliament should be obtained for that purpose, which hath never yet been done:

May it therefore please your Majesty that it may be enacted, and be it enacted by the Queens most excellent Majesty by and with the advice and consent of the Lords Spiritual and Temporal and Comons in this present Parliament assembled and by the authority of the same, that the said Canonry of Christ Church and several Rectoryes of Newelme alias Ewelme Somersham and Terington and every of them, and all members tythes lands tenements hereditaments profitts and emoluments whatsoever to them and every of them respectively belonging or in any wise appertaining, or with the said Canonry and Rectoryes every or any of them used or enjoyed, are and shall hereby be united and for ever annexed unto the several offices or places aforesaid, and shall be held and enjoyed by the respective persons already placed in the said offices or places, and by such other person and persons as shall from time to time for ever hereafter be placed and put into the said offices or places, in as full and ample manner to all intents and purposes as if they were duly presented nominated admitted instituted and inducted thereunto. And the said respective Professors and Reader of the said Lecture and their

The Canonry of Christ Church and the several Rectories herein mentioned, united to the said several offices.

successors for the time being, during such time and times only as they shall continue in their respective offices or places, shall by vertue of such office or place for ever hereafter enjoy the said respective Canonry and also shall have and hold the said Rectoryes without any presentation admission institution or induction or any other act or thing whatsoever to entitle them thereunto; and shall be and are hereby declared to be (during their continuance in the said respective offices or places) full and perfect Canon and Incumbents of the respective Canonry and Rectoryes aforesaid to all intents and purposes whatsoever: which nevertheless shall not be so understood as to make void any other benefice or benefices which the said Professors and Reader of the said Lecture or any of them is at present or shall hereafter be legally possessed of; it being the intention of this Act, that the aforesaid Rectoryes shall consist and be held and enjoyed by the said Professors and Reader of the said Lecture respectively together with any one other ecclesiastical benefice, without any lycence or dispensation for that end to be granted or obtained.

The said Canonry and Rectories to be held and enjoyed by virtue of the said offices only.

2. And it is hereby further enacted and declared, that, as often as it shall happen that any of the said offices or places shall become void by death resignation or otherwise, the Canonry and Rectoryes or the Rectory to such office or place respectively belonging shall at the same time become void, and the person that shall be placed in such office or place so become void shall, by vertue of such office or place only, have and enjoy the Canonry and Rectoryes or the Rectory to such office or place belonging for so long time as he shall continue in such office or place and no longer.

The Professors to do the duty of the said several Rectories.

3. Provided always, that the said Professors shall celebrate Divine Service and performe all other parochial dutyes relating to the cure of souls within the said several Rectoryes which any other Rectors of the said Rectoryes have heretofore done and performed and were by law obliged to do and performe, or shall allow to learned and able Curates (to be lycenced by the Bishop or Ordinary of the diocess), who shall be constantly residing within the said Rectoryes, such competent salaries and stipends as the said Bishop or Ordinary shall judge sufficient.

4. Provided also, that neither this Act nor any thing therein contained shall excuse or be construed to excuse the said Professors or Reader of the Lecture aforesaid or any of them from the payment of first fruits and tenths, or from the payment of all dues of what kind soever to the Bishop or other Ordinary who before the making this Act had lawfull right to claime the same, or from canonical obedience to the Bishop or Ordinary of their respective diocesses; but every such Professor and Reader of the said Lecture shall be obliged to make payment thereof. *The Professors not hereby excused from paying first fruits, tenths, and other dues, or from canonical obedience.*

13 ANNÆ, Cap. VI; *al.* 12 ANNÆ, st. 2, c. 6.

An Act for taking away Mortuaries within the dioceses of [Wales] . . . . , and for confirming several Letters Patents granted by Her Majesty for perpetually annexing a Prebend of Gloucester to the Mastership of Pembroke College in Oxford and a Prebend of Rochester to the Provostship of Oriel College in Oxford and a Prebend of Norwich to the Mastership of Catherine Hall in Cambridge.

8. And whereas Her Majesty has been graciously pleased by her Letters Patents under the Great Seal of Great Britain, bearing date at Westminster the eleventh day of November in the twelfth year of her Reign, to incorporate Collwell Brickenden Doctor in Divinity the Master of Pembroke College in the University of Oxford, and his successors Masters of the same College, by the name stile and title of Master of Pembroke College in the University of Oxford; and did thereby grant to the said Master and his successors Masters of the same College for their better support and maintenance that Canonship or Prebend in the Cathedral Church of the Holy and Undivided Trinity of Gloucester which should first happen to be void and in the gift of Her Majesty her heirs and successors from and *Recital of Letters Patent, 11th Nov. 12 Anne, annexing a Prebend at Gloucester to the Mastership of Pembroke College, Oxford;*

after the date of the said grant, to have and to hold the said Canonship or Prebend to the said Collwell Brickenden Master of the said College and his successors Masters of the same College of Her Majesty her heirs and successors in pure and perpetual alms for and during his and their respective continuance in the said Mastership, and did thereby likewise unite such Canonship or Prebend as aforesaid to the said corporation for ever:

and of Letters Patent, 14th Jan. 12 Anne, annexing a Prebend at Rochester to the Provostship of Oriel College, Oxford;

And whereas Her Majesty has been also graciously pleased by other her Letters Patents under the Great Seal of Great Britain, bearing date at Westminster the fourteenth day of January in the twelfth year of her Reign, to incorporate George Carter Doctor in Divinity the Provost of Oriel College in the University of Oxford, and his successors Provosts of the same College, by the name stile and title of Provost of the House of the Blessed Virgin Mary in Oxon commonly called Oriel College of the foundation of Edward the Second some time King of England of famous memory; and did thereby grant to the said Provost and his successors Provosts of the same College for their better support and maintenance that Canonship or Prebend in the Cathedral Church of Christ and of the Blessed Virgin Mary of Rochester which should first happen to be void and in the gift of Her Majesty her heirs and successors from and after the date of the said grant, saving always the right of the Arch-Deacons of the said Church for the time being to one of the said Canonships by virtue of a former grant, to have and to hold the said Canonship or Prebend to the said George Carter Provost of the said College and his successors Provosts of the same College of Her Majesty her heirs and successors in pure and perpetual alms for and during his and their continuance in the said Provostship, and did thereby likewise unite such Canonship or Prebend as aforesaid to the said corporation for ever:

and of Letters Patent, 26th April 13 Anne, annexing a Prebend at Norwich to the Mas-

And whereas Her Majesty has been further graciously pleased by other her Letters Patents under the Great Seal of Great Britain, bearing date at Westminster the six and twentieth day of April in the thirteenth year of her Reign, to incorporate Thomas Sherlock Doctor in Divinity Master or Warden of St. Katherines College or Hall in the University of Cambridge, and his successors Masters or Wardens of the same College or Hall, by the name stile and title of Master or Warden of St. Katherines College or Hall in the University of Cambridge; and did thereby grant to the said Master or Warden and his successors Masters or Wardens of the same College or Hall for their better support and Maintenance that Canonship or Prebend in the Cathedral Church of the Holy and Undivided Trinity in Norwich of the foundation of King Edward the Sixth which should first happen to be void and in the gift of Her Majesty her heirs and successors from and after the date of the said grant, to have and to hold the said Canonship or Prebend to the said Thomas Sherlock Master or Warden of the said College or Hall and his successors Masters or Wardens of the same College or Hall of Her Majesty her heirs and successors in pure and perpetual alms for and during his and their continuance in the said Mastership or Wardenship, and did thereby likewise unite such Canonship or Prebend as aforesaid to the said corporation for ever: as by the said several and respective recited Letters Patents (relation being thereunto had) may more fully and at large appear: tership of St. Katharino's College, Cambridge.

Be it therefore enacted by the authority aforesaid, that the said several and respective recited Letters Patents and all and singular the clauses articles and things therein respectively contained shall be and are hereby ratified and confirmed, and the said several and respective Canonships or Prebends shall be from time to time for ever held and enjoyed according to the true intent and meaning of the several and respective Letters Patents above recited. The said Letters Patent confirmed

13 ANNÆ, Cap. XIII; *al.* 12 ANNÆ, st. 2, c. 14.

An Act for rendring more effectual an Act made in the third year of the Reign of King James the First intituled An Act to prevent and avoid dangers which may grow by Popish Recusants, and also of one other Act made in the first year of the Reign of their late Majesties King William and Queen Mary intituled An Act to vest in the two Universities the Presentations of Benefices belonging to Papists, and for vesting in the Lords of Justiciary power to inflict the same punishments against Jesuits Priests and other trafficking Papists which the Privy Council of Scotland was impowered to do by an Act passed in the Parliament of Scotland intituled Act for preventing the growth of Popery.

The Acts 3 Jac. I, c. 5, and 1 W. & M. c. 26, s. 2, disabling Popish Recusants convict to present to Benefices, are ineffectual.

FOR as much as by an Act of Parliament made in the third year of the Reign of King James the First intituled an Act to prevent and avoid dangers which may grow by Popish Recusants, and also one other Act made in the first year of the Reign of their late Majesties King William and Queen Mary intituled An Act to vest in the two Universities the Presentations of Benefices belonging to Papists, the presentation nomination collation and donation of and to benefices prebends or ecclesiastical livings schools hospitals and donatives belonging to Popish Recusants and other persons thereby disabled to present collate or nominate are given to the two Universities; but they are so given only where such persons are and stand convicted by such ways and means as in the said recited Acts are mentioned and provided; which Acts do nevertheless prove ineffectual for such purposes, by reason such patrons are not convicted, or not in such manner as the said Acts do direct and appoint: therefore for making the said laws more effectual, and for the speedier and easier vesting the presentations to such benefices in the two

Universities according to the intention of the said laws, be it enacted by the Queens most excellent Majesty by and with the advice and consent of the Lords spiritual and temporal and Commons in this present Parliament assembled and by the authority of the same, that every Papist or person making profession of the Popish religion, and every child not being a Protestant under the age of one and twenty years of every such Papist or person professing the Popish religion, and every mortgagee trustee or person any ways intrusted directly or indirectly mediately or immediately by or for any such Papist or person making profession of the Popish religion or such child as aforesaid, whether such trust be declared by writing or not, shall, from and after the tenth day of July which shall be in the year of our Lord one thousand seven hundred and fourteen, be disabled and is hereby made incapable to present collate or nominate to any benefice prebend or ecclesiastical living school hospital or donative, or to grant any avoidance of any benefice prebend or ecclesiastical living; and that every such presentation collation nomination and grant, and every admission institution and induction to be made thereupon, shall be utterly void and of no effect to all intents constructions and purposes whatsoever; and that in every such case the Chancellor and Scholars of the University of Oxford and the Chancellor and Scholars of the University of Cambridge, by what name or names soever they or either of them are incorporated, shall respectively have the presentation nomination collation and donation of and to every such benefice prebend or ecclesiastical living school hospital and donative set lying and being in the respective counties cities and other places and limits in the said Act of the third year of King James mentioned, as in and by the said Act is directed and appointed in the case of a Popish Recusant convict. *Papists, and persons entitled by or for them, disabled to present to Benefices &c.*

Their presentations void.

In such cases the Universities of Oxford and Cambridge to present.

2. And be it further enacted by the authority aforesaid, that from and after the said tenth day of July, when and as often as any presentation to any benefice or ecclesiastical living shall be brought to any Archbishop Bishop or other Ordinary from any person who shall be reputed to be, or whom such Archbishop Bishop or other Ordinary shall have cause to suspect to be, a Papist or trustee of any person making profession of the Popish religion or suspected to be *If a presentation is made by a reputed or suspected Papist, the Ordinary shall tender to him the Declaration in*

such, it shall and may be lawful to and for such Archbishop Bishop or other Ordinary and he is hereby required to tender or administer to every such person, if present, the Declaration against Transubstantiation set down and expressed in an Act of Parliament made in the five and twentieth year of the Reign of the late King Charles the Second, intituled An Act for preventing dangers which may happen from Popish Recusants, to be by such person made repeated and subscribed; and in case such person shall be absent, the said Archbishop Bishop or other Ordinary shall by notice in writing, to be left at the place of habitation of such person, appoint some convenient time and place when and where such person shall appear before such Archbishop Bishop or other Ordinary or some persons to be authorized by such Archbishop Bishop or other Ordinary by commission under his or their seal of office, and upon such appearance the said Archbishop Bishop or other Ordinary or such Commissioners shall tender or administer the said Declaration to the person making such presentation; and in case such person shall neglect or refuse to make repeat and subscribe such Declaration when the same shall be so tendred as aforesaid, or shall neglect or refuse to appear before such Archbishop Bishop or other Ordinary or such Commissioners upon such notice as aforesaid, that then such presentation shall be utterly void and of none effect; and in every such case such Archbishop Bishop or other Ordinary shall, within ten days next after such neglect or refusal, send and give a certificate under his or their seal of office of such neglect or refusal to the Vice-Chancellor for the time being of that University to whom such presentation would of right belong if such person so presenting had been a Popish Recusant convict, and it shall and may be lawful to and for the Chancellor and Scholars of such University to present a person qualified according to the said Acts to such benefice or ecclesiastical living, and the presentation to such benefice or ecclesiastical living for that turn only is hereby given unto and vested in them for that purpose; any matter clause or thing contained in either of the said former recited Acts to the contrary thereof notwithstanding.

3. And for the better discovery of all secret trusts and fraudulent conveyances made by Papists or persons making

Marginal notes:
25 Car. 2, c. 2, s. 8.

If such person refuse to subscribe the same, the presentation shall be void, and the Ordinary shall certify such refusal to the University to which the presentation would belong if the person presenting had been a Popish Recusant convict, and which may then present.

The Ordinary shall examine

profession of the Popish religion of their advowsons and right of presentation nomination and donation to any benefices or ecclesiastical livings, be it further enacted by the authority aforesaid, that when the presentation of any person presented to any benefice or ecclesiastical living shall be brought to any Archbishop Bishop or other Ordinary, the said Archbishop Bishop or Ordinary is hereby required, before he give institution, to examine the person presented upon oath whether to the best and utmost of his knowledge and belief the person or persons who made such presentation be the true and real patron or patrons of the said benefice or ecclesiastical living or made the said presentation in his or her or their own right, or whether such person or persons so presenting be not mediately or immediately directly or indirectly trustee or trustees or any way intrusted for some other and what person or persons by name who is or are Papists or make profession of the Popish religion or the children of such or for any other and what person or persons, or what he knows has heard or believes touching or concerning the same; and if such person or persons so presented shall refuse to be so examined, or shall not answer directly thereto, then and in every such case such presentation shall be void.

upon oath every person presented, before institution, whether the person presenting be the real patron, or the trustee of some Papist, or any other person; and if he refuse to answer, the presentation shall be void.

4. And be it further enacted by the authority aforesaid, that it shall and may be lawful for the Chancellor and Scholars of the respective Universities to whom the presentation to such benefices and ecclesiastical livings should belong in case the rightful patrons had been Popish Recusants convict, and their presentees or Clerks, for the better discovery of such secret and fraudulent trusts had done made and created by or for such Papists or persons professing the Popish religion and their children as aforesaid, to exhibit their bill in any Court of Equity against such person or persons presenting and such person or persons as they have reason to believe to be the cestuyque trust of the advowson of such benefice or ecclesiastical living, or any other person who they have cause to suspect may be able to make any other or further discovery of such secret trusts and practices; to which bill the defendant therein named, being duly served with the process of the Court in which the said bill shall be exhibited, shall forthwith directly answer to the facts charged and

The Universities and their Presentees may exhibit Bills in Equity for the discovery of secret Trusts.

enquired in the said bill at the discretion of the Court where such bill shall be exhibited; and in case the defendants or any of them shall refuse or neglect to answer the said bill in such reasonable time as shall be for that purpose allowed and appointed by discretion of the said Court where the said cause shall be depending (the distance of place and the circumstances of the defendant or defendants considered), that then and in such case the said bill shall be taken pro confesso and be allowed as evidence against such person so neglecting and refusing and his trustee or trustees and his and their Clerk: provided that every person having fully answered such bill in such Court of Equity, and not knowing any thing of any such trust for a Papist or other person disabled as aforesaid, shall be entitled to his costs, to be taxed according to the course of the Court.

<small>Defendants not answering, such bill to be taken pro confesso.</small>

<small>Proviso for costs of defendant answering.</small>

5. And be it further enacted by the authority aforesaid, that it shall and may be lawful for the Court where any Quare impedit shall be hereafter depending, at the instance of either of the said Chancellors or Scholars or their Clerk being plaintiffs or defendants in such suit by motion in open Court, at their discretion to make any rule or order requiring satisfaction upon the oath of such patron and his Clerk who in the said suit shall contest the right of the said University to present to such benefice or ecclesiastical living, by examination of them or either of them in open Court, or by commission under the seal of such Court for examination of them or either of them, or by affidavit, as the said Court shall find most proper in order to the discovery of any secret trust frauds or practices relating to the said presentation then in question; and in case it appear to the Court upon the examination of such patron and Clerk or either of them that the said patron is but a trustee for some other person or persons, that then the said patron and his Clerk shall discover who such person and persons are and where he she or they live or inhabit; and upon their refusal to make such discovery or to give such satisfaction as aforesaid they shall be punished as persons that are guilty of a contempt to the said Court; and in case such patron or his Clerk shall discover the person for whom the said patron is a trustee, that then and in such case the said Court upon motion made in open Court shall

<small>The Court where Quare impedit is depending may take proceedings for discovery of secret Trusts.</small>

<small>If thereupon it appear that the patron is but a Trustee, then the patron or his Clerk shall discover cestuique trust, or be punished for contempt. If discovery be</small>

make a rule or order that the person or persons for whom the said patron is a trustee shall in the said Court, or before Commissioners to be appointed for that purpose under the seal of the said Court, make repeat and subscribe the Declaration against Transubstantiation herein before mentioned, and likewise, on pain of incurring a contempt against the said Court, give such further satisfaction upon oath touching or relating to the said trust as the said Court shall think fit; and such person so required to make repeat and subscribe the said Declaration and refusing or neglecting so to do shall be esteemed as a Popish Recusant convict in respect of such presentation.

made, then such centinue trust shall subscribe the Declaration against Transubstantiation, or be deemed a Popish Recusant convict.

6. And be it further enacted, that the answer of such patron and patrons and the person for whom he or they are any ways intrusted and his and their Clerk or any of them, and his and their or any of their examinations and affidavits taken as aforesaid by order of any Court where such Quare impedit shall be depending, or by any Archbishop Bishop or other Ordinary or the Commissioners as aforesaid, (which examinations shall therefore be reduced into writing and signed by the party examined,) shall be allowed as evidence against such patron so presenting and his Clerk.

Answers and Examinations allowed as evidence against patron presenting and his Clerk.

7. Provided always, that no such bill nor any discovery to be made by any answer thereunto or to any such examination as aforesaid shall be made use of to subject any person making any such discovery or not answering such bill to any penalty or forfeiture other than the loss of the presentation then in question.

No penalty upon such bill or answers, except loss of the presentation.

8. And it is hereby further enacted, that in case of any such bill or bills of discovery as aforesaid, exhibited in any Court of Equity by the Chancellor and Scholars of either of the said Universities or their presentee, no lapse shall incur nor plenarty be a bar against such Chancellor and Scholars in respect of the benefice or ecclesiastical living touching which such bill shall be so exhibited till after three months from the time that the answer to such bill shall be put in, or the same be taken pro confesso, or the prosecution thereof deserted; provided that such bill or bills be exhibited before any lapse incurred.

No Lapse to incur or Plenarty a bar against University, till after the time herein mentioned, if the bill be exhibited before Lapse incurred.

9. And whereas it hath been doubted whether any writ

of Quare impedit brought by the respective Universities for any presentation nomination collation or donation pursuant to the said recited Acts or either of them may be brought by them in or by the name of Chancellor and Scholars, or ought to be by their true name of incorporation respectively; it is hereby declared, that the said respective Chancellors and Scholars of the said Universities are by this Act and were by the said former Acts entitled to sue any writ of Quare impedit by the name of Chancellor and Scholars of the University of Oxford and Chancellor and Scholars of the University of Cambridge respectively, or by their respective proper names of incorporation, at their election.

<small>Proviso for the style by which the Universities may sue Writs of Quare imped.t.</small>

10. And be it further enacted, that in case of any trust for any Papist or person professing the Popish religion, confessed or discovered in and by any answer to such bill as aforesaid or such examination as aforesaid, it shall and may be lawful for the Court where such discovery shall be made, and such Court is hereby enabled, to inforce the producing of the deeds creating and relating to the said trusts by such methods as they shall find proper.

<small>Upon discovery of such secret Trust, the Court may order production of Deeds.</small>

[The two remaining sections of this Act relate to Scotland.]

1 Geo. I, Stat. II, Cap. XIII.

An Act for the further security of His Majesties Person and Government, and the Succession of the Crown in the Heirs of the late Princess Sophia, being Protestants; and for extinguishing the hopes of the Pretended Prince of Wales, and his open and secret abetters.

<small>Oaths of Allegiance, Supremacy, and Abjuration.</small>

[The first section of this Act contains the Oaths of Allegiance and Supremacy, and appoints a new Form of the Oath of Abjuration, which was first prescribed by 13 & 14 Will. III, c. 6, was afterwards altered by 1 Anne, c. 16 (*al.* 22) and 6 Anne, c. 41 (*al.* 7), and subsequently by 6 Geo. III, c. 53; and has since been combined with the two other Oaths by 21 & 22 Vict. c. 48.]

1 GEO. I, st. 2, c. 13.   65

2. And be it further enacted by the authority aforesaid, that all and every person and persons that shall be admitted, entered, placed, or taken into any office or offices, civil or military, ... and all .... Heads or Governors, of what denomination soever, and all other Members of Colleges and Halls in any University, that are or shall be of the Foundation, or that do or shall enjoy any Exhibition, being of or as soon as they shall attain the age of eighteen years, and all persons teaching or reading to pupils in any University or elsewhere, and all schoolmasters and ushers, ... within that part of Great Britain called England, who shall, at any time after the tenth day of August one thousand seven hundred and fifteen, be admitted into or enter upon any of the above-mentioned preferments, benefices, offices, or places, or shall come into any such capacity, or shall take upon him or them any such practice, employment, or business, as aforesaid, shall within three months^q after he or they shall be admitted into or enter upon any such preferment, benefice, office, or place, or come into such capacity, or take upon him or them such practice, employment, or business, as aforesaid, take and subscribe the same Oaths in one of the said Courts at Westminster, or at the General Quarter Sessions of the county, city, or place, where he or they shall reside. *To be taken by all Foundation Members of Colleges, all Tutors, &c.*

12. And be it further enacted by the authority aforesaid, that if any Head or Member of any College or Hall within either of the Universities of Oxford or Cambridge, that are or shall be of the Foundation, or that do or shall enjoy any Exhibition, being of (or as soon as he shall attain) the age of eighteen years, shall neglect or refuse to take and subscribe the several Oaths in this Act mentioned, according to the true intent and meaning of this Act, or to produce a certificate thereof under the hand of some proper officer of the respective Court, and cause the same to be entred in the *If any Foundation Member of any College neglect or refuse to take the Oaths, the rightful Electors may elect another person in his stead: if they*

---

^q By 9 Geo. 2, c. 26, s. 3, the time for taking the Oaths is appointed to be "within six calendar months" after admission. Hitherto it has been usual at the end of each Session of Parliament to pass an Act to indemnify, under certain conditions, all persons who have not complied with the requirements of this and some other Acts. The title of the Act so passed in 1866, 29 & 30 Vict. c. 116, is "An Act to indemnify such persons in the United Kingdom as have omitted to qualify themselves for Offices and Employments, and to extend the time limited for those purposes respectively."

make default, the King may appoint.

Register of such College or Hall within one month after his having taken and subscribed the said Oaths; and if the persons in whom the right of election of such Head or Member shall be do neglect or refuse to elect some other fitting or proper person in the place or stead of such Head or Member, so neglecting and refusing to take and subscribe the said Oaths, as aforesaid, by the space of twelve months after such neglect or refusal; that then, and from thenceforth, it shall and may be lawful unto and for the Kings most excellent Majesty, his heirs and successors, under the Great Seal or Sign Manual, to nominate and appoint some fitting person, qualified according to the local Statutes of such College or Hall, to succeed to the place of such person who shall neglect or refuse to take and subscribe the said Oaths; and that every person so to be nominated and appointed shall have and enjoy such place, to which he shall be nominated and appointed, as aforesaid, to all intents and purposes whatsoever, and all benefits, privileges, and advantages to the same belonging and appertaining, as if such person had been elected and chosen by the proper electors of such College or Hall.

If the Head of any College refuse or neglect to admit any person so appointed by the King, the Visitor shall admit him: if the Visitor neglect or refuse, the Court of King's Bench may issue a writ of Mandamus to him to admit.

13. And be it further enacted by the authority aforesaid, that if the Head of any College or Hall in either of the Universities, or other person or persons lawfully authorized to admit, shall refuse or neglect to admit such person, so nominated and appointed under the Great Seal or Sign Manual, as aforesaid, by the space of ten days after such admission shall be demanded of him or them who ought to make such admission, to such place as he shall be nominated to, as aforesaid, that then and in such case the local Visitor or Visitors of such College or Hall is hereby authorized and required to admit and place such person so nominated and appointed to such place as he shall be nominated to, as aforesaid, within the space of one month after the same shall be demanded of such Visitor; and in case such Visitor shall neglect or refuse to admit, as aforesaid, during the space of one month after the same is lawfully demanded of such Visitor, that then it shall and may be lawful to and for the Court of Kings-Bench at Westminster to issue out a writ of Mandamus to be directed to such Visitor or Visitors

to admit such person to such place, and to proceed upon the said writ according to the course of the said Court in such cases.

9 Geo. II, Cap. XXXVI.

An Act to restrain the Disposition of Lands, whereby the same become unalienable.

[This Act directs that no lands &c., nor any money to be laid out in lands &c., shall be given for any Charitable Uses whatsoever, unless by indenture executed twelve calendar months before the death of the donor and enrolled in the Court of Chancery within six months after execution, and unless the gift is to take effect immediately and without any power of revocation or any limitation whatsoever for the benefit of the donor.]

[margin: No lands &c., nor money to be laid out in lands, shall be given for any Charitable Uses, unless by deed 12 months before the death of the donor and without power of revocation &c.]

4. Provided always, that this Act shall not extend, or be construed to extend, to make void the dispositions of any lands, tenements, or hereditaments, or of any personal estate to be laid out in the purchase of any lands, tenements, or hereditaments, which shall be made in any other manner or form than by this Act is directed, to or in trust for either of the two Universities within that part of Great Britain called England, or any of the Colleges or Houses of Learning within either of the said Universities, or to or in trust for the Colleges of Eton, Winchester, or Westminster, or any or either of them, for the better support and maintenance of the Scholars only upon the foundations of the said Colleges of Eton, Winchester, and Westminster[r].

[margin: But not to prejudice the two Universities, or the Colleges of Eton, Winchester, or Westminster.]

---

[r] The fifth section of this Act, which limited the number of advowsons which any College might hold to half the number of Fellows in it, was totally repealed by 45 Geo. 3, c. 101.

11 Geo. II, Cap. XVII.

An Act for securing the Estates of Papists conforming to the Protestant Religion against the disabilities created by several Acts of Parliament relating to Papists; and for rendering more effectual the several Acts of Parliament made for vesting in the two Universities in that part of Great Britain called England the Presentations of Benefices belonging to Papists.

<small>Recital of 13 Ann. c. 13, *al.* 12 Ann. st. 2, c. 14.</small>

5. And whereas by an Act made in the twelfth year of the Reign of Queen Anne, for rendring more effectual an Act made in the third year of the Reign of King James the First intituled An Act to prevent and avoid dangers which may grow by Popish recusants, and also one other Act made in the first year of the Reign of King William and Queen Mary intituled An Act to vest in the two Universities the Presentations of Benefices belonging to Papists, it was enacted, that every Papist or person making profession of the Popish religion, and every child not being a Protestant under the age of one and twenty years of every such Papist or person professing the Popish religion, and every mortgagee trustee or person any ways intrusted directly or indirectly mediately or immediately by or for any such Papist or person making profession of the Popish religion or such child as aforesaid, whether such trust be declared by writing or not, should be disabled and made incapable to present, collate, or nominate to any benefice, prebend, or ecclesiastical living, school, hospital, or donative, or to grant any avoidance of any benefice, prebend, or ecclesiastical living; and that every such presentation, collation, nomination, and grant, and every admission, institution, and induction to be made thereupon, should be utterly void and of no effect to all intents, constructions, and purposes whatsoever; and that in every such case the Chancellor and Scholars of the University of Oxford and the Chancellor and Scholars of the University of Cambridge should respectively have the presentation, nomination, colla-

tion, and donation of and to every such benefice, prebend, or ecclesiastical living, school, hospital, and donative, set, lying, and being in the respective counties, cities, and other places and limits in the said Act of the third year of King James mentioned, as in and by the said Act is directed and appointed in the case of a Popish recusant convict:

And whereas, for the better discovery of all secret trusts and fraudulent conveyances made by Papists or persons making profession of the Popish religion of their advowsons and right of presentation, nomination, and donation to any benefices or ecclesiastical livings, several provisions were made by the said Act of the twelfth year of the Reign of Queen Anne, which have been fraudulently evaded by persons obtaining from such Papists, without a full and valuable consideration, grants of such advowsons and right of presentation, nomination, and donation, upon confidence only that such grantees will, at the request of such Papists, present to such benefices or ecclesiastical livings Clerks nominated by such Papists; who have been presented accordingly, contrary to the true intent and meaning of the said Acts, and to the great hurt of the Protestant interest of this Kingdom:

Be it therefore enacted by the authority aforesaid, that every grant to be made, from and after the sixth day of May one thousand seven hundred and thirty eight, of any advowson or right of presentation, collation, nomination, or donation of and to any benefice, prebend, or ecclesiastical living, school, hospital, or donative, and every grant of any avoidance thereof, by any Papist or person making profession of the Popish religion, or any mortgagee, trustee, or person any ways intrusted directly or indirectly, mediately or immediately, by or for any such Papist or person making profession of the Popish religion, whether such trust be declared by writing or not, shall be null and void, unless such grant shall be made bona fide and for a full and valuable consideration to and for a Protestant purchaser or Protestant purchasers, and meerly and only for the benefit of a Protestant or Protestants; and that every such grantee, or person claiming under any such grant, shall be deemed to be a trustee for a Papist or person professing the Popish religion, as aforesaid, within the true intent and meaning of the said Act; and that all such gran-

Every grant or devise of any Ecclesiastical Living &c. made by any Papist, or by the Trustee &c. of any Papist, shall be void, unless made for a valuable consideration to a Protestant purchaser.

tees, or persons claiming under such grants, and their presentees, shall be compelled to make such discovery relating to such grants and presentations made thereupon, and by such methods, as in and by the said Act of the twelfth year of the Reign of Queen Anne are directed in the case of trustees of Papists or persons professing the Popish religion; and that every devise to be made, from and after the said sixth day of May, by any Papist or person professing the Popish religion of any such advowson, or right of presentation, collation, nomination, or donation, or any such avoidance, with intent to secure the benefit thereof to the heirs or family of such Papist or person professing the Popish religion, shall be null and void; and that all such devisees, and persons claiming under such devises, and their presentees, shall in like manner, and by such methods, be compelled to discover whether, to the best of their knowledge and belief, such devises were not made with the said intent.

17 GEO. II, Cap. XL.

An Act to continue the several laws therein mentioned . . ., and to prevent the retailing of Wine within either of the Universities in that part of Great Britain called England without Licence.

Against selling Wine without Licence at either of the Universities. 11. And whereas divers persons have of late taken cellars, vaults, or warehouses within the University of Oxford and the precincts thereof, in which they retail great quantities of wine, not having licence from the Chancellor or Vice-Chancellor of the said University, in violation of the rights of the said University, and in prejudice of his Majesty's revenues; and whereas the like offences may be committed within the University of Cambridge and the precincts thereof by persons selling wine by retail, not being duly licensed by the said University; and whereas the Acts of Parliament relating to wine licences do not extend to the said Universities: be it enacted by the authority aforesaid, that, from and after the twenty fourth day of June one thousand seven hundred and forty four, no person or persons shall sell wine by retail within either of the said Universities or the precincts of either of them, unless such person or persons shall be duly licensed or authorized so to do by the Chancellor or Vice-Chancellor of the said University of Oxford and by the Chancellor, Masters, and Scholars of the said University of Cambridge respectively, upon pain of forfeiting for every offence the sum of five pounds, one moiety thereof to the use of his Majesty, his heirs, and successors, and the other moiety to the informer; and that all persons offending against this Act shall and may be prosecuted and proceeded against for the said forfeitures in the Courts of the Chancellors or Vice-Chancellors of the said Universities respectively, in a summary way, by summoning the party accused to appear in the said Courts respectively; and on appearance, or contempt of the party accused by not appearing, being duly summoned, and oath thereof made, such Courts may examine the matter, and upon confession of the party accused, or on the oath of one credible witness, of such party's having offended against this Act, such Courts respectively shall and may give sentence against such party, and issue their warrant or warrants for levying the said forfeitures by distress and sale of the goods of the party offending, rendering the overplus, if any, to the party on whom such distress shall be made; and for want of such distress shall and may commit such offender or offenders to the House of Correction, there to remain without bail or mainprize for the space of one month; and such sentence or sentences shall be and are hereby declared to be taken and adjudged to be good, valid, and effectual in the law; and that no writ of certiorari or other process shall issue or be issuable to remove any such sentence from the said Courts of the said Chancellors or Vice-Chancellors respectively, or to remove any order or other proceedings made or taken by the said Courts respectively upon, touching, or concerning any such sentence, into any of his Majesty's Courts of Record at Westminster, until the party or parties against whom such sentence shall be given, before the allowance of such writ of certiorari or other process, shall find two sufficient sureties, to become bound to the prosecutor or prosecutors of such offenders in the sum of fifty pounds

The Penalty.

with condition to prosecute the same with effect within twelve months, and to pay unto the prosecutor or prosecutors his or their full costs and charges of the removal of such sentence and the proceedings thereon, in case such sentence shall be affirmed; any law, statute, provision, or usage to the contrary notwithstanding.

<small>This Act not to affect the privileges of the Mayor, &c., of Oxford.</small>

12. Provided always, that this Act, or any thing herein contained, shall not in any wise be construed to prejudice or confirm any of the liberties, privileges, franchises, jurisdictions, powers, and authorities appertaining or belonging to the Mayor, Bailiffs, and Commonalty of the City of Oxford, or to any of them; but that they, and every of them, and their successors, may have, hold, use, and enjoy all their liberties, privileges, franchises, jurisdictions, powers, and authorities, in such large and ample wise, as though this present Act had never been had or made.

18 Geo. II, Cap. XX.

An Act to amend and render more effectual an Act passed in the fifth year of his present Majesty's reign, intituled, An Act for the further Qualification of Justices of the Peace.

[This Act provides that no person, with some few exceptions, shall act as a Justice of the Peace for any County, who is not possessed of an estate in lands worth £100 clear, or entitled to the reversion of an estate in lands worth £300 a year clear.]

<small>Property qualification not required for Heads of Colleges or Halls, or for Vice-Chancellors, in either University.</small>

15. Provided always, that this Act, or any thing herein contained, shall not extend, or be construed to extend, to any of the Heads of Colleges or Halls in either of the two Universities of Oxford and Cambridge, or to the Vice-Chancellor of either of the said Universities, or to the Mayor of the City of Oxford or of the Town of Cambridge; but that they may be and act as Justices of the Peace of and in the several Counties of Oxford, Berks, and Cambridge, and the

cities and towns within the same, and execute the office thereof as fully and freely in all respects as heretofore they have lawfully used to execute the same, as if this Act had never been made; any thing herein before contained to the contrary notwithstanding.

32 Geo. II, Cap. XXXIII.

An Act to explain and amend an Act made in the last Session of Parliament, intituled, An Act for granting to His Majesty several Rates and Duties upon Offices and Pensions, and upon Houses, and upon Windows . . ., *so far as the same relates to the Rates and Duties on Offices and Pensions.*

13. Provided always, and be it further enacted by the authority aforesaid, that nothing in this Act contained shall extend, or be construed to extend, to charge any Offices or Employments in either of the two Universities in that part of Great Britain called England with the Duty by this Act imposed. Offices in both Universities exempted from the Duty.

5 Geo. III, Cap. XVII.

An Act to confirm all Leases already made by Archbishops and Bishops and other Ecclesiastical persons of Tythes and other Incorporeal Hereditaments for one, two, or three life or lives, or twenty one years; and to enable them to grant such Leases, and to bring Actions of Debt for recovery of Rents reserved and in arrear on Leases for life or lives.

WHEREAS it may be doubtful whether, by the laws now in being, Archbishops or Bishops, Master and Fellows or any other Head and Members of Colleges or Halls, Deans and Chapters, Precentors, Prebendaries, Masters Preamble and Guardians of Hospitals, or any other person or persons having any spiritual or ecclesiastical promotions, heretofore had, or now have, any power to make or grant any Lease or Leases of tythes or other incorporeal hereditaments only, which lie in grant and not in livery, for one, two, or three lives, or for any term or terms of years not exceeding twenty one years, although the ancient rent or yearly sum is thereby mentioned to be reserved, and all other requisites prescribed by the Acts of Parliament now in being to that end, or any of them, were or are justly and truly observed and performed, by reason that there is generally no place wherein a distress can be had or taken for such rent or yearly sum; and it may be also doubtful whether, in cases of such Leases for life or lives, there is any remedy in law for such ecclesiastical or other persons, by action of debt or otherwise, for recovering the rent or yearly sum due and arrear* which is mentioned to be reserved on such Leases for life or lives: therefore, for obviating all doubts touching the same, and enabling the said Archbishops and Bishops, Masters and Fellows or other Heads and Members of Colleges or Halls, Deans and Chapters, Precentors, Prebendaries, Masters and Guardians of Hospitals, and other ecclesiastical persons, to make valid Leases of such their incorporeal hereditaments, and to recover the rents or yearly sum mentioned to be reserved on any Leases by them already granted, or to be granted, for one, two, or three lives, as aforesaid; and also to make good and effectual all such Leases as have already been granted by them or any of them; may it please your Majesty that it may be enacted, and be it enacted by the King's most excellent Majesty, by and with the advice and consent of the Lords spiritual and temporal and Commons in this present Parliament assembled, and by the authority of the same, that all Leases for one, two, or three life or lives, or any term not exceeding twenty one years, already made and granted, or which shall at any time from and after the passing this Act be made or granted, of any tythes, tolls, or other incorporeal hereditaments, solely, and without any lands or corporeal hereditaments, by any Archbishop or Bishop, Master and Fellows or other Head and Members of Colleges or Halls, Deans and Chapters, Precentors, Prebendaries, Masters

So in orig. Read and in arrear.

Leases of Tithes and other Incorporeal Hereditaments made by Bishops, Colleges, &c., for Life or Lives, or for 21 Years, and Guardians of Hospitals, and every other person and persons who are enabled by the several Statutes now in being, or any of them, to make any Lease or Leases for one, two, or three life or lives, or any term or number of years not exceeding twenty one years, of any lands, tenements, or other corporeal hereditaments, shall be, and are hereby deemed and declared to be, as good and effectual in law against such Archbishop, Bishop, Masters and Fellows or other Heads and Members of Colleges or Halls, Deans and Chapters, Precentors, Prebendaries, Masters and Guardians of Hospitals, and other persons so granting the same, and their successors, and every of them, to all intents and purposes, as any Lease or Leases already made or to be made by any such Archbishop or Bishop, Master and Fellows or other Heads and Members of Colleges or Halls, Deans and Chapters, Precentors, Prebendaries, Masters and Guardians of Hospitals, and other persons having spiritual promotion, of any lands or other corporeal hereditaments now are by virtue of the Statute of the thirty second year of King Henry the Eighth, or any other Statute now in being; any law, custom, or usage to the contrary thereof in any wise notwithstanding.

<small>declared to be as good in law, as Leases of Lands or other Corporeal Hereditaments made in virtue of 32 Hen. 8 c. 28.</small>

2. Provided always, that nothing herein contained shall extend, or be construed to extend, to enable any Master and Fellows or other Head and Members of Colleges or Halls, Deans and Chapters, Precentors, Prebendaries, Masters and Guardians of Hospitals, or other ecclesiastical persons as aforesaid, to grant Leases for any longer or other terms than by the local Statutes of their several foundations they are now respectively enabled to do.

<small>Colleges &c. may not grant Leases for any longe term than their Statutes allow.</small>

3. And be it further enacted and declared by the authority aforesaid, that in case the rent or rents, or yearly sum or sums, reserved or made payable in or by any Lease or Leases already made, or to be made, by any Archbishop or Bishop, Master and Fellows or other Head and Members of Colleges or Halls, Deans and Chapters, Precentors, Prebendaries, Masters and Guardians of Hospitals, and every other person and persons so enabled to make Leases as aforesaid, for one, two, or three life or lives, or years, in pursuance of the several Acts of Parliament already in being, or by this present Act, or any part thereof, shall be behind or unpaid by the space

<small>Actions of Debt may be brought by Bishops Colleges, &c. for recovery of Rents reserved and in arrear on Leases for Life or Lives.</small>

of twenty eight days next over or after any of the days whereon the same, by such Lease or Leases, now are or hereafter shall or may be reserved or made payable; then, and so often, and from time to time as it shall so happen, it shall and may be lawful for such Archbishop or Bishop, Master and Fellows or other Head and Members of Colleges or Halls, Deans and Chapters, Prebendaries, Precentors, Masters and Guardians of Hospitals, and other persons so making or granting, or having made or granted, such Leases as aforesaid, or their executors, administrators, and successors respectively, to bring an action or actions of debt against the Lessee or Lessees, to whom any such Lease or Leases for life or lives or years now are or hereafter shall be made and granted, his, her, or their heirs, executors, administrators, or assigns, for recovering the rent or rents which shall be then due and in arrear to any such Archbishop or Bishops, Masters and Fellows or other Heads and Members of Colleges or Halls, Deans, Chapters, Precentors, Prebendaries, Master and Guardians of Hospitals, and other person or persons before mentioned, his or their executors, administrators, or successors, in such and the same manner, and as fully and effectually to all intents and purposes, as any landlord or lessor or other person or persons could or might do for recovering of arrears of rent due on any Lease or Leases for life or lives or years by the laws now in being; any law, statute, usage, or custom to the contrary notwithstanding.

7 GEO. III, Cap. XCIX.

An Act for establishing and well governing a General Hospital to be called Addenbrooke's Hospital *in the Town of Cambridge.*

[The Preamble of this Act recites, that John Addenbrooke, Doctor of Physic, deceased, by his will dated 1 May 1719, after making several devises and bequests, directed that the residue of his property should at the death of his wife be vested in certain Trustees for the purpose of establishing "a small Physical Hospital in the Town of Cambridge for poor people;" that, after sundry proceedings and orders in Chancery, lands have been purchased and a Hospital has been built and furnished, but the capital of the Charity is insufficient for carrying on the design; that "several noblemen, gentlemen, clergy, and others, have entered into a voluntary subscription for making the said Hospital a General Hospital;" and that the Trustees assent to this extension of the Testator's plan.

[Section 1 enacts that from and after the 24th of June 1767 there "shall be a Corporation, to continue for ever, for establishing and well governing a General Hospital in the Town of Cambridge, to be called *Addenbrooke's Hospital;*" that the Lord Lieutenant of the County of Cambridge, the Chancellor of the University, the Lord Bishop of Ely, the High Steward of the Corporation, the High Sheriff of the County, the Representatives in Parliament for the County, University, and Town, the Vice-Chancellor of the University, and the Mayor of the Town of Cambridge, each for the time being, together with donors of certain sums of money, shall be Governors of the Hospital, and shall be a Body Corporate by the name of *The President and Governors of Addenbrooke's Hospital in the Town of Cambridge*, with perpetual succession, a common seal, and the right to sue and be sued; "and that they by the name aforesaid shall and may at any time hereafter, without licence in mortmain, purchase, take, or receive any lands, tenements, or hereditaments, or any estate or interest arising or derived out of any lands, tenements, or hereditaments, for the purposes aforesaid."]

Governors of Addenbrooke's Hospital incorporated.

11 Geo. III, Cap. XIX.

An Act for amending certain of the Mile-Ways leading to Oxford; for making a commodious Entrance through the Parish of St. Clement; for Rebuilding or Repairing Magdalen Bridge; for making commodious Roads from the said Bridge through the University and City and the Avenues leading thereto; for Cleansing and Lighting the Streets, Lanes, and Places within the said University and City and the Suburbs thereof and the said Parish of St. Clement; for removing Nuisances and Annoyances therefrom, and preventing the like for the future; for empowering Colleges and Corporations to alienate their Estates there; for Removing, Holding, and Regulating Markets within the said City; and for other Purposes.

[The first portion of this Act, comprising seventy six sections, made provision, by the appointment of a body of Commissioners and otherwise, for erecting Turnpike Gates and Toll Houses, for repairing, widening, turning, or altering the several Mileways, for rebuilding or repairing and widening Magdalen Bridge, for repairing, paving, and widening the streets which lead from Magdalen Bridge to the great roads lying on the North, South, and West sides of Oxford, and for cleansing and lighting all the streets and lanes in Oxford and St. Clement's. Sections 74 and 75 empowered "any body corporate or collegiate, whether of University or City, aggregate or sole, to alienate and sell for ever any tenements or hereditaments" in Oxford or its suburbs or in St. Clement's.

[By 28 & 29 Vict. c. 108 all this is repealed, except what relates to Magdalen Bridge and the Mileways, the Tolls to be demanded and taken in respect of the same, and the Mortgages of the Tolls. But the term during which Tolls may be taken is now so near expiring that it does not seem worth while to print any of these sections here.]

77. And whereas the holding of a Market, as heretofore accustomed, for selling of meat, fish, and garden-stuff in the High Street and Butcher Row in the said City hath been found very inconvenient, by reason of the great number of coaches, carts, and other carriages, and travellers passing and repassing through the same to and from the roads above mentioned; and whereas it is necessary for the benefit and accommodation of the inhabitants of the said University, City, and Suburbs, and of all persons resorting thereto, that a Market should be still continued for the sale of all kinds of meat, fish, poultry, and garden-stuff; and the Chancellor, Masters, and Scholars of the said University, and Mayor, Bailiffs, and Commonalty of the said City, are desirous to erect, hold, and maintain such Market: it is hereby further enacted, that the said Commissioners, or any fifteen or more of them, shall have full power and authority to view, set out, and describe such plot or piece of ground between the High Street and the lane called Jesus College Lane within the said City, as they shall adjudge most convenient and proper for holding the said Market, and to and for making proper avenues thereto. *Power to set out a site for a new Market.*

78. And it is hereby further enacted by the authority aforesaid, that the said Chancellor, Masters, and Scholars of the said University, and their successors, by and with the consent and approbation of the said Mayor, Bailiffs, and Commonalty of the said City, and their successors, shall have power and authority, and they are hereby authorized and impowered to remove, or cause to be removed, the Markets for all kinds of meat, fish, poultry, and garden-stuff, and to establish and hold, or cause to be established and held,* within the limits of the said plot or piece of ground, so to be set out and described by the said Commissioners as aforesaid for the site of the said Market; and that it shall and may be lawful to and for the said Chancellor, Masters, and Scholars, by and with the consent and approbation of the said Mayor, Bailiffs, and Commonalty, to cause such Market to be held within the limits aforesaid, daily and every day, or less frequently, according as the same shall to them appear necessary for the *Power to remove th present Markets to the site so set out.*

* *So in orig.*

convenience and accommodation of the inhabitants of the said University, City, and Suburbs, and of persons resorting thereto.

79. Provided, that nothing herein contained shall extend, or be construed to extend, to take away the right of the said Chancellor, Masters, and Scholars to appoint or nominate one or more Clerk or Clerks of the said Market, and otherwise to govern, regulate, and superintend the same, as heretofore accustomed with respect to the ancient Market Place or Places; or to take away the right of the said Mayor, Bailiffs, and Commonalty to such Pitching-pence or Tolls as have been heretofore paid to them or their Toll-gatherer by butchers, gardeners, and others; but the same respectively shall remain and belong to the said Chancellor, Masters, and Scholars, and the said Mayor, Bailiffs, and Commonalty, severally, as before the passing this Act; and the said Chancellor, Masters, and Scholars, and Mayor, Bailiffs, and Commonalty, respectively, shall and may prescribe and have such remedies for the same in such new Market, as they could have and were intitled to in the places where the ancient Markets were usually or commonly held.

80. And, for preventing any encroachments which might hereafter be made on the said Market, be it further enacted by the authority aforesaid, that from and after the same shall be completed and used as a Market, it shall not be lawful for any person or persons to erect or hold any other Market within the said University, City, or Suburbs, except the present Markets for corn, pigs, and butter[*], or to vend or expose to sale any manner of flesh, or other raw victuals, fish, poultry, herbs, roots, or garden-stuff, which are usually sold in public markets, in any other place whatsoever within the said University, City, or Suburbs; and every person who shall so vend or expose to sale any manner of flesh, or other raw victuals, fish, poultry, herbs, roots, or garden-stuff out of the said Market within the said University, City, or Suburbs, and shall be convicted thereof before any one or more of his Majesty's Justices of the Peace for the County or City of Oxford aforesaid, shall for every such offence forfeit and pay the sum of five pounds; to be recovered by

[*] As to butter, see 21 Geo. 3, c. 47, s. 26.

distress and sale of the goods and chattels of the offender, rendering the overplus, (if any there be,) after deducting the expence of such distress and sale, to the owners thereof; one moiety whereof shall go to the informer, and the other moiety to the poor of the parish where the offence or offences shall be committed.

81. Provided always, that nothing herein contained shall be construed to extend to prevent fishmongers or poulterers from selling fish or poultry in their own shops or houses, as heretofore accustomed, in the said University, City, and Suburbs. *Fishmongers and Poulterers may sell in their own Houses.*

82. Provided also nevertheless, that it shall and may be lawful to and for the said Justices, where they shall see cause, to mitigate or lessen any such penalties or forfeitures, according to their discretion. *Justices may mitigate l'enalties.*

83. And, for enabling the said Chancellor Masters and Scholars and the said Mayor Bailiffs and Commonalty to effect the several purposes of this Act, be it further enacted, that it shall and may be lawful to and for the said Chancellor Masters and Scholars in Convocation assembled, from time to time, to nominate, depute, and appoint six of the Members of Convocation resident within the said University, and for the said Mayor Bailiffs and Commonalty in Council assembled, from time to time, to nominate, depute, and appoint six of the Members of the Council of the said City residing within the said City or Suburbs, to be a Committee to treat and agree with the owners and occupiers and all other persons interested in the houses and buildings standing on the said plot or piece of ground, so to be set out as aforesaid for the said Market, and to do all matters and things, for and in the names of the said Chancellor Masters and Scholars and the said Mayor Bailiffs and Commonalty, necessary for carrying this Act into execution, so far as the same relates to the said Market; and such Committee, from time to time, so to be nominated, deputed, and appointed by the said Chancellor Masters and Scholars and the said Mayor Bailiffs and Commonalty respectively, shall continue to act until others shall be by them severally nominated, deputed, and appointed in their stead. *Power to appoint a Committee of Members of each Body.*

[Sections 84–89 give powers for the sale to the University

and the City of "any messuages, lands, tenements, or hereditaments, which shall be necessary to be purchased for the holding the said Market and to and for making proper avenues thereto."

[Sections 90–94, which gave powers to the Market Committee to raise money by borrowing a sum not exceeding £5000, or by granting building leases, or by the sale of Life Annuities, were repealed by 5 & 6 Will. IV, c. lxix, s. 37.]

Market vested in the University and City, in Trust to pay all Debts incurred on account thereof, and afterwards equally between them.

95. And be it further enacted by the authority aforesaid, that the houses, buildings, and ground to be purchased by virtue and under the authority of this Act for the scite of the said Market as aforesaid, and all sheds, stalls, standings, and other erections to be built or set thereupon, and the rents and profits arising from the same, shall be and are hereby vested in the said Chancellor Masters and Scholars and the said Mayor Bailiffs and Commonalty and their successors for ever; and that they should stand seized thereof, in trust, for the several uses, intents, and purposes herein after mentioned and declared of and concerning the same; (that is to say,) the said Chancellor Masters and Scholars and the said Mayor Bailiffs and Commonalty, or the said Committee, or any seven or more of them, shall, out of the first monies to be borrowed or arising by granting of Leases or the sale of Annuities as aforesaid, or by any other ways and means under the authority of this Act, pay off and discharge all debts that shall be incurred by the purchases of the said plot or piece of ground and the houses and buildings thereon for the erection of the said Market, and all such charges and expences as shall necessarily attend the erecting and constituting the same; and the rents and profits arising thereby shall be applied in paying the annuity or annuities to be granted to such purchaser or purchasers as aforesaid, so long as any of them shall live; and all such savings as shall, from time to time, be made by the death of any such annuitants shall, after the discharge of all debts accrued on account of the said Market, be vested in the said Chancellor Masters and Scholars and the Mayor Bailiffs and Commonalty equally; and the savings, together with the rents and profits of the said Markets, after the death

of all such annuitants, shall be and remain an estate for the use and benefit of the said Chancellor Masters and Scholars and the said Mayor Bailiffs and Commonalty, and their successors for ever, equally, share and share alike.

[Sections 96–101 have either been repealed or relate to proceedings at law which may be taken under this Act.]

102. Provided also, and it is hereby further enacted, that nothing in this Act shall extend, or be deemed or construed to extend, to take away, diminish, or impede the exercise of any privilege or right whatsoever of the said University, or of any of the Magistrates, Officers, Ministers, or Servants thereunto belonging, or of any privilege or right whatsoever of the said City, or of any of the Magistrates, Officers, or Servants thereunto belonging. Saving Clause.

12 Geo. III, Cap. XC.

An Act for repairing and widening the Road from the West end of Saint Ives Lane in the Town of Saint Neots in the County of Huntingdon to the Pavement at the end of Bell Lane in the Town of Cambridge.

[The Vice-Chancellor and the Heads of the several Colleges and Halls in the University of Cambridge for the time being are appointed Trustees under this Act; which was continued by 33 Geo. III, c. 151, and again by 54 Geo. III, c. iv, and has of late been continued annually.]

15 Geo. III, Cap. LIII.

An Act for enabling the two Universities in England, the four Universities in Scotland, and the several Colleges of Eton, Westminster, and Winchester, to hold in Perpetuity their Copy Right in Books given or bequeathed to the said Universities and Colleges for the Advancement of useful Learning and other purposes of Education.

Preamble.

WHEREAS authors have heretofore bequeathed or given, and may hereafter bequeath or give, the copies of books composed by them to or in trust for one of the two Universities in that part of Great Britain called England, or to or in trust for some of the Colleges or Houses of Learning within the same, or to or in trust for the four Universities in Scotland, or to or in trust for the several Colleges of Eaton, Westminster, and Winchester; and in and by their several wills or other instruments of donation have directed or may direct, that the profits arising from the printing and reprinting such books shall be applied or appropriated as a fund for the advancement of learning and other beneficial purposes of education within the said Universities and Colleges aforesaid: and whereas such useful purposes will frequently be frustrated, unless the sole printing and reprinting of such books, the copies of which have been or shall be so bequeathed or given as aforesaid, be preserved and secured to the said Universities, Colleges, and Houses of Learning respectively in perpetuity: may it therefore please your Majesty that it may be enacted, and be it enacted by the King's most excellent Majesty, by and with the advice and consent of the Lords spiritual and temporal and Commons in this present Parliament assembled, and

Universities &c. in England

by the authority of the same, that the said Universities and Colleges respectively shall, at their respective presses, have for ever the sole liberty of printing and reprinting all such books as shall at any time heretofore have been, or (having not been heretofore published or assigned) shall at any time hereafter be, bequeathed or otherwise given by the author or authors of the same respectively, or the representatives of such author or authors, to or in trust for the said Universities, or to or in trust for any College or House of Learning within the same, or to or in trust for the said four Universities in Scotland, or to or in trust for the said Colleges of Eaton, Westminster, and Winchester, or any of them, for the purposes aforesaid, unless the same shall have been bequeathed or given, or shall hereafter be bequeathed or given, for any term of years or other limited term; any law or usage to the contrary hereof in any-wise notwithstanding.

and Scotland to have, for ever, the sole Right of printing &c. such Books as have been, or shall be, bequeathed to them, unless the same have been, or shall be, given for a limited time.

2. And it is hereby further enacted, that if any bookseller, printer, or other person whatsoever, from and after the twenty fourth day of June one thousand seven hundred and seventy-five, shall print, reprint, or import, or cause to be printed, reprinted, or imported, any such book or books; or, knowing the same to be so printed or reprinted, shall sell, publish, or expose to sale, or cause to be sold, published, or exposed to sale, any such book or books; then such offender or offenders shall forfeit such book or books, and all and every sheet or sheets, being part of such book or books, to the University, College, or House of Learning respectively, to whom the copy of such book or books shall have been bequeathed or given as aforesaid; who shall forthwith damask and make waste paper of them; and further, that every such offender or offenders shall forfeit one penny for every sheet which shall be found in his, her, or their custody, either printed or printing, published, or exposed to sale, contrary to the true intent and meaning of this Act; the one moiety thereof to the King's most excellent Majesty, his heirs and successors, and the other moiety thereof to any person or persons who shall sue for the same; to be recovered in any of his Majesty's Courts of Record at Westminster, or in the Court of Session in Scotland, by action of debt, bill, plaint, or information, in which no wager of law, essoin, privilege, or protection, or more than one imparlance shall be allowed.

After June 24, 1775, persons printing or selling such Books shall forfeit the same, and also 1d. for every Sheet.

One Moiety to his Majesty, and the other to the Prosecutor.

Nothing in this Act to extend to grant any exclusive Right longer than such Books are printed at the Presses of the Universities.

3. Provided nevertheless, that nothing in this Act shall extend to grant any exclusive right otherwise than so long as the books or copies belonging to the said Universities or Colleges are printed only at their own printing presses within the said Universities or Colleges respectively and for their sole benefit and advantage; and that if any University or College shall delegate, grant, lease, or sell their copy rights or exclusive rights of printing the books hereby granted, or any part thereof, or shall allow, permit, or authorise any person or persons or bodies corporate to print or reprint the same, that then the privileges hereby granted are to become void and of no effect, in the same manner as if this Act had not been made; but the said Universities and Colleges, as aforesaid, shall nevertheless have a right to sell such copies so bequeathed or given as aforesaid, in like manner as any author or authors now may do under the provisions of the Statute of the eighth year of her Majesty Queen Anne.

Universities may sell Copy Rights in like manner as any Author.

No Person subject to Penalties for printing &c. Books already bequeathed, unless they be entered before June 24, 1775.

4. And whereas many persons may through ignorance offend against this Act, unless some provision be made whereby the property of every such book as is intended by this Act to be secured to the said Universities, Colleges, and Houses of Learning within the same, and to the said Universities in Scotland, and to the respective Colleges of Eaton, Westminster, and Winchester, may be ascertained and known; be it therefore enacted by the authority aforesaid, that nothing in this Act contained shall be construed to extend to subject any bookseller, printer, or other person whatsoever to the forfeitures or penalties herein mentioned for or by reason of the printing or reprinting, importing, or exposing to sale any book or books, unless the title to the copy of such book or books which has or have been already bequeathed or given to any of the said Universities or Colleges aforesaid be entered in the Register Book of the Company of Stationers kept for that purpose, in such manner as hath been usual, on or before the twenty-fourth day of June one thousand seven hundred and seventy-five; and of all and every such book or books as may or shall hereafter be bequeathed or given as aforesaid be entered in such Register within the space of two months after any such bequest or gift shall have come to the knowledge of the Vice-Chan-

All Books that may hereafter be bequeathed, must be entered within two

cellors of the said Universities, or Heads of Houses and Colleges of Learning, or of the Principal of any of the said four Universities respectively; for every of which entries so to be made as aforesaid, the sum of sixpence shall be paid, and no more; which said Register Book shall and may, at all seasonable and convenient times, be referred to and inspected by any bookseller, printer, or other person, without any fee or reward; and the Clerk of the said Company of Stationers shall, when and as often as thereunto required, give a certificate under his hand of such entry or entries, and for every such certificate may take a fee not exceeding sixpence.

Months after such Bequest shall be known. 6d. to be paid for each Entry in the Register Book, which may be inspected without Fee.

Clerk to give a Certificate being paid 6d.

5. And be it further enacted, that if the Clerk of the said Company of Stationers for the time being shall refuse or neglect to register or make such entry or entries, or to give such certificate, being thereunto required by the agent of either of the said Universities or Colleges aforesaid, lawfully authorised for that purpose, then either of the said Universities or Colleges aforesaid, being the proprietor of such copy right or copy rights as aforesaid, (notice being first given of such refusal by an advertisement in the Gazette,) shall have the like benefit as if such entry or entries, certificate or certificates, had been duly made and given; and the Clerk so refusing shall for every such offence forfeit twenty pounds to the proprietor or proprietors of every such copy right, to be recovered in any of his Majesty's Courts of Record at Westminster, or in the Court of Session in Scotland, by action of debt, bill, plaint, or information, in which no wager of law, essoin, privilege, protection, or more than one imparlance shall be allowed.

If Clerk refuse or neglect to make Entry &c., Proprietor of such Copyright to have like Benefit as if such Entry had been made, and the Clerk to forfeit £20.

7. And be it further enacted by the authority aforesaid, that if any action or suit shall be commenced or brought against any person or persons whatsoever for doing or causing to be done any thing in pursuance of this Act, the defendants in such action may plead the general issue†, and give the special matter in evidence; and if upon such action a verdict, or, if the same shall be brought in the Court of Session in Scotland, a judgement, be given for the defendant,

Limitation of Actions.

General Issue†.

---

† Section 6, and so much of s. 7 as relates to plea of General Issue, are repealed by 24 & 25 Vict. c. 101.

or the plaintiff become non-suited, and discontinue his action, then the defendant shall have and recover his full costs, for which he shall have the same remedy as a defendant in any case by law hath.

17 Geo. III, Cap. LIII.

An Act to promote the residence of the Parochial Clergy, by making Provision for the more speedy and effectual building, rebuilding, repairing, or purchasing Houses, and other necessary Buildings and Tenements, for the Use of their Benefices.

[This Act enables every Incumbent, for the purpose of building, rebuilding, or repairing a Residence-House for his Benefice, to borrow, with the consent of the Ordinary and the Patron, money not exceeding two years' net income of his living, and to mortgage the glebe &c. for twenty five years as a security.]

Colleges in Oxford and Cambridge, and other Corporate Bodies Patrons of Livings, may lend any Sums without Interest, to aid the execution of this Act.

13. And be it further enacted, that it shall and may be lawful for any College or Hall within the Universities of Oxford and Cambridge, or for any other corporate bodies possessed of the patronage of ecclesiastical livings or benefices, to advance and lend any sum or sums of money, of which they have the power of disposing, in order to aid and assist the several purposes of this Act, for the building, rebuilding, repairing, or purchasing of any houses or buildings for the habitation and convenience of the Clergy upon livings or benefices under the patronage of such College or Hall, upon the mortgage and security directed by this Act for the repayment of the principal, without taking any interest for the same.

21 Geo. III, Cap. XLVII.

An Act to amend and enlarge the Powers of an Act, passed in the eleventh year of his present Majesty's Reign, for performing several Works and making Improvements within the University and City of Oxford and the Suburbs thereof and in the adjoining Parish of Saint Clement.

[Sections 1–24 and 31–48 of this Act extended the term for taking the Tolls granted by 11 Geo. III, c. 19; made provision for cleansing and lighting Magdalen Bridge, for widening the upper part of High Street by taking down houses on the north side of it, for repairing and paving all streets and lanes in Oxford and its suburbs and in St. Clement's, and for widening the Turl[u] by taking down houses on both sides of it; and gave larger powers for lighting and cleansing and for preventing nuisances.]

25. And whereas, in pursuance of the directions and powers contained in the before recited Act, the Committee respectively deputed and appointed by the Chancellor Masters and Scholars of the University of Oxford and the Mayor Bailiffs and Commonalty of the City of Oxford have proceeded to erect and build a new Market, and have completed the same, on a plot or piece of ground set out and described by the Commissioners appointed by or acting under the said Act: and whereas, by the several laws now in force for recovering rents in arrear, the person distraining any goods or chattels cannot sell or dispose of the same until the expiration of five days next after such distress taken, and notice thereof given to the party distrained upon; which has been found inconvenient in distresses made for arrears of rents due from persons occupying shops and other erections

---

[u] "In case the street or passage .... called *The Turl*, which is at present very narrow, was made sufficient to admit carriages to pass commodiously, a very convenient communication would be made between" Broad Street and High Street. Section 20.

in the said Market, by reason of the goods being of a perishable nature: be it therefore further enacted, that in all cases where any rent shall henceforth become due and be in arrear for or in respect of any of the said shops and other erections in the said Market, and any goods or chattels shall be taken in distress for the same, and the tenant or owner of the goods or chattels so distrained shall not, within the space of twenty-four hours next after such distress taken, and notice thereof (with the cause of such distress) given to the person distrained upon, or left at his usual place of abode or upon some notorious part of the premises charged with the rent distrained for, replevy the same, with sufficient sureties, as in the cases of other distresses, then, after such distress and notice as aforesaid and expiration of the said twenty-four hours, the goods and chattels so taken in distress shall and may be appraised, and afterwards sold and disposed of in such manner and for such purposes, and under and subject to such provisions and regulations, as are mentioned and enacted with respect to other distresses for rent; any law, statute, or usage to the contrary notwithstanding.

<small>Distress taken therein may be sold in Twenty-four Hours, if not replevied.</small>

26. And whereas it will be more convenient that the present Market for butter and eggs should be removed into the said new Market; and some doubts have arisen whether apples, cherries, and other fruit, which are sold or exposed to sale in the said University and City and Suburbs thereof, are obliged, under and by force of the before recited Act, to be brought into and sold in the said new Market: be it therefore further enacted, that it shall not be lawful for any person or persons hereafter to vend or expose to sale any butter, eggs, apples, cherries, or other fruit in any other place whatsoever within the said University, City, or Suburbs, than in the said new Market; (other than and except such apples, cherries, and fruit, as shall be sold by persons inhabiting within the said University, City, or Suburbs, within their own houses or shops, and which shall be bona fide their property, and which shall be raised within their own gardens or plantations within the said University or City, or shall have been by them purchased in the said new Market;) and every person who shall hereafter vend or expose

<small>Butter, Eggs, and Fruit (except as excepted) to be sold in the New Market only.</small>

21 GEO. III, c. 47.   91

to sale any butter, eggs, apples, cherries, or other fruit, (except as aforesaid,) in any other place within the said University, City, or Suburbs, than in the said new Market, shall be subject and liable to the same penalty, and to be recovered and disposed of in the same manner, as is mentioned and directed by the said Act in respect of persons vending or exposing to sale any manner of flesh, or other raw victuals, fish, poultry, herbs, roots, or garden-stuff in any other place within the said University, City, or Suburbs, than in the said new Market.

27. Provided always, that nothing herein contained shall prevent, or be construed to prevent, any person or persons from exposing to sale or selling any oranges, lemons, or other fruit, which shall be the growth or produce of foreign parts, within their own houses or shops. *Foreign Fruit excepted.*

28. And whereas the north part of the said new Market consists of an area, or void space of ground, which is occupied upon market days by persons resorting to the said Market with apples, peas, potatoes, and other garden-stuff, in their several seasons, and various other marketable goods and commodities, and no provision is made by the said Act for payment of any sum or sums of money in respect thereof: be it therefore enacted, that the said Chancellor Masters and Scholars and Mayor Bailiffs and Commonalty, and their respective successors, or the Committee by them respectively from time to time appointed as aforesaid, shall and may demand and take of and from the said several persons so occupying the said area with their respective goods as aforesaid any reasonable sum or sums of money by way of and as a compensation for, and in proportion to, the space of ground so by them respectively occupied. *Persons to pay for selling anything in the Area on the North of the Market.*

[Section 29 confirms agreements made with the parishes of All Saints and St. Michael for rating the Market to the Land Tax.

[Section 30 imposes a penalty for obstructing the avenues from High Street into the Market.]

21 Geo. III, Cap. LVI.

An Act for granting to his Majesty an additional Duty upon Almanacks printed on one side of any one Sheet or piece of Paper; and for allowing a certain annual Sum out of the said Duty to each of the Universities of Oxford and Cambridge, in lieu of the Money heretofore paid to the said Universities by the Company of Stationers of the City of London for the Privilege of printing Almanacks.

Preamble.

10. And whereas the power of granting a liberty to print Almanacks and other books was heretofore supposed to be an inherent right in the Crown; and whereas the Crown hath, by different charters under the great Seal, granted to the Universities of Oxford and Cambridge, among other things, the privilege of printing Almanacks; and whereas the Universities did demise to the Company of Stationers of the City of London their privileges of printing and vending Almanacks and Calendars, and have received an annual sum of one thousand pounds and upwards as a consideration for such privilege; and whereas the money so received by them has been laid out and expended in promoting different branches of literature and science, to the great increase of religion and learning, and the general benefit and advantage of these realms; and whereas the privilege or right of printing Almanacks has been, by a late decision at law, found to have been a common right, over which the Crown had no controul, and consequently the Universities no power to demise the same to any particular person or body of men, whereby the payments so made to them by the Company

Out of the Duties granted by this Act, there shall be paid £500 a year to

of Stationers have ceased and been discontinued: be it therefore enacted by the authority aforesaid, that, from and after the twenty-fourth day of June one thousand seven hundred and eighty-one, there shall be issued, paid, and applied, in every year, out of the monies which shall arise by the duty hereinbefore granted, the sums of money following to the two Universities of Oxford and Cambridge; that is to say, the sum of five hundred pounds to the University of Oxford, and the sum of five hundred pounds to the University of Cambridge; which said several and respective sums of money shall be and are hereby charged upon the duty herein-before granted, and shall be paid thereout yearly and every year, at the two usual feasts, that is to say, the Feast of the Nativity of Saint John the Baptist, and the Birth of our Lord Christ; the first payment to be made, on the Feast of the Birth of our Lord Christ after passing this Act, by the Receiver General of his Majesty's Stamp-duties, free and clear of all fees, dues, duties, taxes, and deductions whatsoever, unto the Chancellors Masters and Scholars of the said Universities of Oxford and Cambridge, and to be received by the hands of the Vice-Chancellor of each University respectively, or by some person or persons duly authorized by each respective Vice-Chancellor under his hand to receive the same, to and for the sole use and benefit of each of the said Universities; and the receipt of the Vice-Chancellor of each University, or of the person or persons duly authorized as aforesaid by him to receive the same, shall be a sufficient receipt to the said Receiver General of the Stamp-duties, and shall be allowed by the Auditor and Auditors of the Imprest, and all other persons concerned in passing his accounts, as a full and sufficient discharge for the making such payments out of the aforesaid duty [x].

[x] This grant is confirmed by 44 Geo. 3, c. 98 (a Stamp Act), by the following words in Schedule (C.) under "Allowances": "To the two Universities of Oxford and Cambridge respectively, the annual sum of £500 each."

28 Geo. III, Cap. LXIV.

An Act for the better paving, cleansing, and lighting the Town of Cambridge, for removing and preventing Obstructions and Annoyances, and for widening the Streets, Lanes, and other Passages within the said Town.

[Sections 1–22 appoint, or provide for the appointment of, Commissioners for putting the Act in execution, and give directions concerning their meetings, officers, &c.

[Section 23 empowers the Commissioners to raise money "by a Rate, not exceeding one shilling in the pound for each year, upon the several tenants or occupiers of all houses, buildings, gardens, tenements, and hereditaments within the said Town, according to the annual value of the same" from time to time, such value being determined by the assessment of them to the Poor's Rate: provided "that nothing in this Act contained shall extend, or be construed to extend, to subject the Chancellor Masters and Scholars of the University aforesaid to pay any rates or assessments for or in consideration of the Botanick Garden in the said University."

Botanic Garden not to be rated.

[Sections 24–36 all relate to rating.

[Section 25 enacts that "one third part of the said Rates or Assessments shall be borne and defrayed by the respective landholders, and two third parts thereof by the respective tenants or occupiers."]

One-third part of Rates to be borne by Landlords.

26. Provided always, and be it further enacted, that nothing herein contained shall be deemed or taken to make void any contract, covenant, or agreement between any landlord and tenant, touching or concerning the repairing any of the pavements in the streets and other places within the said Town: and the Lessees of Colleges or Halls to the University estates in the said Town shall, in all cases, be deemed the Landlord for the purposes of this Act.

Not to make void any Contract between Landlord and Tenant.

[Section 33 enacts, that in case any tenant shall remove before payment of Rates, or shall not have sufficient goods and chattels to defray them, or in case any rated premises shall be empty and untenanted, then the premises shall be chargeable with one third part only of such Rates, and this may be recovered from the Owner or Owners.]

34. And whereas some doubts may hereafter arise who shall be deemed the Owner or Owners of the several houses, buildings, yards, lands, tenements, and hereditaments in the said Town, for the purposes and within the true intent and meaning of this Act; for removing whereof be it further enacted, that neither the Chancellor Masters and Scholars of the University, nor any College or Hall, nor the Mayor Bailiffs and Burgesses of the Town of Cambridge, or any other person or persons, shall, on account of any ground rent or other acknowledgement, sum or sums of money, in nature of a ground rent or rents issuing out of or payable for any messuage, yard, garden, land, tenement, or hereditament in the said University and Town, or on account of their reversion or interest of or in the messuage, yard, garden, land, tenement, or hereditament for which such ground rent, acknowledgement, sum or sums of money shall be payable, be considered, deemed, taken or adjudged to be the Owner or Owners, Proprietor or Proprietors of such messuage, yard, garden, lands, tenements, or hereditaments; but the Lessee or Lessees of the said Chancellor Masters and Scholars of the said University, or of any College or Hall, or of the Mayor Bailiffs and Burgesses, or of such other person or persons, or their assigns, shall, during the existence of the term for which such messuage, yard, garden, lands, tenements, or hereditaments shall be demised, be considered, deemed, taken, and adjudged, for all and every the purposes of this Act, to be the Owner or Owners, Proprietor or Proprietors of such messuage, yard, garden, lands, tenements, or hereditaments; and shall, during such term, bear and pay all expences and impositions whatsoever by force or virtue hereof to be borne or defrayed by the Owner or Owners, Proprietor or Proprietors of the said messuage, yard, garden, lands, tenements, and hereditaments; any thing in this Act contained to the contrary thereof in anywise notwithstanding.

Who shall be deemed Owners.

[Section 37 provides for cases of dispute concerning wages

of labourers employed, and s. 38 for complaints of defective pavements.

[Sections 39–42 empower the Commissioners to raise money by Tolls *y*.

[Sections 43–46 empower them to raise money, not exceeding £6000 in the whole, by mortgage or by life-annuities.

[Section 47 vests all moneys so raised in the Commissioners.

[Sections 48–57 enable the Commissioners to purchase any houses, shambles, buildings, grounds, and estates within the Town in order to widen, turn, or alter any of the streets, lanes, and public passages.

[Section 58 vests in the Commissioners the property of all pavements, sewers, drains, or watercourses in the streets, lanes, and other public passages and places in the Town, and of all lamps and lamp-posts.

[Section 59 empowers the Commissioners to alter and improve all public pavements, sewers, and drains, and to cause all streets, lanes, and public passages and places to be cleansed and lighted, and all nuisances and encroachments to be removed.]

Nothing in this Act to extend to any College Courts.
60. And be it further enacted, that nothing herein contained shall extend, or be construed to extend, to the inside of any Court or other place within any College or Hall in the said Town of Cambridge, or within the scite or walls thereof.

[Sections 61–67 empower the Commissioners to make contracts for paving and other works, to dig gravel, and to regulate private drains.

[Section 68, concerning the sweeping of foot paths, is repealed by 34 Geo. III, c. 104, s. 20, following.

[Sections 69–73 contain provisions for scavenging.]

Penalty on breaking or damaging Lamps by matriculated or
74. And be it further enacted by the authority aforesaid, that if any matriculated person or persons, or member or members of any College or Hall in the said University, shall wilfully break, throw down, or otherwise damage any of

---

y By 9 & 10 Vict. c. cccxlv, the Eastern Counties Railway Company is charged with a yearly payment of £1000 to the Commissioners in lieu of all Tolls levied under this Act or under 34 Geo. 3, c. 104.

the lamps which shall be erected by virtue of this Act, or any of the posts, irons, or other furniture thereof, and complaint shall be made by the Commissioners appointed by this Act or their Surveyor to the Vice-Chancellor or his Deputy against such person or persons, the said Vice-Chancellor or his Deputy shall and he is hereby required to summon the party or parties so complained of to appear before him, and shall proceed to examine upon oath any witness or witnesses who shall appear or be produced to give information touching such offence (which said oath the said Vice-Chancellor, or his Deputy, is hereby impowered to administer); and if the party or parties so complained of shall be convicted of such offence, either by his or their own confession, or upon such information as aforesaid, he or they shall be sentenced, over and above any Academical punishment, to pay to the Commissioners or their Surveyor the full amount of the damages by him or them done as aforesaid; and in case such offender or offenders shall refuse to pay the amount of such damages, the Tutor of the College of which the offender shall be a Member shall be answerable for the same. [The remainder of this section provides for the punishment of persons guilty of the like offences, not being Members of any College or Hall, and increases the penalty for the second and for the third offence.] *other persons.*

[Sections 75–86 give the Commissioners powers to prevent certain specified nuisances and encroachments.]

87. And whereas many houses, edifices, shops, and warehouses within the said University and Town belong to bodies corporate, and are irregularly built, and by reason of their contingent tenure are frequently suffered to fall into a ruinous state, be it therefore enacted, that it shall and may be lawful for any body corporate or collegiate, aggregate or sole, to alienate and sell for ever any tenements or hereditaments, and the scite thereof, with their appurtenances, standing or being within the University and Town of Cambridge: provided, that all and every sum and sums of money to be paid to any body corporate or collegiate, aggregate or sole (except the Corporation of the Town of Cambridge), for the purchase of such houses, tenements, or hereditaments, be lodged in any of the publick funds in the names of the three Royal *Colleges and Corporations impowered to sell Houses, &c.*

Professors of Divinity, Law, and Physick for the time being within the said University, in trust for the use of the said body corporate or collegiate, aggregate or sole, for houses belonging to such body corporate or collegiate, as aforesaid; and for houses, tenements, and hereditaments belonging to the Corporation, in the name of the Mayor Bailiffs and Burgesses; to be by them laid out in the purchase of lands and hereditaments without the University and Town of Cambridge, or otherwise settled and appropriated for such uses and trusts as the houses, tenements, or hereditaments so sold by such Corporation, College, or Body Corporate, were settled and limited at the time of such sale so made.

[Sections 88 and 89 provide for the re-investment of purchase moneys to the uses and trusts to which the property sold was limited.]

[Sections 90–94 contain provisions concerning penalties and prosecutions.]

Corporation may hereafter alter the Market Place.

95. And be it further enacted, that, if at any time hereafter the said Mayor Bailiffs and Burgesses of the said Town of Cambridge shall, for the accommodation of the inhabitants of the said Town, make and erect, or cause to be made and erected, a publick market with shambles or other conveniencies for the sale of goods and victuals in any other place or places within the said Town than where the markets are now usually kept or held, then and in such case it shall not be lawful for any person or persons whomsoever to expose to sale any goods, victuals, or other commodities whatsoever in any other part or parts of the Town or place than shall be so made, erected, or set out as and for a market-place, other than in their own shops, houses, warehouses and yards within the said Town, under the forfeiture of paying for every offence the sum of forty shillings, to be recovered in like manner as the penalties are herein-after directed to be recovered.

Reservation of the Right of the University to superintend and regulate the Mar-

96. Provided, that nothing herein contained shall extend, or be construed to extend, to take away the right of the said Chancellor Masters and Scholars to govern, regulate, and superintend the same, as heretofore accustomed with respect to the ancient market-place or places, or to take away the right of the said Mayor Bailiffs and Burgesses of the Tolls

as have been heretofore paid to them or their Toll-gatherer; but the same respectively shall remain and belong to the said Chancellor Masters and Scholars and the said Mayor Bailiffs and Burgesses severally, as before the passing of this Act; and the said Chancellor Masters and Scholars and Mayor Bailiffs and Burgesses respectively shall and may prescribe and have such remedies for the same in such new market, as they could have and were intitled to in the places where the ancient markets were usually or commonly held.

kets, and the Right of the Corporation to Tolls.

[Sections 97–108 contain various provisions for holding fairs, for numbering houses, for regulating Hobson's Conduit, for proceedings at law.]

109. Provided also, and it is hereby further enacted, that nothing in this Act shall extend, or be deemed or construed to extend, to take away, diminish, or impede the exercise of any privilege or right whatsoever of the said University or Corporation, or of any persons being Members of the same, or of any of the Magistrates, Officers, Ministers, or Servants thereunto belonging, or of the Mayor Bailiffs and Burgesses of the Corporation of Cambridge.

Saving Clause for the Rights of the University and of the Corporation.

[Section 110 saves all rights of the Mayor Bailiffs and Burgesses to collect Tolls.]

111. And for raising money towards answering and defraying the charges and expences of passing this Act, and for further carrying the same into execution, be it further enacted, that the said Commissioners, or any five or more of them, at a meeting to be held for that purpose, shall and they are hereby authorized and required, annually, or as often as they shall judge necessary, to ascertain the sum or sums of money which may be wanted for the purposes of defraying the expences of passing this Act, and for widening, improving, new paving, and fixing lamps in the several streets, lanes, and alleys, publick passages and ways of the Town of Cambridge, and for doing all other works necessary to the execution of this Act; and, within two days after such sum shall have been so agreed upon, give notice thereof, specifying the sum or sums, to the Vice-Chancellor of the University and to the Mayor of the said Town, in writing under the hands of five or more of them, to be delivered to the Vice-

Proportion of the Monies to be raised by the University and Town for the first Pavements &c. to be settled.

Chancellor and Mayor, or left at their respective places of abode; two fifths of which respective sum (such sum being into five parts equally divided) shall be paid by or on account of the said University in manner herein-after directed; and one twelfth of the remaining three fifth parts shall be paid by or on account of the Corporation of the said Town in the manner herein-after directed; and the remaining part of the sum so ascertained the said Commissioners are hereby authorized and impowered to borrow, on the security of the tolls herein granted, and on the rates and assessments to be levied on the several tenants and occupiers of all houses, buildings, gardens, tenements, and hereditaments within the said Town, as herein mentioned.

University may borrow Money.

112. And be it further enacted, that the said Chancellor, Vice-Chancellor, Masters or Heads of the several Colleges or Halls within the said University, shall and are hereby authorized and impowered to borrow any sum or sums of money, not exceeding in the whole the sum of four thousand pounds, on their part or quota of the rates and assessments for defraying of the expences of carrying this Act into execution; and such security shall be signed by the Vice-Chancellor for the time being, and five at the least of the other Masters or Heads of the Colleges or Halls in the said University.

Proportion of annual sums for Paving &c. to be raised by the University and Town, to be settled.

113. And, for raising money towards answering and defraying the annual charges and expences of repairing, cleansing, and lighting the several streets within the said Town, be it further enacted, that the said Commissioners, or any five or more of them, at a meeting to be held for that purpose, shall and are hereby authorized and required, annually, or as often as they shall judge necessary, to ascertain the sum or sums wanted for the purposes aforesaid; and, within two days after such sum shall have been agreed upon, give notice thereof, specifying the sum or sums, to the Vice-Chancellor of the University and to the Mayor of the said Town, in writing under the hands of any five or more of them; two fifths of which sum (such sum being in five equal parts divided) shall be paid by or on account of the said University in manner herein mentioned; and ten pounds of such annual sum to be paid by or on account of the said Corporation; and the remaining part of such annual sum to

be paid by and out of the money to be raised by tolls herein granted, and rates and assessments herein directed to be levied on the several tenants or occupiers of all houses, buildings, gardens, tenements, and hereditaments within the said Town.

114. And be it further enacted by the authority aforesaid, that the Chancellor or Vice-Chancellor, and Masters or Heads of the several Colleges and Halls within the said University, or in their absence their Deputies or Locum Tenentes, shall and they are hereby required to meet upon summons of the Vice-Chancellor within seven days after notice aforesaid (which summons the said Vice-Chancellor is hereby required to issue), and make, or cause to be made, an account of such sum or sums of money, as they shall deem the quota or proportion of the sum to be paid out of the University Chest for the pavement and other works to be done under this Act, belonging to the University, and of the quotas or proportions of the different Colleges and Halls; which said respective sums so assessed shall amount to two fifths as aforesaid: and in case the Chancellor, Vice-Chancellor, and Heads of Colleges or Halls in the said University, or in their absence their Deputies or Locum Tenentes, shall neglect or refuse to meet, and make or cause to be made an assessment of the different quotas or proportions of the said two fifth parts, to be paid as the share of the said University and several Colleges and Halls as aforesaid, for the space of fourteen days after notice delivered to the Vice-Chancellor as aforesaid, then, and in such case, the said Vice-Chancellor is hereby authorized and required to make out such assessment himself, and deliver or cause to be delivered a copy thereof to the Collector who shall or may be appointed, by virtue of this Act, to collect and receive the monies for the carrying the same into execution, and shall demand of the Vice-Chancellor, and of the Bursar of each College or Hall in the said University, payment of the sum or sums so assessed by the said Vice-Chancellor upon the said University and the several Colleges and Halls aforesaid: and upon nonpayment thereof, or in case the said Vice-Chancellor, or any of the said Bursars, shall neglect or refuse, for the space of fourteen days after demand thereof made, to pay the said

How the sums to be raised by the University are to be recovered.

sum or sums so respectively assessed as aforesaid, then the said Vice-Chancellor is hereby required, upon complaint made by the Collector of such neglect or refusal, to issue a warrant of distress under his hand and seal, to seize and take any of the goods and chattels of the said University or the several Colleges or Halls aforesaid, and, if the sum so assessed is not paid within three days, to cause the same to be sold, and after payment of the demand or assessment, together with all charges attending the seizing, detaining, and selling the same, to return the overplus to the said Vice-Chancellor or Bursar in whose College such distress was made as aforesaid: and, in case the said Vice-Chancellor shall neglect or refuse to proceed in the manner herein-before directed for the space of seven days after the expiration of the respective times aforesaid, then it shall and may be lawful for the said Commissioners, or any five or more of them, to proceed in like manner as the said Vice-Chancellor is hereby authorized and required to do, and levy the amount on the goods and chattels of the said University or College or Hall, as hereinbefore mentioned.

Remaining Proportion to be raised by the Town. 115. And it is hereby also enacted, that one twelfth part of the remaining three fifth parts of the sum or sums of money ascertained for the first expence of paving the said Town shall be paid and defrayed by the Mayor Bailiffs and Burgesses of the said Town, to be applied to the purposes of this Act; and in case of refusal to pay the same within seven days after the next common day after the same shall be demanded, it shall be lawful for the said Commissioners to cause the same to be levied by distress and sale of the goods and chattels of the said Mayor Bailiffs and Burgesses, rendering the overplus (if any be), after deducting the costs and charges of making such distress and selling the same; and the said Mayor Bailiffs and Burgesses shall yearly and every year, for ever afterwards, pay to the said Commissioners, for the purposes of this Act, the sum of ten pounds, to be recovered and levied in manner aforesaid; and such payments, so to be made by the said Mayor Bailiffs and Burgesses, shall be deemed and taken to be a full equivalent and satisfaction for the paving, repairing, cleansing, and lighting such part of the streets, lanes, and ways belonging to the said Mayor Bailiffs and Burgesses, who are and shall be exonerated and discharged from such paving, repairing, cleansing, and lighting for the future.

34 Geo. III, Cap. CIV.

An Act to amend and enlarge the powers of an Act, passed in the twenty-eighth year of the Reign of His present Majesty, intituled, An Act for the better paving, cleansing, and lighting the Town of Cambridge, for removing and preventing Obstructions and Annoyances, and for widening the Streets, Lanes, and other Passages, within the said Town. 28 Geo. 3, c. 64.

WHEREAS an Act was passed in the twenty-eighth year of the reign of His present Majesty for the better paving, cleansing, and lighting the Town of Cambridge, for removing and preventing obstructions and annoyances, and for widening the streets, lanes, and other passages, within the said Town; and whereas great progress hath been made in executing the said Act, in the doing of which the whole of the money authorized by the said Act to be raised and borrowed hath been expended, and a considerable debt hath been contracted by the Commissioners for executing the same, which now remains due; and whereas divers works necessary to be done for the completion of the improvements in the said Town still remain unfinished, and cannot be executed, nor can the above-mentioned debt be discharged, without the further aid of Parliament; and whereas several amendments and further regulations are wanting to the said Act, to render it more extensively useful: Preamble.

May it therefore please your Majesty that it may be enacted, and be it enacted by the King's most excellent Majesty, by and with the advice and consent of the Lords spiritual and temporal and Commons in this present Parliament assembled, and by the authority of the same, that it shall be lawful for the Com- Commissioners em-

powered to raise a further Sum of Money.

missioners for executing this Act, and they are hereby authorized and empowered, to raise (over and above the monies allowed to be raised by the said former Act) any sum or sums of money not exceeding five thousand pounds, the same to be raised and paid in the following proportions; (that is to say), two fifth parts of such sum or sums, so to be raised in pursuance of this Act, shall be paid by and on account of the University of Cambridge, one twelfth part of the remaining three fifths shall be paid by or on account of the Corporation of the said Town, and the remaining part of such sum or sums the said Commissioners are hereby authorized and empowered to borrow on the security of the rates and assessments, duties and tolls, made and levied, or to be made and levied, by virtue of this and the said former Act; such sum and sums, so to be borrowed on security, to be raised and borrowed by any or either of the ways and means of borrowing money mentioned in the said former Act; and the proportion of the said sum and sums of money, payable as above-mentioned by the said University and Corporation, shall be enforced in like manner as is provided and directed with respect to the payment of the sums of money payable by the said University and Corporation by virtue of the said former Act; and the said sum and sums of money, when paid and raised, shall be applied by the said Commissioners, in the first place, in the paying and discharging the costs and expences of applying for and passing this Act, and then in discharging all debts contracted by the said Commissioners in the execution of the said recited Act, and now due and owing, and the residue shall be applied by the said Commissioners in finishing, completing, and making the several improvements in the said Town yet remaining unfinished, in manner, and under the rules, orders, and regulations herein and in the said former Act specified and provided.

The University enabled to borrow Money.

2. And be it further enacted, that it shall be lawful for the Chancellor, Vice-Chancellor, Masters or Heads of the several Colleges or Halls within the said University, and they are hereby authorized and empowered, to borrow any sum or sums of money, not exceeding in the whole their quota of the said money so to be raised and borrowed as above-mentioned, in such manner as is directed touching the sum or

sums of money authorized in and by the said former Act to be borrowed by the said University.

3. And be it further enacted, that the clauses in the said former Act relating to the original appointment of Commissioners for carrying the same into execution shall be, and the same are hereby repealed; and that, from and after the passing of this Act, the following Magistrates and Officers for the time being of the University of Cambridge, and of the Colleges and Halls therein, (to wit), the Chancellor, High Steward, Representatives in Parliament, the Vice-Chancellor or his Deputy, all the Heads or Masters of Colleges or Halls, or in their absence their respective Deputies or Locum Tenentes, and the Commissary, or in his absence his Deputy, also two persons for Trinity College, two persons for Saint John's College, and one person for each of the remaining Colleges and Halls in the said University, being Fellows or Masters of Arts or of the Degree hereinafter mentioned, and also the following Magistrates and persons of the Corporation of Cambridge, (to wit), the High Steward, Recorder, or his Deputy, Representatives in Parliament, and the Mayor, or his Deputy, and the Aldermen, for the time being, together with [*here follow the names of several persons*], shall be, and they are hereby appointed Commissioners for putting this and the said former Act into execution.

For appointing Commissioners, and repealing Provision in former Act relating thereto

4. And be it further enacted, that it shall and may be lawful to and for the Head or Master of each College and Hall within the said University, except the said Colleges of Trinity and Saint John, and the Masters of Arts and persons of superior Academical Degree resident for the time being within such College and Hall, and on the Foundation thereof, to meet together in the usual place for transacting the College business in the respective Colleges and Halls, between the hours of nine and twelve in the forenoon of the second Monday after the passing of this Act, or as soon after as conveniently may be, and the major part of such persons then resident and there assembled shall and may proceed to elect one of the Fellows or Masters of Arts or persons of superior Degree on the Foundation of such their respective College or Hall to be a Commissioner for such respective College or Hall; and the Head or Master, Masters of Arts, and

Commissioners to be elected from each College.

persons of superior Academical Degree, resident for the time being within the said Colleges of Trinity and Saint John, and on the Foundation thereof, are hereby empowered to proceed in the same manner to the election of two persons of the like Degree as above-mentioned to be Commissioners for each of their respective Colleges; and in case of an equality of votes in the election of a Commissioner or Commissioners for any such College or Hall respectively, the Head or Master, or in his absence his Deputy, or in their absence the senior Fellow present of such College or Hall, shall have the casting voice; and such person or persons so elected shall and may continue to act and be a Commissioner or Commissioners for putting into execution the powers in this or the said former Act contained, during the time he or they shall actually remain a Fellow or Fellows of such College or Hall or on the Foundation thereof: provided, that when and as often as any of the said Commissioners, to be chosen by their respective Colleges or Halls as aforesaid, shall happen to die, resign, or refuse to act, or his Fellowship or other place on the Foundation shall become vacant, it shall and may be lawful, within one month after such disqualification, death, resignation, refusal, or vacancy, for the several voters in the College or Hall of which such Commissioner was a Member to proceed to elect another Commissioner in manner above-mentioned, and so *toties quoties*, as occasion shall be or require.

Commissioners so appointed may act without proving any other Qualification.

5. Provided always, and be it further enacted, that all persons who have been or shall be named or appointed by any College or Hall, and all Members of the said University appointed Commissioners in or by virtue of the said former Act, or to be hereafter appointed as above-mentioned, shall be, to all intents and purposes, Commissioners for putting the said former Act and this Act in execution, in all respects, without proving any other qualification, or taking any oath in respect thereto; any thing in the said former Act or this Act or in any other Law or Statute to the contrary in anywise notwithstanding.

[Sections 6–19 contain various provisions for the annual election of two Commissioners for each Parish, for making a further Rate of three pence in the pound annually on all rateable property, for increasing the Tolls, for paying the land tax and poor rates for buildings taken down, for selling surplus land, for stopping private drains, if necessary.]

20. And be it further enacted, that, from and after the passing of this Act, the clause contained in the said former Act, directing the footpaths of the said Town to be swept and cleansed, and every part thereof, shall be, and the same is hereby declared to be repealed; and that from thenceforth all and every inhabitant and inhabitants of the Town of Cambridge, and the Master of every College within the University, shall cause to be swept and cleansed the whole of the footway, including the kirb stone, before their respective houses, buildings, walls, Colleges, and Halls, every day (except Saturday and Sunday) between the hours of six and ten in the forenoon, and between the hours of three in the afternoon of every Saturday and nine in the morning of every Sunday in the year; and the Vice-Chancellor for the time being shall cause the footpath before the Senate House and Senate House Walk, and the Churchwardens of every parish in Cambridge for the time being the footpath before the walls of their respective parish churches and church yards, to be swept and cleansed in like manner, and at the days and times above specified; and in case of neglect in the premises such inhabitant or inhabitants, Masters of Colleges and Halls, Vice-Chancellor, and Churchwardens shall respectively forfeit and pay for every such neglect the sum of five shillings, to be recovered by distress and sale of goods, and applied in such manner as is directed for the recovery and application of penalties and forfeitures by the said former Act; and in case any person or persons shall give information to any Justice of the Peace in and for the said Town of any of the said footpaths being dirty and unswept, (which information the said Justice may take without oath,) such Justice shall and may summon the person or persons who ought, by virtue of this Act, to cause the footpath complained of to be swept; and such person or persons shall prove, to the satisfaction of the said Justice, that the directions of the Act have been complied with by him, her, or them, or otherwise shall be liable to pay the said penalty.*New Clause for sweeping Footways.*

21. And, whereas some of the penalties laid by the said *Further Penalty of*

breaking Lamps.

former Act upon persons wilfully breaking or damaging lamps have not proved sufficient to prevent such offences, be it further enacted, that, from and after the passing of this Act, if any person or persons shall wilfully break, throw down, or otherwise damage any of the lamps erected by virtue of the said Act, or any of the posts, iron, or other furniture thereof, or shall extinguish any of the said lamps, every such offender shall forfeit and pay any sum or sums of money not exceeding the sum of five pounds nor less than forty shillings for each lamp so broken or thrown down, damaged, or extinguished as aforesaid; the amount of such sum or sums to be fixed and adjudged by the Justice of Peace before whom such offender shall be convicted of the said offence, any thing in the said former Act as to the first or second offence to the contrary notwithstanding; and the same methods shall be pursued for enquiring into, recovering, and levying the said penalties, and otherwise punishing the offenders, as are respectively prescribed by the said former Act with respect to the like offences committed by persons matriculated or being Members of the said University, or by any other person or persons: one moiety of the penalty so adjudged to be paid by such offender and offenders shall, upon the conviction of him, her, or them, be paid to the informer or informers upon whose oath such offender or offenders shall be convicted, and the other moiety of the penalty to the Treasurer or Treasurers of the said Commissioners for the purposes of this and the said former Act.

[Sections 22–24 contain provisions respecting sundry nuisances.]

Purchase Money for College Property to be placed out in the name of the Master of the College as well as of the three Royal Professors.

25. And whereas power is given in and by the said former Act to and for any body corporate or collegiate, aggregate or sole, to alienate and sell for ever any tenements or hereditaments, and the scite thereof, with their appurtenances, standing or being within the University and Town of Cambridge; and it is provided that all and every sum and sums of money to be paid to any body corporate or collegiate, aggregate or sole, (except the Corporation of Cambridge,) for the purchase of such houses, tenements, or hereditaments, should be lodged in any of the publick funds in the names of the three Royal Professors of Divinity, Law, and Physick

for the time being within the said University, for the use of the said body corporate or collegiate, aggregate or sole; and whereas the blending of money belonging to different Colleges in one account in the publick funds has been found inconvenient, and, in order to keep the property of the several Colleges of the said University distinct, it is thought expedient to add the name of the Master of the College so alienating and selling as aforesaid to the said three Royal Professors: be it therefore enacted, that, from and after the passing of this Act, all and every sum and sums of money heretofore paid or hereafter to be paid as aforesaid to any body corporate or collegiate, aggregate or sole, in or belonging to the said University of Cambridge, for the purchase of any houses, tenements, or hereditaments by them or either of them heretofore or hereafter to be alienated and sold, vested or to be vested in the publick funds, shall be transferred into placed out and stand in the name of the Master of the College so alienating and selling for the time being, as well as of the said three Royal Professors, in trust and to be applied to such uses, intents, and purposes as in the said former Act are mentioned and directed of and concerning the same.

[Sections 26–29 relate to compulsory purchase of property by the Commissioners; and section 30 to appeals from rates or penalties.]

35 Geo. III, Cap. LXXVII.

An Act for improving the Drainage of the Middle and South Levels ....; and for altering and improving the Navigation of the said River Ouze ....; and for improving and preserving the Navigation of the several rivers communicating with the said river Ouze.

[By section 3 "the Vice-Chancellor of Cambridge for the time being" and "the Conservators of the river Cam[z] for the time being," together with many other persons, are " appointed Commissioners for Navigation."]

[z] See 14 & 15 Vict. c. xcii.

37 Geo. III, Cap. CLXX.

An Act for more effectually repairing, improving, and keeping in repair the Road leading from the Guide Post in the Village of Adderbury in the County of Oxford through Kidlington to the end of the Mileway in the City of Oxford.

["The Vice-Chancellor, Heads of Colleges and Halls, Proctors, and Professors in the University of Oxford for the time being, ... and the Canons of Christ Church, Oxford, for the time being," are appointed Trustees for the purposes of this Act; which was continued by 59 Geo. III, *c.* cxxii, and has of late been continued annually.]

37 Geo. III, Cap. CLXXIX.

An Act for amending, altering, improving, and keeping in repair the Road leading from the Town of Cambridge into the old North Road near Arrington Bridge, all in the County of Cambridge.

[The Heads of the respective Colleges in the University of Cambridge for the time being are appointed Trustees under this Act; which was continued by 57 Geo. III, *c.* lxviii, and has of late been continued annually.]

38 Geo. III, Cap. V.

An Act for granting an Aid to His Majesty by a Land Tax to be raised in Great Britain for the service of the year one thousand seven hundred and ninety eight [a].

25. Provided, that nothing in this Act contained shall extend to charge any College or Hall in either of the two Universities of Oxford or Cambridge, or the Colleges of Windsor, Eaton, Winton, or Westminster, or the Corporation of the Governors of the Charity for the Relief of the Poor Widows and Children of Clergymen, or the College of Bromley, or any Hospital in England, Wales, or Berwick upon Tweed, for or in respect of the scites of the said Colleges, Halls, or Hospitals, or any of the buildings within the walls or limits of the said Colleges, Halls, or Hospitals; or any Master, Fellow, Scholar, or Exhibitioner of any such College or Hall, or any Reader, Officer, or Master [b] of the said Universities, Colleges, or Halls, or any Masters or Ushers of any Schools in England, Wales, or Berwick upon Tweed, for or in respect of any stipend, wages, rents, profits, or exhibitions whatsoever arising or growing due to them in respect of the said several places or employments in the said Universities, Colleges, or Schools [c]; or to charge any of the houses

Colleges &c. in the University, &c., not chargeable.

---

[a] The Land Tax was made perpetual by 38 Geo. 3, c. 60.

[b] The word "Master" is wrong: the right word is "Minister," which is found in the Act an. 1656, c. 12, cited in the next note, and in all the Land Tax Acts until 7 Geo. 1, c. 4, when "Master" first appears. By "Minister" is not meant a person in Holy Orders: the word is to be taken in the sense which it bears in the Statutes of the University and of most Colleges in Oxford.

[c] These exemptions were granted in the first Land Tax Act, 4 W. & M. c. 1; and previously in 22 & 23 Car. 2, c. 3, from which many clauses in the first Land Tax Act were taken. The exemption "in respect of the said several places or employments in the said Universities, Colleges, or Schools" is of still earlier date. It was granted in the time of the Commonwealth in an Act for an "Assessment upon England at the rate of sixty thousand pounds by the moneth for three moneths," an. 1656, c. 12, which contains the substance of the scheme of our existing Land Tax. See Scobell's Acts, cited by Christian on Blackstone's Commentaries, I, viii, p. 312, n. 18.

or lands, which, on or before the five and twentieth day of March one thousand six hundred and ninety-three, did belong to the scites of any College or Hall in England, Wales, or Berwick upon Tweed, or to Christ's Hospital, &c.

39 Geo. III, Cap. LXXIII.

An Act for exempting certain specifick Legacies which shall be given to Bodies Corporate, or other Publick Bodies, from the Payment of Duty; and also the Legacy of Books and other Articles given by the Will of the late Reverend Clayton Mordaunt Cracherode to the Trustees of the British Museum.

<small>Preamble.</small> WHEREAS it is expedient that certain specifick legacies given to bodies corporate and other publick bodies and societies should be exempted from the duties imposed on Legacies; be it enacted by the King's most excellent Majesty, by and with the advice and consent of the Lords spiritual and temporal and Commons in this present Parliament assembled, and by the authority of the same, that, <small>No Legacy of Books &c. bequeathed to any Body Corporate &c., to be preserved, shall be liable to any Duty.</small> from and after the passing of this Act, no Legacy, consisting of books, prints, pictures, statues, gems, coins, medals, specimens of natural history, or other specifick articles, which shall be given or bequeathed to or in trust for any body corporate, whether aggregate or sole, or to the Society of Serjeants Inn, or any of the Inns of Court or Chancery, or any endowed School, in order to be kept and preserved by such Body Corporate, Society, or School, and not for the purposes of sale, shall be liable to any duty imposed on Legacies by any law now in force [d].

[Section 2 relates to Mr. Cracherode's bequest.]

---

[d] This exemption is repeated in the Schedule annexed to the Stamp Act, 55 Geo. 3, c. 184.

39 Geo. III, Cap. LXXIX.

An Act for the more effectual suppression of Societies established for seditious and treasonable purposes, and for better preventing treasonable and seditious practices.

[This Act, among other things, prohibits the delivery of any lectures or discourses for the purpose of raising money or upon payment of money in any place not licensed; and it also requires printers to register their presses with the Clerk of the Peace.] *Every place for lecturing &c. must be licensed. Printers must register their Presses.*

22. Provided always, that nothing in this Act contained shall extend, or be construed to extend, to any lecture or discourses to be delivered in any of the Universities of these kingdoms by any Member thereof, or any person authorized by the Chancellor, Vice-Chancellor, or other proper Officers of such Universities respectively°,   *   *   *   *. *Not to extend to Lectures in any University.*

24. Provided also, that nothing herein contained shall extend to His Majesty's Printers for England and Scotland, or to the public Presses belonging to the Universities of Oxford and Cambridge respectively. *Exception for the Presses of the two Universities.*

39 & 40 Geo. III, Cap. XLI.

An Act for explaining and amending several Acts, made in the thirty-second year of King Henry the Eighth, and the first, thirteenth, and fourteenth years of the Reign of Queen Elizabeth, so far as respects Leases granted by Archbishops, Bishops, Masters and Fellows of Colleges, Deans and Chapters of Cathedral and Collegiate Churches, Masters and Guardians of Hospitals, and others having any Spiritual or Ecclesiastical Living or Promotion.

WHEREAS doubts have arisen whether Archbishops, Bishops, Masters and Fellows of Colleges, Deans *Preamble.*

° This provision is repeated in 57 Geo. 3, c. 19, "An Act for the more effectually preventing seditious meetings and assemblies."

and Chapters of Cathedral and Collegiate Churches, Masters and Guardians of Hospitals, and others having any spiritual or ecclesiastical living or promotion, who are by several Acts, passed in the Reigns of their late Majesties King Henry the Eighth and Queen Elizabeth, restrained from granting any Leases of their estates whereon the accustomed yearly rent is not reserved, can lawfully grant separate Leases of parts of lands or tenements which have been usually demised by one Lease and under one rent, reserving on the several parts so demised less than the rent anciently reserved on the demise of the whole, though the aggregate amount of the rents so reserved on such separate demises should be equal to or exceed the amount of the annual accustomed rent for the whole: and whereas many such separate Leases have been granted, and great inconvenience may arise to persons claiming under such Leases, if such Leases should not be deemed valid and effectual, in case the amount of the rent anciently reserved on demises of the whole shall appear to have been reserved on the separate demises of the different parts; and the power of dividing tenements, anciently so demised in one parcel at one rent, may in many cases tend to improve the value of the estates belonging to such ecclesiastical persons and bodies respectively, as well as to the benefit of their lessees and the publick:

May it therefore please your Majesty that it may be enacted, and be it enacted by the King's most excellent Majesty, by and with the advice and consent of the Lords spiritual and temporal and Commons in this present Parliament assembled, and by the authority of the same, that in all cases where any honours, castles, manors, messuages, lands, tythes, tenements, or other hereditaments, being parcel of the possessions of any Archbishop, Bishop, Master and Fellows, Dean and Chapter, Master or Guardian of any Hospital, or any other person or persons, or body or bodies politick or corporate, having any spiritual or ecclesiastical living or promotion, and having been anciently or accustomably demised by one Lease under one rent or divers rents issuing out of the whole, now are or shall hereafter be demised by several Leases to one or several persons under an apportioned or several rents, or where a part only of such honours, manors, messuages, lands,

Where any part of the possessions of any Archbishop &c. or person having any Ecclesiastical Living shall be demised by several Leases, which was formerly demised by one; or where a

tythes, tenements, or other hereditaments as last mentioned, are or shall be demised by a separate Lease or Leases under a less rent or less rents than was or were accustomably reserved for the whole by such former Lease, and the residue thereof is or shall be retained in the possession or occupation of the Lessor or Lessors, the several and distinct rents reserved on the separate demises of the several specifick parts thereof, comprized in and demised by such several Leases, shall be deemed and taken to be the ancient and accustomed rents for such specifick parts respectively, within the intent and meaning of an Act, passed in the thirty-second year of the Reign of His late Majesty King Henry the Eighth, intituled, Lessees to enjoy the Farm against the Tenants in Tail; and of an Act, passed in the first year of the Reign of Her late Majesty Queen Elizabeth, intituled, An Act giving authority to the Queen's Majesty, upon the avoidance of any Archbishop or Bishop, to take into Her Hands certain of the temporal possessions thereof, recompensing the same with parsonages impropriate and tythes; and of another Act, passed in the thirteenth year of the same Queen, intituled, Fraudulent Deeds made by Spiritual Persons, to defeat their successors of remedy for Dilapidations, shall be void, &c.; and of another Act, passed in the fourteenth year of the Reign of the same Queen, intituled, An Act for the continuation, explanation, perfecting, and enlarging of divers Statutes.

Part shall be demised for less than the ancient Rent, and the Residue shall be retained in the possession of the Lessor; the several Rents reserved on the separate demises of the specific Parts shall be taken to be the ancient Rents within the meaning of 32 Hen. 8, c. 28, 1 Eliz. c. 19, 13 Eliz. c. 5, and 14 Eliz. c. 11.

2. Provided always, that nothing herein contained shall extend to confirm or render valid any demise made before the passing of this Act, unless the several rents reserved upon the separate demises of separate parts of tenements, theretofore accustomably demised under one entire Lease, shall be equal to or more than the rent or rents theretofore accustomably reserved on the entire demise of the whole; or, in case the whole should not be demised, but part reserved in the possession of the Lessor or Lessors, unless the rents reserved on the parts demised should be so far equal to or more than the whole amount of the ancient rent or rents, that the part not demised should be sufficient to answer the difference.

Demise made before passing this Act not valid, unless the Rents reserved be equal to or more than the Rents accustomably reserved, &c.

3. Provided also, that where the whole of any such honours, *Where the whole of*

castles, manors, messuages, lands, tythes, tenements, or other hereditaments, accustomably demised by one Lease, shall be demised in parts by several Leases after the passing of this Act, the aggregate amount of the several rents which shall be reserved by such separate Leases be not less than the old accustomed rent or rents theretofore reserved by such entire Lease; and that where a part only shall be so demised by any such separate Lease, and the residue shall be retained in the possession of the Lessor or Lessors, the rent or rents to be reserved by such separate Lease or Leases shall not be less, in proportion to the fine or fines to be received on granting such Lease or Leases, than the rent or rents accustomed to be reserved for the whole of the said premises was in proportion to the fine received on granting the last entire Lease.

such Premises shall be demised in Parts, the aggregate Rents reserved shall not be less than the old accustomed Rent, and so in proportion where a Part shall be retained in possession by the Lessor.

4. Provided also, that no greater proportion of the accustomed rent be reserved by any separate Lease hereby confirmed or allowed to be granted, than the part of the premises thereby severally demised will reasonably bear and afford a competent security for.

No greater Proportion of the accustomed Rent shall be reserved by any separate Lease than the Premises demised will bear.

5. Provided also, that where any specifick thing, incapable of division or apportionment, shall have been reserved or made payable to the Lessor or Lessors, his or their heirs or successors, either by way of rent, or by any covenant or agreement contained in any such entire Lease, the same may be wholly reserved and made payable out of a competent part of such lands or tenements demised by any such several Lease as aforesaid; and in case, in any Lease already granted, and intended hereby to be confirmed, any such provision shall appear to have been made for the payment and delivery of any such sum or sums of money, stipends, augmentations, or other things as aforesaid, the same shall be deemed and taken to have been lawfully made, in case the lands and tenements charged therewith shall be of a greater annual value than the payment or other things so charged, exclusive of the rent or other annual payment reserved to the Lessor or Lessors.

Where any specifick thing shall have been reserved by the Lessor, it may be a Charge on the Premises demised, &c.

6. Provided further, that nothing herein contained shall extend to authorize or confirm any Lease whereon no annual rent is or shall be reserved to the Lessor or Lessors, his or their successors or assigns.

No Lease confirmed whereon no annual Rent to the Lessor is reserved.

7. Provided also, and be it further enacted, that this Act, or any thing herein contained, shall not authorize the reservation or payment of any rent or rents upon any such several Lease made or to be made, under authority of this Act, by any Master, Provost, President, Warden, Dean, Governor, Rector, or Chief Ruler of any College, Cathedral Church, Hall, or House of Learning in the Universities of Oxford and Cambridge, or by the Warden or other Head Officer of the Colleges of Winchester and Eaton, in any other manner or proportions than is required by an Act passed in the eighteenth year of the Reign of Her said late Majesty Queen Elizabeth, intituled, An Act for Maintenance of the Colleges in the Universities, and of Winchester and Eaton.

<small>Not to authorize the Reservation of any Rent on any such Lease made by any Master &c. of any College in the Universities &c. in any other manner than is required by 18 Eliz. c. 6.</small>

8. Provided also, that where any such accustomably entire Leases as aforesaid shall have usually contained covenants on the part of the Lessee or Lessees for the payment or delivery, or shall have in any other manner subjected or charged such Lessee or Lessees to or with the payment or delivery, of any sum or sums of money, stipend, augmentation, or other thing, to or for the use of any Vicar, Curate, Schoolmaster, or other person or persons, other than and besides the Lessor or Lessors, and his or their heirs or successors, all or any such Leases as shall hereafter be granted of the same lands or tenements in severalty as aforesaid shall and may lawfully provide for the future payment and delivery of such sum or sums of money, stipends, augmentations, or other things, by and out of any part or parts of the lands or tenements accustomably charged therewith, not being of less annual value than three times the amount of the payment so to be charged thereon, exclusive of the proportion of rent or other annual payments to be reserved to the Lessor or Lessors.

<small>Where Payments have been reserved to Vicars &c. other than the Lessors, provision shall be made in Leases for the future Payment thereof out of Premises of three times the annual Value.</small>

9. Provided always, that nothing in this Act shall extend to establish or confirm the claim of any Vicar, Curate, Schoolmaster, or other person or persons, to any such sum or sums, salary, stipend, or other thing as aforesaid, the payment and continuance whereof shall depend only on the will of the person or persons, or body or bodies politick or corporate, granting or renewing such Lease or Leases respectively.

<small>Not to confirm the Claim of any Vicar &c. to such Payment, where it depends only on the will of the person granting or renewing the Lease.</small>

10. And be it further enacted, that where any person or

Persons holding such Leases in Trust, or having granted any under Leases of specific Parts with Covenants of Renewal, may surrender them, in order that separate Leases may be granted by the original Lessors to the Cestuique Trusts and under Lessees on reasonable Terms, subject to the accustomed Rent, &c.

persons, now holding, or who shall hereafter hold, any such Lease or Leases as in this Act mentioned, shall or may hold the same, or any specifick part of the lands or tenements thereby demised, in trust for any other person or persons or for any body or bodies politick or corporate, or shall have granted any under Lease or under Leases of any specifick part or parts of his, her, or their respective holdings, and be under any covenant or engagement for renewal thereof to any other person or persons, body or bodies politick or corporate, when and as often as his, her, or their own Lease or Leases shall be renewed, it shall and may be lawful for such person or persons as first mentioned, at any time or times after the passing of this Act, to surrender his, her, or their Lease or Leases, in order that separate and distinct Leases may be granted by the original Lessor or Lessors of such specifick parts of the same premises as shall have been held in trust, or subject to such covenants or engagements for renewal as aforesaid, to the respective under Lessees and Cestuique Trusts, upon fair and reasonable terms, subject to an apportionment of the accustomed rent or rents and other payments, according to the intent and meaning of this Act; and every such surrender so made, and the new Leases to be granted thereon, according to the intent and meaning of this Act, shall be good and effectual in law and equity, notwithstanding such under Lessees and Cestuique Trusts, or any of them, shall or may be infants, issue unborn, femes covert, persons absent from the realm, or otherwise incapacitated to act for themselves, provided that such new Leases respectively be for the benefit of the several persons entitled to the benefit of such surrendered Lease or Leases respectively, and be expressly so declared in the body of each such new Leases respectively.

42 Geo. III, Cap. XC.

An Act for amending the laws relating to the Militia in England, and for augmenting the Militia.

43. And be it further enacted, that no Peer of this realm, ... nor any person being a resident Member of either of the Universities, ... shall be liable to serve personally or provide a substitute to serve in the Militia. No resident Member of either University liable to serve in the Militia.

42 Geo. III, Cap. CXVI.

An Act for consolidating the provisions of the several Acts passed for the Redemption and Sale of the Land Tax into one Act, and for making further provision for the Redemption and Sale thereof; &c.

17. And be it further enacted, that where the Land Tax charged upon the glebe lands, tythes, or other profits of any living or livings in the patronage of any College, Cathedral Church, Hall, or House of Learning in either of the Universities of Oxford or Cambridge, or in the patronage of either of the Colleges of Eton or Winchester, or of any trustee or trustees for any such College, Cathedral Church, Hall, or House of Learning as aforesaid, or in the patronage of any other bodies politick or corporate, or companies, or feoffees or trustees for charitable or other publick purposes, or other person or persons, shall not then have been redeemed by the Incumbent or Incumbents of such living or livings, it shall be lawful for the corporations of such Colleges, Cathedral Churches, Halls, or Houses of Learning respectively, or for such other bodies politick or corporate, or companies, or other person or persons aforesaid, in whose patronage any such living or livings shall be, to contract and agree for the redemption of such Land Tax, upon the same terms and with the same benefits and advantages as the Incumbent or Patrons of Livings may contract for the Redemption of the Land Tax thereon, not redeemed by Incumbents.

Incumbents of such living or livings could or might have contracted to redeem the same.

Where the Land Tax on any Living belonging to any College &c. shall be redeemed, it may be provided for by sale of any Lands belonging thereto, or by grant of a Rent Charge; but such College &c. shall be entitled to a Rent Charge out of the Living, unless it be declared otherwise at the time of Presentation.

78. And be it further enacted, that where the Land Tax charged upon the glebe lands, tythes, or other profits of any living or livings in the patronage of any College, Cathedral Church, Hall, or House of Learning in either of the Universities of Oxford and Cambridge, or in the patronage of either of the Colleges of Eton or Winchester, or of any trustee or trustees for any such College, Cathedral Church, Hall, or House of Learning, or in the patronage of any other corporation aggregate, shall have been or shall be redeemed by or on the behalf of any such College, Cathedral Church, Hall, or House of Learning, or by any such corporation aggregate, by virtue of any of the provisions of the said recited Acts or of this Act, it shall be lawful for any such College, Cathedral Church, Hall, or House of Learning, or for any such trustee or trustees thereof respectively as aforesaid, or for any such corporation aggregate, to provide for such redemption by sale of any lands, tenements, or hereditaments belonging to such corporations respectively, or by the grant of any rent charge which they could or might respectively lawfully make for the redemption of any Land Tax charged on the lands belonging to such corporations, and the Land Tax so redeemed shall be forthwith extinguished; but every such College, Cathedral Church, Hall, or House of Learning respectively, or such corporation aggregate, shall nevertheless be entitled to an annual rent charge issuing out of such living, equivalent to the amount of the Land Tax redeemed, unless it shall be declared in writing under the common seal of the body or bodies having such right of patronage or nomination, at the time of presenting or nominating any Clerk or Clerks to such living or livings, that such rent charge shall be suspended during his or their incumbency or respective incumbencies, which declaration the body or bodies entitled to nominate to such living or livings shall from time to time be competent to make: provided always, that such suspension shall be without prejudice to the right of the said body or bodies respectively to recover such rent charge after the next or any future avoidance: provided also, that any declaration made by any such body at the time of redeeming

the said Land Tax shall be as available during the incumbency of the then Rector, Vicar, or Curate, as if it had been made at the time of his being preferred to such living.

46 Geo. III, Cap. cxlvii.

An Act for enabling a married person to hold and enjoy the Office of Warden of Wadham College in the University of Oxford.

[This Act consists of seven Sections.

[Sections 1 and 2 declare null and void so much of the Statutes of Wadham College as ordains that the Warden of the College shall at the time of his election be, and whilst he shall be Warden continue to be, a bachelor and unmarried, and that he shall take an Oath that he hath not contracted nor will enter into any contract of matrimony so long as he shall be Warden; and so much as imposes any restraint on the Fellows of the College from electing a married man (otherwise duly qualified) to the Office of Warden, or from permitting the Warden after his election to marry.

[Section 3 enacts that so much of the Warden's Oath as declares that he hath not contracted nor will enter into any contract of matrimony so long as he shall be Warden, or tends in any manner to restrain him from marrying, and also the reading, at the time of the election of a Warden, of so much of the Statutes of the College as relates to the Warden not marrying or contracting matrimony, shall be omitted.

[Sections 4 and 5 enact that after the passing of this Act every Warden of the College may marry and continue Warden, and any married person, otherwise duly qualified, may be elected Warden, and may accept of and hold and enjoy the Office; and that the Fellows of the College may elect any married person to be Warden, provided he shall in every other respect be duly qualified; the Statutes of the College, or any other law or statute, matter or thing, to the contrary notwithstanding.

[Section 6 provides that nothing in this Act contained shall alter, annul, or make void any other parts of the Statutes of the College; and that the Warden Fellows and Scholars of the College shall have, hold, and enjoy all estates, rights, privileges, benefits, and emoluments belonging to the College, in the same manner to all intents and purposes as they might have held and enjoyed the same if this Act had not been made.

[Section 7 enacts that a copy of this Act printed by the King's Printer shall be admitted as evidence in all Courts.]

47 GEO. III, Sess. 2, Cap. lx.

An Act for inclosing lands in the parish of St. Andrew the Less, otherwise called Barnwell, in the Town of Cambridge in the County of Cambridge, and certain lands in the parishes of Saint Andrew the Great, Saint Mary the Great, and Saint Mary the Less, or some or one of them, in the said Town of Cambridge, lying intermixed with the lands in the said parish of Saint Andrew the Less, otherwise called Barnwell.

The Watercourse supplying the Town of Cambridge to be protected.   31. And whereas there is a channel or watercourse, which for a great length of time has been enjoyed by the inhabitants of the University and Town of Cambridge, running from the Nine Wells in the bounds of Shelford in the said County of Cambridge to the Town of Cambridge aforesaid, and supplying the said Town with water; and part of such channel or watercourse doth run through part of the lands and grounds hereby intended to be allotted and divided: now therefore, for the preservation of such channel or watercourse, as far as respects such part as runs through the lands and grounds hereby intended to be allotted and divided, and in order that the same may for ever hereafter be had and enjoyed by the residents and inhabitants of the University and Town of Cambridge aforesaid without any interruption or disturbance whatsoever, be it further enacted, that nothing in this Act contained shall extend or be construed to extend to give the said Commissioners, or the Proprietors of the said open and common fields, common meadows, commonable lands, and waste grounds, or any part thereof, or any or either of them, any power or authority over the said channel or watercourse, or six feet of the soil next and immediately adjoining thereto on both sides thereof; but such channel or watercourse, and six feet of the soil next and immediately adjoining thereto on both sides thereof, as far as the same is situate in and part of the said open and common fields, common meadows, commonable lands, and waste grounds, shall for ever hereafter be appropriated and set apart to and for the exclusive purpose of conveying water to the said Town, as the same hath heretofore been had, used, and enjoyed, as if this Act had not been passed; and the person or persons who shall be empowered to superintend, direct, and manage such channel or watercourse on behalf of the said residents and inhabitants of the said University and Town shall and may stake out and use such six feet of the soil adjoining such watercourse on both sides thereof for the protection and support of the said channel or watercourse; and it shall not be lawful for the said Commissioners and Proprietors, or any or either of them, or any other person or persons whomsoever, to plough, dig up, cut into, or otherwise use or meddle with the said channel or watercourse, or the water within the same, or such six feet of the soil next adjoining thereto as aforesaid; and in case any or either of them should so plough, dig up, cut into, use, or otherwise intermeddle with the said channel or watercourse, or such six feet of the soil as aforesaid, such ploughing, digging up, cutting into, using, or otherwise intermeddling with the same as aforesaid shall be considered as a wilful trespass, and the person or persons guilty thereof shall be deemed a wilful trespasser or trespassers, and shall be answerable for such ploughing, digging up, cutting into, using, or otherwise intermeddling with the premises, in an action at law for damages, which action shall and may be brought by and in the name of the Vice-Chancellor of the University of Cambridge in the County of Cambridge for the time being, or in the name of the Clerk to the Commissioners for the time being, appointed by virtue of [the Acts 28 Geo. III, c. 64, and 34 Geo. III, c. 104. The remainder of the section contains provisions for saving the rights of the lord of the manor of Trumpington de la Pole, for empowering the Commissioners under the said Acts to erect bridges over and to lay tunnels under the watercourse, for saving the rights of Emanuel and Christ Colleges, and for keeping the powers of the said Commissioners.]

52 Geo. III, Cap. CII.

An Act for the registering and securing of Charitable Donations.

Not to extend to the Universities, or to Colleges, &c.

11. And be it further enacted, that nothing in this Act shall be construed to extend to any Hospital, School, or other Charitable Institution whatsoever, which shall have been founded, improved, or regulated by or under the authority of the King's most excellent Majesty or any of his royal predecessors; .... nor to either of the Universities of Oxford or Cambridge, nor to any College or Hall thereto belonging, or to any charitable bequest, devise, gift, or foundation whatsoever belonging thereto, or under the control, direction, superintendence, or management of the said Universities or either of them or any College or Hall therein respectively; nor to the Radcliffe Infirmary within the University of Oxford; nor to the Colleges of Westminster, Eton, or Winchester, or any of them; nor to any Cathedral or Collegiate Church within England and Wales; nor to the Charter House; * * * *.

52 Geo. III, Cap. lxxii.

An Act for enlarging the term and powers of two Acts of His present Majesty for amending certain Mileways leading to Oxford, and making improvements in the University and City of Oxford, the Suburbs thereof, and adjoining Parish of Saint Clement, and for other Purposes.

[The whole of this Act related to the Commissioners of the Streets, enlarging in some respects the powers given to them by 11 Geo. III, c. 19, and 21 Geo. III, c. 47, and extending their term for taking Tolls. Those sections of it which are still in force are now so near expiring that it does not seem worth while to print any of them here.]

52 Geo. III, Cap. cxli.

An Act for making and maintaining a Navigable Canal, with Aqueducts, Feeders, and Reservoirs, from the Stort *Navigation at or near Bishop's Stortford in the County of Hertford to join the River* Cam *near Clay-hithe Sluice in the County of Cambridge, with a Navigable Branch or Cut from the said Canal at Sawston to Whaddon in the County of Cambridge.*

43. And whereas there is in the Town of Cambridge a certain Conduit called Hobson's Conduit, which is vested in trustees or feoffees for the benefit of the inhabitants of the said Town, and of the Masters, Fellows, and Scholars of the several Colleges of Christ and Emanuel in the University of Cambridge, and other persons; and whereas the said Conduit is supplied with water from certain springs and watercourses in the vicinity of the said Town, near to which the

For protecting Hobson's Conduit.

line of the intended Canal is proposed to be carried, and, a plentiful supply of pure and wholesome water being essential to the health and comfort of the said inhabitants, Masters, Fellows, and Scholars, it is just and reasonable that the said Company of Proprietors be prohibited from using, diverting, intercepting, or injuring any of the springs, waters, or watercourses from whence the said Conduit is supplied with water: be it therefore enacted, that nothing in this Act contained shall authorize or empower the said Company of Proprietors, or any of their servants, agents, or workmen, to take, use, injure, or diminish, or cause or suffer to be taken, used, injured, or diminished, any of the springs of water, waters, rivers, or brooks by or from which the Conduit in the Town of Cambridge called Hobson's Conduit now is or usually hath been supplied with water, or to divert, intercept, alter, obstruct, or diminish, or cause or suffer to be diverted, intercepted, altered, obstructed, or diminished, any stream, watercourse, or channel along or through which the water for supplying the said Conduit is or would otherwise be carried or conveyed; and that the said Company of Proprietors shall and they are hereby required, at their own proper costs and charges, as soon as the said Canal shall be cut, at all times thereafter to lay, make, construct, and form, and to maintain and keep in good repair, in all places where it may be requisite to prevent the intended Canal from intercepting or intersecting any such stream, watercourse, or channel, proper soughs, tunnels, arches, or pipes, of sufficient size and dimensions, in order that the waters for supplying the said Conduit may flow, undiminished and without any adulteration or injury, in their present courses and channels, to the said Conduit called Hobson's Conduit; and that if at any time the said Company of Proprietors, their servants, agents, or workmen, shall take, use, injure, or diminish, divert, intercept, alter, or obstruct, or cause or suffer to be taken, used, injured, diminished, diverted, intercepted, altered, or obstructed, any of such springs of water, waters, rivulets, brooks, streams, or watercourses, or shall neglect so to lay, make, construct, or form, or to maintain and keep in repair any such sough, tunnel, arch, or pipe, as herein-before directed to be laid, made, maintained, or kept in repair, the said Company of

Proprietors shall in every case forfeit the sum of ten thousand pounds to the Feoffees or Trustees of the said Conduit called Hobson's Conduit, and the Masters, Fellows, and Scholars of the said two Colleges, to be paid out of the monies to be raised, received, or collected by virtue of this Act, and to be recovered from the said Company of Proprietors by any three or more of the said Feoffees or Trustees, Masters, Fellows, and Scholars, by action of debt in any of His Majesty's Courts of Record at Westminster, in which no essoign, protection, or wager of law, or more than one imparlance shall be allowed; and every such penalty, when recovered, shall be applied for the purposes and benefit of the said trust.

44. And be it further enacted, that if the wells, streams, watercourses, or channels by means or from which the said Conduit called Hobson's Conduit is now supplied with water shall at any time or times be used, diverted, injured, obstructed, intercepted, or intersected by any works executed or to be executed by or by the direction or authority of the said Company of Proprietors, and they or their Clerk or Treasurer shall have received notice in writing under the hands of three or more of the Feoffees or Trustees of the said Conduit called Hobson's Conduit, or of the said Masters, Fellows, and Scholars of the said two Colleges, to remove or alter any such works so using, diverting, injuring, obstructing, intercepting, or intersecting such waters, streams, watercourses, or channels, and shall for the space of six days after such notice neglect to remove or alter such works, it shall be lawful for any person and persons having the order and direction in writing of any three or more of such Feoffees or Trustees, Masters, Fellows, and Scholars, at the costs and expences of the said Company of Proprietors, to remove, take away, and destroy any such work so using, diverting, injuring, obstructing, intercepting, or intersecting the said waters, streams, watercourses, or channels, and to do all further and requisite acts and deeds which may be necessary to restore and retain the said streams, waters, and watercourses in all respects to and in the usual and accustomed course and channel, without becoming subject or liable to any suit, action, prosecution, fine, penalty, or other proceedings on account thereof, any thing in this Act contained to the con-

For restoring Streams supplying Hobson's Conduit.

trary thereof in anywise notwithstanding; and this Act shall be a sufficient authority for an indemnity to all persons so acting under such order and direction as aforesaid; and it shall and may be lawful for any Justice of the Peace for the County of Cambridge, (not interested in the premises,) to ascertain and settle such last-mentioned costs and expences; and such costs and expences, when so ascertained, shall and may be levied by distress and sale of the goods and chattels of the said Company of Proprietors, by virtue of a warrant under the hand and seal of any Justice of the Peace for the county, town, or place in which any of the goods and chattels of the said Company of Proprietors can or may be found, (and which warrant such Justice is hereby empowered and required to grant,) rendering the overplus (if any), after deducting the expences of such distress and sale, on demand to the Clerk or Treasurer to the said Company of Proprietors; and it shall and may also be lawful to and for such Justice of the Peace to ascertain and settle the compensation to be made to the owners and occupiers of any lands so entered upon for the purpose aforesaid, for any injury sustained by such owners and occupiers by reason or means of such entry; and the same, when so ascertained, shall and may be levied by distress and sale of the goods and chattels of the said Company of Proprietors, in like manner as the said costs and expences last-mentioned.

The River Cam.

[Section 54 enacts, that if after the opening of the London and Cambridge Junction Canal the tolls of the River Cam ⸠ shall in any year fall short of the sum of 1032*l*. 0*s*. 6¼*d*., being the annual amount of them upon an average of eight years last past, the Canal Company shall make good the deficiency.

[Section 55 empowers the Canal Company to cleanse the River Cam from Clayhithe Ferry to the Queen's Mill with consent of the Conservators of the River.

[Section 56 saves all rights of the Conservators of the Cam.]

⸠ See 14 & 15 Vict. c. xcii.

55 Geo. III, Cap. CXLVII.

An Act for enabling Spiritual Persons to exchange the Parsonage or Glebe Houses or Glebe Lands belonging to their Benefices for others of greater Value or more conveniently situated for their residence and occupation, and for annexing such Houses and Lands, so taken in exchange, to such Benefices as Parsonage or Glebe Houses and Glebe Lands, and for purchasing and annexing Lands to become Glebe in certain cases, and for other purposes.

[This Act, among other things, enables Incumbents in some cases to borrow money in order to purchase additional glebe land, and to mortgage their tithes &c. for twenty five years as a security.]

9. And be it further enacted, that it shall and may be lawful for any College or Hall within the Universities of Oxford or Cambridge, or for any other corporate bodies, being owners of the patronage of ecclesiastical livings or benefices, to advance and lend any sum or sums of money of which they have the power to dispose, for the convenience of the Parson, Vicar, or other Incumbent for the time being of any benefice, perpetual curacy, or parochial chapelry within the patronage of such College or Hall, upon mortgage as herein-before directed, either upon interest or without any interest. *Colleges may lend any Sum with or without Interest.*

55 Geo. III, Cap. CLXXXIV.

An Act for repealing the Stamp Duties on Deeds, Law Proceedings, and other written or printed Instruments, and the Duties on Fire Insurances, and on Legacies and Successions to Personal Estate upon Intestacies, now payable in Great Britain; and for granting other Duties in lieu thereof.

SCHEDULE.

PART THE FIRST: Containing the Duties on Admissions to Offices, &c.; * * * *.

	Duty.
	£ s. d.
Testimonial or Certificate of the Admission of any person to the Degree of a Bachelor of Arts in either of the Universities in England	3 0 0[a]
Testimonial or Certificate of the Admission of any person to any other Degree in either of the said Universities	10 0 0[a]

55 Geo. III, Cap. CXCIV.

An Act for better regulating the practice of Apothecaries throughout England and Wales.

<small>Saving Rights.</small> 29. Provided always, and be it further enacted, that nothing in this Act contained shall extend or be construed

---

[a] These Duties are not repealed in the case of Oxford by 18 & 19 Vict. c. 36, nor in the case of Cambridge by 21 & 22 Vict. c. 11.

to extend to lessen, prejudice, or defeat, or in anywise to interfere with any of the rights, authorities, privileges, and immunities heretofore vested in and exercised and enjoyed by either of the two Universities of Oxford or Cambridge, the Royal College of Physicians, the Royal College of Surgeons, or the said Society of Apothecaries respectively, other than and except such as shall or may have been altered, varied, or amended in and by this Act, or of any person or persons practising as an Apothecary previously to the first day of August one thousand eight hundred and fifteen; but the said Universities, Royal Colleges, and the said Society, and all such persons or person shall have, use, exercise, and enjoy all such rights, authorities, privileges, and immunities, save and except as aforesaid, in as full, ample, and beneficial a manner, to all intents and purposes, as they might have done before the passing of this Act, and in case the same had never been passed.

55 Geo. III, Cap. xlix.

An Act for more effectually repairing the Road from Jesus Lane in the Town of Cambridge to the first Rubbing House on Newmarket Heath in the County of Cambridge.

["The Vice-Chancellor and Masters or Heads of the several Colleges and Halls in the University of Cambridge" for the time being are appointed Trustees of the Road to which the Act relates, known as "the Paper Mills Turnpike Road."]

56 Geo. III, Cap. CXXXVI.

An Act to enable His Majesty to grant certain lands, tenements, and hereditaments, escheated and devolved to His Majesty by the dissolution of Hertford College in the University of Oxford, and the site of the said College and buildings thereon, to the Chancellor Masters and Scholars of the said University in trust for the Principal and other Members of Magdalen Hall for the purpose of their removing to such site; and to enable the said Chancellor Masters and Scholars of the said University and the President and Scholars of Saint Mary Magdalen College to do all necessary acts for such removal.

[The Preamble of this Act recites a Charter, dated 5 Sept. 14 Geo. II, for the incorporation of Hertford College within Hart Hall in the University of Oxford; that part of the site of that College was held by lease from Magdalen College and part by lease from the University under certain reserved rents; that other parts of the site were subject to a rent charge of 1*l*. 13*s*. 4*d*. payable to Exeter College and to a rent charge of fourpence payable to Christ Church; that, under two Commissions of Escheat lately issued, it has been found by Inquisition in Oxfordshire and in Berkshire that Hertford College became dissolved on the 28th of June 1805, being then seised in fee of a certain piece of land [h], and possessed for certain terms of years of other pieces of land under lease from the University and from Magdalen College, with build-

---

[h] This piece of land is described as containing by admeasurement 1982 square yards, and as bounded on the West partly by Cat Street and partly by land in private occupation, on the North partly "by a certain street leading from a Gate anciently called Smith's Gate to New College" and partly by the land held under lease from the University and from Magdalen College, on the East partly by New College Lane and partly by the stables of New College, and on the South by All Souls College.

ings thereon, situate in the parishes of St. Peter in the East and St. Mary the Virgin in Oxford, and also seised in fee of certain lands[1] in North Moreton in Berkshire, and that all these lands and terms of years had escheated to His Majesty by virtue of his prerogative royal; that the buildings of Hertford College are in a very ruinous state, and there is no fund applicable to putting them into repair; that Magdalen Hall is contiguous to Magdalen College, and an ancient School for the education of sixteen Choristers of the College forms part of the buildings of the Hall, and the freehold of the site of both Hall and School is vested in the College; that, the removal of the Hall and School being necessary to the completion of certain intended improvements at Magdalen College and being likely to conduce to the general improvement and ornament of the University, the President and Scholars of Magdalen College, with the concurrence and approbation of the Principal of Magdalen Hall, and with the consent of the Chancellor of the University as visitor and patron of the Hall, have proposed to the University to transfer the establishment of the Hall to the site of Hertford College, engaging to put the whole of the buildings thereof into complete repair, to relinquish to the use of the Hall all right and title to the part of Hertford College now held by lease under them, and to be at the sole expense of carrying this arrangement into effect; and that the University has agreed to the proposal.

[Section 1 enables His Majesty to grant the site of Hertford College and all or any part of the other lands to the University in trust for the Principal and other Members for the time being of Magdalen Hall.

[Sections 2 and 3 enable the President and Scholars of Magdalen College to make all needful alterations and repairs in the buildings of Hertford College, and to take down and rebuild such parts as in the judgment of the Vice-Chancellor and Delegates of Estates of the University cannot be effectually repaired; and also to convey the fee simple of the ground and buildings held by lease under them, without

---

[1] These lands are described as "fourteen acres and three rods by estimation of arable land, and one acre and a half of meadow ground, more or less, lying dispersed in common fields and meadows of North Moreton."

consideration in money and without any rent or charge, to the University in trust for Magdalen Hall.

[Sections 4 and 5 provide that, as soon as the repairs are complete and the conveyance is made, the Principal and other Members of Magdalen Hall shall surrender possession of the Hall to the President and Scholars of Magdalen College, and shall " remove to and become established at the said dissolved College," which shall thenceforth " be called Magdalen Hall in the University of Oxford"; and that the removal shall in no way affect the rights and privileges appertaining to Magdalen Hall or to the Principal or any Member thereof, or to the University in relation thereto.

[Section 6 enables the Chancellor Masters and Scholars of the University to make the ground and buildings forming part of Hertford College which were held by lease under them a component part of Magdalen Hall, extinguishing the rents, and declaring by deed that they stand seised of the ground and buildings in trust for the Principal and other Members of the Hall.

[Sections 7, 8, and 9 provide that Magdalen College shall yearly pay to the Principal of Magdalen Hall the sum of 1*l*. 13*s*. 4*d*., being the amount of the yearly rent charge due to Exeter College for part of the site, to the intent that such rent charge may be regularly paid, and that the Principal may be indemnified.

[Section 10 empowers Magdalen College to appropriate and annex the site and buildings of Magdalen Hall and the School adjoining, so soon as the Principal and other Members of the Hall shall have removed to the site of Hertford College, and a suitable School shall have been provided for the Choristers.

[Sections 11–17, after reciting that " the site and buildings of the said dissolved College may be greatly improved and made more ornamental, and the occupation of the same by its intended possessors rendered more convenient and desirable, if the front of the said dissolved College and also certain houses[J] at the north and south ends thereof with a house in the occupation of Richard Paine leading to New

---

[J] One of these houses, apparently towards the south end, comprised a "shop under Hertford College Library." Schedule to the Act.

College Lane were taken down," empower the University to purchase the houses and ground, paying for the same out of any money that shall be received for that purpose either by subscription or by public or private donation or bequest, to take down the buildings, and to add to the site of Hertford College so much of the ground as may be necessary for the intended improvements, for the use and benefit of the Principal and other Members of Magdalen Hall.]

18. Provided also, and be it further enacted, that nothing in this Act shall extend or be deemed or construed to extend to take away, diminish, or impede the exercise of any privilege or right whatsoever of the said University, or of any of the Magistrates, Officers, Ministers, or Servants thereunto belonging.

[Section 19 is a general saving of all rights and titles.]

58 Geo. III, Cap. lxiv.

An Act for lighting with Gas the University and City of Oxford and the Suburbs of the said City.

[The Preamble of this Act begins with the averment that "the University and City of Oxford and the suburbs of the said City is a large and populous place," and that "it would be of great benefit to the Members of the said University and the citizens and inhabitants of the said City and to the public at large, if the Colleges, Halls, public highways, lanes, streets, passages, and other places were better lighted": and the first section of the Act declares certain persons named in it and their successors "to be one body politic and corporate by the name of 'The Oxford Gas Light and Coke Company,'" with perpetual succession, a common seal, and certain powers.]

11. Provided always, and be it further enacted, that no gasometer or depôt of gas, or buildings or machinery for the manufacturing or production of gas, shall be erected, made, or established or used within two hundred yards of any public building, garden, or walk belonging to, or held or

Situation of the Gasometer &c. not to be within two hundred yards of any

College or Dwelling House, &c. repaired or maintained by, the said Chancellor Masters and Scholars of the said University, without first obtaining their consent under their Common Seal; or within two hundred yards of the Cathedral Church of Christ in the said University, or of the precincts, gardens, or walks of the same, without first obtaining the consent of the Dean and Chapter of the said Cathedral Church under their Common Seal; or within two hundred yards of any College in the said University, or of the precincts, gardens, or walks of any College, without first obtaining the consent of such College under its Common Seal; or within two hundred yards of any Hall in the said University, or of the precincts, gardens, or walks of any Hall, without first obtaining the consent of the Chancellor Masters and Scholars of the said University under their Common Seal and of the Principal of such Hall for the time being under his hand; or within two hundred yards of any public building, garden, or walk vested in or held by Doctor Radcliffe's Trustees, or the Trustees of the Oxford Market, or any Trustees for charitable or other purposes, without first obtaining the consent of the said respective Trustees in writing under their hands: provided also, that the said gasometer or depôt of gas, or buildings or machinery, shall not be made or established within two hundred yards of any messuage, tenement, or dwelling house in any place or situation in the said City of Oxford and suburbs and liberties and precincts of the said City, without first obtaining the consent and approbation of the owner or owners lessee or lessees for the time being of such messuage, tenement, or dwelling house under his, her, or their hand or hands.

Limiting the profits of the Company. 33. Provided always, and be it further enacted, that the clear profits to be received by the said Company of Proprietors from the said undertaking shall never exceed the sum of ten pounds per annum upon each share of one hundred pounds; and, in order to ascertain the amount of the clear profits of the said undertaking, the said Company shall and are hereby required, from the thirty-first day of December next after the expiration of two years from the time of passing this Act, to cause a true, exact, and particular account to be kept and annually made up and balanced to the said thirty-first day of December of the money collected or received by them or for their use by virtue of this Act, and of the charges and expences attending the supporting, maintaining, and using the said works; and if the clear profits of the said undertaking shall at any time amount to a larger sum of money than shall be sufficient to make a distribution amongst the said Proprietors of ten pounds per annum upon every such share, such per-centage to be computed and take place from the time of the passing of this Act, then and in such case the excess or surplus which shall be more than sufficient for the purposes aforesaid shall from time to time be placed in the hands of such person or persons, or on such Government or other security or securities, to answer any deficiencies that may happen in the next or any succeeding year or years, as the said Company shall for that purpose order or direct, until such excess or surplus shall amount to the sum of four thousand pounds; and the interest or dividends of such sum or sums so to be invested shall be paid and applied in like manner as the money * to be received   * *So in orig.* by or for the use of the said company by virtue of this Act are * to be paid or applied; and the total amount of every such annual account as aforesaid, together with an account of the dividends and interest to be from time to time received on all such money so to be placed out as aforesaid, shall be laid before the Vice-Chancellor of the said University of Oxford, or any other Magistrate acting for the said University, and the Mayor of the said City, or any other Magistrate acting for the said City, not interested in the undertaking, twenty-one days next after the making up of every such annual account, to be made on the twenty-sixth day of December; and if it shall appear that the clear profits of the said undertaking, after such sum shall have been so vested, including the said dividends and interest, shall, upon the average of three years then next preceding, have exceeded the rate of ten pounds per annum upon every such share, then and in every such case the said Company of Proprietors shall pay such surplus of the said clear profits, dividends, and interest to the said Commissioners for lighting, paving and cleansing the said University and City of Oxford, to be by them applied and disposed of towards and in aid of any rate or assessment, rates or assessments, made or to be made under the said Act[k]; any thing in this Act to the contrary notwithstanding.

The soil or pavement of the Market not to be broken up without the consent of the Market Committee.

44. Provided also, and be it further enacted, that nothing in this Act contained shall give any power or authority to the said Company to break up any soil or pavement whereon the Market is erected in the said City of Oxford, except with the consent and under the direction of the Chancellor Masters and Scholars of the said University and the Mayor Bailiffs and Commonalty of the said City, or of the Committee by them appointed for regulating the said Market.

No sewer, &c. to be made in any place belonging to the University &c. without consent.

48. Provided always, and be it further enacted, that nothing in this Act contained shall in any manner authorize or empower the said Company, or any person acting in their behalf, to carry, lay, or put any sewer, cut, main, trench, or pipe, or any other matter or thing, through or into any place belonging (whether in their own occupation or otherwise) to the Chancellor Masters and Scholars of the said University, or to the Cathedral Church of Christ in Oxford, or to any of the said Colleges or Halls, without first obtaining the consent of the said Chancellor Masters and Scholars, or of the said Dean and Chapter, or of such College, under their Common Seal respectively, or, in the case of a Hall, without first obtaining the consent of the said Chancellor Masters and Scholars under their Common Seal and of the Principal of the said Hall under his hand.

No drain for carrying off the washings to be made, or the contents of any drain to be emptied, within the University or City

49. Provided also, and be it further enacted, that it shall not be lawful for the said Company to make or cause to be made any drain, cut, or sewer for the purpose of carrying off the washings or other waste liquid or materials which may flow from or be used in the prosecution of the works aforesaid, or to empty or cause to be emptied the contents of any drain, cut, or sewer, within the said University or

---

[k] The Act here cited is 52 Geo. 3, c. lxxii. The "Commissioners" are now represented by the Local Board.

City, or of* the liberties or precincts of either of them, without consent, &c. without the consent in writing of the Chancellor Masters and Scholars of the said University, and of the Mayor Bailiffs and Common Council of the said City, under their respective Common Seals, first had and obtained.

So in orig.

67. And be it further enacted, that all penalties and forfeitures for all and every the offences in this Act mentioned, in relation to which the manner of convicting the offenders is not particularly mentioned or directed, shall be adjudged by and recovered before any Justice of the Peace for the said University or City of Oxford (as the case may be), in a summary way, by information upon the oath of any person or persons, or on the confession of the party offending, (which oath such Justice is hereby authorized to administer); * * * *.

Recovery and application of penalties.

69. Saving always to the Chancellor Masters and Scholars of the University of Oxford, and to all persons matriculated therein or being members thereof, their rights and privileges of civil and criminal judicature and trial in the Courts of the said University alone, as the same have been granted by the Charters of the said University, and confirmed by divers Acts of Parliament.

Saving the rights of the Chancellor Masters and Scholars &c.

70. Saving always to the King's most excellent Majesty, his heirs and successors, and to the Chancellor Masters and Scholars of the said University and their successors, the several bodies politic, corporate, collegiate, or sole of the said University and their successors, the Mayor Bailiffs and Commonalty of the City of Oxford and their successors, the Commissioners for lighting, cleansing, and paving the said University and City and their successors, the Commissioners of Sewers and their successors, and to the Commissioners of the Thames Navigation and their successors, and all persons whomsoever, their respective rights, privileges, and franchises, in such and the same manner as if this Act had not been passed.

General saving of all rights.

5 Geo. IV, Cap. XXXVI.

An Act to amend and render more effectual the several Acts for the issuing of Exchequer Bills for Public Works.

Loans may be made in like manner to Colleges in the Universities of Oxford or Cambridge for increasing the accommodation of Students, and the rents of the rooms or other rents shall be mortgaged for the repayment within 20 years with Interest at Four per Cent.

4. And whereas applications have been made to the Commissioners for the execution of the said recited Acts, for advances to be made to certain Colleges for the purpose of enabling them to increase the number of apartments for Students within such Colleges respectively, so as to avoid the necessity of many Students having lodgings out of such Colleges; but doubts are entertained whether the said Commissioners are authorized to make advances for such purposes, and whether such Colleges can give any adequate security for the repayment of such advances under the provisions of the said recited Acts: be it therefore enacted, that from and after the passing of this Act, upon any application on behalf of any College or Hall in either of the Universities of Oxford or Cambridge, made in writing under the Common Seal of such College or Hall, (duly affixed by the authority of such person or persons as may for the time being be empowered, by the Statutes of any such College or Hall respectively, to use or affix such Common Seal to leases or other deeds or instruments in writing), it shall be lawful for the Commissioners for the execution of the said recited Acts, and such Commissioners are hereby authorized and empowered, to make any loan or advance, under the powers, authorities, provisions, and regulations of the said recited Acts, of any sum or sums, in Exchequer Bills or money, for the building, rebuilding, enlarging, improving, or fitting up any such additional or existing rooms, buildings, and offices as may by such Commissioners be deemed requisite and necessary for the purpose of increasing the accommodation of the Students of any such College or Hall respectively, in like manner in every respect as if such Colleges and Halls had been included in the provisions of the said recited Acts or any of them; and it shall be lawful for the Treasurer, Bursar, or other

proper Officer of any such College or Hall to receive any sums so advanced for the purposes aforesaid; and it shall be lawful for the proper Officers or Members of any such College or Hall respectively, and they are hereby authorized and required, under the Common Seal of any such College or Hall respectively, to mortgage, assign, and make over the rents and profits which shall arise from such additional or existing rooms so to be built, rebuilt, enlarged, improved, and fitted up, or to mortgage, assign, and make over any other rents, revenues, or receipts which shall be payable and belonging to any such College or Hall respectively, or any part of the same, to such person or persons and in such manner and form as the said Commissioners shall direct and appoint, so as to secure the repayment of all sums so advanced for such purposes, with interest thereon at the rate of four pounds per centum per annum, by annual or half-yearly instalments on the principal money advanced, within the period of twenty years at farthest from the advancing thereof, or at such times not exceeding the said period of twenty years and in such manner as the said Commissioners shall think fit to appoint; and all such mortgages and assignments shall be good and effectual in the law, and binding on the said Colleges and Halls entering into the same, and their successors, as bodies corporate; any charter, statute, law, rule, or regulation of or relating to any such College, or any general or particular law, statute, usage, or custom to the contrary in anywise notwithstanding.

5. Provided always, and be it enacted, that nothing in this Act contained shall extend or be construed to extend to grant to any College or Hall, to which any such advances shall be made under the authority of this Act, any power or authority whatsoever to mortgage or pledge the rents, revenues, or receipts of any such College or Hall otherwise than to the said Commissioners for the execution of the said recited Acts in the manner and for the purposes in this Act mentioned and specified.

Act not to empower Colleges to mortgage their revenues otherwise than to the Commissioners for the purposes hereinmentioned

6 Geo. IV, Cap. XCVII.

An Act for the better preservation of the peace and good order in the Universities of England.

<small>Chancellor or Vice-Chancellor of Universities may appoint Constables.</small>

WHEREAS it is expedient to add to the means anciently provided for maintaining peace and good order in the Universities of Oxford and Cambridge; be it enacted by the King's most excellent Majesty, by and with the advice and consent of the Lords spiritual and temporal and Commons in this present Parliament assembled, and by the authority of the same, that it shall be lawful for the Chancellor or Vice-Chancellor of the said Universities respectively to appoint such number of able men as he shall think fit to be Constables in and for the said Universities respectively, who shall continue in office either during good behaviour, or during pleasure, or for such period of time, either defined or dependant on future circumstances, as such Chancellor or Vice-Chancellor shall direct; and to every man so appointed such Chancellor or Vice-Chancellor shall administer an oath well and faithfully to execute the office of Constable, within the precincts of the University for which he shall be appointed, during his continuance in office, and shall deliver to every such man a certificate of his having been so sworn, expressing the duration of his continuance in office, which certificate shall be evidence of his having been duly appointed; and every man so sworn shall have full power to act as a Constable within the precincts of the University for which he shall be appointed, and four miles of the same University, for the time expressed in the certificate, unless he shall be sooner dismissed therefrom by the Chancellor or the Vice-Chancellor for the time being; and shall, within the precincts of the University and four miles of the same, and during his continuance in office, be subject to the like powers and authorities of His Majesty's Justices of the Peace within the limits of their respective jurisdictions, as other Constables are subject to, and have and enjoy all such powers and authorities, privileges, immunities, and advantages as any Constables* hath or shall have within his constablewick:

<small>* So in orig.</small>

provided always, that every such Constable, for any act done by him in the execution of his office, shall be liable to be sued or indicted in the Courts of Common Law, notwithstanding such Constable may be a Member of the University, and notwithstanding any claim of cognizance or privilege whatsoever.

2. And be it further enacted, that in the absence of the Chancellor and Vice-Chancellor it shall be lawful for any Pro-Vice-Chancellor or Deputy Vice-Chancellor to execute the powers given by this Act. *In absence of Chancellor and Vice-Chancellor Deputy may act.*

3. And be it further enacted, that every common prostitute and night-walker, found wandering in any public walk, street, or highway within the precincts of the said University of Oxford, and not giving a satisfactory account of herself, shall be deemed an idle and disorderly person, within the true intent and meaning of an Act passed in the last Session of Parliament, intituled An Act for the Punishment of idle and disorderly Persons and Rogues and Vagabonds in that part of Great Britain called England, and shall and may be apprehended and dealt with accordingly [1]. *Punishing Prostitutes. 5 Geo. 4, c. 83.*

4. And be it further enacted, that this Act shall be deemed to be a public Act, and shall be judicially taken notice of as such by all Judges, Justices, and other persons whomsoever, without being specially pleaded. *Public Act.*

---

[1] By 5 Geo. 4, c. 83, s. 3, any Justice of the Peace may commit any "idle and disorderly person" (being "convicted before him by his own view, or by the confession of such offender, or by the evidence on oath of one or more credible witness or witnesses) to the House of Correction, there to be kept to hard labour for any time not exceeding one calendar month."

7 & 8 Geo. IV, Cap. LXXV.

An Act to appoint Commissioners for carrying into execution several Acts granting an Aid to His Majesty by a Land Tax to be raised in Great Britain, and continuing to His Majesty certain Duties on Personal Estates Offices and Pensions in England [m].

[Among the Commissioners appointed by this Act are the following.]

For the University of Cambridge.

The Vice-Chancellor for the time being, the Representatives in Parliament for the time being, the Heads and Presidents of all Colleges and Halls for the time being, all Doctors in Divinity, all Doctors of Laws and Physic resident in the University and the Liberties thereof, the Proctors and Bedels for the time being [n].

For the University of Oxford.

The Vice-Chancellor, Heads of Houses, all Professors and Proctors for the time being, the Keeper of Bodleian and Keeper of Radclivian Libraries for the time being [o].

7 & 8 Geo. IV, Cap. xlvii.

An Act for improving the Drainage of part of the South Level of the Fens within the Great Level commonly called the Bedford Level, *and the Navigation of the Rivers passing through the same, in the Counties of Cambridge, Suffolk, and Norfolk, and in the Isle of Ely.*

[By Section 2 "The Vice-Chancellor of the University of Cambridge for the time being or a Deputy to be appointed

---

[m] By 5 & 6 Vict. c. 35, s. 4, the Commissioners of Income Tax in any district are to be appointed from and amongst the Commissioners of Land Tax for the same district.

[n] The same persons are again appointed Commissioners for the University of Cambridge by 6 & 7 W. 4, c. 80.

[o] See also 29 & 30 Vict. c. 59.

by writing under his hand, a Deputy to be appointed by the Conservators of the River Cam[p] for the time being under an order made at some public meeting of the said Conservators," and other official and private persons, are appointed " The Navigation Commissioners."]

7 & 8 Geo. IV, Cap. cxi.

An Act for building a new Gaol for the Town of Cambridge, and for other purposes connected therewith.

56. And be it further enacted, that nothing in this Act contained shall extend or be construed to extend to take away, lessen, or diminish any of the rights, liberties, immunities, exemptions, franchises, and privileges of the Chancellor Masters and Scholars of the University of Cambridge, or any of the Colleges or Halls within the said University; or to lessen or diminish the rights, liberties, immunities, franchises, and privileges of the Mayor Bailiffs and Burgesses of the Town of Cambridge; anything herein contained to the contrary in any wise notwithstanding. *[margin: Act not to affect Rights of University or Town of Cambridge.]*

9 Geo. IV, Cap. LXI.

An Act to regulate the granting of Licences to Keepers of Inns, Alehouses, and Victualling Houses in England.

36. Provided always, and be it further enacted, that nothing in this Act contained shall extend to alter or in any manner to affect any of the rights or privileges of the Universities of Oxford or Cambridge, or the powers of the Chancellors or Vice-Chancellors of the same, as by law possessed under the respective charters of the said Universities or otherwise. *[margin: Not to affect the privileges of the Universities.]*

[p] See 14 & 15 Vict. c. xcii.

10 Geo. IV, Cap. VII.

An Act for the relief of His Majesty's Roman Catholic subjects.

Not to extend to Offices &c. in Universities, Colleges, or Schools;

16. Provided also, and be it enacted, that nothing in this Act contained shall be construed to enable any persons, otherwise than as they are now by law enabled, to hold, enjoy, or exercise ..... any office or place whatever of, in, or belonging to any of the Universities of this realm; or any office or place whatever, and by whatever name the same may be called, of, in, or belonging to any of the Colleges or Halls of the said Universities, or the Colleges of Eton, Westminster, or Winchester, or any College or School within this realm; or to repeal, abrogate, or in any manner to interfere with any local statute, ordinance, or rule, which is or shall be established by competent authority within any University, College, Hall, or School, by which Roman Catholics shall be prevented from being admitted thereto,

nor to Presentations to Benefices.

or from residing or taking Degrees therein: provided also, that nothing herein contained shall extend or be construed to extend to enable any person, otherwise than as he is now by law enabled, to exercise any right of presentation to any ecclesiastical benefice whatsoever; or to repeal, vary, or alter in any manner the laws now in force in respect to the right of presentation to any ecclesiastical benefice.

11 Geo. IV & 1 Gul. IV, Cap. LXIV.

An Act to permit the general sale of Beer and Cyder by retail in England.

Not to affect the privileges of the Universities.

29. Provided always, and be it further enacted, that nothing in this Act contained shall extend to alter or in any manner to affect any of the rights or privileges of the Universities of Oxford or Cambridge, or any of the powers

and authorities vested by charter or otherwise in the Chancellors Masters and Scholars of the said Universities and their successors [q].

1 Gul. IV, Cap. 5.

An Act to effect an exchange between the Chancellor Masters and Scholars of the University of Cambridge and the Master Fellows and Scholars of the College or Hall of the Holy Trinity, commonly called Trinity Hall, in the same University, of lands situate in the parish of Saint Andrew the Less in the Town of Cambridge in the County of Cambridge, and for authorizing the removal of the present Botanic Garden of the said University to a new and more eligible site, and for other purposes.

[The preamble, after reciting indentures of lease and release whereby in August 1762 Richard Walker D.D. Vice-Master of Trinity College conveyed to the University certain messuages and garden ground in the parish of St. Edward in Cambridge for the purpose of making and establishing a public Botanic Garden for the use of the University and of appointing a Reader on Botany and a Curator of the Garden, sets forth that a Botanic Garden has in consequence been duly made, that its site at the time was near the outskirts of the town, but is now nearly surrounded by buildings, and that it is also much too small; that there is in the parish of St. Andrew the Less a parcel of ground belonging to Trinity Hall, which contains about 38 acres and is well suited for the site of a Botanic Garden, and another parcel of ground belonging to the University, which contains nearly 8 acres, and that an agreement has been made for the exchange of the two parcels and for the payment of a sum

---

[q] This provision is repeated verbatim in sect. 22 of 3 & 4 Vict. c. 61, "An Act to amend the Acts relating to the general sale of Beer and Cider by retail in England."

of money by the University to Trinity Hall in compensation for the difference in their value:

[And then the Act proceeds to sanction the exchange; provides for the purchase of land for Trinity Hall with the money to be paid by the University for equality of exchange; directs that a new Botanic Garden shall be formed on the parcel of ground so about to pass into the possession of the University, and that this shall be subject to all the conditions, regulations, and government appointed for the present Garden by the Founder; authorises the removal of all plants and buildings from the present Garden to the new one; empowers the University to purchase additional land to the extent of six acres adjoining the new site, and to sell the site of the present Garden; and enables Trinity Hall to lease for 99 years the parcel of ground which is about to pass into its possession.]

1 & 2 GUL. IV, Cap. XLV.

An Act to extend the provisions of an Act passed in the twenty-ninth year of the reign of His Majesty King Charles the Second, intituled An Act for confirming and perpetuating Augmentations made by Ecclesiastical Persons to small Vicarages and Curacies, *and for other purposes.*

WHEREAS by an Act passed in the twenty-ninth year of the reign of His late Majesty King Charles the Second, intituled An Act for confirming and perpetuating Augmentations made by Ecclesiastical Persons to small Vicarages and Curacies, it was amongst other things enacted, that all and every augmentation, of what nature soever, granted, reserved, or agreed to be made payable, or intended to be granted, reserved, or made payable, since the first day of June in the twelfth year of His said Majesty's reign, or which should at any time thereafter be granted, reserved, or made payable to any Vicar or

29 Car. 2, c. 8.

Curate, or reserved by way of increase of rent to the Lessors, but intended to be to or for the use or benefit of any Vicar or Curate, by any Archbishop, Bishop, Dean, Provost, Dean and Chapter, Archdeacon, Prebendary, or other ecclesiastical corporation, person, or persons whatsoever, so making the said reservation out of any rectory impropriate or portion of tithes belonging to any Archbishop, Bishop, Dean, Provost, Dean and Chapter, or other ecclesiastical corporation, person, or persons, should be deemed and adjudged to continue and be, and should for ever thereafter continue and remain, as well during the continuance of the estate or term upon which the said augmentations were granted, reserved, or agreed to be made payable, as afterwards, in whose hands soever the said rectories or portion of tithes should be or come, which rectories or portion of tithes should be chargeable therewith, whether the same should be reserved again or not; and the said Vicars and Curates respectively were thereby adjudged to be in the actual possession thereof for the use of themselves and their successors, and the same should for ever thereafter be taken, received, and enjoyed by the said Vicars and Curates and their successors, as well during the continuance of the term or estate upon which the said augmentations were granted, reserved, or agreed to be made payable, as afterwards; and the said Vicars and Curates should have remedy for the same, either by distress upon the rectories impropriate or portions of tithes charged therewith, or by action of debt against that person who ought to have paid the same, his executors or administrators, any disability in the person or persons, bodies politic or corporate so granting, or any disability or incapacity in the Vicars or Curates to whom or to or for whose use or benefit the same were granted or intended to be granted, the Statute of Mortmain, or any other law, custom, or other matter or thing whatsoever to the contrary notwithstanding; provided always, that no future augmentation should be confirmed by virtue of the said Act which should exceed one moiety of the clear yearly value above all reprises of the rectory impropriate out of which the same should be granted or reserved; and it was thereby also enacted, that if any question should thereafter arise concerning the validity of such grants, or any other matter or thing in that Act mentioned and contained, such favourable constructions, and such remedy, if need be, should be had and made for the benefit of the Vicars and Curates as theretofore had been had and made or might be had for other charitable uses upon the Statutes for charitable uses: and whereas it is expedient that the powers and provisions of the said Act should be amended and enlarged: be it therefore enacted by the King's most excellent Majesty, by and with the advice and consent of the Lords spiritual and temporal and Commons in this present Parliament assembled, and by the authority of the same, that the said recited provision, by which the amount of any augmentation is restricted and limited to one moiety of the clear yearly value above all reprises of the rectory impropriate out of which the same should be granted and reserved, shall, so far as relates to any augmentation which may be granted after the passing of this Act, be and the same is hereby repealed.

Provision in recited Act limiting any augmentation repealed.

2. And, whereas doubts may arise by reason of the mention of portion of tithes in the said recited Act, be it enacted, that the provisions of the said recited Act shall extend to any augmentation to be made out of tithes, although the same may not be a portion of tithes; and further, that it shall be lawful, under the power given by the said recited Act, to grant, reserve, or make payable any such augmentation as aforesaid to the Incumbent of any Church or Chapel within the parish or place in which the rectory impropriate shall lie, or in which the tithes or portion of tithes shall arise, (as the case may be,) whether such Incumbent shall be a Vicar or Curate, or otherwise: provided also, that no such augmentation shall be made payable to any other person whomsoever.

Explaining doubts as to Portion of Tithes, &c.

3. And be it further enacted, that in every case in which any augmentation shall at any time hereafter be granted, reserved, or made payable to the Incumbent of any Church or Chapel, or reserved by way of increase of rent to the Lessors, but intended to be to or for the

Recited Act to extend to augmentations by Colleges and Hospitals.

use or benefit of any Incumbent, by the Master and Fellows of any College, or the Master or Guardian of any Hospital, so making the said grant or reservation out of any rectory impropriate or tithes or portion of tithes belonging to the Master and Fellows of such College, or the Master or Guardian of such Hospital, all the provisions herein-before recited and set forth, except the provision herein-before repealed, shall apply to such case in the same manner as if the same provisions, except as aforesaid, (with such alterations therein as the difference between the cases would require,) were herein expressly set forth and enacted with reference thereto: provided always, that every such augmentation shall be made to the Incumbent of some Church or Chapel within the parish or place in which the rectory impropriate shall lie, or in which the tithes or portion of tithes shall arise, (as the case may be).

4. And be it further enacted, that in every case in which any augmentation shall at any time hereafter be granted, reserved, or made payable to the Incumbent of any Church or Chapel being in the patronage of the Grantor or Grantors, or Lessor or Lessors, or be reserved by way of increase of rent to the Lessor or Lessors, but intended to be to or for the use or benefit of any such Incumbent, by any Archbishop, Bishop, Dean, Dean and Chapter, Archdeacon, Prebendary, or other ecclesiastical corporation, person, or persons whatsoever, or the Master and Fellows of any College, or the Master or Guardian of any Hospital, so making the said grant or reservation out of any lands, tenements, or other hereditaments belonging to such Archbishop, Bishop, Dean, Dean and Chapter, Archdeacon, Prebendary, or other ecclesiastical corporation, person, or persons whatsoever, or the Master and Fellows of such College, or the Master or Guardian of such Hospital, all the provisions herein-before recited and set forth (except the provision herein-before repealed) shall apply to such case in the same manner as if the same provisions, except as aforesaid, (with such alterations therein as the difference between the cases would require,) were herein expressly set forth and enacted with reference thereto.

The same Statute to extend to augmentations made by Spiritual Persons, Colleges, and Hospitals, out of any hereditaments, to any Church or Chapel being in their patronage.

All such augmentations to be in the form of annual rents.

5. Provided also, and be it further enacted and declared, that every augmentation which at any time hereafter shall be granted, reserved, or made payable, either under the power given by the said recited Act, or under either of the powers herein-before contained, shall be in the form of an annual rent; and that the provisions of the said recited Act, and the provisions herein-before contained, shall not apply to any other kind of augmentation whatsoever to be made after the passing of this Act.

Where hereditaments are in lease, a part of the reserved rent may be granted as an augmentation.

6. And be it further enacted and declared, that where any such rectory impropriate or tithes or portion of tithes, or any such lands, tenements, or other hereditaments as aforesaid, shall respectively be subject to any lease on which an annual rent shall be reserved or be payable to the person or persons or body politic making the augmentation, it shall be lawful, during the continuance of such lease, to exercise the power given by the said recited Act, or either of the powers herein-before contained, (so far as the same shall apply,) by granting to the Incumbent of the Benefice intended to be augmented a part of the rent which shall be so reserved or made payable as aforesaid; and then and in every such case the same premises shall for ever, as well after the determination of such lease as during the continuance thereof, be chargeable to such Incumbent and his successors with the augmentation which shall have been so granted to him as aforesaid; and from and after such time as notice of the said grant shall be given to the person or persons entitled in possession under the said lease, and thenceforth during the continuance of the same, such Incumbent and his successors shall have all the same powers for enforcing payment of such augmentation as the person or persons or body politic by whom the augmentation shall have been granted might have had in that behalf in case no grant of the same had been made; and, after the determination of the said lease, the said Incumbent and his successors shall have such remedy for enforcing payment of such augmentation as aforesaid as is provided by the said recited Act with respect to augmentations granted, reserved, or made payable under the authority thereof.

7. And be it further enacted, that where any such rectory impropriate or tithes or portion of tithes, lands, tenements, or other hereditaments as aforesaid, shall be subject to any lease for any term not exceeding twenty-one years or three lives, or, (in the case of such houses as under the provisions of the Act passed in the fourteenth year of the reign of Her Majesty Queen Elizabeth, intituled An Act for continuation, explanation, perfecting, and enlarging of divers Statutes, may lawfully be leased for forty years,) not exceeding forty years, on which lease the most improved rent at the time of making the same shall not have been reserved, it shall be lawful at any time during the continuance of such lease to exercise the power given by the said recited Act, or either of the powers herein-before contained, by granting out of the said premises an augmentation, to take effect in possession after the expiration, surrender, or other determination of such lease; and then and in every such case the said premises shall, from and after the expiration, surrender, or other determination of the said lease, and for ever thereafter, be chargeable with the said augmentation; and the provisions of the said recited Act and of this Act respectively shall in all respects apply to every augmentation which shall be so granted, in the same manner as in other cases of augmentations to be granted under the powers of the said recited Act or of this Act.

8. And whereas it is apprehended that it may be desirable in many cases to make grants of augmentations in the manner last herein-before mentioned, and that such grants would be much discouraged if the augmentation to be granted should necessarily take effect in possession upon a surrender of the lease during which the same had been granted as aforesaid for the purpose of such lease being renewed; be it therefore further enacted, that in any case in which an augmentation shall have been granted to take effect in possession after the expiration, surrender, or other determination of any lease in the manner authorized by the clause last herein-before contained, and a renewal of such lease shall take place before the expiration thereof, it shall be lawful in and by the renewed lease to defer the time

from which such augmentation is to take effect in possession as aforesaid until any time to be therein specified in that behalf: provided always, that the time to which the augmentation shall be so deferred shall be some time not exceeding twenty-one years, or (in the case of such houses as by the said Act of Her Majesty Queen Elizabeth may lawfully be leased for forty years) not exceeding forty years, to be respectively computed from the commencement of the lease during which the augmentation shall have been granted.

Power to apportion augmentations on future leases.

9. Provided always, and be it further enacted, that where any such augmentation as aforesaid shall have become chargeable, under or by virtue of the said recited Act or of this Act, upon any rectory impropriate, tithes, portion of tithes, lands, tenements, or other hereditaments, if any lease shall afterwards be granted of any part of the same premises separately from the rest thereof, then and in every such case, and from time to time so often as the same shall happen, it shall be lawful for the person or persons granting such lease to provide and agree that any part of such augmentation shall during such lease be paid out of such part of the hereditaments previously charged therewith as shall be comprised in the said lease; and then and in such case, and thenceforth during the lease so to be made as aforesaid, no further or other part of the said augmentation shall be charged on the premises comprised in the said lease than such part of the said augmentation as shall be so agreed

Restriction on the exercise of the power of apportionment.

to be paid out of the same: provided always, that in every such case the hereditaments which shall be leased in severalty as aforesaid shall be a competent security for such part of the said augmentation as shall be agreed to be paid out of the same, and the remainder of the hereditaments originally charged with the said augmentation shall be a competent security for the residue thereof.

Repeal of so much of recited Act as requires an express continuance of the augmentation in new leases.

10. And whereas by the said recited Act it was enacted, that, if, upon the surrender, expiration, or other determination of any lease wherein such augmentation had been or should be granted, any new lease of the premises or any part thereof should thereafter be made without express continuance of the said augmentation, every such new lease

should be utterly void; be it further enacted, that the said last-mentioned provision, so far as relates to any augmentation which may be granted after the passing of this Act, shall be and the same is hereby repealed.

11. And be it further enacted, that it shall be lawful for any Archbishop, Bishop, Dean, Dean and Chapter, Archdeacon, Prebendary, or other ecclesiastical corporation or person or persons, or the Master and Fellows of any College, or the Master or Guardian of any Hospital, being in his or their corporate capacity the owner or owners of any rectory impropriate, or of any tithes or portion of tithes arising in any particular parish or place, by a deed duly executed, to annex such rectory impropriate or tithes or portion of tithes as aforesaid, or any lands or tithes being part or parcel thereof, with the appurtenances, unto any Church or Chapel within the parish or place in which the rectory impropriate shall lie, or in which the tithes or portion of tithes shall arise, to the intent and in order that the same may be held and enjoyed by the Incumbent for the time being of such Church or Chapel; and every such deed shall be effectual to all intents and purposes whatsoever, any law or statute to the contrary notwithstanding. *Ecclesiastical corporations, Colleges, &c., holding any impropriate Rectory or Tithes, may annex the same to any Church or Chapel within the parish in which the Rectory lies or the Tithes arise.*

12. And be it further enacted, that it shall be lawful for any Archbishop, Bishop, Dean, Dean and Chapter, Archdeacon, Prebendary, or other ecclesiastical corporation or person or persons, or the Master and Fellows of any College, or the Master or Guardian of any Hospital, being in his or their corporate capacity the owner or owners of any lands, tenements, or other hereditaments whatsoever, and also being in his or their corporate capacity the patron or patrons of any Church or Chapel, by a deed duly executed, to annex such lands, tenements, or other hereditaments, with the appurtenances, unto such Church or Chapel, to the intent and in order that the same premises may be held and enjoyed by the Incumbent for the time being thereof; and every such deed shall be effectual to all intents and purposes whatsoever, any law or statute to the contrary notwithstanding. *Power to annex lands &c. held by them to any Church or Chapel under their patronage.*

13. Provided always, and be it further enacted, that in any case in which any rectory impropriate, tithes, or portion *Such annexations to be sub-*

ject to prior leases, and the rents reserved upon the same, or some portion thereof, to be determined by the Deed of Annoxation.

of tithes, lands, tenements, or other hereditaments shall be annexed to any Church or Chapel, pursuant to either of the powers herein-before in that behalf contained, the annexation thereof shall be subject and without prejudice to any lease or leases which previously to such annexation may have been made or granted of the same premises or any part thereof: provided also, that in every such case any rent or rents which may have been reserved in respect of the said premises in and by such lease or leases, or (in case any other hereditaments shall have been also comprised in such lease or leases) some proportional part of such rent or rents, such proportional part to be fixed and determined in and by the instrument by which the annexation shall be made, shall, during the continuance of the said lease or leases, be payable to the Incumbent for the time being of the Church or Chapel to which the premises shall be annexed as aforesaid; and accordingly such Incumbent for the time being shall, during the continuance of such lease or leases, have all the same powers for enforcing payment of the same rent or rents, or of such proportional part thereof as aforesaid, as the person or persons or body politic by whom the annexation shall have been made might have had in that behalf in case the said premises had not been annexed.

Provisions of 39 & 40 Geo. 3, c. 41, to extend to such Annexations, in certain cases.

14. And be it further enacted and declared, that where any rectory impropriate, tithes, or portion of tithes, lands, tenements, or other hereditaments, which shall be annexed to any Church or Chapel under either of the powers herein-before in that behalf contained, or any part thereof, shall have been anciently or accustomably demised with other hereditaments in one lease, under one rent or divers rents issuing out of the whole, and after such annexation such other hereditaments as aforesaid, or any part thereof, shall be demised by a separate lease or leases, all the provisions of an Act passed in the thirty-ninth and fortieth years of the reign of His late Majesty King George the Third, intituled, An Act for explaining and amending several Acts made in the thirty-second year of King Henry the Eighth, and the first, thirteenth, and fourteenth years of the reign of Queen Elizabeth, so far as respects leases granted by Archbishops, Bishops, Masters, and Fellows of Colleges, Deans and

Chapters of Cathedral and Collegiate Churches, Masters and Guardians of Hospitals, and others, having any spiritual or ecclesiastical living or promotion, shall apply and take effect in the same manner as if the premises which shall be so annexed as aforesaid had been retained in the possession or occupation of the person or persons by whom such lease or leases as aforesaid shall be made.

15. And be it further enacted, that such of the powers herein-before contained, as are restricted to cases in which the corporation or person by whom the same may be exercised shall be the patron of the benefice which it shall be intended or desired to augment, shall apply to and may be exercised in cases in which such corporation or person shall be entitled only to the alternate right of presentation to such benefice. *Certain powers to apply to persons entitled to alternate Presentation.*

16. Provided always, and be it further enacted, that the power given by the said recited Act shall not at any time hereafter, nor shall any of the powers herein-before contained, in any case, be exercised so as to augment in value any benefice whatsoever, which at the time of the exercise of the power shall exceed in clear annual value the sum of three hundred pounds, or so as to raise the clear annual value of any benefice to any greater amount than such sum of three hundred and fifty pounds, or three hundred pounds, not taking account of surplice fees. *Benefices exceeding in yearly value £300 not to be raised, and all others to be limited.*

17. And be it further enacted, that in every case in which it shall be desired, upon the exercise of any of the said powers, to ascertain, for the purposes of this Act, the clear yearly value of any benefice, or of any rectory impropriate, tithes, or portion of tithes, lands, tenements, or other hereditaments, it shall be lawful for the Archbishop or Bishop of the diocese within which the benefice to be augmented shall be situate, or, where the same shall be situate within a peculiar jurisdiction belonging to any Archbishop or Bishop, then for the Archbishop or Bishop to whom such peculiar jurisdiction shall belong, to cause such clear yearly value to be determined and ascertained by any two persons whom he shall appoint for that purpose by writing under his hand, (which writing is hereby directed to be afterwards annexed to the instrument by which the power shall be exercised); and a certificate of such clear yearly value, written or endorsed on the instrument *Power to determine the yearly value of any hereditaments for the purposes of the Act.*

Instruments to be deposited in the Registry of the Diocese.

26. Provided always, and be it further enacted, that, in every case in which the power given by the said recited Act of the twenty-ninth year of the reign of King Charles the Second, or any of the powers herein-before contained, shall be exercised, the instrument by which the same shall be so exercised shall, within two calendar months after the date of the same, be deposited in the Registry of the diocese within which the benefice augmented or otherwise benefited shall be locally situate, or, where the same shall be situate within a peculiar jurisdiction belonging to any Archbishop or Bishop, then in the Registry of such peculiar jurisdiction.

Act to apply to all Heads of Colleges, under whatever denomination.

29. And be it further enacted, that the powers by this Act given to the Master and Fellows of any College shall apply to cases in which the Head of the College shall be called the Warden, Dean, Provost, President, Rector, or Principal thereof, or shall be called by any other denomination; and that such powers shall extend to every College and Hall in the Universities of Oxford and Cambridge, and to the Colleges of Eton and Winchester.

2 & 3 Gul. IV, Cap. XLV.

An Act to amend the Representation of the People in England and Wales.

This Act not to extend to the Universities of Oxford and Cambridge.

78. Provided always, and be it enacted, that nothing in this Act contained shall extend to or in anywise affect the election of Members to serve in Parliament for the Universities of Oxford or Cambridge, or shall entitle any person to vote in the election of Members to serve in Parliament for the City of Oxford or Town of Cambridge in respect of the occupation of any chambers or premises in any of the Colleges or Halls of the Universities of Oxford or Cambridge.

2 & 3 GUL. IV, Cap. LXXX.

An Act to authorize the identifying of lands and other possessions of certain Ecclesiastical and Collegiate Corporations.

WHEREAS the Archbishops and Bishops of the several Dioceses, and the Deans, and Deans and Chapters, Archdeacons, Prebendaries, and Canons, and other Dignitaries and Officers of the several Cathedral and Collegiate Churches and Chapels, and the Masters or other Heads and Fellows and Scholars or other Societies of the several Colleges and Halls in the Universities of Oxford and Cambridge, and of the Colleges of Winchester and Eton, are proprietors of divers manors, messuages, lands, tenements, tithes, and hereditaments; and in many cases the boundaries or quantities and the identity of lands within such manors, and of such messuages, lands, tenements, and hereditaments, and of lands subject to any such tithes, or some part or parts thereof, are unknown or disputed; and it would be a great benefit, as well to such proprietors respectively, as to their lessees, copyhold or customary tenants, sub-lessees, or under-tenants, their, his, or her heirs, executors, administrators, or assigns, if the said manors, messuages, lands, tenements, tithes, and hereditaments were identified, and the boundaries and quantities thereof ascertained and finally settled:

Be it enacted by the King's most excellent Majesty, by and with the advice and consent of the Lords spiritual and temporal and Commons in this present Parliament assembled, and by the authority of the same, that from and after the passing of this Act it shall and may be lawful to and for any Archbishop, Bishop, Dean, Dean and Chapter, or other corporation aggregate or sole herein-before mentioned, to enter into an agreement of reference or deed of submission with his or their lessee or lessees, copyhold or customary tenant or tenants, sub-lessee or sub-lessees, under-tenant or under-tenants, his, her, or their heirs, executors, administrators, or assigns, or with the owner or owners of any other hereditaments adjoining to or intermixed with the said manors, *Archbishops, Bishops, Deans and Chapters, &c., may enter into agreements or deeds of reference with their Lessees,* messuages, lands, tenements, tithes, or hereditaments, whereby it shall be agreed that any unknown or disputed boundaries or quantities of such manors, messuages, lands, tenements, tithes, or hereditaments, or any part thereof, shall be referred to the adjudication of such person or persons as may be agreed upon and named by the said Archbishop, Bishop, Dean, Dean and Chapter, or other corporation aggregate or sole, and by his or their lessee or lessees, copyhold or customary tenant or tenants, sub-lessee or sub-lessees, under-tenant or under-tenants, his, her, or their heirs, executors, administrators, or assigns, or by such owner or owners of any other hereditaments situate as aforesaid; and that such referee or referees shall be fully authorized to make or cause to be made surveys, maps, and admeasurements of the said manors, messuages, lands, tenements, tithes, and hereditaments, or any part thereof, and to summon any persons as witnesses, and examine them on oath (which oath he or they are hereby authorized to administer) touching or concerning any of the matters or things so referred as aforesaid, or in any way relating thereto; and also to call for the production of all surveys, maps, deeds, books, papers, and writings in the custody or power of any of the parties to the said reference, or of any other person or persons, of or concerning the matters in question; and the said referee or referees, having well and sufficiently investigated and considered the same, and all matters to him or them referred, shall and may make his or their award or awards in writing, under his or their hand and seal or hands and seals, with a map or maps drawn thereupon or thereunto annexed, and which said award or awards and map or maps shall be upon parchment or vellum, and shall award and determine, identify, delineate, and describe the boundaries, quantities, particulars, and situations of the said manors, messuages, lands, tenements, tithes, and hereditaments so referred to him or them as aforesaid; and the said award or awards and map or maps shall be laid before all the parties to any such agreement of reference or deed of submission, including the party or parties whose consent is required by this Act, whose approbation thereof shall be written upon the said award or awards, and shall be signed and sealed by them, and thereupon the said award or awards and map or maps shall be for ever afterwards binding upon all parties, and final and conclusive as to all matters therein contained or thereby referred to.

2. Provided always, and be it further enacted, that in every case in which any of the powers herein-before contained shall be exercised by any Bishop, Dean, Archdeacon, Prebendary, or other ecclesiastical corporation sole, the deed of submission or agreement of reference, and also the approbation of the award, shall, in the case of a Bishop, be executed by the Archbishop of the Province testifying his consent thereto; or in case of a Dean, the same shall be executed by the Dean and Chapter testifying their consent thereto; or in the case of an Archdeacon, Prebendary, or other ecclesiastical corporation sole, the same shall be executed by the Archbishop or Bishop of the diocese testifying his consent thereto. *Certain consents required to render valid proceedings under this Act.*

3. And be it further enacted, that from and after the passing of this Act it shall and may be lawful to and for the said lessee or lessees, copyhold or customary tenant or tenants, sub-lessee or sub-lessees, under-tenant or under-tenants, and such other owner or owners as herein-before named, his, her, or their heirs, executors, administrators, or assigns, who at the time of making any reference authorized by this Act shall be tenant or tenants in fee tail, general or special, or for life or lives, and for the guardians, husbands, committees, or attornies of or acting for any such lessee or lessees, copyhold or customary tenant or tenants, sub-lessee or sub-lessees, under-tenant or under-tenants, and such other owner or owners as herein-before named, his, her, or their heirs, executors, administrators, or assigns, who at the time of making any such reference shall be respectively an infant or infants, feme covert or femes covert, or of unsound mind, or beyond the seas, or under any other legal disability, or otherwise disabled to act for themselves, himself, or herself, to sign, seal, and deliver any agreement of reference or deed of submission or approbation of any award or awards and map or maps authorized by this Act to be made, as fully and effectually to all intents and purposes as if such lessee or lessees, copyhold or customary tenant or tenants, sub-lessee or sub-lessees, under-tenant or under- *Power to Infants, married Women, Lunatics, &c., to enter into reference.*

tenants, and such other owner or owners as herein-before named, his, her, or their heirs, executors, administrators, or assigns, had been tenant or tenants in fee simple, and of full age, sole, of sound mind, or within the realm of England, and not under any other legal disability.

<small>Agreements or Deeds of Reference, Awards, and Maps, to be deposited in Registry of Archbishop, Bishop, &c.</small>

4. And be it further enacted, that, immediately after the execution by the parties of the instrument shewing their approbation of any award to be made by virtue of this Act, the agreement of reference or deed of submission, and also the award or awards and map or maps authorized to be made by this Act, and a copy of the minutes of evidence whereupon the same is made, shall be deposited, in the case of any reference by any Archbishop or Bishop, in the office of their own Registrar; and in case of any reference by any Dean, Dean and Chapter, Archdeacon, Prebendary, Canon, and other Dignitary and Officer of a Cathedral or Collegiate Church or Chapel, in the office of the Registrar of the Dean and Chapter thereof; and in case of any reference by any Masters or other Heads, or by any Fellows and Scholars, or other Societies herein-before named, in the office of the Steward or other proper Officer of their said Colleges and Halls; and every such Registrar, Steward, or other Officer,

<small>Documents to be produced for inspection.</small>

or some person or persons on his behalf, shall produce the documents and papers so deposited with him or any of them, at all proper and usual hours of business, to every person interested in the subject matter of such award, or to his or her agent duly authorized, who shall make application to inspect the same or any of them, and shall furnish a copy or copies of the same or any of them to every such person or agent who shall make application for such copy or copies;

<small>Registrar's Fees.</small>

and every such Registrar, Steward, or other Officer shall in every case be entitled to the sum of five shillings and no more for receiving and preserving the agreement of reference or deed of submission, award or awards, map or maps, and copy of the minutes of evidence as aforesaid, and the sum of one shilling and no more for every production of the same or any of them to be inspected, and the sum of sixpence and no more for every folio containing seventy-two words of every copy, and the sum of ten shillings and no more for every copy of a map so made as aforesaid.

5. And be it further enacted, that the expences attending every reference which shall be made under the authority of this Act, and all the proceedings hereby required relating to the same, shall be paid and borne by the parties thereto in such manner, shares, and proportions as they shall agree; and in case the said parties shall not make any agreement relating to such expences, then all such expences, or so much thereof as shall not be provided for by such agreement, shall be paid and borne by the said parties in equal moieties. *Expences of reference how to be paid.*

6. Provided also, and be it further enacted, that this Act shall extend only to that part of the United Kingdom called England and Wales [*]. *Act limited to England and Wales.*

3 & 4 Gul. IV, Cap. XXXI.

An Act to enable the election of Officers of Corporations and other public companies now required to be held on the Lord's Day to be held on the Saturday next preceding or on the Monday next ensuing.

WHEREAS the profanation of the Lord's Day is greatly increased by reason of certain meetings which are usually or occasionally held thereon; and whereas it is the duty of the Legislature to remove as much as possible impediments to the due observance of the Lord's Day; be it therefore enacted by the King's most excellent Majesty, by and with the advice and consent of the Lords spiritual and temporal and Commons in this present Parliament assembled, and by the authority of the same, that every meeting or adjourned meeting of any vestry or corporation, whether ecclesiastical or civil, or of any public company, for the nomination, election, appointment, swearing in, or admission of any officer or officers, or for the transaction of any other secular affair of such vestry, corporation, or company, and *Elections of Officers of Corporations and other public Com-*

---

[*] Where leasehold lands are intermixed with other lands and cannot be certainly identified, the Inclosure Commissioners are empowered by 9 & 10 Vict. c. 70, s. 8, whether an Inclosure be pending or not, to determine the boundaries and to make an award thereon.

panies now required to be held on a Sunday shall be held on the Saturday preceding or the Monday following.

every other meeting of a public and secular nature, which, according to any Act of Parliament, or according to any charter, grant, constitution, deed, testament, law, prescription, or usage whatsoever, is or shall be required to be held on any Lord's Day, or on any day which shall happen to be on a Lord's Day, shall be held on the Saturday next preceding or on the Monday next ensuing, at the like hour, with like form and effect, as if the same had been held on such Lord's Day; and every matter transacted at any such meeting or adjourned meeting held upon any Lord's Day shall be absolutely void and of none effect to all intents and purposes whatsoever:

If election does not take place on the Saturday the person holding the office to continue so to do until the Monday.

provided always, that when no such nomination, election, appointment, swearing in, or admission shall have taken place on such Saturday, every person whose term of office would, according to any such Act, charter, grant, constitution, deed, testament, law, prescription, or usage, have expired on any such Lord's Day, shall continue in office, and exercise and enjoy all the powers and privileges annexed or relating to such office, until and on such Monday next ensuing, in the same manner as if such Monday had been the customary day of nomination, election, appointment, swearing in, or admission.

Elections not made on such Saturday or Monday shall be taken to be within the provisions of 11 Geo. 1, c. 4.

2. And be it further enacted, that whenever the nomination, election, appointment, swearing in, or admission of any such officer or officers as before mentioned shall not take place on such Saturday or Monday, or shall become void, the case shall be and is hereby declared to be within the provisions of an Act made and passed in the eleventh year of His late Majesty King George the First, intituled, An Act for preventing the inconveniences arising for want of Elections of Mayors or other chief Magistrates of Boroughs or Corporations being made upon the days appointed by charter or usage for that purpose, and directing in what manner such Elections shall be afterwards made, as fully and effectually as if such officer or officers had been expressly named in the said Act †.

† By 11 Geo. 1, c. 4, it is provided that where an election is not made on the proper day the electors may meet on the next day for the purpose and may then make a valid election; and that if this be not done the Court of King's Bench may award a writ of Mandamus for an election to be made on a day named in the writ.

5 & 6 GUL. IV, Cap. LXII.

An Act to repeal an Act of the present Session of Parliament, intituled An Act for the more effectual Abolition of Oaths and Affirmations taken and made in various Departments of the State, and to substitute Declarations in lieu thereof, and for the more entire Suppression of voluntary and extra-judicial Oaths and Affidavits, *and to make other provisions for the Abolition of unnecessary Oaths.*

6. Provided always, and be it enacted, that nothing in this Act contained shall extend or apply to the Oath of Allegiance in any case in which the same now is or may be required to be taken by any person who may be appointed to any Office; but that such Oath of Allegiance shall continue to be required, and shall be administered and taken, as well and in the same manner as if this Act had not been passed. *Oath of Allegiance on admission to any Office still to be required in all cases.*

8. And be it enacted, that it shall be lawful for the Universities of Oxford and Cambridge, and for all other bodies corporate and politic, and for all bodies now by law or statute, or by any valid usage, authorized to administer or receive any Oath, solemn Affirmation, or Affidavit, to make statutes, bye laws, or orders authorizing and directing the substitution of a Declaration in lieu of any Oath, solemn Affirmation, or Affidavit now required to be taken or made: provided always, that such statutes, bye laws, or orders be otherwise duly made and passed according to the charter, laws, or regulations of the particular University, other body corporate and politic, or other body so authorized as aforesaid. *Universities of Oxford and Cambridge, and other Bodies, may substitute a Declaration in lieu of an Oath.*

5 & 6 Gul. IV, Cap. LXIII.

An Act to repeal an Act of the fourth and fifth year of His present Majesty relating to Weights and Measures, and to make other provisions instead thereof.

Saving the rights of the Universities of Oxford and Cambridge.

44. Provided always, and be it enacted, that nothing in this Act contained shall extend to prohibit, defeat, injure, or lessen the rights or privileges of either of the Universities of Oxford or Cambridge; but that the custody of the assize, assay, and overlooking of Weights and Measures in the City of Oxford and its Suburbs and in the Town of Cambridge shall continue as heretofore and be in the Chancellor, Vice-Chancellor, or his Deputy, of the said Universities respectively; and that the Chancellor, Vice-Chancellor, or his Deputy, of each of the said Universities for the time being, and none other, shall have the power, and is or are hereby authorized, as occasion may require, to appoint in and for the said City and Suburbs and in and for the said Town respectively an Inspector or Inspectors of Weights and Measures, and shall have full power and authority to perform and execute all such matters and things as are required or are granted to Justices of the Peace of any county, city, town, or other jurisdiction in England and Wales under the provisions of this Act or by any or either of the said recited Acts; and every such Inspector is hereby authorized and empowered to put in force and execute all such powers and provisions as are by this Act, or by any or either of the said recited Acts, granted to or required of any Inspector or Inspectors of Weights and Measures appointed as aforesaid by the Justices of the Peace in Quarter Sessions assembled.

5 & 6 GUL. IV, Cap. LXV.

An Act for preventing the Publication of Lectures without consent.

[This Act provides that the authors of Lectures, or their assigns, shall have the sole right of publishing them; and that persons having leave to attend Lectures have not thereby leave to publish them.]

5. Provided further, that nothing in this Act shall extend .... to any Lecture or Lectures delivered in any University or public School or College, or on any public Foundation, or by any individual in virtue of or according to any gift, endowment, or foundation; and that the law relating thereto shall remain the same as if this Act had not been passed. Not to extend to Lectures delivered in any University &c.

5 & 6 GUL. IV, Cap. LXXVI.

An Act to provide for the regulation of Municipal Corporations in England and Wales.

[Section 1 enacts], that so much of all laws, statutes, and usages, and so much of all royal and other charters, grants, and letters patent now in force relating to the several boroughs[u] named in the Schedules (A.) and (B.) to this Act annexed, or to the inhabitants thereof, or to the several bodies or reputed bodies corporate named in the said Schedules or any of them, as are inconsistent with or contrary to the provisions of this Act, shall be and the same are hereby repealed and annulled. Repeal of all laws, charters, and customs, inconsistent with this Act.

[u] In the construction of this Act the word "Borough" is to be construed to mean City &c. Cambridge and Oxford are two of the boroughs named in Schedule (A.)

Exclusive rights of trading abolished.

[Section 14 enacts], that every person in any borough may keep any shop for the sale of all lawful wares and merchandizes by wholesale or retail, and use every lawful trade, occupation, mystery, and handicraft, for hire, gain, sale, or otherwise, within any borough, [notwithstanding any custom or bye-law limiting rights of trading to persons free of the place or of certain guilds or companies.]

All chartered exemptions from serving on Juries abolished.

[Section 123 enacts], that after the passing of this Act no person in any borough shall continue to be exempt from serving on juries in any of the King's Courts of Record at Westminster, ... or in any Court of Assize, Nisi Prius, Oyer and Terminer, Gaol Delivery, or Sessions of the Peace, or in any other of the King's Courts, by virtue of any writ, grant, charter, prescription, or otherwise.

Saving of the rights of the Universities of Oxford and Cambridge.

137. And be it enacted, that nothing in this Act contained shall be construed to alter or affect the rights or privileges, duties or liabilities, of the Chancellor Masters and Scholars of the Universities of Oxford or Cambridge respectively, as by law possessed under the respective charters of the said Universities or otherwise, or to entitle any person to be enrolled a Citizen of the City of Oxford or Burgess of the Borough of Cambridge by reason of his occupation of any rooms, chambers, or premises in any of the Colleges or Halls of the Universities of Oxford or Cambridge or either of them, or to compel any resident Member of either of the said Universities to accept any office in or under the body corporate of the Mayor and Citizens of the City of Oxford or of the Mayor and Burgesses of the Borough of Cambridge, or to authorize the levy of any rate within the precincts of the said Universities, or of any of the Colleges or Halls of the same, which now by law cannot be levied therein.

5 & 6 GUL. IV, Cap. lxix.

An Act for continuing the Term and amending and enlarging the Powers of three Acts of His Majesty King George the Third, for amending certain Mileways leading to Oxford, and making Improvements in the University and City of Oxford, the Suburbs thereof, and adjoining Parish of Saint Clement, and for other purposes in the said Acts mentioned. 11 Geo. 3, c. 19; 21 Geo. 3, c. 47; 52 Geo. 3, c. lxxii.

[Sections 1–10, 32–36, 64–73, of this Act concern the Commissioners of Streets, and have either been repealed by 28 & 29 Vict. c. 108, or are now so near expiring that it does not seem worth while to print any of them here.]

11. And whereas the said City of Oxford and its neighbourhood have of late years greatly increased, and are still increasing in population and buildings, and there is reason to apprehend that the Market established by virtue of the said recited Acts will soon become inadequate for the same; be it therefore enacted, that it shall be lawful for the Committee for the time being, appointed by the Chancellor Masters and Scholars of the University of Oxford and the Mayor Bailiffs and Commonalty of the City of Oxford respectively, pursuant to the provisions of the said recited Act of the eleventh year of the reign of King George the Third, or any five or more of them, and they are hereby authorized and empowered, when and as they shall think fit, to extend and enlarge the said present Market Place, or any part or parts thereof, and, if they shall deem it expedient, to appropriate and set apart a sufficient space of ground, if the same can be purchased or obtained, in some convenient part of the said City of Oxford or the Suburbs thereof, as or for a second or additional Market for the sale of all or any of the marketable commodities now usually sold or exposed to sale in the present Market of the said City. *Power to enlarge the present Market, or erect and appropriate another.*

[Sections 12–26 enable the Market Committee to purchase

such houses, lands, &c., as may be necessary; but sections 15-20, giving a compulsory power of purchase within three years, have expired.]

Power to Market Committee to appropriate £10,000 of the savings;

27. And be it further enacted, that, notwithstanding anything in the said recited Acts or this Act mentioned or contained, the said Market Committee for the time being, or any five or more of them, shall, after all the monies already borrowed under the said recited Acts shall have been paid off, discharged, or satisfied, have full power and authority to apply, lay out, and expend, out of the rents and profits which may from time to time arise from the said present or extended Market or any new or additional Market, and out of the savings which may from time to time be made by the falling in of annuities, any sum not exceeding ten thousand pounds in, about, and towards the improvement of the said present or extended Market, or the building, erecting, or improvement of any new or additional Market that may be made as aforesaid, in such manner and at such times as the said Committee for the time being, or any five or more of them, shall deem expedient.

and to contribute £4000 towards widening Jesus College Lane.

28. And be it further enacted, that it shall be lawful for the said Market Committee for the time being, or any five or more of them, from and out of the said rents and profits and savings as aforesaid, to contribute and apply any sum not exceeding four thousand pounds towards the costs and expences of widening a certain street or lane in the said City, called Jesus College Lane, running from the Corn Market into the Turl[x].

[Section 29 prescribes a Form of Conveyance.

[Section 30 directs that, if any works effected or intended under this or the former Acts be abandoned, the land purchased for them shall revert to the original owners.

[Section 31 exempts the Commissioners of Streets and the Market Committee from personal responsibility in contracts.

[Section 37 repeals ss. 90-94 of 11 Geo. III, c. 19, by which the Market Committee had power to borrow £5000: and sections 38-47 give the Committee power to borrow

---

[x] The power given in s. 28 is not exhausted.

money to the amount of £20,000 for the purchase of land &c. for the purposes of the Market [y].

[Sections 48 and 49 make provision for the establishing of a second Market, if necessary.

[Sections 50 and 51 relate to the letting of shops and stalls in the Market.

[Section 52 prohibits all slaughtering of animals in the Market.

[Sections 53–56 empower the Market Committee, " with the consent and approbation of the Vice-Chancellor of the University of Oxford for the time being by writing under his hand," to make Bye-laws.

[Sections 57 and 58 relate to the appointment of Officers.]

59. Provided always, and be it further enacted, that nothing in this Act contained shall extend or be construed to extend in any manner to abridge or rescind the rights which the said Chancellor Masters and Scholars now enjoy of appointing or nominating one or more Clerk or Clerks of the said present or of any new or additional Market, and of otherwise governing, regulating, and superintending the same as heretofore accustomed, according to the saving and reservation in this respect contained in the said Act of the eleventh year of the reign of His Majesty King George the Third; nor shall anything in this Act contained extend or be construed to prejudice or affect any of the remedies now by law given to the said Chancellor Masters and Scholars and the said Mayor Bailiffs and Commonalty for the recovery of the said rents, stallages, sum or sums of money, or extend to take away the right of the said Mayor Bailiffs and Commonalty to such pitching-pence or tolls as before the passing of the said last mentioned Act were paid to them or their toll-gatherer by butchers, gardeners, and others; but that the same rights respectively shall remain and belong to the said Chancellor Masters and Scholars and the said Mayor Bailiffs and Commonalty respectively, as they had before the passing of this Act. *The ancient rights of the University and City with reference to the Markets reserved.*

[Section 60 imposes a penalty on persons obstructing any Market Officers, or damaging buildings, or defacing notices.

[y] This power of borrowing is not exhausted.

[Section 61 applies to any enlargement of the Market and to any additional Market all the powers, penalties, &c., contained in 11 Geo. III, c. 19, and 21 Geo. III, c. 47.

[Section 62 enables the Market Committee to sue and be sued in the name of their Clerk.]

Commissioners may allow Market Carts to stand in the streets.

63. And be it further enacted, that the said Commissioners, or any five or more of them, shall and may and they are hereby empowered to permit and allow any waggon, carts, or carriages, wherein any meat, fish, poultry, eggs, butter, vegetables, fruit, and other provisions, or any goods, wares, or merchandizes, commodities, articles, and things shall be brought for sale in the said new Market erected by virtue of the said first-recited Act, or in any additional or other Market made or established by virtue of this Act, to be placed and to stand in such parts of the streets, lanes, ways, and public places within the said City and Suburbs, and on such days and times, and under such regulations, as well in respect to loading or unloading as in all other respects, as they the said Commissioners, or any five or more of them, shall and may from time to time direct, order, and appoint; any thing in this or the said recited Acts to the contrary thereof notwithstanding [z].

[Sections 74–85 empower the Commissioners of Streets "to set up and establish a manufactory of Gas [a]."

[Sections 86–97 relate to proceedings which may be taken at law under this Act.

[Section 98 directs how the expenses of procuring the Act shall be paid.

[Section 99 continues and renews all the clauses and provisions of the three former Acts now in force and not by this Act repealed or varied.]

Saving the privileges of the University and the City.

100. Provided always, and be it further enacted, that nothing in this Act or the said recited Acts shall extend, or be deemed or construed to extend, to take away, diminish, or impede the exercise of any privilege or right whatsoever of the said University, or of any of the Magistrates, Officers,

---

[z] By 28 & 29 Vict. c. 108, the Local Board of Oxford are in the place of the Commissioners.

[a] This power to make Gas is expressly reserved to the Local Board by 28 & 29 Vict. c. 108.

Ministers, or Servants thereunto belonging, or of any privilege or right whatsoever of the said City, or any of the Magistrates, Officers, or Servants thereunto belonging.

101. And be it further enacted, that this Act shall be deemed and taken to be a Public Act, and shall be judicially taken notice of as such by all Judges, Justices, and others. Public Act.

102. And be it further enacted, that so much of the said recited Acts, passed in the eleventh, twenty-first, and fifty-second years of the reign of His Majesty King George the Third, and this Act, as relates to the Tolls thereby and hereby respectively granted, and to the Mileways, Bridge, and Avenues thereto, shall commence and take effect from and after the passing of this Act [b], and shall from thenceforth continue and be in full force and effect for and during the term of thirty-one years, and from thence to the end of the then next Session of Parliament [c]. Term and continuance of this Act.

6 & 7 GUL. IV, Cap. CV.

An Act for the better Administration of Justice in certain Boroughs.

[The preamble of the Act recites, that " by reason of certain defects in an Act passed in the last Session of Parliament, intituled *An Act to provide for the regulation of Municipal Corporations in England and Wales,* the administration of civil and criminal justice is injuriously hindered and delayed in certain Boroughs."] 5 & 6 W. 4, c. 76.

12. And whereas doubts have been entertained whether, under the provisions of the said recited Act, it may be lawful for His Majesty from time to time to constitute and appoint the Vice-Chancellor of the University of Cambridge for the time being a Justice of the Peace in and for the Town and Borough of Cambridge; be it therefore enacted, that it shall be lawful for His Majesty, His heirs and successors, from time to time, if His Majesty shall so think fit, in and by His His Majesty may appoint the Vice-Chancellor of Cambridge University to be a Justice of the Borough.

---

[b] This Act received the Royal assent on the 21st of July 1835.

[c] In 1848 another Act was passed, 11 & 12 Vict. c. xxxvii, concerning the rates to be raised for paving and lighting; but it is entirely repealed by 28 & 29 Vict. c. 108.

Commission of the Peace for the said Town and Borough to constitute and appoint the Vice-Chancellor of the University for the time being a Justice of the Peace for the said Town and Borough, any thing in the said recited Act or in this Act to the contrary notwithstanding: provided always, that no Vice-Chancellor of the said University, by reason of his being named in any Commission of the Peace for the said Town and Borough, shall thereby have, as touching the grant of licences to alehouses, any greater authority as Justice of the Peace than any other Justice of the Peace named in any such Commission; but that nothing in this Act shall be construed to alter or in any way to affect the rights and privileges which the Vice-Chancellor by virtue of his office now lawfully has or enjoys, or might have lawfully had and enjoyed if the Vice-Chancellor had not been appointed under the provisions of this Act a Justice of the Peace for the said Town and Borough.

Proviso as to Vice-Chancellor's power of licensing Alehouses.

1 & 2 VICT., Cap. XXIII.

An Act to amend the law for providing fit Houses for the Beneficed Clergy.

[This Act enlarges the powers given by 17 Geo. III, c. 53, by enabling every Incumbent to borrow, for the purposes and in the manner prescribed by the Act, money not exceeding three years' net income of his living, and to mortgage the glebe &c. for thirty-five years as a security.]

5. And be it enacted, that it shall be lawful for any College or Hall within the Universities of Oxford or Cambridge, or for any other corporate bodies possessed of the patronage of ecclesiastical benefices, to advance and lend any sum or sums of money of which they have the power of disposing in order to aid and assist the several purposes of this Act, for the building, rebuilding, repairing, or purchasing of any houses or buildings for the habitation or convenience of the clergy, or sites for such houses and buildings, upon benefices in the patronage of such Colleges or Halls respectively, upon the mortgage and security directed by this Act for the repayment of the principal, without taking any interest for the same.

Colleges &c. may advance money interest-free for Houses upon Benefices in their patronage.

1 & 2 VICT., Cap. CVI.

An Act to abridge the holding of Benefices in Plurality, and to make better provision for the Residence of the Clergy.

37. And be it enacted, that no spiritual person, being Head Ruler of any College or Hall within either of the Universities of Oxford or Cambridge, or being Warden of the University of Durham, or being Head Master of Eton, Winchester, or Westminster School, or Principal or any Professor of the East India College, having been appointed such Principal or Professor before the time of the passing of this Act, and not having respectively more than one benefice with cure of souls, shall be liable to any of the penalties or forfeitures in this Act contained for or on account of non-residence on any benefice [d]. Certain persons exempt from penalties for non-residence.

38. And be it enacted, that no spiritual person being Dean of any Cathedral or Collegiate Church, during such time as he shall reside upon his Deanery, and no spiritual person having or holding any Professorship or any public Readership in either of the said Universities, while actually resident within the precincts of the University and reading Lectures therein, (provided always that a Certificate under the hand of the Vice-Chancellor or Warden of the University, stating the fact of such residence and of the due performance of such duties, shall in every such case be transmitted to the Bishop of the diocese wherein the benefice held by such spiritual person is situate within six weeks after the thirty first day of December in each year,) . . . . and no spiritual person being Provost of Eton College, or Warden of Winchester College, or Master of the Charter House, or Principal of Saint David's College, or Principal of King's College, London, during the time for which he may be required to reside and shall actually reside therein respectively, shall be liable to any of the penalties or forfeitures in this Act contained for or on account of non-residence on any benefice for the time in any year during which he shall be so as aforesaid resident, Privileges for temporary non-residence.

[d] See however 13 & 14 Vict., c. 98, s. 6.

engaged, or performing duties, as the case may be; but every such spiritual person shall, with respect to residence on a benefice under this Act, be entitled to account the time in any year during which he shall be so as aforesaid resident, engaged, or performing duties, as the case may be, as if he had legally resided during the same time on some other benefice; any thing in this Act contained to the contrary notwithstanding.

<small>Performance of Cathedral duties &c. may be accounted as residence, under certain restrictions.</small>

39. And be it enacted, that it shall be lawful for any spiritual person, being Prebendary, Canon, Priest Vicar, Vicar Choral, or Minor Canon in any Cathedral or Collegiate Church, or being a Fellow of one of the said Colleges of Eton or Winchester, who shall reside and perform the duties of such office during the period for which he shall be required to reside and perform such duties by the charter or statutes of such Cathedral or Collegiate Church or College, as the case may be, to account such residence as if he had resided on some benefice: provided always, that nothing herein contained shall be construed to permit or allow any such Prebendary, Canon, Priest Vicar, Vicar Choral, Minor Canon, or Fellow to be absent from any benefice on account of such residence and performance of duty for more than five months altogether in any one year, including the time of such residence on his prebend, canonry, vicarage, or fellowship: provided also, that it shall be lawful for any spiritual person having or holding any such office in any Cathedral or Collegiate Church or College in which the year for the purposes of residence is accounted to commence at any other period than the first of January, and who may keep the periods of residence required for two successive years at such Cathedral or Collegiate Church or College, in whole or in part, between the first of January and the thirty-first of December in any one year, to account such residence, although exceeding five months in the year, as reckoned from the first of January to the thirty-first of December, as if he had resided on some benefice, any thing in this Act contained to the contrary notwithstanding.

[Section 62 enacts, that on the avoidance of any benefice not having a fit house of residence the Bishop shall raise money, not exceeding four years' net income of the benefice, by mortgage of the glebe &c. for thirty-five years, for the purpose of building and repairing; and section 70 enables the Bishop in certain cases to raise money for purchasing a house, or land on which a house may be built, by mortgage in like manner.]

73. And be it enacted, that it shall be lawful for any College or Hall within the Universities of Oxford and Cambridge, or for any other corporate bodies possessed of the patronage of ecclesiastical benefices, to advance and lend any sum or sums of money of which they have the power of disposing in order to aid and assist the several purposes of this Act for the building, rebuilding, repairing, or purchasing of any houses or buildings for the habitation and convenience of the clergy upon benefices under the patronage of such College or Hall, upon the mortgage and security directed by this Act for the repayment of the principal, without taking any interest for the same. *Colleges in Oxford and Cambridge and other Corporate Bodies, Patrons of Livings, may lend any sum without interest, to aid the execution of this Act.*

2 & 3 VICT. Cap. XII.

An Act to amend an Act of the thirty-ninth year of King George the Third for the more effectual suppression of Societies established for seditious and treasonable purposes, and for preventing treasonable and seditious practices, and to put an end to certain proceedings now pending under the said Act.

[Section 1 repeals 39 Geo. III, c. 79, s. 27.]

2. And be it enacted, that every person who after the passing of this Act shall print any paper or book whatsoever, which shall be meant to be published or dispersed, and who shall not print upon the front of every such paper, if the same shall be printed on one side only, or upon the first or last leaf of every paper or book which shall consist of more than one leaf, in legible characters, his or her name and usual place of abode or business, and every person who *Penalty upon Printers for not printing their name and residence on every paper or book; and on persons publishing the same.*

Proviso.

shall publish or disperse, or assist in publishing or dispersing, any printed paper or book on which the name and place of abode of the person printing the same shall not be printed as aforesaid, shall for every copy of such paper so printed by him or her forfeit a sum not more than five pounds: provided always, that nothing herein contained shall be construed to impose any penalty upon any person for printing any paper excepted out of the operation of the said Act, either in the said Act or by any Act made for the amendment thereof.

As to books or papers printed at the University Presses.

3. And be it enacted, that in the case of books or papers printed at the University Press of Oxford, or the Pitt Press of Cambridge, the printer, instead of printing his name thereon, shall print the following words: "Printed at the University Press, Oxford," or the "Pitt Press, Cambridge," as the case may be.

No actions for penalties to be commenced, except in the name of the Attorney or Solicitor General in England, or the Queen's Advocate in Scotland.

4. Provided always, and be it enacted, that it shall not be lawful for any person or persons whatsoever to commence, prosecute, enter, or file, or cause or procure to be commenced, prosecuted, entered, or filed, any action, bill, plaint, or information in any of Her Majesty's Courts, or before any Justice or Justices of the Peace, against any person or persons, for the recovery of any fine, penalty, or forfeiture made or incurred, or which may hereafter be incurred under the provisions of this Act, unless the same be commenced, prosecuted, entered, or filed in the name of Her Majesty's Attorney General or Solicitor General in that part of Great Britain called England, or Her Majesty's Advocate for Scotland (as the case may be respectively); and if any action, bill, plaint, or information shall be commenced, prosecuted, entered, or filed in the name or names of any other person or persons than is or are in that behalf before mentioned, the same, and every proceeding thereupon had, are hereby declared and the same shall be null and void to all intents and purposes.

Former Acts and this Act to be construed as one Act.

6. And be it enacted, that the said Act, and all Acts made for the amendment thereof, except so far as herein repealed or altered, shall be construed as one Act together with this Act.

2 & 3 Vict. Cap. ix.

An Act to amend an Act of the seventh and eighth of King George the Fourth for building a new Gaol for the Town of Cambridge, and for making further provision for payment of creditors under the said Act.

11. And be it further enacted, that nothing in this Act shall extend, or be construed to extend, to take away, lessen, or diminish any of the rights, liberties, immunities, exemptions, franchises, and privileges of the Chancellor Masters and Scholars of the University of Cambridge, or any of the Colleges or Halls within the said University, any thing herein contained to the contrary in anywise notwithstanding. *Act not to affect Rights of the University.*

3 & 4 Vict. Cap. LXXVII.

An Act for improving the condition and extending the benefits of Grammar Schools.

[This Act empowers the Court of Chancery to make decrees for altering the system of education in any endowed school, and the right and terms of admission to it, and to establish schemes for the application of its revenues.] *Court of Chancery may order new schemes for endowed Schools.*

24. Provided always, and be it enacted, ... that this Act shall not be construed as extending to any of the following institutions; (that is to say,) to the Universities of Oxford or Cambridge, or to any College or Hall within the same, or to the University of London, or any Colleges connected therewith, or to the University of Durham, or to the Colleges of Saint David's or Saint Bee's, or the Grammar Schools of Westminster, Eton, Winchester, Harrow, Charter House, Rugby, Merchant Tailors, Saint Paul's, Christ's Hospital, Birmingham, Manchester, or Macclesfield, or Louth, or such schools as form part of any Cathedral or Collegiate Church. *Not to extend to the Universities, &c.*

3 & 4 Vict. Cap. CXIII.

An Act to carry into effect, with certain modifications, the fourth Report of the Commissioners of Ecclesiastical Duties and Revenues.

[The preamble of this Act recites, among other things, that the Commissioners in their fourth Report, dated June 24, 1836, " made certain recommendations touching Cathedral and Collegiate Churches."]

Canonry at Christchurch annexed to a Professorship instead of Canonry at Worcester.

5. And be it enacted, that in the Chapter of Christchurch in Oxford the first vacant Canonry, not being one of the two Canonries which are respectively annexed to Regius Professorships in the University of Oxford, shall immediately become and be permanently annexed and united to the Lady Margaret's Professorship of Divinity in the said University, and shall and may be held by the present and every future Lady Margaret's Professor of Divinity therein; and that upon such annexation as aforesaid the Canonry in the Cathedral Church of Worcester, which is now annexed to the last-mentioned Professorship, shall be *ipso facto* detached therefrom, and shall become vacant; and the Canonry secondly vacant in the said Chapter of Christchurch shall be subject to the provisions herein-after contained respecting the endowment of Archdeaconries by the annexation of Canonries thereto [a].

Two Canonries at Christchurch annexed to new Professorships in the University of Oxford.

6. And whereas Her Majesty has graciously intimated to Parliament Her Royal will and intention to found two new Professorships in the said University of Oxford, and it is expedient that the same should be competently endowed; be it therefore enacted, that the two Canonries in the said Chapter of Christchurch (not being either of them a Canonry annexed or to be annexed to any of the Professorships already founded in the

---

[a] By section 34, "any Archdeaconry may be endowed by the annexation either of an entire Canonry, or of a Canonry charged with the payment of" some "portion of its income .... towards providing for another Archdeacon in the same diocese, or with such last-mentioned portion of the income of a Canonry."

said University) which shall be thirdly and fourthly vacant shall, upon the vacancies thereof respectively, and the foundation of such Professorships respectively, become and be permanently annexed and united thereto, in such order as Her Majesty shall, in and by Her Royal Letters Patent founding such professorships, direct and appoint; and if either of such last-mentioned Canonries be vacant before the foundation of such Professorships, the same shall not be filled up until after such foundation; and after such annexation the said Canonries shall and may be held by the holders of such Professorships respectively for the time being: provided, that if the* Member of any College or Hall in the said University except Christchurch shall hereafter accept any Professorship to which a Canonry of Christchurch is or shall be annexed, he shall thereby cease to be a Member of such other College or Hall.

* *So in orig.* Read any.

7. And be it enacted, that, except as herein particularly specified, nothing in this Act contained shall in any manner affect or apply to the Cathedral Church of Christ in Oxford.

Act not to apply otherwise to Christchurch.

[Sections 4, 8–11, 13, and 14, direct the suspension of many Canonries.]

12. And be it enacted, that, so soon as conveniently may be, and by the authority herein-after provided, the two Canonries in the Chapter of the Cathedral Church of Ely which shall be secondly and thirdly vacant shall be permanently annexed and united to the Regius Professorships of Hebrew and Greek respectively in the University of Cambridge.

Two Canonries at Ely to be annexed to Professorships at Cambridge.

15. Provided always, and be it enacted, that the provisions hereinbefore contained respecting the suspension of Canonries shall not be construed to extend to the suspension .... of any Canonry in the said Chapter of Ely which may be annexed to any Professorship in the University of Cambridge, ... or of the Canonry in the said Cathedral Church of Gloucester which is annexed to the Mastership of Pembroke College in Oxford, or of either of the Canonries in the said Cathedral Church of Rochester which are respectively annexed to the Provostship of Oriel College in Oxford and to the Archdeaconry of Rochester, or of the Canonry in the said Cathedral Church of Norwich which is annexed to the Mastership of Catherine Hall in Cambridge.

Canonries annexed to certain Professorships and Headships of Colleges not to be suspended.

Qualification of Deans, Archdeacons, and Canons.

27. And be it enacted, that no person shall hereafter be capable of receiving the appointment of Dean, Archdeacon, or Canon until he shall have been six years complete in Priest's Orders, except in the case of a Canonry annexed to any Professorship, Headship, or other office in any University.

Exercise of Patronage of Chapters.

44. And be it enacted, that, upon the vacancy of any benefice in the patronage of the Chapter of any Cathedral or Collegiate Church, the Chapter shall present or nominate thereto either a Member of such Chapter, or one of the Archdeacons of the diocese, or a non-residentiary Prebendary or Honorary Canon, as the case may be, or any spiritual person who shall have served for five years at the least in the office of Minor Canon or Lecturer of the same Church, or of Master of the Grammar or other School (if any) attached to or connected with such Church, or as Incumbent or Curate in the same diocese, or as Public Tutor in either of the Universities of Oxford and Cambridge, ... and that every such office of Minor Canon, Lecturer, Schoolmaster, Professor, Reader, Lecturer, or Tutor shall immediately upon the expiration of one year from the time of his institution to such benefice, if not previously resigned, become and be vacant.

[Section 51 enacts, that all estates of non-residentiary Prebends and of certain other Dignities and Offices in Cathedral or Collegiate Churches shall be vested in the Ecclesiastical Commissioners for England:] provided always, that nothing herein contained shall in any manner apply to or affect any Dignity, Office, or Prebend which is permanently annexed to any Bishoprick, Archdeaconry, Professorship, or Lectureship, or to any School or the Mastership thereof, or the Prebends of Burgham, Bursalis, Exceit, and Wyndham in the Cathedral Church of Chichester.

Benefices annexed to Headships of Colleges may be sold.

69. And be it enacted, that, so soon as conveniently may be, and by the authority herein-after provided, such arrangements may be made with respect to benefices which are annexed by Act of Parliament or otherwise to the Headships of Colleges in the Universities of Oxford and Cambridge, as may enable the respective Colleges, if they shall think fit, to sell, or themselves to purchase, the advowsons of such

benefices, and to invest the proceeds in proper securities with provisions for the payment of the interest and annual profits thereof to the respective Heads of the Colleges for the time being; and that, upon the completion of the said arrangements respectively, the existing Incumbents of such benefices respectively shall be at liberty, upon resigning the same, to receive the interest and annual profits of the proceeds arising from such sales respectively.

70. And be it enacted, that, so soon as conveniently may be, and by the like authority, arrangements may be made to enable the University of Cambridge, if they shall so think fit, to sell the advowsons of the benefices annexed to the Regius Professorship of Divinity in the said University or any of them, and to invest the proceeds of any such sale in proper securities with a provision for the payment of the interest and annual profits thereof to the Regius Professor of Divinity for the time being; and that, upon the completion of the sale of any such advowson, the existing Incumbent of the benefice shall be at liberty, upon resigning the same, to receive such interest and annual profits. *Benefices annexed to the Regius Professorship of Divinity in Cambridge may be sold.*

71. And be it enacted, that, with respect to any benefice with cure of souls which is held together with or in the patronage of the holder of any prebend or other sinecure preferment belonging to any College in either of the Universities, or to any private patron, arrangements may be made by the like authority, and with the consents of the respective patrons, for permanently uniting such preferment with such benefice: provided, that this Act shall not apply to or affect any prebend or other sinecure preferment in the patronage of any College or of any lay patron in any other manner than as is herein expressly enacted. *Sinecure preferments may be annexed to benefices with cure of souls, with consent of Patrons.*

5 & 6 VICT. Cap. XIV.

An Act to amend the laws for the Importation of Corn.

14. And whereas it is expedient that the Inspectors of Corn Returns for the City of Oxford and the Town of *Universities of Oxford*

and Cambridge to appoint and remove Inspectors of Corn Returns for the said City and Town.

Cambridge respectively should, as heretofore, be appointed and removed by the Chancellors Masters and Scholars of the respective Universities of Oxford and Cambridge, and should perform, as heretofore, the duties of their respective offices, and that the Chancellors Masters and Scholars of the said respective Universities should have power to suspend such Inspectors respectively as herein-after is mentioned; be it therefore enacted, that the Chancellors Masters and Scholars of the Universities of Oxford and Cambridge respectively shall and they are hereby respectively authorized and required to nominate and appoint some fit and proper person to be the Inspector of Corn Returns for the City of Oxford and the Town of Cambridge respectively; and it shall be lawful for the said Chancellors Masters and Scholars respectively, from time to time as occasion may require, upon any misbehaviour or neglect of duty of any such Inspector, or for any other good and sufficient cause to them respectively appearing, to remove or suspend any such Inspector from his office; and, upon the death, resignation, removal, or suspension of any such Inspector of Corn Returns for the City of Oxford or Town of Cambridge, it shall be lawful for the said respective Chancellors Masters and Scholars, and they are hereby authorized and required, respectively to nominate and appoint some fit and proper person to succeed to the said office vacant by such death, resignation, or removal, or to hold the same during the continuance of such suspension (as the case may be).

No person dealing in corn, flour, or malt to be appointed Inspector or Deputy Inspector of Corn Returns for the Cities of London or Oxford or Town of Cambridge.

15. And be it enacted, that no person shall be eligible or shall be appointed to the office of Inspector or Deputy Inspector of Corn Returns for the City of London, or to the office of Inspector of Corn Returns for the City of Oxford or the Town of Cambridge, who, within six months next preceding the time of any such appointment, shall have been engaged in trade or business as a miller, maltster, or corn factor, or who during that period shall, as a merchant, clerk, agent, or otherwise, have bought corn for sale, or for the sale of meal, flour, malt, or bread made or to be made thereof; and if any Inspector or Deputy Inspector of Corn Returns for the City of London, or any Inspector of Corn Returns for the City of Oxford or the Town of Cambridge, shall,

during his continuance in such his office, engage in trade or business as a miller, maltster, or corn factor, or shall, as a merchant, clerk, agent, or otherwise, buy corn for sale, or for the sale of meal, flour, malt, or bread made or to be made therefrom, he shall in manner aforesaid be removed from such his office, and from and after the time of such removal shall become incapable of acting as Inspector of Corn Returns under this Act.

16. And be it enacted, that every nomination and appointment so to be made as aforesaid of any Inspector of Corn Returns for the City of London, or of any Inspector of Corn Returns for the City of Oxford or the Town of Cambridge, shall be enrolled at the next Session of the Peace to be holden in and for such City or Town; and the said enrolment, or a copy thereof, certified under the hand of the Clerk of the Peace for the said City of London, or under the hand of the Town Clerk of the said City of Oxford, or of the Town Clerk of the said Town of Cambridge, as the case may be, to be a true copy, shall for all intents and purposes be, and be deemed and taken to be, good and conclusive evidence of any such appointment as aforesaid having been duly made. *Appointments of Inspectors for London, Oxford, and Cambridge to be enrolled.*

19. And be it enacted, that the Comptroller and Deputy Comptroller of Corn Returns, and the Inspectors of Corn Returns for the City of London, the City of Oxford, and the Town of Cambridge respectively, who at or immediately before the passing of this Act shall respectively hold such offices or appointments under and by virtue of the said recited Act of the ninth year of the reign of His late Majesty King George the Fourth, shall and they are hereby authorized and required respectively, without further appointment, to hold and forthwith to act in such their offices or appointments under and by virtue of this present Act, and to discharge the several duties of and belonging to such their former offices or appointments, in such and the same manner, and as fully and effectually, to all intents and purposes, as if they had been respectively appointed to such their offices or appointments as aforesaid under and by virtue of this present Act. *The present Comptroller, Deputy Comptroller, and Inspectors of Corn Returns for London, Oxford, and Cambridge to continue in office.*

5 & 6 Vict. Cap. XXXV.

An Act for granting to Her Majesty duties on profits arising from Property, Professions, Trades, and Offices, until the sixth day of April one thousand eight hundred and forty five[f].

[Section 60 is immediately followed by Rules for assessing and charging the duties payable under Schedule (A) for all lands, tenements, and hereditaments, or heritages in Great Britain, in respect of the property thereof. *No. V* comprises *Particular Deductions and Allowances in respect of the Duties under Schedule (A)*, of which the Third is as follows:]

Deductions.

Repairs of Chancels. For repairs of Collegiate Churches and Chapels, and Chancels of Churches, or of any College or Hall in any of the Universities of Great Britain, by any Ecclesiastical or Collegiate Body, Rector, Vicar, or other person bound to repair the same, on an average of twenty one years preceding as aforesaid, or as nearly thereto as can be produced.

* * * * *

Allowances to Ecclesiastical Bodies &c., how to be made. Provided always, that the Allowances to be granted in pursuance of the .... Third case may be granted to the Ecclesiastical or Collegiate Body, Rector, Vicar, or other person aforesaid liable to the charges therein mentioned, in one sum, either by deducting the same from the Assessment upon him (if any), or by Certificate.

[Section 61 is immediately followed by]

No. VI. Allowances to be made in respect of the said Duties in Schedule (A).

Allowances for Colleges and Halls in Universities. For the Duties charged on any College or Hall in any of the Universities of Great Britain, in respect of the public buildings and offices belonging to such College or Hall, and not occupied by any individual Member thereof or by any person paying rent for the same, and for the repairs of the public buildings and offices of such College or Hall, and the gardens, walks, and grounds for recreation repaired and maintained by the funds of such College or Hall.

[f] The portions of the Act here printed have not been altered by any subsequent Act. See the first note on 7 & 8 Geo. 4, c. 75.

5 & 6 VICT. Cap. XLV.

An Act to amend the law of Copyright.

8. And be it enacted, that a copy of the whole of every book, and of any second or subsequent edition of every book containing additions and alterations, together with all maps and prints belonging thereto, which after the passing of this Act shall be published, shall, on demand thereof in writing, left at the place of abode of the publisher thereof at any time within twelve months next after the publication thereof, under the hand of the Officer of the Company of Stationers who shall from time to time be appointed by the said Company for the purposes of this Act, or under the hand of any other person thereto authorized by the persons or bodies politic and corporate, proprietors and managers of the Libraries following, (*videlicet,*) the Bodleian Library at Oxford§, the Public Library at Cambridge, the Library of the Faculty of Advocates at Edinburgh, the Library of the College of the Holy and Undivided Trinity of Queen Elizabeth near Dublin, be delivered, upon the paper of which the largest number of copies of such book or edition shall be printed for sale, in the like condition as the copies prepared for sale by the publisher thereof respectively, within one month after demand made thereof in writing as aforesaid, to the said Officer of the said Company of Stationers for the time being; which copies the said Officer shall and he is hereby required to receive at the Hall of the said Company for the use of the Library for which such demand shall be made within such twelve months as aforesaid; and the said Officer is hereby required to give a receipt in writing for the

A copy of every book to be delivered within a month after demand to the Officer of the Stationers Company, for the following Libraries: the Bodleian at Oxford, the Public Library at Cambridge, that of the Faculty of Advocates at Edinburgh, and that of Trinity College, Dublin.

---

§ This provision for the Bodleian Library originated in an agreement made between Sir Thomas Bodley himself and the Stationers' Company, which was embodied in an Indenture between the Company and the University dated December 20, 1610, and was somewhat extended by an Ordinance of the Company made at Stationers' Hall January 28, 1612. See Arch. Univ. Oxon. WP, P, fasc. 11, 6; SEP, A, 27. It was enforced upon every printer by s. 33 of the Decree of the Court of Star Chamber concerning Printing made 11 July 1637 (Rushworth's Historical Collections, III, Append. 315); and again by 8 Anne, c. 21 (al. 19), s. 5; 15 Geo. 3, c. 53, s. 6; 54 Geo. 3, c. 156, s. 2.

same, and, within one month after any such book shall be so delivered to him as aforesaid, to deliver the same for the use of such Library.

Publishers may deliver the copies to the Libraries, instead of at Stationers' Hall.

9. Provided also, and be it enacted, that if any publisher shall be desirous of delivering the copy of such book as shall be demanded on behalf of any of the said Libraries at such Library, it shall be lawful for him to deliver the same at such Library, free of expence, to such Librarian or other person authorized to receive the same (who is hereby required in such case to receive and give a receipt in writing for the same), and such delivery shall to all intents and purposes of this Act be held as equivalent to a delivery to the said Officer of the Stationers Company.

Penalty for default in delivering copies for the use of the Libraries.

10. And be it enacted, that if any publisher of any such book, or of any second or subsequent edition of any such book, shall neglect to deliver the same, pursuant to this Act, he shall for every such default forfeit, besides the value of such copy of such book or edition which he ought to have delivered, a sum not exceeding five pounds, to be recovered by the Librarian or other Officer (properly authorized) of the Library for the use whereof such copy should have been delivered, in a summary way, on conviction before two Justices of the Peace for the county or place where the publisher making default shall reside, or by action of debt or other proceeding of the like nature, at the suit of such Librarian or other Officer, in any Court of Record in the United Kingdom, in which action, if the plaintiff shall obtain a verdict, he shall recover his costs reasonably incurred, to be taxed as between attorney and client.

Saving the rights of the Universities, and the Colleges of Eton, Westminster, and Winchester.

27. Provided always, and be it enacted, that nothing in this Act contained shall affect or alter the rights of the two Universities of Oxford and Cambridge, the Colleges or Houses of Learning within the same, the four Universities in Scotland, the College of the Holy and Undivided Trinity of Queen Elizabeth near Dublin, and the several Colleges of Eton, Westminster, and Winchester, in any copyrights heretofore and now vested or hereafter to be vested in such Universities and Colleges respectively, any thing to the contrary herein contained notwithstanding.

6 & 7 Vict. Cap. LXVIII.

An Act for regulating Theatres.

[Section 1 repeals, among other Acts, "so much of an Act passed in the tenth year of the reign of King George the Second for the more effectual preventing the unlawful playing of Interludes within the precincts of the two Universities in that part of Great Britain called England, and the places adjacent, as is now in force."

[By sections 5, 6, 7, and 9, Justices of the Peace are required to hold special Sessions "for granting licences to houses for the performance of Stage Plays," and to "make suitable rules for ensuring order and decency at the several Theatres licensed by them within their jurisdiction, and for regulating the times during which they shall severally be allowed to be open."]

10. Provided always, and be it enacted, that no such licence shall be in force within the precincts of either of the Universities of Oxford or Cambridge, or within fourteen miles of the City of Oxford or Town of Cambridge, without the consent of the Chancellor or Vice-Chancellor of each of the said Universities respectively; and that the rules for the management of any theatre which shall be licensed with such consent within the limits aforesaid shall be subject to the approval of the said Chancellor or Vice-Chancellor respectively; and in case of the breach of any of the said rules, or of any condition on which the consent of the Chancellor or Vice-Chancellor to grant any such licence shall have been given, it shall be lawful for such Chancellor or Vice-Chancellor respectively to annul the licence, and thereupon such licence shall become void. *Proviso for the Universities of Oxford and Cambridge.*

11. And be it enacted, that every person who for hire shall act or present, or cause, permit, or suffer to be acted or presented, any part in any stage play, in any place not being a patent theatre or duly licensed as a theatre, shall forfeit such sum as shall be awarded by the Court in which or the Justices by whom he shall be convicted, not exceeding ten pounds for every day on which he shall so offend. *Penalty on persons performing in unlicensed places.*

What shall be evidence of acting for hire.

16. And be it enacted, that in every case in which any money or other reward shall be taken or charged, directly or indirectly, or in which the purchase of any article is made a condition for the admission of any person into any theatre to see any stage play, and also in every case in which any stage play shall be acted or presented in any house, room, or place in which distilled or fermented exciseable liquor shall be sold, every actor therein shall be deemed to be acting for hire.

Proof of licence in certain cases to lie on the party accused.

17. And be it enacted, that in any proceedings to be instituted against any person for having or keeping an unlicensed theatre, or for acting for hire in an unlicensed theatre, if it shall be proved that such theatre is used for the public performance of stage plays, the burden of proof that such theatre is duly licensed or authorized shall lie on the party accused, and until the contrary shall be proved such theatre shall be taken to be unlicensed.

Interpretation of Act.

23. And be it enacted, that in this Act the word "stage-play" shall be taken to include every tragedy, comedy, farce, opera, burletta, interlude, melodrama, pantomime, or other entertainment of the stage, or any part thereof: provided always, that nothing herein contained shall be construed to apply to any theatrical representation in any booth or show which by the Justices of the Peace, or other persons having authority in that behalf, shall be allowed in any lawful fair, feast, or customary meeting of the like kind.

6 & 7 VICT. Cap. x.

An Act for making a Railway from the Great Western Railway to the City of Oxford.

Officers of the University of Oxford to have access to Railway Stations.

304. And be it enacted, that the Vice-Chancellor, the Proctors, and Pro-Proctors for the time being of the University of Oxford, and Heads of Colleges and Halls, and the Marshal of the said University, or other person or persons (provided such other person or persons shall have been deputed by writing under the hand of the Vice-Chancellor of the said

University for the time being, or of the Head or Governor, or, in his absence, the Vicegerent of any College or Hall in the said University), shall, at or about the times of trains of carriages upon the said Railway starting or arriving, and at all other reasonable times, have free access to every depôt or station for the reception of passengers proceeding by the trains upon the said Railway, and to every part thereof, and to every booking office, ticket office, or other office or place for passengers upon the said Railway, wheresoever such office or place shall be, and shall then and there be entitled to demand and take and have, without any unreasonable delay, from the proper officer or servant of the Company, such information as it may be in the power of any officer or servant of the Company to give with reference to any passenger or person having passed or applying to pass on the said Railway, or otherwise coming to or being in or upon the said depôt or station or place, who shall be a Member of the said University or suspected of being such; and in case the said Company, or their officers, or servants, or any of them, shall not permit such free access to the said depôts or stations as aforesaid, or shall not furnish such information as hereinbefore mentioned, the said officer or servant of the said Company shall for each default forfeit and pay a sum not exceeding five pounds.

305. And be it enacted, that if the said Vice-Chancellor or Proctors or Pro-Proctors for the time being of the said University, or Heads of Colleges and Halls, or the Marshal of the said University, or other person or persons deputed as aforesaid, shall, at any time or times previous to the starting of any train of carriages upon the said Railway, notify to the proper officer, book-keeper, or servant of the said Company that any person or persons about to travel in or upon the said Railway is a Member of the University not having taken the degree of Master of Arts or Bachelor in Civil Law, and shall identify such Member to such proper officer, book-keeper, or servant of the Company at the time of giving such notice, and require such officer, book-keeper, or servant to decline to take such Member of the University as a passenger upon the said Railway, the proper officer, book-keeper, or servant of the said Company shall immediately thereupon, and for the space *Company not to convey such Members of the University as the said Officers of the University shall require them not to convey.*

of twenty-four hours after such notice, identification, and requirement, refuse to convey such Member of the said University in or upon the said Railway, and which he is hereby authorized to do, notwithstanding such Member may have paid his fare; and in case any such Member of the said University shall be knowingly and wilfully allowed to be conveyed thereon after such notice within the time aforesaid, the said Company shall for each passenger so conveyed forfeit and pay a sum not exceeding five pounds: provided always, that no Member of the University represented as such to the said Company, or any of their officers or servants, by the said Vice-Chancellor, Proctors, Pro-Proctors, Heads of Colleges and Halls, Marshal, or other person or persons deputed as aforesaid, or any of them, who shall be refused to be carried by the said Company, or by any of their officers or servants, shall on that account be entitled to claim or recover any damage or compensation from the said Company, or such officers, book-keepers, or servants, provided that, in case such Member shall have paid his fare, the same shall have been tendered or returned to him on demand.

Company to take up and set down Members of the University at appointed Stations only.

306. And be it enacted, that it shall not be lawful for the said Company to take up or set down any person or persons being Members of the University, but not having taken the degree of Master of Arts or Bachelor in Civil Law, on any part of the said Railway, except at the regularly appointed stations of the line; and in case the said Company shall take up or set down any such person or persons, except at such regularly appointed stations of the line, they shall forfeit a sum not exceeding five pounds for each such person so taken up or set down.

Saving rights of the University of Oxford.

308. And be it enacted, that nothing herein contained shall in any manner alienate, prejudice, alter, interfere with, or impede the exercise of any of the rights, privileges, or authorities whatsoever of the said University, or of any of the Officers, Ministers, or servants thereto belonging [h].

---

[h] The Acts for making the Railway from Oxford to Bletchley do not contain these or any similar provisions.

7 & 8 VICT. Cap. lxii.

An Act to enable the Eastern Counties Railway Company to make a Railway from the Northern and Eastern Railway at Newport by Cambridge to Ely, and from thence Eastward to Brandon and Westward to Peterborough.

184. And be it enacted, that the Vice-Chancellor, the Proctors, and Pro-Proctors for the time being of the University of Cambridge, with or without their servants, and the Heads and Tutors of Colleges and Halls, and the Marshal and the Yeoman Bedel of the said University, or other person or persons, provided such other person or persons shall have been deputed by writing under the hand of the Vice-Chancellor of the said University for the time being, or of the Head or Governor, or, in his absence, the Vicegerent of any College or Hall in the said University, shall, at or about the times of trains of carriages upon the said Railway starting or arriving, and at all reasonable times, have free access to every depôt or station for the reception of passengers proceeding by the trains upon the said Railway, and to every part thereof, and to every booking office, ticket office, or other office or place for passengers upon the said Railway, wheresoever such office or place shall be, and shall then and there be entitled to demand and take and have, without any unreasonable delay, from the proper officer or servant of the Company, such information as it may be in the power of any officer or servant of the Company to give with reference to any passenger or person having passed or applying to pass on the said Railway, or otherwise coming to or being in or upon the said depôt or station or place, who shall be a Member of the said University or suspected of being such; and in case the said Company, or their officers or servants, or any of them, shall not permit such free access to the said depôts or stations as aforesaid, or shall not furnish such information as herein-before mentioned, the said officer or

Officers of the University of Cambridge to have access to Railway Stations.

servant of the said Company shall for each default forfeit a sum not exceeding five pounds.

Company not to convey such Members of the University as the said Officers of the University shall require them not to convey.

185. And be it enacted, that if the said Vice-Chancellor or Proctors or Pro-Proctors for the time being of the said University, or Heads or Tutors of Colleges and Halls of the said University, or any of them, or any other person or persons deputed as aforesaid, shall, at any time or times previous to the starting of any train of carriages upon the said Railway, notify to the proper officer, book-keeper, or servant of the said Company that any person or persons about to travel in or upon the said Railway is a Member of the University not having taken the degree of Master of Arts or Bachelor in Civil Law or Medicine, and shall identify such Member to such proper officer, book-keeper, or servant of the Company at the time of giving such notice, and require such officer, book-keeper, or servant to decline to take such Member of the University as a passenger upon the said Railway, the proper officer, book-keeper, or servant of the said Company shall immediately thereupon, and for the space of twenty-four hours after such notice, identification, and requirement, refuse to convey such Member of the said University in or upon the said Railway, and which he is hereby authorized to do, notwithstanding such Member may have paid his fare; and in case such Member of the said University shall be knowingly and wilfully allowed to be conveyed thereon after such notice within the time aforesaid, the said Company shall for each passenger so conveyed forfeit a sum not exceeding five pounds: provided always, that no Member of the University represented as such to the said Company, or any of their officers or servants, by the said Vice-Chancellor, Proctors, Pro-Proctors, Heads or Tutors of Colleges and Halls, or other person or persons deputed as aforesaid, or any of them, who shall be refused to be carried by the said Company, or by any of their officers or servants, shall on that account be entitled to claim or recover any damage or compensation from the said Company, or such officers, book-keepers, or servants, provided that, in case such Member shall have paid his fare, the same shall have been tendered or returned to him.

Company to take up

186. And be it enacted, that it shall not be lawful for the

said Company to take up or set down any person or persons who shall be known to the Company or their officers as Members of the University, but not having taken the degree of Master of Arts or Bachelor in Civil Law or Medicine, on any part of the said Railway, except at the regular appointed stations of the line; and in case the said Company shall take up or set down any such person or persons, except at such regular appointed stations of the line, they shall forfeit a sum not exceeding five pounds for each person so taken up or set down. *and set down Members of the University at appointed Stations only.*

188. And be it enacted, that it shall not be lawful for the said Company to take up or set down any passenger or passengers at the Cambridge Railway Station, or at any place within three miles of the same, between the hours of ten in the morning and five in the afternoon on any Sunday, unless it should happen that any train usually arriving at or departing from the said station at or before the said hour of ten in the morning has been delayed by some unavoidable accident; and that for every person so taken up or set down the said Company shall forfeit a sum not exceeding the sum of five pounds, to be recoverable and levied by summary conviction and distress and sale before any Justice of the Peace for the County of Cambridge not holding any office in the said University; and that such Justice of the Peace shall have jurisdiction, whether the said person or persons or any of them shall have been taken up or set down within the Borough of Cambridge or the precincts of the said University, or at any place within the said County; the said forfeiture or penalty to be paid and applied to and for the benefit and use of Addenbrooke's Hospital, or other County charity that may in lieu thereof be hereafter from time to time declared for the purpose under the seal of the said University. *Company not to take up or set down passengers at the Cambridge Station between certain hours on Sundays.*

[Sections 189 and 190 contain provisions for protecting the springs and watercourses which supply the University and Town of Cambridge with water.]

191. And be it enacted, that nothing herein contained shall in any manner alienate, prejudice, alter, interfere with, or impede the exercise of any of the rights, privileges, or authorities whatsoever of the said University, or of any of the Officers, Ministers, or servants thereto belonging. *Saving rights of the University of Cambridge.*

9 & 10 Vict. Cap. XCV.

An Act for the more easy Recovery of Small Debts and demands in England.

[This Act provides for the regulation and establishment of County Courts.]

Not to affect the privileges of the Universities, or the jurisdiction of the Chancellors' Courts.

140. Provided always, and be it enacted, that nothing in this Act contained shall be construed to alter or affect the rights or privileges of the Chancellor Masters and Scholars of the Universities of Oxford or Cambridge respectively, as by law possessed, or the jurisdiction of the Courts of the Chancellors or Vice-Chancellors of the said Universities, as holden under the respective charters of the said Universities or otherwise.

9 & 10 Vict. Cap. clxxii.

An Act for making a Railway from Chesterford to Newmarket with a branch to Cambridge.

[Sections 33, 34, 35, 37, and 38 agree verbatim with sections 184, 185, 186, 188, and 191 of 7 & 8 Vict. c. lxii.][1]

11 & 12 Vict. Cap. LXIII.

An Act for promoting the Public Health.

Local Board of Health in Oxford and Cambridge to consist of Oxford and Cambridge Improvement Commissioners.

31. Provided always, and be it enacted, that nothing herein-before contained with respect to the appointment, selection, or election of any Local Board of Health, or member thereof, shall apply to the City of Oxford, or the parts within the jurisdiction of the Commissioners for amending certain Mileways leading to Oxford, and making improvements in the University and City of Oxford, the Suburbs thereof, and the adjoining Parish of Saint Clement, (which Commissioners

---

[1] By 9 & 10 Vict. c. cccxlv the Eastern Counties Railway Company is exempted from the Tolls levied under the Cambridge Improvement Acts, 28 Geo. 3, c. 64, and 34 Geo. 3, c. 104, and is required in lieu thereof to pay £1000 yearly to the Commissioners.

are herein-after called the Oxford Commissioners,) or to the Borough of Cambridge, or the parts within the jurisdiction of the Commissioners acting under an Act of the thirty-fourth year of the reign of King George the Third, for amending and enlarging the powers of a former Act of the same reign, for the better paving, cleansing, and lighting the Town of Cambridge, for removing and preventing obstructions and annoyances, and for widening the streets, lanes, and other passages within that Town (which Commissioners are herein-after called the Cambridge Commissioners); and if the City of Oxford, or the parts within the first-mentioned jurisdiction, become a district under this Act, the same shall be called the Oxford District, and the said Oxford Commissioners for the time being shall, within and for such District, be the Local Board of Health under this Act; and if the Borough of Cambridge, or the parts comprised within the jurisdiction secondly above mentioned, become a District under this Act, the same shall be called the Cambridge District, and the said Cambridge Commissioners for the time being shall, within and for such District, be the Local Board of Health under this Act.

34 Geo. 3, c. 104.

34. And be it enacted, that the Local Board of Health of every noncorporate district shall hold an annual meeting, and other meetings for the transaction of business under this Act once at least in each month, and at such other times as may be necessary for properly executing its powers and duties under this Act, and shall from time to time make bye laws with respect to the summoning, notice, place, management, and adjournment of such meetings, and generally with respect to the transaction and management of business by such Board under this Act: provided always, that no business shall be transacted at any such meeting unless at least one third of the full number of members be present thereat, except in either of the Districts to be called the Oxford or Cambridge Districts, in which cases business may be transacted if at least seven members be present: and all questions shall be decided by a majority of votes; and the names of the members present, as well as of those voting upon each question, shall be recorded; and the said Local Board shall at their first meeting under this Act, and afterwards from

Meetings of Local Boards of noncorporate districts, and regulation of business, &c.

time to time at their annual meeting, appoint one of their number to be Chairman for one year at all meetings at which he is present; and in case the Chairman so appointed be absent from any meeting at the time appointed for holding the same, the Members present shall appoint one of their number to act as Chairman thereat; and in case the Chairman appointed as first aforesaid die, resign, or become incapable of acting, another Member shall be appointed to be Chairman for the period during which the person so dying, resigning, or becoming incapable would have been entitled to continue in office, and no longer; and the Chairman at any meeting shall have a second or casting vote in case of an equality of votes; but nothing herein contained with respect to the appointment of Chairman shall apply to any District to be called the Oxford or Cambridge District, and in such Districts the Oxford or Cambridge Commissioners respectively shall appoint a Chairman as heretofore.

Water Rate.

93. And be it enacted, that whenever and so long as any premises are supplied with water¹ by the Local Board of Health for the purposes of domestic use, cleanliness, or drainage, they shall make and levy, in addition to any other rate, a water rate upon the occupier, except as herein-after provided; and the rate so made shall be assessed upon the net annual value of the premises, ascertained in the manner herein-before prescribed with respect to the said special and general district rates; and when several houses in the separate occupation of several persons are supplied by one common pipe, the respective houses shall be charged with the payment of water rates in the same manner as if each house had been supplied with water by a separate pipe: provided always, that in any District to be called the Oxford or Cambridge District the Local Board of Health, with the consent of the said General Board, may supply water to any Hall, College, or premises of the University within such District, upon such terms with respect to the mode of paying for such supply as shall from time to time be agreed upon between such

Agreements with Universities.

---

¹ By sections 75–80 Local Boards of Health are enabled to provide their districts with a supply of water, and to establish and maintain waterworks for that purpose.

University, or any Hall or College thereof, and the said Local Board.

105. Provided always, and be it enacted, that nothing in this Act shall be deemed to alter or interfere with the liability of the Universities of Oxford or Cambridge respectively to contribute in the proportion and manner specified in any Local Act under which the Oxford and Cambridge Commissioners respectively now act towards the expense of paving and pitching, repairing, lighting, and cleansing, under the powers of any such Local Act, the several streets, lanes, ways, alleys, passages, and places within the jurisdiction of such Commissioners respectively; and in case any difference shall arise between either of the said Universities and the Local Board of Health with respect to the proportion and manner in which the University shall contribute towards any expenses under this Act, and to which the University is not liable under any such Local Act, the same shall be settled by the General Board of Health: provided also, that all rates, contributions, and sums of money which may become payable under this Act by the said Universities respectively, and their respective Halls and Colleges, may be recovered from such Universities, Halls, and Colleges in the same manner in all respects as rates, contributions, and sums of money may now be recovered from them by virtue of any such Local Act. *[margin: Quota of Rates to be paid by the Universities, &c.]*

13 & 14 Vict. Cap. XCVIII.

An Act to amend the law relating to the holding of Benefices in Plurality.

[The Preamble recites the Act 1 & 2 Vict. c. 106.]

5. And be it enacted, that it shall not be lawful for any person appointed after the passing of this Act to the Deanery of any Cathedral Church to hold the office of Head Ruler of any College or Hall within either of the Universities of Oxford or Cambridge, or the office of Provost of Eton College, or of Warden of Winchester College, or of Master of the Charter House, together with his Deanry: provided always, that nothing herein contained shall apply to the Dean of *[margin: Deans of Cathedrals not to hold office of Heads of Colleges or Halls in the Universities.]*

the Cathedral Church of Christ in Oxford as Chief Ruler of the College there maintained.

Heads of Colleges in the Universities not to hold Cathedral preferments except in certain cases.

6. And be it enacted, that (anything in the said recited Act to the contrary notwithstanding) it shall not be lawful for any spiritual person, being Head Ruler of any College or Hall within either of the Universities of Oxford or Cambridge, or being Warden of the University of Durham, and also holding any benefice, to take after the passing of this Act and hold therewith any Cathedral preferment or any other benefice, or for any such spiritual person, also holding any Cathedral preferment, to take after the passing of this Act and hold therewith any benefice: provided always, that nothing in this Act contained shall be construed to prevent any such spiritual person from holding any benefices or Cathedral preferment permanently attached to or forming part of the endowment of his office.

13 & 14 VICT. Cap. xxxvii.

An Act for regulating the Markets and Fairs held within the Borough of Cambridge and at Reach in the County of Cambridge, and for enlarging the Market Place, and for rebuilding or altering the Guildhall of the said Borough, and for the improvement of the said Borough, and the better regulation of the Police within the same.

Saving rights of the University of Cambridge.

51. And be it enacted, that neither this Act nor the Acts incorporated therewith [k] shall be construed to alter or affect the rights or privileges, duties or liabilities, of the Chancellor Masters and Scholars of the University of Cambridge, as by law possessed under the charters of the said University or otherwise.

[k] With this Act are incorporated provisions of "The Lands Clauses Consolidation Act, 1845" (8 & 9 Vict. c. 18), of "The Markets and Fairs Clauses Act, 1847" (10 & 11 Vict. c. 14), of "The Commissioners Clauses Act, 1847" (10 & 11 Vict. c. 16), of "The Towns Improvement Clauses Act, 1847" (10 & 11 Vict. c. 34), and of "The Town Police Clauses Act, 1847" (10 & 11 Vict. c. 89).

14 & 15 Vict. Cap. XXXVI.

An Act to repeal the Duties payable on Dwelling Houses according to the number of windows or lights, and to grant in lieu thereof other Duties on Inhabited Houses according to their annual value.

[This Act imposes Duties on Inhabited Dwelling Houses worth the rent of £20 per annum, and provides, among other things, that such Duties shall be levied in accordance with the Rules for charging Duties on Dwelling Houses set forth in Schedule (B) annexed to the Act 48 Geo. III, c. 55. The fourth Rule in that Schedule is as follows: "Every chamber or apartment in any of the Inns of Court or of Chancery, or in any College or Hall in any of the Universities of Great Britain, being severally in the tenure or occupation of any person or persons, shall be charged thereto as an entire house, and on the respective occupiers thereof."] *Every separate apartment in Colleges and Halls to be charged with House Tax as an entire house.*

14 & 15 Vict. Cap. xcii.

An Act for repealing and amending the provisions of the Acts relating to the Navigation of the River Cam or Cham, alias Grant, between Clayhithe Ferry and the King's Mill in the Town of Cambridge; for altering the Navigation Tolls; for enabling the Conservators of the said River to sue and be sued in the name of their Clerk; for conferring additional powers; and other purposes.

[The first section of this Act repeals 1 Anne, st. 2, c. 11, and 53 Geo. III, c. 214, being the two former Acts relating to the navigation of the river.] *Former Acts repealed.*

14. That three persons to be nominated by the Chancellor of the University of Cambridge for the time being or his *Act to be carried into exe-*

cution by eleven Conservators.

Deputy, and the Heads of the Colleges of the said University for the time being or, in their absence, their Deputies, or the major part of them, five persons to be nominated by the Justices of the Peace for the said County of Cambridge, three persons to be nominated by the Council of the said Borough of Cambridge, to be from time to time nominated as by this Act provided, shall be Conservators for executing this Act; and such Conservators, and other the Conservators for the time being, whether appointed under the said recited Acts or this Act, shall be called "the Conservators of the River Cam in the County of Cambridge," and may and shall exercise the several powers by this Act conferred on the Conservators, and, subject to the provisions of this Act, they shall be the Conservators of the river within the limits of this Act, and shall have power to purchase and hold lands and to improve the said River within such limits, subject to the provisions and restrictions contained in this Act and the Acts incorporated herewith [1].

University to appoint three Conservators.

15. That it shall be lawful for the Chancellor of the said University or his Deputy, and the Heads of the Colleges of the said University for the time being or their Deputies, or the major part of them, to appoint three persons to be Conservators to represent the said University, and to act as such Conservators, from and after the first Tuesday in the month of June one thousand eight hundred and fifty-one, and every person who at the time of such appointment shall be a Conservator appointed for the said University shall be eligible for re-appointment.

How vacancies in University Conservators to be filled up.

16. That if the Chancellor of the said University or his Deputy, and the Heads of the Colleges of the said University for the time being or their Deputies, or the major part of them, shall at any time think fit to remove or change any of the Conservators for the time being appointed for the said University, or if any of such Conservators shall die, or become unfit for the service, or shall neglect or decline to act as a Conservator, it shall be lawful for the said Chancellor or his Deputy, and the Heads of the Colleges of the said University for the time being or their Deputies, or the major

---

[1] This Act leaves the number of Conservators the same as in 1 Anne, st. 2, c. 11, and makes no material alteration in the mode of choosing them.

part of them, from time to time, as occasion shall require, to appoint some other person to be a Conservator in the room of every Conservator who shall be so removed, or who shall so die, or become unfit or neglect or decline to act as a Conservator.

[Section 21 directs that there shall be six Auditors of the accounts of the Conservators.] *Auditors to be six in number.*

22. That one of such Auditors shall be the Chancellor of the University of Cambridge for the time being, or his Deputy; .... that one other of such Auditors shall be one of the Heads of the Colleges of the University, to be from time to time appointed by the Chancellor or his Deputy, and the Heads of Colleges in the said University or their Deputies, or the major part of them. *Appointment of Auditors.*

23. That the accounts of the Conservators, when audited under the provisions of this Act, shall be fairly entered into three several books to be kept for that purpose, one whereof shall be kept amongst the Evidences of the said University, one other among the Records of the Sessions of the Peace for the said County of Cambridge, and the other shall remain in and among the Records of the Sessions of Peace of the said Town of Cambridge; the which said books may be inspected and perused by any person or persons requiring the same, without any fee for such inspection; and if the Conservators shall omit to prepare and transmit such books or any of them, they shall be liable for every such omission to a penalty of twenty pounds. *Accounts, when audited, to be entered in three several Books.*

27. That so much and such part of the said River Cam or Cham, alias Grant, as lies within the following limits, that is to say, between a certain place called the King's Mill in the said Town of Cambridge and a certain place about seven miles below the said Town in the said River called Clayhithe alias Clayhive Ferry, shall be and be deemed to be the portion of the said River within the jurisdiction of the Conservators, and subject to the powers and provisions of this Act. *Limits of jurisdiction of Conservators.*

83. That if any owner or other person having charge of or employed in navigating any boat, barge, or other vessel upon the said River shall on any account or pretence whatsoever (except for the purpose of repairs on the said River, *Penalty for vessels or boats lying or making fast between the*

small Bridge and north-west Buttress of the Library of Saint John's College.

or during such repairs,) permit such boat, barge, or other vessel to stop and remain or lie in any part of the said River between the small Bridge which adjoins the south side of Queen's College in the University of Cambridge and the north-west buttress of the Library of Saint John's College in the said University, unless for the purpose of taking on board or landing passengers or goods, and during such time only as shall be necessary for those purposes, or shall in any manner damage, injure, or deface any part of the buildings, walls, bridges, walks, grounds, trees, hedges, gates, posts, pales, rails, or fences, or trespass upon any of the premises, belonging to any of the Colleges or Halls in the said University abutting upon or adjoining to any part of the said River, every such owner or other person so offending shall forfeit and pay for every such offence a sum not exceeding five pounds.

Vice-Chancellor invested with the power of Chancellor during his absence.

88. That it shall be lawful for the Vice-Chancellor of the University of Cambridge, or his Deputy, at all times hereafter, in the absence of the Chancellor of the said University, to do, perform, and execute all and every such Acts, powers, and things as the said Chancellor is by this Act authorized and empowered to do in case he was present, anything in this Act to the contrary notwithstanding.

This Act not to lessen the privileges of the University, or of the Mayor &c. of Cambridge.

89. That there shall always be reserved unto the Chancellor Masters and Scholars of the said University and their successors, and also unto the Mayor Aldermen and Burgesses of the Borough of Cambridge, and all and every person or persons, all and singular customs, tolls, duties, privileges, immunities, dockage, wharfage, and right of fishing in the said River within the limits aforesaid which they or either of them might lawfully have and enjoy before the passing of this Act.

[By the other sections, "The Lands Clauses Consolidation Act, 1845," the greatest part of "The Commissioners Clauses Act, 1847," and certain clauses of "The Railways Clauses Consolidation Act, 1845," are incorporated with this Act; directions are given respecting the meetings of the Conservators, and the appointment of Conservators; provision is made for investing surplus sums of money now in the possession of the Conservators, for vesting existing works in the Conservators, and for the continuance of deeds, engagements, actions, and rights, and of officers until removed, notwithstanding the repeal of the former Acts; the powers and duties of the Conservators are specified; they are enabled to make Bye-laws; regulations are made concerning Tolls and Toll Collectors; Masters of Boats are made accountable for damage done; penalties are imposed for assaults on Officers, and for injuries to toll houses or works; the Conservators are empowered "at any time and from time to time, as occasion shall require, to borrow on mortgage" of the Tolls, "for the purposes of this Act, any sum or sums of money not exceeding in the whole at any one time the sum of £3000;" and the Act is styled "The River Cam Navigation Act, 1851."]

16 & 17 VICT. Cap. LXVIII.

An Act to limit the time for proceeding to Election in Counties and Boroughs in England and Wales, and for Polling at Elections for the Universities of Oxford and Cambridge, and for other purposes.

1. The writ for making any election of a Member or Members to serve in Parliament for the Universities of Oxford and Cambridge .... shall hereafter be directed to the Vice-Chancellors of the said Universities .... respectively; and such Vice-Chancellors .... shall thereupon in due course of law proceed to election, and after such election certify the same, together with the writ, according to the directions thereof: all such writs hereafter to be issued, and all mandates, precepts, instruments, proceedings, and notices consequent upon such writs, shall be and the same are hereby authorized to be framed and expressed in such manner and form as may be necessary for carrying the provisions of this Act into effect. *Writs for Election for either University to be directed to the Vice-Chancellor.*

Writs &c. to be made conformable to this Act.

3. That the Act of the third and fourth Victoria, chapter eighty-one, be and the same is hereby repealed, and in every city or town being a county of itself, and in every borough, *Elections in cities, boroughs, &c., to be within six*

Days after the receipt of the writ, three clear days notice being given.

town corporate, port, or place, returning or contributing to return a Member or Members to serve in Parliament in England and Wales, the officer to whom the duty of giving notice for the election of such Member or Members belongs shall proceed to election within six days after the receipt of the writ or precept, giving three clear days notice at least of the day of election, exclusive of the day of proclamation and the day of election.

Polling at the Universities to continue for five days only.

4. At any election of a Member or Members to serve in Parliament for either of the Universities of Oxford and Cambridge the polling shall not continue for more than five days at the most, Sunday, Christmas Day, Good Friday, and Ascension Day being excluded.

Vice-Chancellors to appoint additional Polling Places, and appoint Pro-Vice-Chancellors &c. for conducting the Poll.

5. At every such election the Vice-Chancellor shall have power to appoint any number of polling places not exceeding three, in addition to the House of Convocation or Senate House, and to direct at which of such polling places the Members of Convocation and of the Senate according to their Colleges shall vote, and also to appoint any number of Pro-Vice-Chancellors, any one of whom may receive the votes and decide upon all questions during the absence of such Vice-Chancellor; and such Vice-Chancellor shall have power to appoint any number of Poll Clerks and other officers, by one or more of whom the votes shall be entered in such number of poll books as shall be judged necessary by such Vice-Chancellor.

16 & 17 Vict. Cap. CXXXVII.

An Act for the better administration of Charitable Trusts.

Not to extend to the Universities &c.

62. This Act shall not extend to the Universities of Oxford, Cambridge, London, or Durham, or any College or Hall in the said Universities of Oxford, Cambridge, and Durham, or to any Cathedral or Collegiate Church.

16 & 17 VICT. Cap. xxiii.

An Act for supplying the inhabitants of the University and Borough of Cambridge and other places adjoining thereto with Water.

[By section 4 a Company is incorporated by the name of "The Cambridge University and Town Waterworks Company."]

14. That inasmuch as the University of Cambridge is largely interested in the execution of the undertaking by this Act authorized, and it is expedient that the Heads of Colleges, Halls, and Houses and the Bursars and resident Fellows of Colleges, Halls, and Houses in that University should be empowered to participate in the management of the said undertaking, notwithstanding that they may be spiritual persons; therefore so much of any Act of Parliament as prohibits any spiritual person holding any cathedral preferment, benefice, curacy, or lectureship, or who shall be licensed or allowed to perform the duties of any ecclesiastical office, from acting as a director or managing partner of any association or copartnership, or from carrying on any trade or dealing in person, shall not (so far as regards the Directors named in this Act, or any Directors or Managing Partners of the Company who may hereafter be elected or appointed,) extend or apply to any Heads of Colleges, Halls, or Houses, or Bursars or resident Fellows of Colleges, Halls, or Houses, in the said University: provided always, that if any of the aforesaid spiritual persons being Directors or Managing Partners of the Company shall cease to be the Head of a College, Hall, or House, or a resident Fellow of any such College, Hall, or House in the said University, he shall thereupon become disqualified and incompetent to act as a Director or Managing Partner, and shall cease to be a Director of the Company.

Provision as to spiritual persons being Directors

50. That neither this Act nor the Acts incorporated therewith shall be construed to alter or affect the rights or privileges, duties or liabilities, of the Chancellor Masters and Scholars of the University of Cambridge, as by law possessed under the charters of the said University or otherwise.

Saving rights of the University of Cambridge

17 & 18 Vict. Cap. LXXXI.

An Act to make further provision for the good Government and Extension of the University of Oxford, of the Colleges therein, and of the College of Saint Mary Winchester [m].

[Sections 1–4 of this Act appoint Commissioners for the purposes thereof with powers to continue, if Her Majesty shall think fit, until January 1, 1858.]

Establishment of Hebdomadal Council.

5. Upon the fourteenth day of Michaelmas Term one thousand eight hundred and fifty-four, all powers, privileges, and functions now possessed or exercised by the Hebdomadal Board of the said University shall cease, and upon the fifteenth day of the said Michaelmas Term one thousand eight hundred and fifty-four there shall be elected in manner herein-after mentioned a Council, which shall be called the Hebdomadal Council, to which shall be transferred immediately after the election thereof all powers, privileges, and functions now possessed or exercised by the Hebdomadal Board of the said University.

Composition of Hebdomadal Council.

6. The Hebdomadal Council shall consist of the Chancellor, the Vice-Chancellor, the Proctors, six Heads of Colleges or Halls, six Professors of the University, and six Members of Convocation of not less than five years standing, such Heads of Colleges or Halls, Professors, and Members of Convocation to be elected by the Congregation herein-after mentioned of the said University, and the Chancellor, or in his absence the Vice-Chancellor or his Deputy, being a Member of the Hebdomadal Council, shall be the President of such Hebdomadal Council: provided always, that nothing herein contained shall

As to Heads of Colleges and Professors being returned or sitting as Professors, or Members of Convocation.

be held to prevent the Head of any College or Hall who is a Professor being returned or continuing to sit as one of the six Professors, or the Head of any College or Hall, or a Professor, being returned or continuing to sit as one of

---

[m] This Act is published entire at the beginning of "Ordinances and Statutes framed or approved by the Oxford University Commissioners," printed at the Clarendon Press in 1863.

the six Members of Convocation; and if any person shall be elected a Member of the Hebdomadal Council in two or more classes he shall, when he first takes his seat in the Council, declare under which class he desires to sit, and his seat for the other shall be forthwith vacated. *[Persons elected in two or more Classes to declare under which Class they will sit.]*

7. The Hebdomadal Council shall meet for the despatch of business on the fifteenth day of Michaelmas Term one thousand eight hundred and fifty-four. *[Date of meeting.]*

8. Of the six persons to be then elected together out of each of the classes of Heads of Colleges or Halls, Professors, and Members of Convocation, the three juniors of each class in academical standing, reckoned from matriculation, shall vacate their seats at the expiration of the third year from such day within the then current academical year as shall be named by the Hebdomadal Council in that behalf; and all the other persons to be then elected shall vacate their seats at the expiration of the sixth year from the said day; and all other persons elected from time to time, except such as shall be so elected upon casual vacancies, shall vacate their seats at the expiration of six years; and the election to supply the places of the persons so vacating their seats shall be made upon the day on which seats are vacated. *[Periodical vacating of seats.]*

9. All such persons whatsoever shall be capable of re-election. *[Members may be re-elected.]*

10. Any casual vacancy occurring by death, resignation, or otherwise among such persons shall be filled by the election of a qualified person, according to the directions of this Act; but the person so elected shall be subject to the same rules and conditions in all respects as the person to whose place he succeeds would have been subject to if no such vacancy had taken place. *[Filling up of casual vacancies.]*

11. If the Vice-Chancellor for the time being shall not be also an elected Member of the said Council, then, on the expiration of his term of office, he shall, in virtue of his late office, continue to be a Member thereof until the next triennial election, or for the space of one year if such election shall take place at an earlier period. *[Vice-Chancellor to continue a Member.]*

12. No Professor shall be ineligible for the said Council *[Professors eligible.]*

by reason of anything contained in the Statutes of his foundation.

Non-residence to create a vacancy.

13. If any of the Members of the Hebdomadal Council other than the Chancellor of the University shall reside for less than twenty-four weeks during Term time in any year, his seat shall at or before the close of such year be declared by the Vice-Chancellor and shall thereupon become vacant.

Vice-Chancellor to make Register of Congregation; also regulations respecting Hebdomadal Council.

14. The Vice-Chancellor shall, before the twenty-fifth day of September one thousand eight hundred and fifty-four, and before the same day in each succeeding year, make and promulgate a Register of the persons qualified to the best of his knowledge to be Members of the Congregation of the University of Oxford according to this Act, and shall also make and promulgate all such regulations as to the said Register, and as to all matters relating to the voting for, election, resignation, and return of Members of the Hebdomadal Council, as may be necessary for the assembling together of the Congregation and for the election and assembling together of the said Hebdomadal Council according to this Act, and for keeping the number of such Council complete, and shall appoint the time of the day and place at which they shall so assemble together; and if the Vice-Chancellor fails to comply with the provisions of this section, the Commissioners shall thereupon carry the same into effect, and thereupon make such regulations in respect of the matters aforesaid as they may think fit; and no persons shall be admitted to vote in the election of Members of the Hebdomadal Council but those included in such Register, and mentioned or described in the sixteenth section and the Schedule therein referred to.

Power to Hebdomadal Council to make rules for regulation of its own proceedings.

15. Subject to the provisions of this Act, and without prejudice to the rights of Congregation and Convocation in the making of Statutes for the University of Oxford, the Hebdomadal Council shall have power to make, from time to time, rules for the regulation of its own proceedings, and to revise the regulations and Register herein-before directed to be made by the Vice-Chancellor.

Composition of Congregation.

16. On and after the fifteenth day of Michaelmas Term one thousand eight hundred and fifty-four the Congregation of the University of Oxford shall be composed of the

following persons only, the said persons being Members of Convocation:
1. The Chancellor.
2. The High Steward.
3. The Heads of Colleges and Halls.
4. The Canons of Christ Church.
5. The Proctors.
6. The Members of the Hebdomadal Council.
7. The Officers named in Schedule (A) to this Act annexed.
8. The Professors.
9. Assistant or Deputy Professors.
10. The Public Examiners.
11. All Residents.
12. All such persons as shall be provided to be added by election or otherwise to the said Congregation by any Statute of the University approved by the Commissioners, or (after the expiry of the Commission) passed by licence of the Crown.

The Chancellor, or in his absence the Vice-Chancellor or his Deputy, shall preside in the said Congregation, and the Congregation so constituted as aforesaid shall have power to frame regulations for the order of its own proceedings, but subject to any Statute which the University may make in respect thereof. *Power to Congregation to frame regulations for its own proceedings.*

17. Every Statute framed by the Hebdomadal Council shall, after due notice of the contents thereof, be promulgated in Congregation, and shall also be proposed there for acceptance or rejection after an interval of seven days, or such other interval as the University by Statute may appoint, and if accepted by Congregation shall be, after an interval of fourteen days, or such other interval as the University by Statute may appoint, submitted to Convocation for final adoption or rejection as a Statute of the University. *As to promulgation of Statutes.*

18. Any Member of Congregation may, upon the promulgation of any such Statute, propose, in writing, amendments thereof to the Hebdomadal Council, which the said Council shall consider, and thereupon may adopt, alter, or reject. *Proposal of amendments.*

19. If after the promulgation of a Statute the said Council *If change made, Sta-*

shall make any change in it, it shall thereupon be promulgated afresh in manner aforesaid.

Congregation may speak in English.

20. The Members of Congregation shall upon the occasion of the promulgation of any Statute have the right to speak thereon in the English tongue, but without the power of moving any amendment, and subject to such regulations as the University may make by Statute for the due order of debate.

As to election of Hebdomadal Council.

21. Upon any occasion of electing Members of the Hebdomadal Council, every person entitled to vote in such election shall have the power of giving votes in each class as follows: for one vacancy, one vote; for two or three vacancies, two votes; for four vacancies, three votes; for five or six vacancies, four votes: provided always, that no elector shall give more than one vote for any one candidate.

Powers of Convocation retained.

22. The Convocation of the University of Oxford shall not, save as herein provided, be deprived of any of the powers by it now lawfully possessed.

University may provide that votes may be given by proxy at election of Chancellor.

23. It shall be lawful for the University to provide by Statute, if it shall think fit, that votes may be given either personally or by proxies, being Members of Convocation authorized by writing under the hand of the Member of Convocation nominating such proxy, at any election of a Chancellor of the University.

Certain oaths illegal.

24. Every oath directly or indirectly binding the juror—
- Not to disclose any matter or thing relating to his College, although required so to do by lawful authority;
- To resist or not concur in any change in the Statutes of the University or College;
- To do or forbear from doing anything the doing or the not doing of which would tend to any such concealment, resistance, or non-concurrence—

shall from the time of the passing of this Act be an illegal oath in the said University and the Colleges thereof, and no such oath shall hereafter be administered or taken.

Power to Vice-Chancellor to license Members of Convocation to open their residences

25. It shall be lawful for any Member of Convocation, of such standing and qualifications as may be provided by any Statute hereafter to be made, to obtain a licence from the Vice-Chancellor to open his residence, if situate within one mile and a half of Carfax, for the reception of students, who shall be matriculated and admitted to all the privileges of

the University without being of necessity entered as Members of any College or existing Hall; but no such licence as aforesaid shall be granted by the Vice-Chancellor until such regulations as are herein-after mentioned have come into operation. *for reception of Students;*

26. Every person to whom such licence is granted shall be called a Licensed Master, and his residence so opened as aforesaid shall be called a Private Hall. *who shall be called Licensed Masters.*

27. For the purpose of carrying into effect the objects proposed by this Act in relation to Private Halls, the University is hereby specially empowered, at any time before the first day of Michaelmas Term one thousand eight hundred and fifty-five, by Statute, to be approved as herein-after mentioned[n], to do the following things: *Power of University to make Statutes.*

 To fix the terms and conditions of granting licences to Licensed Masters, and the qualifications of such Masters:

 To make regulations for the government of Private Halls, the instruction and discipline of the Students therein, their attendance on Divine worship, and their status in the event of the withdrawal or suspension of the licence of any such Private Hall:

 To make provision for punishing neglect or breach of regulation on the part of a Licensed Master by the withdrawal or suspension of his licence, and on the part of any Students by such reasonable penalties or other punishments as they may think fit:

 To make provision for the aggregation of all or any Private Halls, with the consent of the Masters thereof, into one or more Great Halls of the University:

 To make provision for the appointment of one or more officers for the due execution of any regulation relating to the aforesaid matters, and, if considered expedient, for the appointment of any such officer Head of any such Great Hall for the better accomplishment of the said purpose:

 To fix the conditions upon which a Private Hall of the University may become an ordinary or Public Hall thereof.

[Section 28 enables all Colleges to alter and amend their

---

[n] That is, by the Commissioners first, and afterwards by Her Majesty in Council, according to the terms of ss. 35–37.

Statutes in various respects before the first day of Michaelmas Term 1855, subject to the approval of the Commissioners.

[Section 29 empowers the Commissioners to make Ordinances and Regulations, subject to the approval of Her Majesty in Council, for effecting the same objects in the case of any College which shall not before the day limited have exercised effectually the powers given in s. 28.]

Power of University to alter trusts.

30. And further, if, in the case of any gift or endowment held by the University which has taken effect for more than fifty years, it shall appear to the said University that the interests of religion and learning, and the main design of the donor, may be better advanced by an alteration of the trusts or directions affecting such gift or endowment, it shall be lawful for the University to alter or modify such trusts or directions, and to frame a new Statute for the application of such gift or endowment in such manner as may better advance the purposes aforesaid; but no such Statute shall take effect until the same shall have been assented to by the Commissioners under their Seal, and shall also have received the approbation of Her Majesty, to be signified by an order in Council.

[Sections 31–33 relate to Regulations or Ordinances which may be proposed by any College or by the Commissioners "for the abolition of any right of preference in elections to any emolument within any College now lawfully belonging to and enjoyed by any School or other place of education beyond the precincts of the University."

[Section 34 subjects Winchester College to the provisions of this Act.

[Sections 35 and 36 direct how Regulations and Ordinances of Colleges and of the Commissioners, "and every Statute passed by the University under the power lastly hereinbefore contained" (in s. 30), shall be laid before Her Majesty in Council, published in the London Gazette, and laid before both Houses of Parliament, and how they may ultimately become valid.

[Section 37 grants to the University in relation to Halls and Private Halls the powers before granted to Colleges with respect to themselves severally, subject to the approval of the Commissioners; and directs that, if the University fails to exercise them sufficiently before the first day of Michaelmas Term 1855, the Commissioners shall make Statutes for the purpose, subject to the approval of Her Majesty in Council.

[Section 38 states the objects which the Commissioners are to keep in view.]

39. Every Statute made by the University of Oxford, or by any of the Colleges thereof, by virtue of the powers of this Act, shall be subject to repeal or alteration in the same manner and to the same extent, but not otherwise, in and to which other Statutes of the said University or College, as the case may be, are or may be subject to repeal or alteration by the authorities thereof. *Power to repeal Statutes.*

40. Every Statute made by the Commissioners in pursuance of the provisions of this Act, and likewise all provisions herein-before contained, respecting the election, constitution, powers, and proceedings of the Hebdomadal Council, and respecting the constitution, powers, and proceedings of the Congregation, shall be subject to repeal and alteration by the University or College, as the case may be, with the approval of Her Majesty in Council. *Statutes by Commissioners subject to repeal, &c.*

41. For the purposes of this Act, the Cathedral or House of Christ Church in Oxford shall be considered to be to all intents and purposes a College of the University. *Christ Church deemed a College.*

[Section 42 bars vested interests after the passing of this Act.]

43. From and after the first day of Michaelmas Term one thousand eight hundred and fifty-four it shall not be necessary for any person, upon matriculating in the University of Oxford, to make or subscribe any declaration, or to take any oath, any law or statute to the contrary notwithstanding. *Not necessary to make declaration or take an oath on matriculating;*

44. From and after the first day of Michaelmas Term one thousand eight hundred and fifty-four it shall not be necessary for any person, upon taking the degree of Bachelor in Arts, Law, Medicine, or Music in the University of Oxford, to make or subscribe any declaration, or take any oath, any law or statute to the contrary notwithstanding; but such degree shall not as such constitute any qualification for the holding of any office which has been heretofore always held by a member of the United Church of England and Ireland, and for which such degree in the said University has hereto- *nor on taking certain degrees.*

fore constituted one of the qualifications, unless the person obtaining such degree shall have taken such oaths and subscribed such declarations as are now by law required to be made and taken on obtaining such degree, either at the time of taking such degree or subsequently.

[Section 45, relative to the Chancellor's Court, is repealed by 25 & 26 Vict. c. 26, s. 12.]

Stamp duties abolished.
46. The Stamp duties now payable on Matriculations and Degrees shall be abolished so soon as provision shall have been made by the University, to the satisfaction of the Lords Commissioners of Her Majesty's Treasury, in lieu of the monies heretofore voted annually by Parliament[o].

Powers of University to continue in force, except as altered by this Act.
47. Except in so far as they are expressly altered or taken away by the provisions of this Act, the powers and privileges of the University and its Officers, and of the Colleges and their Officers, shall continue in full force.

Interpretation of terms.
48. In the construction of this Act, the expression "University or College emolument" shall include all Fellowships, Studentships, Scholarships, Exhibitions, Demyships, Postmasterships, Taberdarships, Bible Clerkships, Servitorships, and every other such place of emolument payable out of the revenues of the University or of any College, or to be held and enjoyed by the Members of any College or Hall as such within the University; the word "Scholarship" shall include the Bursaries appropriated to any College in Scotland; and the word "School" shall include Colleges in Scotland; and the words "Professor" and "Professorship" shall be taken to include respectively Public Readers, Prælectors, and their several offices; and the words "Public Examiner" shall be taken to include Moderators and Masters of the Schools; and the word "Hall" shall be taken to mean all Halls other than affiliated Halls or such Private Halls as are authorized by this Act; and the governing body of any College shall mean and include the Head and all actual Fellows thereof, being Graduates, but in the case of Christ Church shall mean the Dean and Canons thereof; and the word "Residents" shall mean and include all Members of Convocation who shall have resided twenty weeks within one mile and a half of Carfax during the year that shall expire on the first day

[o] See 18 & 19 Vict. c. 36.

of September next preceding the making and promulgation of the Register as directed by the fourteenth section of this Act.

SCHEDULE A.

Deputy Steward.
Public Orator.
Keeper of the Archives.
Assessor of the Vice-Chancellor's Court.
Registrar of the University.
Counsel to the University.
Bodley's Librarian.
Radcliffe Librarian.
Radcliffe Observer.
Librarian and Sub-Librarians of University Libraries. } If authorized for the purposes of this Schedule by Statute of the University.
Keepers of University Museums and Repositories of Art or Science.

17 & 18 VICT. Cap. ccxix.

An Act to repeal an "Act for better regulating the Poor within the City of Oxford," and to grant further and more effectual powers in lieu thereof, and also to provide for rating to the relief of the Poor certain hereditaments within the University of Oxford.

WHEREAS by a certain Act of Parliament made and passed in the eleventh year of the reign of King George the Third, intituled An Act for better regulating the Poor within the City of Oxford, certain provisions were made for the maintenance, support, regulation, and employment of the poor of several parishes in the City of Oxford, (that is to say,) the Parish of All Saints, the Parish of Saint Aldate (with the Liberty of Grandpont in the County of Berks), the Parish of Saint Ebbe, the Parish of Holywell (otherwise called Saint Cross), the Parish of Saint Martin, the Parish of Saint Mary Magdalen, the Parish of Saint Mary the Virgin,

11 Geo. 3, c. 16.

the Parish of Saint Michael, the Parish of Saint Peter le Bailey, the Parish of Saint Peter in the East, and the Parish of Saint Thomas, under one Board of Guardians, consisting of the Mayor, Recorder, Aldermen, Assistants, Town Clerk, and Solicitor of the said City for the time being, and also of certain Guardians elected by the Ratepayers of the said several parishes in vestry assembled, and which said Guardians were thereby incorporated by the name of "The Guardians of the Poor within the City of Oxford:"

And whereas the said several Parishes have ever since been united for the relief and maintenance of their poor, and the poor thereof have been and are maintained, supported, regulated, and employed under and by virtue of the provisions of the said Act:

And whereas the said Act does not contain any provisions for the assessment of the University of Oxford in respect of the Colleges and Halls or other property of the said University to the Poor Rates authorized to be levied thereby, and the Members of the said University form a distinct and separate body, possessing many special rights and privileges, and particularly the privilege that in cases of taxation they shall be assessed by their own Officers, and not by the City:

And whereas the ancient sites of the several Colleges and Halls in the University have been reputed to be extra-parochial, and have hitherto been exempt from rates for the relief of the poor; but doubts have for some time past existed as to the validity of such exemption, and disputes have arisen between the said University and the said Guardians respecting the same:

And whereas, for putting an end to such disputes, it is agreed, by and between the Chancellor Masters and Scholars of the said University on behalf of themselves and of the Colleges and Halls herein-after mentioned, (that is to say,) the Colleges of All Souls, Balliol, Brasenose, Exeter, Jesus, Lincoln, New, Oriel (in respect of such part thereof as is comprised within the perambulations of the Parish of Saint Mary the Virgin), Pembroke, Queen's, Saint John Baptist (in respect of such part thereof as is comprised within the perambulations of the Parish of Saint Mary Magdalen), Saint Mary Magdalen, Trinity, University, Wadham, and Worcester, and the Halls of New Inn, Saint Edmund, Saint

Mary, and Saint Mary Magdalen, of the one part, and the Mayor Aldermen and Citizens of the City of Oxford, and the said several Parishes, by their present Guardians, of the other part, that the Board of Guardians for the said Union shall hereafter consist of the whole number of Guardians to be elected by or on behalf of each of the parties aforesaid in certain proportions herein-after mentioned; and it is further agreed by the parties aforesaid, that the rateable property in the said University and in the said Colleges and Halls shall hereafter be rated to the relief, maintenance, and employment of the poor of the said Union:

And whereas it is further agreed between the said parties, that for the purpose of carrying the said agreement into effect it is deemed expedient that the said recited Act should be repealed, and other provisions made instead thereof:

Be it therefore enacted by the Queen's most excellent Majesty, by and with the advice and consent of the Lords spiritual and temporal and Commons in this present Parliament assembled, and by the authority of the same,

1. That the said recited Act shall from and after the day on which this Act shall pass into a law be and the same is hereby repealed. *Recited Act repealed.*

2. That hereafter there shall be elected for the City of Oxford, the several Parishes herein-before mentioned, and for the said University of Oxford, and for the said Colleges and Halls therein, in manner herein-after mentioned, thirty-three Guardians of the poor; (that is to say,) eleven Guardians for the said City, who shall consist of the Mayor for the time being and the ten Aldermen of the said City for the time being; eleven Guardians for the said Parishes, one to be elected by each Parish; three Guardians for the said University, consisting of the Vice-Chancellor for the time being, and two other Members of the said University, being Graduates thereof; and eight Guardians to be elected by the said Colleges and Halls: provided nevertheless, that whenever the Mayor for the time being shall be one of the said Aldermen it shall be lawful for the Council of the said City to elect a Member thereof for such period as the said Mayor shall continue in office, in order to make up the eleven Guardians for the said City. *Election of Guardians of the Poor.*

3. That, with respect to the election of Guardians for the *Guardians for the*

Colleges and Halls, how elected.

Colleges and Halls in the said University, it shall be lawful for the Governor or Head and Senior Bursar of each of the following Colleges, (that is to say,) the College of All Souls, Balliol, Brasenose, Exeter, Jesus, Lincoln, New, Oriel, Pembroke, Queen's, Saint John Baptist, Saint Mary Magdalen, Trinity, University, Wadham, and Worcester Colleges, and for the Governor or Head of each of the following Halls in the said University, (that is to say,) New Inn, Saint Edmund, Saint Mary, and Saint Mary Magdalen Halls, to meet together in such place as the Vice-Chancellor of the said University shall for that purpose appoint on the third Thursday after the passing of this Act, or as soon after as conveniently may be; and the major part of the persons assembled for that purpose shall proceed to elect eight Members of the said University, being Graduates of the same, to be Guardians for such Colleges and Halls; and in case of an equality of votes in any such election the person presiding at the meeting shall have the casting vote; and the persons so elected shall continue to act and be Guardians for putting this Act in execution until the twenty-fifth day of March then next ensuing, or in case that day shall be a Sunday then until the day following, and from thence until other Guardians shall be elected in their stead; and in like manner the Governors or Heads and Senior Bursars of the said Colleges, and the Governors or Heads of the said Halls, shall meet on the said twenty-fifth day of March or the day following, as the case may be, and on the like day in every succeeding year, or as soon after as conveniently may be, to elect Guardians for such Colleges and Halls, to serve as such until the twenty-fifth day of March in the year next following, and from thence until other Guardians shall be elected in their stead [p].

Guardians for the University, how elected.

4. That, with respect to the election of Guardians for the University, it shall be lawful for the Chancellor Masters and Scholars of the said University, in a Convocation to be held on the third Thursday after the passing of this Act, or as

---

[p] By an order of the Poor Law Board, made January 15, 1863, with consent of the Dean and Chapter of Christ Church and of the Board of Guardians, under the Act for the relief of the Poor in Extra-parochial Places, 20 Vict. c. 19, s. 8, Christ Church was annexed to the Oxford Incorporation, and the Dean and Chapter were empowered to elect two Guardians annually in addition to the thirty-three provided by this Act.

soon after as conveniently may be, and afterwards annually on the twenty-fifth day of March, or in case that day shall be a Sunday then on the day following, or as soon after as conveniently may be in every succeeding year, to elect two persons, being Members of the said University and Graduates of the same, to be Guardians, together with the Vice-Chancellor for the time being, for and on behalf of the University, in putting this Act into execution, for the same time as Guardians for the Colleges and Halls are hereinbefore directed to be elected; and all Members of the University, being Graduates of the same, who shall be appointed Guardians under this Act, whether by and for and on behalf of the Chancellor Masters and Scholars of the said University, or by and for and on behalf of the said Colleges and Halls respectively, shall be Guardians to all intents and purposes, without showing or proving, or being liable to show or prove, any other qualification whatsoever. Qualification.

6. That on the third Thursday after the passing of this Act, or within ten days thereof, the rate-payers of each of the said Parishes, or any seven or more of them, who shall then by law have power to vote at a vestry meeting of the said Parish, shall and may meet in vestry, and elect one rate-payer of the said Parish to serve as Guardian, and represent the said Parish at the Board of Guardians, until the twenty-fifth day of March then next following, and from thence until another shall be elected in his stead, as hereafter mentioned; and on the twenty-fifth day of March in each and every year, or on some other day within ten days next after the said twenty-fifth day of March, the said rate-payers shall and may meet in vestry, and elect one rate-payer of the said Parish to serve as Guardian, and represent the said Parish at the said Board of Guardians, until the twenty-fifth day of March in the next following year, and from thence until another shall be elected in his stead: provided, that nothing herein shall be construed to prevent the said electors at such vestry meeting from re-electing any person, with his consent, who may have served the office of Guardian for the previous year; and provided, that no Member of the said University entitled to vote for any Guardian of any College or Hall shall vote at such election of Guardians for any of the said Parishes. Time when election shall take place.

Guardians a corporation.

24. With respect to the powers and authorities of the said Guardians, it is enacted, that the Guardians so elected and appointed as aforesaid shall be and are hereby declared to be incorporated, and shall for ever be one body corporate to all intents and purposes, and shall have a perpetual succession and a common seal, and shall be and be called "The Guardians of the Poor within the City of Oxford," and may sue and be sued by that name in all courts and places of judicature within that part of the United Kingdom called England, and by that name may and are hereby empowered to convey, assign, release, transfer, or dispose of any lands, tenements, or hereditaments, money, goods, or chattels, for the benefit and use of the said Corporation, as there shall be occasion.

Property in Parishes, in the University, and in Colleges and Halls to be valued.

29. And for the purpose of assessing the rateable property in the said several Parishes, and in the said University and the Colleges and Halls thereof aforesaid, it is enacted, that immediately after the passing of this Act, or as soon thereafter as conveniently may be, a valuation shall be made of the annual value of all lands, houses, and other property by law rateable to the relief of the poor, situate within the said several Parishes, and within the said University and the Colleges and Halls thereof aforesaid; and, for the purpose of making such valuation, the Vice-Chancellor of the said University (acting for and on behalf of the said University and of the said Colleges and Halls) of the one part, and the Guardians of the Poor elected or to be elected for the City and the several Parishes aforesaid of the other part, shall procure the Poor Law Board to appoint a valuer to value the same, and which valuer shall be paid for his labour and trouble in that behalf out of the first monies to be raised by virtue of this Act; and the said Vice-Chancellor shall appoint one person, and the said Guardians shall appoint another, to be paid by them respectively, to represent respectively the said University, Colleges, and Halls, and the said several Parishes, before the said valuer, and who shall attend and assist the said valuer in his valuation of the rateable property aforesaid; and the said valuer shall have full power and authority to receive evidence from either or both of the said parties, and to make a particular survey and valuation

of the whole of such rateable property or of any part thereof, if necessary, or if he shall think fit so to do; and the valuation to be made by such valuer shall be deemed binding and conclusive on the said University and the Colleges and Halls thereof as aforesaid, and on the several Parishes herein-before mentioned, until some other valuation of such properties shall afterwards be made in the manner aforesaid; and the like valuation shall be made from time to time at the end of every ten years, upon the requisition of either of the said parties: provided nevertheless, that if the persons so appointed to assist the said valuer shall themselves agree in the valuation of the whole or any part of the said properties without the interference of such valuer, such valuation shall be deemed valid, binding, and conclusive, as if the same had been made by the said valuer.

31. And whereas the said University, and the said Colleges and Halls thereof, claim that certain land and buildings within or appertaining to the same are exempted by law from being rated to the relief of the poor, and the Vice-Chancellor of the said University of the one part, and the Guardians of the Poor of the several Parishes aforesaid of the other part, have agreed that a case shall be stated (to be prepared by their respective solicitors, and settled, if there should be any difficulty or disagreement, by some barrister-at-law to be chosen by them for that purpose) for the purpose of obtaining the opinion of Her Majesty's Court of Queen's Bench whether by law the same, or any and which of them, are or ought to be exempt from being rated to the relief of the poor: be it enacted, that, upon such case being so stated as aforesaid, it shall be lawful for the said Court to receive and determine such case, although no appeal against any rate shall then be pending; and the decision of such Court thereupon shall be final and binding upon the parties aforesaid; and the costs attending the same shall be borne by the respective parties, and those incurred by the University, Colleges, and Halls shall be paid by them, and those incurred by the said Guardians shall, when duly taxed, be paid out of the funds under their control q. *Exemptions from rate claimed, how to be decided.*

q See Queen's Bench Reports, Ellis and Blackburn, viii, 184. Case of the Oxford Poor Rate.

Poor Rate.

32. With respect to the amount of Poor Rate to be made on the said several Parishes, and on the Colleges and Halls, and to that portion in the said University, it is enacted, that the Guardians shall, as often as occasion shall require, at special courts or assemblies to be called for that purpose, ascertain the sum which they shall judge necessary to be raised for the relief and maintenance of the poor of the said several Parishes, and for the other purposes of this Act, and shall, within three days after such sum shall be so ascertained and agreed upon, give notice thereof to the Vice-Chancellor of the University in writing, under the hand of the Chairman or Clerk to the Guardians, such notice to be delivered to the Vice-Chancellor or left at his place of abode; and which sum, together with the amount of the expenses of collecting the same, shall be raised by equal pound rates or assessments on the rateable property in the said several Parishes within the limits of this Act, and on the rateable property within the said University and the Colleges and Halls aforesaid, in manner herein-after mentioned.

How Rate to be assessed for the Colleges and Halls.

33. That the Vice-Chancellor of the University for the time being, for the purpose of assessing the rateable property within the said University, Colleges, and Halls as aforesaid, shall and he is hereby empowered and required from time to time, immediately on receipt of the notice from the Clerk to the Guardians or the Chairman of the sum required by the Guardians, and of the rate in the pound at which it is to be raised and levied, to rate and assess the several properties in the occupation of the University and the several Colleges and Halls aforesaid, according to the full rateable value of such properties, in such manner as rates are directed to be made under the Act of the sixth and seventh of

6 & 7 Will. 4, c. 96.

William the Fourth, Chapter ninety-six, intituled An Act to regulate Parochial Assessments, and, in and by the rates and assessments which shall be so made, to direct the time within which the monies to be raised thereby shall be paid to the Vice-Chancellor or to the University Bailiff for the time being, or such other person or persons as the Vice-Chancellor shall appoint to collect or receive the same; and the rates upon the Colleges shall be paid by the Bursars for the time being, or other Officers employed in or usually receiving the rents of their estates; and the rates upon the Halls shall be paid by the Principals of the said Halls for the time being; and in case of non-payment of the rates by any of the said parties within the time appointed, the same shall be recovered by the Vice-Chancellor for the time being, after demand made of such rate by the Bailiff or other person appointed to receive the rates, by distress and sale of the goods, chattels, and effects of the College or Hall or other party making default, or the same may be sued for and recovered by the Vice-Chancellor* Masters and Scholars of the University by action of debt in any of Her Majesty's Courts of Record at Westminster, or in the Courts of the said University; and the sums received from such rates shall be paid by the Vice-Chancellor of the University for the time being to the Treasurer of the Guardians on or before the expiration of eight weeks from the time that notice of the ascertainment of the sum required shall have been given as herein-before provided; and in default of payment of any such sum within the time herein-before limited for that purpose, the same, or such part thereof as shall be due and unpaid, shall and may be recovered of and from the Vice-Chancellor, or the Chancellor Masters and Scholars of the said University, by action of debt in any of Her Majesty's Courts of Record at Westminster, to be commenced and prosecuted by and in the name of the Corporation aforesaid.

* *So in orig.*

34. That in the making of any rate or assessment by the Vice-Chancellor as aforesaid it shall be sufficient to rate and assess the following parties; (that is to say,) the Chancellor Masters and Scholars of the University of Oxford in respect of the Clarendon Buildings and the University Press, the superintendents or other occupiers for the time being of the houses within the quadrangle of the Press, the occupiers for the time being of the houses and rooms of the Professors and others in the Botanic Garden, Ashmolean Museum, and in the Taylor Institution and University Galleries; and in the Colleges and Halls it shall be sufficient to rate and assess the Head of each College and Hall in respect of his house in or attached to the same; and in the Colleges to rate the Bursar for the time being (without further naming him) in respect of the rooms and other rateable parts of each College;

Who to be rated.

Inspection of University Rate.

35. That every rate or assessment that shall be made by the Vice-Chancellor of the University under the authority of this Act shall be signed by him, and shall be deposited with the Registrar of the University for the time being; and every such rate or assessment shall at all reasonable times be open to the inspection of every person therein rated or assessed, and of the Members of the several Colleges and Halls, who may take copies of or extracts from such rate or assessment.

Appeal against University Rate.

36. That if any College or Hall or other party charged or assessed by the Vice-Chancellor to any such rate or assessment shall feel themselves or himself aggrieved by any such rate or assessment, such College, Hall, or party shall state in writing the grounds of such dissatisfaction, and deliver the same to the Vice-Chancellor; and if the Vice-Chancellor shall refuse or omit to amend the rate, then such College, Hall, or party, after paying the amount charged in such rate or assessment, may, within two months after the making of such rate or assessment, appeal against the same to the Delegates of Appeal, to be appointed as herein-after mentioned.

Delegates of Appeal, how appointed.

37. That, annually, in the same Convocation which shall be held for the appointment of Guardians by the Chancellor Masters and Scholars as herein-before is provided, the Proctors of the University for the time being shall nominate persons, being Masters of Arts or of some superior academical Degree in the University, who shall be called " Delegates of Appeal in cases of Poor Rates," who shall have power to hear and determine throughout the year following all such cases of appeal as aforesaid, and their determination thereof shall be final.

Act not to affect the privileges of the University or City.

51. Provided that this Act, or anything herein contained, shall not be deemed or construed to affect or interfere with the rights or privileges of the said University, or with the rights and privileges of the said City of Oxford, except as in and by this Act is enacted.

[The remaining sections relate to the Elections of Guardians for the Parishes, the meetings, duties, and powers of the

Guardians, the appointment of Officers, the assessment and collection of the Poor Rate on the Parishes, Proceedings for Penalties, and possible Actions against Guardians or their Officers.]

18 & 19 Vict. Cap. XXXVI.

An Act to repeal the Stamp Duties payable on Matriculation and Degrees in the University of Oxford.

WHEREAS by an Act passed in the last Session of Parliament (chapter eighty-one) to make further provision for the good Government and Extension of the University of Oxford, of the Colleges therein, and of the College of Saint Mary Winchester, it was enacted, that the stamp duties then payable on Matriculations and Degrees should be abolished so soon as provision should have been made by the University, to the satisfaction of the Commissioners of Her Majesty's Treasury, in lieu of the monies theretofore voted annually by Parliament: and whereas by a Statute of the said University, adopted by Convocation on the thirty-first day of May one thousand eight hundred and fifty-five, provision has been made for the payment out of the University Chest of the salaries and allowances to certain Professors of the said University mentioned in the Schedule to this Act (being the same salaries and allowances as were theretofore annually voted by Parliament to the same Professors), and the Commissioners of Her Majesty's Treasury are satisfied that such Statute is a due provision in lieu of the monies theretofore voted annually by Parliament, as intended by said Act: be it enacted by the Queen's most excellent Majesty, by and with the advice and consent of the Lords spiritual and temporal and Commons in this present Parliament assembled, and by the authority of the same, as follows: [17 & 18 Vict. c. 81.]

1. All stamp duties payable under the Act of the fifty-fifth year of King George the Third, chapter one hundred and eighty-four, or under any other Act of Parliament, on the admission or matriculation of any person in the said [Stamp duties on matriculation and degrees in Oxford repealed.]

University of Oxford, and on the admission of any person to any degree in the said University (whether conferred in the ordinary course of the University or otherwise), or for the registry or entry of any such admission, shall from and after the said thirty-first day of May cease to be payable [r].

Salaries payable under University Statute not to be discontinued without consent of the Treasury.

2. No salary or allowance payable under the said Statute of the said University to any Professor mentioned in the Schedule to this Act shall be discontinued or reduced without the consent of the Commissioners of Her Majesty's Treasury.

SCHEDULE.

	£
To the Professor of Mineralogy	100
To the Professor of Geology	100
To the Professor of Experimental Philosophy	100
To the Professor of Chemistry	100
To the Professor of Modern History	371
To the Professor of Botany	182

19 & 20 Vict. Cap. XXXI.

An Act to amend the Act of the seventeenth and eighteenth years of Her Majesty concerning the University of Oxford and the College of Saint Mary Winchester [s].

[The first six sections of this Act give certain additional powers to be used during the continuance of the Commission under 17 & 18 Vict. c. 81.

[The 7th and last section is superseded by 20 & 21 Vict. c. 25, s. 4.]

---

[r] The Stamp Duties repealed by this Act were as follow. On matriculation of any person, £1. On admission of any person to the degree of B.A., for the register or entry thereof, if conferred in the ordinary course, £3, if by special grace, £5: on admission to any other degree, for the register or entry thereof, if conferred in the ordinary course, £6, if by special grace, £10.

[s] This Act is published entire at the beginning of "Ordinances and Statutes framed or approved by the Oxford University Commissioners," printed at the Clarendon Press in 1863.

19 & 20 VICT. Cap. LXXXVIII.

An Act to make further provision for the good Government and Extension of the University of Cambridge, of the Colleges therein, and of the College of King Henry the Sixth at Eton.

[The first four sections of this Act appoint Commissioners for the purposes thereof, with powers to continue, if Her Majesty shall think fit, until January 1, 1860 †.]

5. Upon the sixth day of November one thousand eight hundred and fifty-six all powers, privileges, and functions now possessed or exercised by the Caput Senatus of the said University shall cease, and upon the seventh day of the said month of November one thousand eight hundred and fifty-six there shall be elected in manner herein-after mentioned a Council, which shall be called the Council of the Senate, and which shall consider and prepare all Graces to be offered to the Senate, whether proceeding from individual Members of the Senate or from Syndicates, and no Grace shall be offered to the Senate without the sanction of the major part of those voting upon it in the Council. *Constitution of the University.*
Establishment of Council of the Senate.

6. The Council of the Senate shall consist of the Chancellor, the Vice-Chancellor, four Heads of Colleges, four Professors of the University, and eight other Members of the Senate, such eight Members to be chosen from the Electoral Roll herein-after mentioned, and such Heads of Colleges, Professors, and Members of the Senate to be elected by the persons whose names shall be on such Electoral Roll: provided always, that there shall never be more than two Members of the same College among such eight elected Members. *Composition of Council.*

7. The Vice-Chancellor shall, on or before Monday the thirteenth day of October one thousand eight hundred and fifty-six, and also on or before the second Monday in October in every year, cause to be promulgated, in such way as may *Vice-Chancellor to promulgate Lists of Members of Senate.*

---

† By 22 & 23 Vict. c. 34, s. 1, the powers of the Commissioners were continued until January 1, 1861.

to him seem expedient for the purpose of giving publicity thereto, a list of the Members of the Senate whom he shall ascertain to have resided within one mile and a half of Great Saint Mary's Church for fourteen weeks at the least between the first day of the preceding Michaelmas Term and the first day of the said month of October; and such list, together with the following persons, (that is to say,) all Officers of the University, being Members of the Senate, the Heads of Houses, the Professors, and the Public Examiners, shall be the Electoral Roll of the University for the purposes of this Act.

<small>Lists may be objected to and amended.</small>
8. The Vice-Chancellor shall at the same time fix some convenient time and place, not more than fourteen nor less than seven days from the time of such promulgation, for publicly hearing objections to the said List, which any Member of the Senate may make on the ground of any person being improperly placed on or omitted from the said List; and if any such objections shall appear to the Vice-Chancellor to be well founded, he shall correct the said List accordingly, and he shall thereupon sign and promulgate the said List, which shall thenceforth be the Electoral Roll for the year thence next ensuing, and until a new Roll shall in like manner have been promulgated.

<small>As to vacating of seats of Members of Council.</small>
9. Two of the Heads of Colleges, two of the Professors, and four of the other Members of the Council to be elected on the seventh day of November one thousand eight hundred and fifty-six, shall be elected to hold office for two years only, and shall vacate their seats at the end of two years; and the other Members of the Council to be then elected shall hold office for four years, and shall vacate their seats at the end of four years; and the election of the two Heads of Colleges, two Professors, and four other Members of the Council, who are to hold office for two years only, shall be made separately from the election of the other Heads of Colleges and Professors and other Members of the Council.

<small>For supply of periodical vacancies in Council.</small>
10. The places of the Members of the Council vacating their seats shall be supplied by a new election, to be made on the seventh of November or, in case the seventh of November should be Sunday, on the eighth of November in every other year, in the same manner as is herein-before

prescribed as to the election to take place on the seventh day of November one thousand eight hundred and fifty-six, save only that all Members of the Council to be then elected shall be elected to hold office for four years; and all Members so vacating their seats shall (if otherwise eligible) be capable of re-election. *Members vacating may be re-elected.*

11. Any casual vacancy occurring by death, resignation, or otherwise among the Members of the Council shall be filled by the election of a qualified person, according to the directions of this Act, upon a day not later than twenty-one days or sooner than seven days after such occurrence, to be fixed by the Vice-Chancellor and publicly notified by him; but if such vacancy shall occur during Vacation the occurrence shall be deemed for the purpose of such notice to have taken place on the first day of the ensuing Term; and the person so elected shall be subject to the same rules and conditions as to the tenure of office, and in all other respects, as the person to whose place he succeeds would have been subject to if no such vacancy had taken place. *As to filling up of casual vacancies.*

12. In all elections of Members of the Council every elector may vote for any number of persons, being Heads of Colleges, Professors, or Members of the Senate as aforesaid respectively, not exceeding the number of Heads of Colleges, Professors, or Members of the Senate respectively to be then chosen; and in case of an equality of votes for any two or more of such Heads of Colleges, Professors, or Members of the Senate respectively, the Vice-Chancellor shall name from amongst those persons for whom the number of votes shall be equal as many as shall be requisite to complete the number of Heads of Colleges, Professors, or Members of the Senate to be then chosen. *Votes of Electors.*

13. If any Member of the Council, other than the Chancellor or the Vice-Chancellor, shall have been absent from all the meetings of the Council during the whole of one Term, his seat shall at the close of such Term become and shall be declared by the Vice-Chancellor to be vacant. *Absence from meetings for a certain time to create a vacancy.*

14. If any Member of the Council shall become Vice-Chancellor, his seat shall not thereby become vacant; nor shall the seat of any Member of the Council become vacant by reason that after his election he may have become or may *Member of Council becoming Vice-Chancellor not to vacate seat.*

have ceased to be a Professor or a Head of a College: provided always, that if any of the eight Members of the Senate chosen from the Electoral Roll as aforesaid shall afterwards cease to be on the Electoral Roll, his seat shall thereupon become and be declared to be vacant.

Professors eligible.

15. No Professor shall be ineligible for the Council by reason of anything contained in the Statutes of his Foundation.

Vice-Chancellor to make regulations respecting Council.

16. The Vice-Chancellor shall, before the tenth day of October one thousand eight hundred and fifty-six, make and promulgate all such regulations as to the voting for, election, resignation, and return of Members of the Council, as may be necessary for the election and assembling of the Council according to this Act, and for keeping the number of such Council complete, and shall appoint the time and place at which they shall assemble; and if the Vice-Chancellor fails to comply with the provisions of this section, the Commissioners shall thereupon make such regulations in respect of the matters aforesaid as they may think fit.

Power to Council to make rules for regulation of its own proceedings.

17. Subject to the provisions of this Act, and without prejudice to the rights of the Senate in the making of statutes, regulations, and ordinances for the University of Cambridge, the Council shall have power from time to time to make rules for the regulation of its own proceedings, and to revise or alter the regulations herein-before directed to be made by the Vice-Chancellor, or, in the case of his failing to do so, by the Commissioners, and also to appoint Committees for the purpose of examining all questions referred to them by the said Council.

Date of Meeting.

18. The Council shall meet for the despatch of business on the eighth day of November one thousand eight hundred and fifty-six.

Who shall be President of the Council.

19. The President of the Council shall be the Chancellor, or in his absence the Vice-Chancellor, or a Member of the Council appointed by the Vice-Chancellor to act as his Deputy, or if at any Council duly convened and assembled neither the Chancellor nor the Vice-Chancellor nor any Deputy so appointed shall be present, then some Member to be chosen by the Members of the Council then assembled.

Quorum of Council.

20. No business shall be transacted in the Council unless

five Members at least be present; and all questions in the Council shall be decided by the majority of the votes of the Members present, and the President shall have a second or casting vote when the votes are equally divided: provided always, that in case of a difference of opinion between the Chancellor, or the Vice-Chancellor or his Deputy, and the majority of the Members present at any meeting of the Council, the question as to which such difference may exist shall not be deemed to be carried by such majority unless the same shall constitute a majority of the whole Council, but in such case the question shall be adjourned to the next meeting of the Council, and such adjourned question shall be finally decided by the majority of the Members of Council then present. *Questions in the Council to be decided by the majority.*

21. The Council shall nominate two qualified persons to the Senate, of whom the Senate shall choose one, in the manner heretofore accustomed, to fill every vacant office in the University to which the Heads of Colleges have heretofore nominated two persons to the Senate: provided always, that the persons nominated as aforesaid to the office of Vice-Chancellor shall be Heads of Colleges. *Council to nominate to offices.*

22. Every oath directly or indirectly binding the juror— *Certain oaths deemed illegal, and not to be administered.*

    Not to disclose any matter or thing relating to his College, although required so to do by lawful authority;

    To resist or not concur in any change in the Statutes of the University or College;

    To do or forbear from doing anything the doing or the not doing of which would tend to any such concealment, resistance, or non-concurrence,—

shall from the time of the passing of this Act be an illegal oath in the said University and the Colleges thereof, and no such oath shall hereafter be administered or taken.

23. Any Member of the University, of such standing and qualifications as may be provided by any Statute hereafter to be made, may obtain a licence from the Vice-Chancellor to open his residence, if situate within one mile and a half of Great Saint Mary's Church, for the reception of Students, who shall be matriculated and admitted to all the privileges of the University without being of necessity entered as Members of any College; but no such licence as aforesaid shall *Power to Vice-Chancellor to license Members of the University to open their residences for reception of Students.*

be granted by the Vice-Chancellor until such regulations as are herein-after mentioned have come into operation.

Hostels. 24. Every person to whom such licence is granted shall be called a Principal, and his residence so opened as aforesaid shall be called a Hostel.

Power of University to make Statutes as to Hostels. 25. The University, before the first day of January one thousand eight hundred and fifty-eight, may proceed to frame Statutes,

For regulating the terms and conditions of granting licences to Principals, and the qualifications of such Principals;

For the government of Hostels, the discipline of the Students therein, and their status in the event of the death or removal of any such Principal, or of the withdrawal or suspension of his licence;

For punishing neglect or breach of regulation on the part of a Principal by the withdrawal or suspension of his licence, and on the part of any Students by such reasonable penalties or other punishments as the University may think fit;

but no such Statute shall be of any force or effect unless and until it shall have been approved in the manner hereinafter mentioned ⁿ.

[Section 26 directs the Commissioners to frame Statutes for the establishment and regulations of Hostels, in case the University shall not have done so by January 1, 1858.

[Section 27 enables all Colleges to make Statutes for various purposes before January 1, 1858, subject to the approval of the Commissioners.

[Section 28 enables Colleges to make Statutes, before the same day and subject to the same approval, for the severance of Benefices from Headships.

[Section 29 empowers the Commissioners to frame Statutes, subject to the approval of Her Majesty in Council, for effecting the objects specified in s. 27 in the case of any College which shall not before the day limited have exercised effectually the powers given in that section.

[Sections 30 and 31 empower the University before January 1, 1858, and the Commissioners after that day, to

---

ⁿ That is, by the Commissioners first, and afterwards by Her Majesty in Council, according to the terms of ss. 26, 39, and 40.

frame Statutes, subject to the approval of Her Majesty in Council,

"1. for repealing, altering, or adding to any of the existing Royal Statutes of the University;

"2. or, in order to promote useful learning and religious education, and the main designs of the Founders and Donors so far as is consistent with these purposes, for altering or modifying the trusts, statutes, or directions affecting any gift or endowment held or enjoyed by the University, or by any Professor, Lecturer, Reader, Preacher, or Scholar therein, or the endowment of Lady Sadler for Lecturers in the several Colleges, or the endowment of the offices of Christian Preacher and Christian Advocate, or the endowment of William Worts for Bachelors of Arts."]

32. The University may provide by Statute that Members of the Senate may vote at any election of a Chancellor or High Steward of the University by proxy, such proxy being a Member of the Senate authorized by an instrument in writing signed by the Member nominating such proxy; but no Member shall be entitled to vote as a proxy unless the instrument appointing him has been transmitted to the Vice-Chancellor not less than forty-eight hours before the time appointed for holding such election of a Chancellor or High Steward, as the case may be; and such instrument may be in the form contained in the Schedule to this Act annexed.

[Sections 33–35 relate to Statutes which may be proposed by any College or by the Commissioners "for the abolition of any right of preference in elections to any emolument within any College now lawfully belonging to any School or other place of education beyond the precincts of the University."

[Section 36 enables Trinity College and the Dean and Chapter of Westminster respectively, with the consent of the Dean and Chapter of Christ Church on certain matters, to frame Statutes, subject to the approval of the Commissioners, as to the Scholarships in the College which have been annually appropriated to Scholars elected from Westminster School, and as to the studies to be prosecuted in the School, and the mode of electing the Head Master and Under

Master, and the conditions for holding Exhibitions to be established in Trinity College for persons elected from the School.

[Section 37 enables Pembroke College, with the consent of the Governors of St. Bees School, to frame Statutes, subject to the approval of the Commissioners, for converting the Grindal Fellowship and Grindal Scholarships in that College partly into open Scholarships and partly into Exhibitions, such Exhibitions to be given to meritorious scholars educated at that School and proceeding to any College in Cambridge.

[Section 38 subjects Eton College to the provisions of this Act.

[Sections 39 and 40 direct how Statutes made in virtue of this Act by the University, by Colleges, or by the Commissioners, shall be laid before Her Majesty in Council, published in the London Gazette, and laid before both Houses of Parliament, and how they may ultimately become valid.]

Statutes made by Queen Elizabeth in 1570 for regulation of the University repealed.

41. After the first day of January one thousand eight hundred and sixty the Statutes made by Queen Elizabeth in the year of our Lord one thousand five hundred and seventy for the government and regulation of the University, or such and so much of them or of any of them as shall be then unrepealed by any Statute made under the authority of this Act, shall be repealed, but not so as to revive any Statute of the University thereby repealed [x].

Power to the Chancellor to settle doubts as to meaning of University Statutes.

42. If any doubt shall arise with respect to the true intent and meaning of any of the new Statutes of the University framed and approved as aforesaid, or of any Statute which may hereafter be approved in the manner herein-after mentioned for amending or altering the same, the Council may apply to the Chancellor of the University for the time being, and it shall be lawful for him to declare in writing the intent and meaning of the Statute on the matter submitted to him, and such declaration shall be registered by the Registrary of the University, and the intent and meaning of the Statute as therein declared shall be deemed the true intent and meaning thereof.

[x] By 22 & 23 Vict. c. 34, s. 2, the repeal of the Statutes of Queen Elizabeth was deferred to January 1, 1861.

43. Every Statute made in pursuance of the provisions of this Act by the University, or by any College, or by the Commissioners, and likewise all provisions herein-before contained respecting the election, constitution, powers, and proceedings of the Council of the Senate, or respecting Hostels, shall be subject to repeal, amendment, and alteration from time to time by the University or College, as the case may be, with the approval of Her Majesty in Council. *Statutes to be subject to repeal &c.*

44. No person who after the passing of this Act shall become a Member of any College, or shall be elected or become eligible to any University or College emolument, shall be deemed or taken to have acquired or to possess an existing interest within the meaning of this Act. *Persons becoming Members not to possess vested interests.*

45. From the first day of Michaelmas Term one thousand eight hundred and fifty-six no person shall be required, upon matriculating, or upon taking, or to enable him to take, any Degree in Arts, Law, Medicine, or Music, in the said University, to take any oath or to make any declaration or subscription whatever; but such Degree shall not, until the person obtaining the same shall, in such manner as the University may from time to time prescribe, have subscribed a declaration stating that he is *bona fide* a Member of the Church of England, entitle him to be or to become a Member of the Senate, or constitute a qualification for the holding of any office, either in the University or elsewhere, which has been heretofore always held by a Member of the United Church of England and Ireland, and for which such Degree has heretofore constituted one of the qualifications. *Not necessary to make Declaration or take an Oath on Matriculating, nor on taking certain Degrees;*

46. From and after the first day of Michaelmas Term one thousand eight hundred and fifty-six it shall not be necessary for any person, on obtaining any Exhibition, Scholarship, or other College emolument available for the assistance of an Undergraduate Student in his academical education, to make or subscribe any declaration of his religious opinion or belief, or to take any oath, any law or statute to the contrary notwithstanding. *nor on obtaining any Exhibition, Scholarship, or other College emolument.*

47. The Stamp duties now payable on Matriculations and Degrees shall be abolished so soon as provision shall have been made by the University, to the satisfaction of the *Stamp duties on Matriculations &c. abolished.*

Commissioners of Her Majesty's Treasury, in lieu of the monies heretofore voted annually by Parliament[y].

<small>Colleges, with consent of Church Estate Commissioners, may sell estates, &c.</small>

48. It shall be lawful for any College, with the consent of the Church Estates Commissioners, to sell any estate in lands or hereditaments vested in such College, or to exchange any estate in lands or hereditaments for any other lands or hereditaments, or either of them, and upon any such exchange to receive or pay any money by way of equality of exchange; and all monies which on any such sale or exchange shall be received by or become payable to or for the benefit of such College shall be paid into the Bank of England, for the benefit of such College, to such account as the said Church Estates Commissioners shall appoint in that behalf; and the receipt of the said Church Estates Commissioners shall be an effectual discharge to any purchaser for any money therein expressed to be received, and shall be evidence of their consent as aforesaid; and all monies so paid into the Bank of England shall be applied in payment for equality of exchange as aforesaid, or shall be laid out by such College, with such consent as aforesaid, in the purchase of the absolute estate of freehold in other lands and hereditaments, or either of them, to be conveyed to the use or for the benefit of such College; and such lands and hereditaments, and any lands and hereditaments received in exchange by such College, shall be held by the College upon the like trusts and for the like purposes as the lands and hereditaments sold or given in exchange by such College respectively; and the monies from time to time remaining unapplied for the purposes aforesaid shall be invested, by and in the names of the said Church Estates Commissioners, in the purchase of Government stocks, funds, or securities, which the said Church Estates Commissioners shall hold in trust for such College; and the said Church Estates Commissioners may sell and dispose of the same for the purpose of effecting any such purchase of lands and hereditaments, or either of them, as aforesaid, or of paying money for equality of exchange as aforesaid, as occasion may require; and in the meantime the interest, dividends, and annual proceeds of such monies, stocks, funds, and securities shall be paid to such College

[y] See 21 & 22 Vict. c. 11.

to be applied to the same purposes as the annual income was applicable which arose out of those lands and hereditaments from the sale or exchange of which the money invested in such stocks, funds, and securities was produced: provided, that nothing in this section contained shall apply to any estate of the College in reversion in lands or hereditaments expectant upon any lease for lives, or for a term of years determinable upon any life or lives, or for a term of years whereof more than seven shall be unexpired, on which a rent less than three fourths of the clear yearly value of such lands or hereditaments shall have been reserved.

49. Except in so far as they are expressly altered or taken away by the provisions of this Act, the powers and privileges of the University and its Officers, and of the Colleges and their Officers, shall continue in full force. *Powers of University to continue in force, except as altered by this Act.*

50. In the construction of this Act, the expression "University or College emolument" shall include all Headships, Downing Professorships, Fellowships, Bye-Fellowships, Scholarships, Exhibitions, Bible Clerkships, Sizarships, Subsizarships, and every other such place of emolument payable out of the revenues of the University or of any College, or to be held and enjoyed by the Members of any College as such within the University; and the word "Professor" shall be taken to include the three Royal Professors of Hebrew, Greek, and Divinity, and Public Readers or Lecturers in the University, except the Barnaby Lecturers; and the Governing Body of any College shall mean the Head and all actual Fellows thereof, Bye-Fellows excepted, being Graduates, and in Downing College shall mean the Head, Professors, and all actual Fellows thereof, Bye-Fellows excepted, being Graduates; and the word "Statutes" shall be taken to include all ordinances and regulations of the University, and all ordinances and regulations contained in any charter, deed of composition, or other instrument of foundation or endowment of a College, and all bye-laws, ordinances, and regulations; and the word "Vacation" shall be taken to include that part of Easter Term which falls after the division of Term. *Interpretation of terms.*

51. The Lands Clauses Consolidation Act, 1845, except the parts and enactments of that Act with respect to the *Parts of Lands Clauses*

Act, 1845, incorporated herewith.

purchase and taking of lands otherwise than by agreement, and with respect to the recovery of forfeitures, penalties, and costs, and with respect to lands required by the promoters of the undertaking, but which shall not be wanted for the purposes thereof, shall be incorporated with and form part of this Act, so far as relates to land within the Town of Cambridge required for the erection of any buildings for the extension of the buildings of the said University, or of any College therein, and as if the corporate name of the University or College, as the case may be, had been inserted therein instead of the expression " the promoters of the undertaking."

[Section 52 enacts that the powers given by ss. 27–31 may be exercised, notwithstanding anything contained in any Act of Parliament, or any instrument of foundation or endowment.

[Section 53 enacts that elections in Colleges may be suspended by the Commissioners.]

SCHEDULE.

A. B., a Member of the Senate, doth hereby appoint *C. D.*, a Member of the Senate, to be the proxy of the said *A. B.* in his absence, and to vote in his name at the election of a Chancellor, *or* High Steward, *as the case may be*, for the University of Cambridge, on the   day of   next, in such manner as he the said *C. D.* may think proper. In witness whereof the said *A. B.* hath hereunto set his hand, the   day of

(Signature)   *A. B.*

19 & 20 VICT. Cap. xvii.

An Act to confirm an Award for the settlement of matters in difference between the University and Borough of Cambridge, and for other purposes connected therewith.

WHEREAS by a Letter bearing date the twenty-seventh day of December one thousand eight hundred and fifty-four, addressed to the Right Honourable Sir John Patteson, Knight, one of Her Majesty's most Honourable Privy Council, by the Chancellor Masters and Scholars of the University of Cambridge, and the Masters Fellows and Scholars, Masters and Fellows, Provost and Scholars, President and Fellows, and Master Professors and Fellows respectively of the several Colleges and Halls in the said University, and the Mayor Aldermen and Burgesses of the Borough of Cambridge, and sealed with their respective seals, after reciting, amongst other things, that differences had arisen and were still pending between them, they requested the said Sir John Patteson to hear them by their respective counsel, attorneys, agents, or witnesses, and to determine all the matters in difference between them; and they further respectively agreed with each other respectively to abide by and keep such Award as the said Sir John Patteson might make in writing concerning the premises, and to apply to the Legislature for an Act or Acts of Parliament, and to take all such steps as might be necessary for the purpose of making his Award valid and binding on each of them, or which he in his Award might think fit to direct to be taken by them or any of them respectively; whereupon the said Sir John Patteson accepted the reference thereby made to him, and was attended by the counsel, attorneys, and agents of the respective parties, and heard such arguments and perused and examined such documents, papers, and evidences as they thought proper to lay before him respecting the matters in difference, and, having maturely considered the same, made his Award in writing concerning the premises on the thirty-first day of August one thousand eight hundred and fifty-five: and whereas it is expedient to confirm the said Award, with certain variations made with the approbation of the said arbitrator; but the purposes aforesaid cannot be effected without the authority of Parliament: may it therefore please Your Majesty that it may be enacted, and be it enacted and declared by the Queen's most excellent Majesty, by and with the advice and consent of the Lords spiritual and temporal and Commons in this present Parliament assembled, and by the authority of the same, as follows; (that is to say,)

Preliminary.

Short Title. 1. This Act may be cited for all purposes as "The Cambridge Award Act, 1856."

Commencement of Act. 2. This Act shall, except in cases where it is otherwise expressly provided, come into operation immediately after the passing thereof.

Interpretation of Terms. 3. In the construction of this Act (if not inconsistent with the context) the following terms shall have the respective meanings herein-after assigned to them; (that is to say,)

"University," "Chancellor Masters and Scholars," "Senate," "Vice-Chancellor," "Proctors," "Pro-Proctors," "Registrary," shall respectively be understood to refer to the University of Cambridge:

"Borough," "Mayor Aldermen and Burgesses," "Council," "Borough Fund," "Mayor," "Bailiffs," "Aldermen," "Justices of the Peace," "Town Clerk," "Treasurer," "Clerk to the Justices," "Councillor," "Watch Committee," "Burgess," "Inhabitant," "Inspector of Weights and Measures," shall respectively be understood to refer to the Borough of Cambridge:

"Alehouse Licences" shall mean licences for keeping inns, alehouses, and victualling houses within the Borough:

"College" shall include every Collegiate Foundation and every Public Academical Hall now established or hereafter to be established within the University or within the limits and bounds of the Borough; and, when applied to a place and not to a body corporate, shall mean every building, room, and chamber within the University or Borough occupied or used by any Collegiate Corporation or Society, and the official residence of the Head or any other Member thereof, and all walks, grounds, gardens, and groves appertaining thereto:

"Municipal Corporation Act" shall mean the Act fifth and sixth William the Fourth, chapter seventy-six, and the respective Acts passed to amend the same:

"Improvement Acts" shall mean the Cambridge Improvement Acts, twenty-eighth George the Third, chapter sixty-four, thirty-fourth George the Third, chapter one hundred and four, and ninth and tenth Victoria, chapter three hundred and forty-five:

"Improvement Commissioners" shall mean the Commissioners acting in execution of the said last-mentioned Acts, or any one or more of them:

"Rates" shall mean all local and parochial rates, but shall not include the land tax or any other tax payable or to be payable to the Crown:

"Constabulary Force" shall mean the High and Chief Constables and the Police Constables of the Borough, and the Constables of the respective Parishes therein, but shall not include the Proctors or Pro-Proctors, or their servants respectively, or Constables appointed under the Act sixth George the Fourth, chapter ninety-seven.

4. The Mayor and Bailiffs shall not be required to take any oath or to make any declaration for the conservation of the liberties and privileges of the University. *Oaths. Oaths of Mayor and Bailiffs.*

5. The oaths required of certain Aldermen, Burgesses, and Inhabitants by the Letters Patent of King Henry the Third, dated the twentieth day of February in the fifty-second year of his reign, shall be abolished and not taken henceforth. *Oaths of Aldermen, &c.*

6. The power of the University exercised by the Proctors shall be continued as it now by law exists. *Proctors. Continuance of power of the Proctors.*

7. And whereas it is expedient that the Acts of the Proctors, Pro-Proctors, and their men, in the exercise of such power, should not be subject to any summary jurisdiction of Justices of the Peace; be it further declared and enacted, that the Proctors, Pro-Proctors, and their men are and shall be exempt from and not subject to the summary jurisdiction of Justices of the Peace under the Statute ninth George the *Exemption of Proctors from summary jurisdiction of Justices.*

Fourth, chapter thirty-one, or any other Statute, in respect of any act done or purporting to be done in the exercise of the authority of the Proctor, but without prejudice to the right of any person to proceed against the Proctors, Pro-Proctors, or their men, civilly or criminally, in any of Her Majesty's Courts.

Alehouse Licences.

Exclusive privilege of Vice-Chancellor abrogated.

8. The power of the Vice-Chancellor to grant alehouse licences within the Borough is hereby abrogated, subject to the provision herein-after contained with respect to certain of such licences, and saving to the Vice-Chancellor the same power as other Justices of the Peace may lawfully exercise.

Power to revoke Licenses.

9. The Justices of the Peace may at any time revoke any alehouse licence within the Borough, on the complaint in writing of the Vice-Chancellor, sent to the Clerk to the Justices, who shall forthwith upon the receipt of such complaint summon a special Session of the Justices of the Peace to consider the same, and give written notice of the complaint to the person complained of, in order that he may make his answer or defence at such special Session.

Existing Licences to continue in force for a limited period.

10. Every alehouse licence granted by any Vice-Chancellor, and now in force, shall so continue till the next general annual licensing meeting, unless such licence shall previously be revoked, on the complaint of the Vice-Chancellor, by the Justices of the Peace.

Wine Licences.

No money to be taken for Licences.

11. The power of granting wine licences within the Borough shall continue in and be exercised by the Chancellor Masters and Scholars of the University in the same manner as it is now exercised under ancient usage, and the provisions of the Statutes tenth George the Second, chapter nineteen, and seventeenth George the Second, chapter forty; but no sum whatever shall be taken by the University from the persons to whom wine licences are granted for or in respect of the grant of the same.

Power may be delegated to Vice-Chancellor.

12. The Chancellor Masters and Scholars lawfully can and may from time to time delegate to the Vice-Chancellor the power to grant wine licences, and it is not and shall not be necessary that they should be under the common seal of the University.

Weights and Measures.

Certain

13. All powers and authorities with respect to the supervision of Weights and Measures in the Borough (except

powers and authorities incidental to the office of Inspector shall be transferred from the University and its officers to the Justices of the Peace of the Borough. *Powers of University to be exercised by Justices.*

14. The Vice-Chancellor shall have authority from time to time to appoint an Inspector or Inspectors of Weights and Measures, and the Council shall have the like authority, provided that the Inspectors appointed by the Vice-Chancellor and the Council respectively have only concurrent power, and the University shall provide from its own funds for the remuneration of every Inspector appointed by the Vice-Chancellor. *Appointment of Inspectors.*

15. The privileges, powers, and authorities heretofore exercised by the University and its officers with respect to the Markets and Fairs of and within the Borough shall be abolished. *Markets and Fairs. Abolition of privileges of University.*

16. No occasional public exhibition or performance, whether strictly theatrical or not, other than performances in Theatres which are regulated by the Act sixth and seventh Victoria, chapter sixty-eight, shall take place within the Borough (except during the period of Midsummer Fair, or in the Long Vacation), unless with the consent in writing of the Vice-Chancellor and the Mayor, and every person who shall offend against this enactment shall be liable to forfeit a sum not exceeding twenty pounds, recoverable in like manner as penalties imposed by the said Act. *Public Exhibitions. Occasional public Exhibitions.*

17. The power of discommuning, by which Members of the University *in statu pupillari* are prohibited from dealing with such persons as have or shall have infringed or not complied with rules or decrees made from time to time by the authorities of the University, and publicly proclaimed, shall be continued: provided nevertheless, that notice shall be given to the person in respect to whom the power is proposed to be exercised, in order that he may attend, if he think fit, to show that the rules have not been infringed, or to explain the circumstances under which they have been infringed; and provided further, that the said power shall not extend to discommune any person for adopting legal remedies for the recovery of a debt without having given previous notice to the University or College authorities, or to the deprivation or suspension of a wine licence. *Discommuning. Continuance of discommuning power, with certain limitation.*

Conusance of Pleas &c.

Abolition of Conusance of Pleas in certain cases.

18. The right of the University or any officer thereof to claim conusance of any action or criminal proceeding wherein any person who is not a Member of the University shall be a party shall cease and determine.

Convictions of Members of the University.

Notice to Vice-Chancellor of certain convictions, &c.

19. As often as any Member of the University shall be convicted by any Justice of the Peace of any offence, a duplicate or copy of his conviction shall be forthwith sent by the Clerk to the Justices to the Vice-Chancellor; and in such case, and also in the case of any dismissal by any Justice of the Peace of any charge against any Member of the University, the Clerk to the Justices shall forthwith, after application made to him by the Vice-Chancellor for a copy of the depositions, furnish the same to the Vice-Chancellor without making any charge for the same.

University Constables.

Copies of Certificates to be sent to Town Clerk.

20. The Vice-Chancellor shall send to the Town Clerk a duplicate or copy of every certificate of the appointment of a Constable under the Act sixth George the Fourth, chapter ninety-seven, as soon as practicable after such certificate shall be made.

Rates on University and College Property.

University Property.

21. The property of the University herein-after specified is situate within the Parishes in the Borough herein-after respectively mentioned; (that is to say,)

The Senate House in the Parish of Saint Mary the Great;

The Senate House Yard in the Parishes of Saint Mary the Great and Saint Edward;

The University Library, with the Lecture Rooms, Schools, and Museums thereunder, in the Parishes of Saint Mary the Great and Saint Edward, what was lately King's College Old Court in the Parish of Saint John;

The Pitt Press in the Parish of Saint Botolph;

The Fitzwilliam Museum in the Parish of Saint Mary the Less;

The Old Botanic Garden in the Parishes of Saint Edward and Saint Benedict;

The Theatre of Anatomy and the Lecture Rooms adjacent in the parish of Saint Benedict;

The New Botanic Garden in the Parish of Saint Andrew the Less;

The Spinning House in the Parish of Saint Andrew the Great;

The Observatory in the Parish of Saint Giles;
and so much of the said property as shall not be exempt from rates under the subsequent provisions of this Act shall be assessed to rates (rates made under the Improvement Acts excepted) in the said Parishes repectively.

22. The property occupied by the several Colleges, and herein-after specified, is situate within the Parishes in the Borough herein-after respectively mentioned; (that is to say,) *College property.*

 Saint Peter's College in the Parish of Saint Mary the Less;
 Clare College in the Parish of Saint John;
 Pembroke College in the Parishes of Saint Mary the Less and Saint Botolph;
 Gonville and Caius College in the Parish of Saint Michael;
 Trinity Hall in the Parish of Saint John;
 Corpus Christi College in the Parishes of Saint Benedict and Saint Botolph;
 King's College in the Parishes of Saint John, Saint Benedict, Saint Edward, Saint Giles, and Saint Mary the Great;
 Queen's College in the Parish of Saint Botolph;
 Saint Catherine's College in the Parishes of Saint Benedict, Saint Botolph, and Saint Edward;
 Jesus College in the Parishes of Saint Rhadegund and All Saints;
 Christ's College in the Parishes of Saint Andrew the Great and Saint Andrew the Less;
 Saint John's College in the Parishes of All Saints, Saint Giles, and Saint Peter;
 Magdalen College in the Parishes of Saint Giles and Saint Peter;
 Trinity College in the Parishes of All Saints, Saint Giles, and Saint Michael;
 Emmanuel College in the Parish of Saint Andrew the Great;
 Sidney Sussex College in the Parish of All Saints;
 Downing College in the Parishes of Saint Benedict, Saint Botolph, and Saint Mary the Less;

and so much of the property of the said several Colleges as shall not be exempt from rates under the subsequent provisions of this Act shall be assessed to rates (rates made

Exemptions from rates.

23. No rate whatever shall be assessed or imposed upon or in respect of the Senate House, the University Library, the Schools or the Museums of Science, Laboratories, or Lecture Rooms for the time being of the University, nor upon or in respect of the Chapels or Libraries for the time being of any College; provided, that the buildings, rooms, or places respectively hereby exempted from rates be used for the purposes aforesaid at the time of making the valuation for assessment then in force.

Colleges to be assessed for property occupied by individual Members.

24. As respects College property, the whole thereof shall be deemed to be in the occupation of the College, although parts may be exclusively occupied by individual Members thereof or Students; and the College, if a corporation, shall be assessed for the same in its corporate name; and for the property of any College not incorporated the Head thereof shall be assessed, and shall be liable to pay all rates, although he himself may not occupy the whole or any part of the property rated.

Valuation of University and College property.

25. The amount at which property occupied by the University or any College shall be assessed shall, as soon as practicable, be determined by two valuers, or their umpire, one of such valuers to be appointed by the Vice-Chancellor, and the other by the Mayor; and such two valuers shall appoint an umpire before entering upon their valuation, or, in case they cannot agree in the choice of an umpire, such umpire shall be chosen by the Poor Law Board.

Ground Plans to define Parochial Boundaries.

26. As respects property occupied by the University or any College situate in more than one parish (whether such property be rateable or exempt from rates), the said valuers or umpire shall make duplicate ground plans thereof, whereupon the parochial boundaries shall be marked, and such ground plans shall be signed by the valuers or umpire, and shall be deemed conclusive evidence of such boundaries, and one duplicate of the valuation and ground plans aforesaid shall be deposited in the Registrary's Office, and the other in the Town Clerk's Office, for the free inspection at all seasonable times of all parties interested.

Provision for fresh Valuations

27. At any time after three years from the completion of the first or any subsequent valuation of property occupied by

the University or any College, the Vice-Chancellor or Mayor respectively may by notice in writing to the other of them require a fresh valuation to be made, and the same shall be made accordingly, in like manner in all respects as the first valuation.

of University and College property.

28. The said valuers and umpire respectively shall have free access to the rate books of every Parish, and also the same powers which by the Act to regulate Parochial Assessments (sixth and seventh William the Fourth, chapter ninety-sixth, section four,) are given to surveyors acting thereunder.

Powers of valuers.

29. Every valuation of property occupied by the University or any College, during the time it continues in force, shall be final and conclusive on all parties interested; nor shall any rate be subject to objection, on appeal or otherwise, in respect of the amount at which any property comprised in the valuation in force for the time being shall be assessed, provided such amount be in conformity with such valuation.

Valuations to be conclusive.

30. The costs of and incidental to the making of the ground plans herein-before directed, and also the costs of and incidental to the first valuation of property occupied by the University or any College, shall be paid in equal proportions by the Vice-Chancellor (on behalf of the University and Colleges), and by the Mayor Aldermen and Burgesses; and the Vice-Chancellor shall have power to demand and collect from the several Colleges their respective shares of such proportion, according to the amount of their respective assessments; and in default of any special agreement as to the costs of and incidental to any subsequent valuation which shall be required by the Vice-Chancellor, such costs shall be paid by the Chancellor Masters and Scholars; and in default of any special agreement as to the costs of and incidental to any subsequent valuation which shall be required by the Mayor, such costs shall be paid by the Mayor Aldermen and Burgesses.

As to cost of Valuations.

31. Any property occupied by the University or by any College which may be acquired by the University or by any College after any valuation shall have been made, or which may be accidentally omitted therefrom, shall (if not exempt from rates under the provisions of this Act or otherwise) be rated in the ordinary manner until a new valuation be made,

As to University and College property acquired after Valuation.

when such property shall be included in such new valuation, if not exempt as aforesaid.

As to certain rates on Magdalen College.
32. Magdalen College shall be exonerated from the payment of all rates imposed before the passing of this Act in the several Parishes of Saint Giles and Saint Peter in respect of any property for which such College had not previously paid rates; and the Council may make such orders as may appear equitable for payment out of the Borough Fund to the said Parishes, or either of them, of compensation for the loss sustained by such Parishes, or either of them, by reason of this enactment.

For cessation of payments under agreement of October, 1650.
33. The liability of the University and Colleges to pay any money under a certain agreement made in October one thousand six hundred and fifty, or under any previous or subsequent agreement on the same subject, shall cease from the time when by the operation of this Act the property occupied by the University and Colleges shall be actually assessed to the Poor Rate of any Parish.

Vestry Meetings.
34. As respects any Vestry to be holden in any Parish wherein the University or any College shall be charged to the rate for the relief of the poor, the Vice-Chancellor, or some Member of the Senate deputed by him, shall be deemed the duly authorized Agent of the University, and the Head of such College, or some Member of the College deputed by him, shall be deemed the duly authorized Agent of such College, within the intent and meaning of the Act fifty-ninth George the Third, Chapter eighty-five, Section two.

Exemption from Municipal and Parochial Offices, &c.
35. No Member of the University or of any College shall, by reason of any rate on the property occupied by the University or by such College, be entitled to be registered as an Elector of the Borough, or to be enrolled as a Burgess thereof, or be compellable to serve any Municipal or Parochial Office, or to serve or to be empannelled on any Jury or Inquest, or to perform any service imposed on Ratepayers.

[Sections 36–49 provide for the establishment of a common fund for the relief of the poor, to which all the Parishes within the Cambridge Union shall contribute rateably.]

Improvement Quota.

Reduction of Univer-
50. So much of the Improvement Acts as enacts that two fifths of the annual sum or sums to be ascertained and raised

under those Acts shall be paid by or on account of the University shall be repealed, and for the future one fourth only of the annual sum or sums which the Improvement Commissioners shall from time to time ascertain and direct to be raised shall be paid by or on account of the University in the manner provided and under the powers given by the Improvement Acts; which Quota shall be in lieu and instead of any assessment or rate on the University or Colleges; and no other assessment or rate shall be made on them under the Improvement Acts; and the remaining part of such annual sum or sums shall be paid in the manner provided by those Acts. *sity Quota under Improvement Acts.*

51. From and after the ninth day of November one thousand eight hundred and fifty-six the Watch Committee of the Borough shall consist of— *Watch Committee.*

Constitution of Watch Committee.

The Mayor for the time being;

Nine other Members of the Council, appointed by the Council;

Five Members of the University, being Members of the Senate, appointed by the Senate;

and at any Meeting of such Committee the Mayor, if present, shall be the Chairman; and in the absence of the Mayor a Chairman shall be chosen by the Members of the Committee then present; and in all cases where the votes are equal the Chairman shall have a second or casting vote.

52. The appointment of Members of the Watch Committee by the Council and Senate respectively shall be made on or before the ninth day of November in each year, unless in any year in which that day shall be Sunday, and in such year the said appointment may be made on the day following; and the Members of the Watch Committee shall continue in office from the tenth day of November in the year of their appointment until and including the ninth day of November in the following year. *Watch Committee to be appointed annually.*

53. Occasional vacancies in the Watch Committee may be filled up by the Council or Senate respectively as the same may occur; and the persons appointed to supply such vacancies shall continue in office for the residue of the current year. *For supply of occasional vacancies.*

54. The Town Clerk shall from time to time, with all practicable despatch, notify in writing to the Vice-Chancellor all *Notice of appointment of*

Members of Watch Committee.

appointments of Members of the Watch Committee made by the Council; and the Registrary shall in like manner notify in writing to the Town Clerk all appointments of Members of the Watch Committee made by the Senate.

Powers of Watch Committee.

55. The determination of the number, the appointment, dismissal, and entire management and direction of the Constabulary Force shall be vested in such Watch Committee; but the said Watch Committee shall not have the power of making orders for the payment of money out of the Borough Fund.

Borough Fund.

Senate to appoint three Auditors to join in auditing Borough Fund.

56. And whereas it is expedient to provide means for giving to the University and Colleges a knowledge of any intended expenditure from or out of the Borough Fund, and for urging any objections they may have to it, as well as for giving the right of removing orders for payment of money into the Court of Queen's Bench, under the Statute seventh William the Fourth and first Victoria, chapter seventy-eight, or other Statutes; be it enacted, that the Senate shall annually appoint three Members of the Senate to audit the accounts of the Treasurer of the Borough conjointly with the three Auditors elected and appointed under the Municipal Corporation Act; but it shall not be necessary that the Auditors so appointed by the Senate (herein-after termed University Auditors) should take any oath or make any declaration.

Duration of office of University Auditors.

57. The University Auditors shall continue in office from the first day of March in the year of their appointment until and including the last day of February in the following year.

For supply of occasional vacancies.

58. Occasional vacancies in the office of University Auditor may be filled up by the Senate as the same may occur; and the persons appointed to supply such vacancies shall continue in office for the residue of the current year.

Notice of appointment of University Auditors.

59. The Registrary shall from time to time notify in writing to the Town Clerk all appointments of University Auditors.

Certain matters to be submitted to Finance Committee before submitted to Council.

60. The Council of the Borough shall annually appoint a Finance Committee, and every question concerning the payment of money out of the Borough Fund shall be submitted to the Finance Committee six days at least before the same is brought under the consideration of the Council.

61. The University Auditors shall have three days' notice of every meeting of the Finance Committee for the purposes herein-before mentioned, and of the business to be transacted at such meeting; and they or any of them shall be at liberty to attend at such meeting, and to be heard on the matters and business then brought forward, but shall not have any right of voting. *University Auditors to have notice of meeting of Finance Committee.*

62. The Vice-Chancellor or his *locum tenens*, and the Head of every College or his *locum tenens*, shall have all the privileges conferred on any Burgess or on any Alderman or Councillor by the Acts fifth and sixth William the Fourth, chapter seventy-six, section ninety-three, and seventh William the Fourth and first Victoria, chapter seventy-eight, section twenty-two, or by this Act, and shall be deemed persons interested in the Borough Fund within the intent and meaning of the forty-fourth section of the last-mentioned Act and of this Act. *Vice-Chancellor and Heads of Colleges to have all privileges and rights conferred by 5 & 6 Will. 4, c. 76, s. 93, and 7 Will. 4 & 1 Vict. c. 78, s. 22.*

[Sections 63 and 64 direct how the costs of the reference and of this Act shall be paid.]

20 & 21 Vict. Cap. XXV.

An Act to continue the powers of the Commissioners under an Act of the seventeenth and eighteenth years of Her Majesty concerning the University of Oxford and the College of Saint Mary Winchester, and further to amend the said Act[z]*.

[Section 1 continues the Commission under 17 & 18 Vict. c. 81 until July 1, 1858.

[Section 2 enables the Commissioners to consolidate the Michel Foundation at Queen's College with the Old Foundation.]

3. It shall be lawful for any College within the University from time to time, with consent of the Visitor, to appropriate and apply any property, or the income of any property, held *Power to Colleges with consent of Visitor to apply*

---

[z] This Act is published entire at the beginning of "Ordinances and Statutes framed or approved by the Oxford University Commissioners," printed at the Clarendon Press in 1863.

property held for purchase of Advowsons for benefit of Colleges, &c.

by or in trust for the College for the purpose that the same or the income thereof may be applied in purchasing Advowsons for the benefit of the College, to the augmentation of the endowment of Livings in the patronage of the College to such amount as may be by law allowed, or towards the building of fit and suitable Parsonage Houses on any Livings in the patronage of the College, or to the foundation or augmentation of Scholarships or Exhibitions, or to other purposes for the advancement of religion, learning, and education within the College; and, in exercise of this power, the College may annex to any Living in the patronage of the College (by way of augmentation of the endowment of such Living) any Tithe Rentcharge which may be vested in the College, or any portion thereof, in consideration of the appropriation to other purposes of the College of a part of the trust property or income, not exceeding the amount which the Visitor shall adjudge to be an adequate consideration for the Tithe Rentcharge so to be annexed: provided, that this power shall not extend to property or income applicable to the purchase of Advowsons for the benefit of Scholars or Exhibitioners on any particular Foundation within a College.

Certain provisions of 8 & 9 Vict. c. 18 incorporated with this Act and with 17 and 18 Vict. c. 81, so far as relates to certain lands.

4. The Lands Clauses Consolidation Act, 1845, except the parts and enactments of that Act with respect to the purchase and taking of lands otherwise than by agreement, and with respect to the recovery of forfeitures, penalties, and costs, and with respect to lands required by the promoters of the undertaking, but which shall not be wanted for the purposes thereof, shall be incorporated with and form part of this Act and of the "Oxford University Act, 1854," so far as relates to land within one mile and a half of Carfax in the City of Oxford required for the erection of any buildings for the extension of the buildings of the said University or of any College or Hall therein, or for purposes of utility or recreation relating to the said University or to any College or Hall therein, and as if the corporate name of the University or College, as the case may be, had been inserted therein instead of the expression "the promoters of the undertaking."

21 & 22 Vict. Cap. XI.

An Act to repeal the Stamp Duties payable on Matriculation and Degrees in the University of Cambridge.

WHEREAS by an Act passed in the Session of Parliament holden in the nineteenth and twentieth years of Her Majesty (chapter eighty-eight) to make further provision for the good government and extension of the University of Cambridge, of the Colleges therein, and of the College of King Henry the Sixth at Eton, it was enacted, that the Stamp duties then payable on Matriculations and Degrees should be abolished so soon as provision should have been made by the University, to the satisfaction of the Commissioners of Her Majesty's Treasury, in lieu of the monies theretofore voted annually by Parliament: and whereas by a Grace or Statute of the said University, passed by the Senate in Congregation on the tenth day of December one thousand eight hundred and fifty-seven, provision has been made for the payment out of the University Chest of the salaries and allowances to certain Professors of the said University, mentioned in the Schedule to this Act, (being the same salaries and allowances as were heretofore annually voted by Parliament to the said Professors,) and the Commissioners of Her Majesty's Treasury are satisfied that such Statute is a due provision in lieu of the monies theretofore voted annually by Parliament, as intended by the said Act: be it enacted by the Queen's most excellent Majesty, by and with the advice and consent of the Lords spiritual and temporal and Commons in this present Parliament assembled, and by the authority of the same, as follows: [19 & 20 Vict. c. 88.]

1. All Stamp duties payable under the Act of the fifty-fifth year of King George the Third, chapter one hundred and eighty-four, or under any other Act of Parliament, on the admission or matriculation of any person in the said University of Cambridge, and on the admission of any person to any degree in the said University (whether conferred in the ordinary course of the University or otherwise), or for the registry [Stamp duties on matriculation and admission to degrees in Cambridge repealed.]

or entry of any such admission, shall, from and after the first day of April next, cease to be payable [a].

Salaries payable to Professors in Schedule not to be discontinued without consent of Treasury.

2. No salary or allowance payable under the said Grace or Statute of the said University to any Professor mentioned in the Schedule to this Act shall be discontinued or reduced without the consent of the Commissioners of Her Majesty's Treasury.

SCHEDULE.

	£
To the Professor of Modern History	371
To the Professor of Civil Law	100
To the Professor of Chemistry	100
To the Professor of Anatomy	100
To the Professor of Botany	182
To the Jacksonian Professor	100
To the Professor of Mineralogy	100

21 & 22 Vict. Cap. XLIV.

An Act to give to the Universities of Oxford, Cambridge, and Durham, and the Colleges in those Universities, and to the Colleges of Saint Mary of Winchester near Winchester and of King Henry the Sixth at Eton, power to sell, enfranchise, and exchange lands under certain conditions, and also to grant Leases for agricultural, building, and mining purposes, and to deal with the interests of their Lessees under proper reservations and restrictions.

WHEREAS it is expedient that the Universities of Oxford, Cambridge, and Durham, and the Colleges in those Universities, and the Colleges of Saint Mary of Winchester near Winchester and of King Henry the Sixth at Eton, should be empowered to sell, enfranchise, and exchange their lands under certain conditions, and also to grant leases for agricultural and building and mining purposes

[a] See the note on 18 & 19 Vict. c. 36, s. 1.

under proper reservations and restrictions, and to deal with the interests of their lessees in manner herein-after provided; and whereas the several Acts now in force in relation thereto are inadequate for such purposes: be it enacted by the Queen's most excellent Majesty, by and with the advice and consent of the Lords spiritual and temporal and Commons in this present Parliament assembled, and by the authority of the same, as follows:

1. It shall be lawful for the said Universities and for any College therein respectively, and for the Colleges of Saint Mary of Winchester near Winchester and of King Henry the Sixth at Eton, with the consent of the Copyhold Commissioners, to sell any estate in lands either at law or in equity which now is or at any time hereafter shall be vested in such Universities respectively or in any such College, and also, with such consent as aforesaid, to enfranchise any copyhold or customary lands held of any manor belonging to such Universities respectively or any such College, or to exchange any estate in lands for any other lands, whether the same shall be of a like nature or not, and upon any such exchange to receive or pay any money by way of equality of exchange; and all monies which on any such sale, enfranchisement, or exchange shall be received by or become payable to or for the benefit of such Universities respectively, or for any such College, shall from time to time be paid into the Bank of England for the benefit of such Universities respectively, or of any such College, to an account to be entitled "The Account of the Copyhold Commissioners *ex parte* the University or the College for whose benefit such monies shall have been so paid in (describing such University or College by its corporate name) in the matter of this Act;" and the receipt of the said Copyhold Commissioners shall be an effectual discharge to any purchaser or other person for any money therein expressed to be received; and all monies so paid into the Bank of England shall be applicable and be applied in payment for equality of exchange as aforesaid, or shall be laid out by such University or College with such consent as aforesaid in the purchase of other lands in fee simple, or of any lands of a leasehold tenure, (such leaseholds to be holden for a term of not less than five hundred

Power to the Universities and Colleges to sell, enfranchise, and exchange lands under certain conditions.

s

years yet to come and unexpired at the time of such purchase at a nominal rent, and to be contiguous to or convenient to be held with any other lands belonging to such Universities respectively or to any such College,) such lands to be conveyed and assigned respectively to the use or for the benefit of such University or College, and to be held together with any lands received in exchange by such University or College upon the like trusts and for the like purposes as the lands sold or given in exchange by such University or College respectively; and the monies from time to time remaining unapplied for the purposes aforesaid shall be invested by and in the names of the said Copyhold Commissioners to the account aforesaid in the purchase of Government stocks, funds, or securities, which the said Copyhold Commissioners shall hold in trust for such University or College; and the said Copyhold Commissioners may sell and dispose of the same for the purposes of this Act as occasion may require; and in the meantime the interest, dividends, and annual proceeds of such monies, stocks, funds, and securities shall be paid to such University or College to be applied to the same purposes as the annual income was applicable which arose out of the lands from the sale, enfranchisement, or exchange of which the money invested in such stocks, funds, or securities was produced: provided that, except as hereafter is mentioned, nothing in this section contained shall apply to any estate of the Universities respectively, or any such College as aforesaid, in reversion in lands expectant upon any lease for a life or lives, or for a term of years determinable upon any life or lives, or for a term of years whereof more than seven shall be unexpired, on which a rent less than three fourths of the clear yearly value of such lands shall have been reserved, except where the lessee has a right of renewal.

Mode in which consents of Copyhold Commissioners are to be evidenced.

2. The consent herein-before required to be given by the Copyhold Commissioners to any sale, enfranchisement, or exchange to be effected under the authority of this Act shall be evidenced in manner following; (that is to say,) the said Commissioners, upon consideration of the proposed sale, enfranchisement, or exchange, and the report thereon of the Surveyor of the University or College proposing the same,

and being satisfied as to the propriety thereof, shall issue an order under their hands and the common seal of their Board, authorizing such proposed sale, enfranchisement, or exchange to be carried into effect by the University or the College making application under the provisions of this Act; and the consent of the said Commissioners herein-before required to the re-investment of the monies to be received upon any such sale, enfranchisement, or exchange in the purchase of other lands shall also be evidenced by a similar order, to be issued by the said Commissioners in manner aforesaid, approving of the proposed purchase, and authorizing the University or College (as the case may be) to carry the same into effect; and it shall not in any case be necessary that the said Commissioners should be made parties to, or should execute, any conveyance, assignment, or other assurance to be made by such University or College for effecting any sale, enfranchisement, exchange, purchase, or mortgage under the powers of this Act, or satisfy themselves as to the title of any lands, the subject of any such exchange or purchase: provided, that, notwithstanding anything herein contained, the said Commissioners shall be at liberty (if they shall think fit) to require a valuation to be made by any surveyor to be selected or approved by them, and also a plan to be furnished of the lands, the subject of any such sale, enfranchisement, exchange, purchase, or mortgage: and all costs and expenses of and incidental to the obtaining such consent shall be borne by the University or College applying for the same.

3. The several orders to be issued by the said Commissioners pursuant to the foregoing provisions shall respectively be in the form or to the effect set forth in the Schedule to this Act, with such variations only as occasion may require. *Form of orders to be issued by Commissioners.*

4. For facilitating such transactions by way of sale and exchange between the University or College and their lessees, it shall be lawful for the said Universities and for any College therein respectively, and for the Colleges of Saint Mary of Winchester near Winchester and of King Henry the Sixth at Eton, upon accepting the surrender of the whole or any part of the lands comprised in any lease for years or for a life or lives, to covenant or agree to grant to the person *Power to accept surrenders from lessees in consideration of annual payments, and to sell and exchange*

to or with such lessees.

so surrendering during the residue then unexpired of the term, or so long as such lease but for such surrender would have continued, such an annual sum as may be agreed upon between such University or College and lessee respectively; and it shall also be lawful for such University or College upon accepting such surrender, and with such consent and so evidenced as aforesaid, to contract with the lessee or person so surrendering for the sale or exchange to or with such lessee or person of the lands comprised in the surrender, such lands being for the purpose of such sale or exchange valued as if in the possession of such University or College discharged of such lease, and to convey the same in pursuance of such contract accordingly.

Repeal of 19 & 20 Vict. c. 95, and of sect. 48 of 19 & 20 Vict. c. 88.

5. The Act passed in the Session of Parliament holden in the nineteenth and twentieth years of the present reign (chapter ninety-five), intituled An Act to give to the University of Oxford and to Colleges in the said University, and to the College of Saint Mary of Winchester near Winchester, power to sell and exchange lands under certain conditions; also the forty-eighth section of the Act passed in the same Session (chapter eighty-eight), intituled An Act to make further provision for the good Government and Extension of the University of Cambridge, of the Colleges therein, and of the College of King Henry the Sixth at Eton, shall be and the same are hereby repealed; so, nevertheless, as not to prejudice or affect any negotiations or arrangements which shall have been entered upon or made under the provisions of the said Act and section, and which shall be actually pending at the time of the passing of this Act, and which negotiations or arrangements the University or College shall, notwithstanding anything herein contained, be at liberty to complete under the said last-mentioned provisions; but all monies which shall become payable thereunder shall be paid and applied in manner herein-before particularly mentioned; and any monies which at the time of the passing of this Act shall be standing to any account appointed by the Church Estates Commissioners by virtue of the said Act and section, and any stocks, funds, or securities in or upon which any such monies shall have been invested, shall be paid and transferred to the like account, as is herein-before

directed in respect of the monies to become payable under the provisions of this Act.

Provisions as to purchase of Lessees' interests.

6. It shall be lawful for the said Universities and any College therein respectively, and the Colleges of Saint Mary of Winchester near Winchester and of King Henry the Sixth at Eton, to purchase by agreement from any lessee holding under any lease for years or for a life or lives granted by such University or College, whereon a rent less than three fourths of the clear yearly value of such lands shall have been reserved, the term, estate, and interest of such lessee in all or any of the lands comprised in such lease for such consideration, either by payment to such lessee of a gross sum of money (to be provided or raised as hereafter mentioned), or by the grant to such lessee during the residue then unexpired of the term, or so long as such lease but for such purchase would have continued, such* an annual sum as may be agreed on between such University or College and lessee respectively. Power to purchase the interests of lessees in consideration of a gross sum of money or by an annual charge.

* So in orig.

7. Upon the purchase by such University or College of the estate or interest of any lessee in a part only of the lands comprised in any lease, it shall be lawful for the Steward, Chapter Clerk, Solicitor, or Agent of such University or College and such lessee, by a memorandum in writing under their respective hands, which may be indorsed on such lease, to apportion the rent reserved thereby, and declare what part thereof shall continue payable thereunder; and thereupon such apportioned part of the rent shall be payable as if the same had been the rent originally reserved in respect of the lands not purchased; and where the rent originally reserved was an ancient and accustomed rent, the part so continuing payable shall be deemed and taken to be the ancient and accustomed rent for the lands not purchased; and the reservations, covenants, and agreements contained in such lease, and the powers and authorities of such University or College, so far as the same shall be applicable to the lands not purchased, shall remain in full force as if such purchase had not been made. Apportionment of rent in case of the purchase of part only of the lands comprised in lease.

Consent of sub-lessee with covenant for renewal.

8. If any lands held under lease from such University or College shall have been sublet with a covenant on the part of the original lessee to renew the under-lease upon any renewal of the original lease, the interest of the lessee in such lands shall not be purchased under this Act by such University or College without the consent in writing of such sub-lessee: provided always, that such University or College shall not be prevented from making such purchase, nor shall their title to any such lands be affected in respect of the existence of any such under-lease, unless such University or College shall have had notice thereof in writing; but the sub-lessee shall, in cases where a purchase shall have been made without such notice, be entitled to recover such damages for the loss of the benefit of such covenant against the party bound by the covenant for the loss to be sustained by him as he would be entitled to in respect of its non-performance on a renewal by the original lessee.

Power to University or College with consent of Copyhold Commissioners to raise money by mortgage, to be applied to such purchases.

9. In case there shall not be any monies, stocks, funds, or securities, belonging to such University or College, properly and conveniently applicable in or towards such last mentioned purchase, it shall be lawful for such University or College, with the consent of the said Copyhold Commissioners (such consent to be evidenced by an order to be issued under their hands and common seal in the form or to the effect set forth in the said Schedule hereto), to raise such sum or sums of money as shall be required for that purpose and be stated in such order, together with all reasonable costs and expenses, by mortgage for a specified determinable term of years of all or any of the lands comprised in any such lease which shall be so purchased as aforesaid.

Leasing Powers.

Power to grant Leases for a term not exceeding 21 years at rack-rent.

10. It shall be lawful for the said Universities and for any College therein respectively, and for the Colleges of Saint Mary of Winchester near Winchester and of King Henry the Sixth at Eton, from time to time after the passing of this Act, by indenture sealed by such University or College with their common seal, to lease all or any of the lands which now are or at any time hereafter shall be either at law or in equity

vested in such University or College (except as herein-after is mentioned), with the appurtenances, for any term or number of years not exceeding twenty-one years, to take effect in possession and not in reversion or by way of future interest, and at the best rent that can be reasonably obtained for the same, so as there be not any fine, premium, or foregift taken for the making thereof, and so as the rent be made payable half-yearly or oftener, and so as sufficient power of entry be reserved for securing the payment of the rent and the performance and observance of the lessee's covenants therein, and so as the lessee be not thereby made dispunishable for waste, and so as the lessee execute a counterpart of the lease; and every such lease may be on such terms and conditions as such University or College may think reasonable.

11. It shall be lawful for the said Universities and for any College therein respectively, and for the Colleges of Saint Mary of Winchester near Winchester and of King Henry the Sixth at Eton, from time to time after the passing of this Act, by indenture sealed by such University or College with their common seal, to lease all or any of the lands which now are or at any time hereafter shall be either at law or in equity vested in such University or College (except as herein-after is mentioned), with the appurtenances, for any term or number of years not exceeding ninety-nine years, to take effect in possession and not in reversion or by way of future interest, to any person or persons who may be willing to improve or repair the present or any future houses thereon or any of them, or to erect other houses and buildings in lieu thereof or in addition thereto, or to erect any houses or other buildings on any land whereon no building shall be standing, or who shall be willing to annex any part of the same lands to buildings erected or to be erected on the said lands or any part thereof, or otherwise to improve the said premises or any part thereof; and with or without liberty for the lessee to take down any buildings standing on the lands in any such lease to be comprised, and to dispose of the materials thereof to such uses and for such purposes as shall in such lease be agreed upon; and with or without liberty for the lessee to lay out and appropriate any part or parts of the lands to be comprised in any such lease, as and for accommodation lands, plantations,

Power to grant Building and Repairing Leases for a term not exceeding 99 years.

gardens, pleasure grounds, yards, or other conveniences or appendages, for the use or convenience of the tenants or occupiers of the said houses or other buildings, and also to set out and allot any part or parts of the lands to be comprised in any such lease, as and for streets, squares, or other similar spaces of ground, roads, avenues, approaches, courts, ways, passages, sewers, drains, wells, reservoirs, yards, or otherwise, for the use and convenience of the tenants or occupiers for the time being of the said houses or buildings or of adjoining houses or buildings, or for the general improvement thereof or of any part thereof; and also with or without liberty for the lessee to dig, take, and carry away, and dispose of such earth, clay, sand, or gravel as it shall be found convenient to remove for effecting any of the purposes aforesaid; and also with or without any other liberties, easements, or privileges which are or may be usual in leases of a similar description; so as there be reserved by every such lease the best and most improved yearly rent that can be reasonably obtained for the premises comprised therein at the time of the granting or making of such lease or the contract for the same, payable half-yearly or oftener during the continuance of the term thereby granted, and to be incident to and go along with the reversion immediately expectant on the determination thereof; and so as any such lease be made without taking any fine, premium, or foregift, or anything in the nature thereof, for or in respect of the making of the same; and so as in every such lease made for the purpose of having buildings erected there shall be contained a covenant on the part of the lessee to build, complete, and finish such buildings within a time to be therein specified for that purpose; and so as in every such lease made for the purpose of having buildings repaired or rebuilt there shall be contained a covenant on the part of the lessee substantially to rebuild or repair the same within a time to be therein specified for that purpose; and so as in every such lease, whether for building or repairing or otherwise, there be contained on the part of the lessee a covenant for the due payment of the rent to be thereby reserved and (subject to the provisions in this behalf hereafter contained) of all taxes, charges, rates, assessments, and impositions whatsoever affecting the lands therein comprised (except only the tax (if any) for the time being upon property or income in respect of the rent reserved); and also a covenant for keeping the buildings erected and built, or to be erected and built, in repair during the term thereby granted; and also a covenant for keeping the houses and buildings (subject to the provision in this behalf hereafter contained) insured from damage by fire, to the amount of three fourths at least of the value thereof, in some or one of the Public Offices of Insurance, to be selected or approved from time to time by such University or College, and to lay out the money to be received by virtue of such insurance, and also all such other sums as shall be necessary, in rebuilding, repairing, and reinstating such houses and buildings as shall be destroyed or damaged by fire; and also to surrender the possession of, and leave in good condition and repair, the houses and buildings erected and to be erected or rebuilt or repaired on the premises therein comprised, on the expiration or other sooner determination of the term to be thereby granted; or such covenants on the part of the lessee as shall be in substance and effect the same as or equivalent to the covenants herein-before specified; and so as in every such lease there be contained a power for such University or College, their Stewards, Surveyors, or Agents, to enter upon the premises and inspect the condition thereof, and also a proviso or condition of re-entry for non-payment of the rent thereby reserved for any space not exceeding forty days, or for non-performance of any of the covenants or agreements on the part of the lessee therein contained; and also with or without a proviso that no breach of any of the covenants or agreements to be therein contained (except the covenant for payment of the rent and other such covenants or agreements (if any) as such University or College shall think it reasonable to except) shall occasion any forfeiture of such lease or of the term thereby granted, or give any right of re-entry, unless or until judgment shall have been obtained in an action for such breach, nor unless the damages and costs to be recovered in such action shall have remained unpaid for the space of three calendar months after judgment shall have been obtained in such action; and so as there be not contained in any such lease any clause or words authorizing the lessee to commit waste or exempting him from punishment for committing waste, save so far as may be necessary for or incident to the purposes aforesaid or any of them; and every such lease may also contain any other covenants, provisoes, conditions, restrictions, and stipulations which shall appear reasonable to such University or College, and particularly any provisions that, where any such lease is granted with liberty to erect thereafter any house or houses on the land thereby demised in addition to the house in respect of which the original yearly rent thereby reserved shall be payable, then, in addition to such original yearly rent to be so reserved as aforesaid, there shall also be reserved any such additional yearly rent, to become payable only in the event of such additional house or houses being thereafter built, as shall be the best and most improved additional yearly rent that can, at the time of making or granting of such lease or for* the contract for the same, and considering the nature and circumstances of the case, be reasonably obtained, and shall* be made payable half-yearly or oftener from a time not later than the time when the respective additional house is fit for habitation and use, and shall continue payable during the remainder of the term granted by such lease, and be incident to and go along with the reversion immediately expectant on the determination thereof; and also a provision for apportioning the rent to be reserved in and by any such lease, and for exonerating any part of the lands to be comprised in any such lease from the payment of any specified portion of the whole rent to be thereby reserved; and so that the respective lessees execute counterparts of their respective leases.

* *So in orig.*

* *So in orig.*

Power to enter into contracts for granting Leases, and afterwards to grant Leases pursuant thereto.

12. It shall be lawful for the said Universities and for any College therein respectively, and for the Colleges of Saint Mary of Winchester near Winchester and of King Henry the Sixth at Eton, by themselves, or by any person or persons acting on their behalf, to enter into any contract in writing, either conditional or absolute, for making or granting any lease authorized to be granted under the provisions of this Act; and in any such contract or contracts (with the consent of the contractor or contractors) to reserve power to rescind and vary the same, and to enter into fresh contracts or not, as such University or College shall think fit; and by

any such contract to agree, when and as any land or buildings thereby agreed to be let, or any part or parts thereof, shall be respectively built upon, rebuilt, or repaired, laid out, formed, or improved in the manner and to the extent to be stipulated in such contract, by one or more indenture or indentures to lease or cause to be leased the same lands or buildings or any part thereof to the person or persons contracting to take the same as aforesaid, or his or her executors, administrators, or assigns, or to his, her, or their nominee or nominees, for and during the remainder of the term to be specified in such contract, and in such parcels, and under and subject to such portion or portions of the yearly rent, to be specified in such contract, as shall be thought proper; and also (if such University or College shall think the same expedient) to agree that the yearly rent agreed to be reserved in any such contract may be made to commence at any such periods within two years from the date of such contract, and may be made to increase periodically, beginning with such portion of the full rent thereby agreed to be paid as shall be thought advisable, and increasing up to the full rent, as shall be thought proper, and as in such contract shall be expressed, regard being had to the quantity of land from time to time agreed to be leased, and the progress of the buildings, rebuildings, or repairs stipulated to be erected or made thereon or on some part thereof; but so, nevertheless, that the full yearly rent shall be made to commence at a period not exceeding five years from the date of the said contract; with liberty, nevertheless, to make provisions in the same contract for the payment of an additional yearly rent or rents, in the event of any house or houses being thereafter built on the land comprised in the same contract, in addition to the house or houses in respect of which such original yearly rent was reserved or made payable; and also to agree that, when and as any lease shall be granted of any part of the lands so contracted to be leased, the lands so for the time being leased shall be discharged from such contract, and that the person with whom such contract shall have been entered into shall remain liable, in respect of such part of the lands comprised in such contract as shall not for the time being be leased, to the payment of such portion only of the rent by such contract agreed to be paid as may be thought proper and shall in such contract be provided for; and also to agree that the person with whom such contract shall be entered into may have, exercise, and enjoy all or any of the liberties, easements, and privileges therein authorized to be granted, except such thereof as such University or College shall think reasonable to except: provided also, that there may be contained in every such contract as aforesaid such further or other agreements and stipulations as to such University or College shall seem reasonable.

Variations in terms between Leases and Contracts not to be material, and Contracts not to form part of title.

13. No lease granted or to be granted under the powers of this Act shall be invalid by reason of any variation between any such lease and any prior contract for a lease which may have preceded the granting of such lease, but every lease to be granted as aforesaid shall be valid and effectual notwithstanding such variation; and no person taking such lease or claiming under such lease shall be bound to inquire whether such lease is in pursuance of or authorized by any such prior contract, nor shall any such person be in any manner affected by anything contained in any such contract; and the contract or contracts which shall have preceded such lease shall not at law or in equity form a part of the necessary evidence of the title of the lessee or lessees named in such lease, or of his, her, or their executors, administrators, or assigns, whether such lease is or is not expressed to be granted under or in pursuance of any such previous contract: provided, that such lease shall not be inconsistent or at variance with the provisions and restrictions herein contained with respect to the leases hereby authorized to be granted.

Power to Universities and Colleges to insure buildings &c. comprised in any Lease, and to charge the tenants with the premiums.

14. It shall be lawful for the University and College, if they shall think fit, in any lease to be granted under the powers of this Act to cause to be omitted the covenant on the part of the lessee, hereinbefore directed to be inserted, for keeping the houses and buildings comprised in such lease, or to be erected and built on the lands therein comprised, insured from loss or damage by fire, and in lieu of such covenant to insert or cause to be inserted in any such lease a covenant on the part of such University or College to keep such houses and buildings insured from loss or damage by fire to the amount of three fourths at least of the value thereof, and to lay out the money which shall be received by

virtue of such insurance in substantially rebuilding, repairing, and reinstating such houses or buildings as shall be destroyed or damaged by fire, and to cause to be inserted in such lease such covenants, stipulations, and provisions for securing to such University or College the repayment of the sum or sums of money which shall be paid by them in effecting or keeping on foot any such insurance as such University or College shall think fit.

15. From and after the passing of this Act it shall be lawful for the said Universities and any College therein respectively, and the Colleges of Saint Mary of Winchester near Winchester and of King Henry the Sixth at Eton, either by themselves or by any person or persons on their behalf, to enter into such contract or contracts in writing as they may deem expedient with any person who may be willing to purchase the liberty or privilege of digging and raising gravel or sand, or earth, loam, or clay, suitable for making bricks or tiles, out of any part of the lands belonging to such University or College, and to grant to such person, either by indenture sealed with the common seal of such University or College, or by such other ways or means as may be deemed expedient, and for such considerations as to such University or College shall appear reasonable or proper, the liberty or privilege of digging and raising such gravel, sand, earth, loam, or clay, and of selling and disposing of the same, together with all such powers as may be requisite for carrying such contract or contracts into effect: provided always, that the net monies which shall be received by the University or College for or in respect of the grant of such liberty or privilege as aforesaid shall be applied and disposed of by such University or College in the manner herein-after directed respecting the net rents, tolls, duties, royalties, and reservations which shall be received by such University or College for or in respect of any lease to be granted under the authority of the twentieth section of this Act. *Power to Universities and Colleges to dispose of brick earth, &c.*

16. From and after the passing of this Act it shall be lawful for the said Universities and any College therein respectively, and the Colleges of Saint Mary of Winchester near Winchester and of King Henry the Sixth at Eton, at any time or times to make or enter into any arrangement *Lessors may enter into arrangements with Lessees as for lighting, paving, &c.*

or arrangements with the lessees or tenants of the lands leased under the authority of this Act or any or either of them, either alone or in conjunction with any other person or persons, for the lighting, paving, draining, and cleansing, or otherwise for the general improvement or more convenient use and enjoyment of such lands, or any part thereof, or the roads, streets, ways, approaches, avenues, or passages in or about the same; and, for such purposes or any or either of them, to give and grant or allow such easements, rights, liberties, and privileges in or over such lands or any part thereof, to any person or persons whomsoever, as by such University or College shall be deemed expedient, and under and subject to such provisoes, conditions, and restrictions as shall be deemed proper; and, for carrying into effect any such arrangement, to enter into and to insert or cause to be inserted in any lease or leases or contract or contracts for any lease or leases, to be made or entered into by virtue of this Act, such covenants, agreements, and stipulations on the part of such University or College, or the said lessee or respective lessees, his, her, or their heirs, executors, administrators, and assigns, as by such University or College shall be thought requisite or proper.

Universities and Colleges may enter into arrangements with Lessees as to payment of land tax and tithe rent-charges.

17. It shall be lawful for the said Universities and any College therein respectively, and the Colleges of Saint Mary of Winchester near Winchester and of King Henry the Sixth at Eton, if they shall think it expedient so to do, to enter into any arrangement for the payment by them of the land tax and tithe rentcharge, or either of them, for the time being payable for or in respect of any of the lands comprised in any lease to be granted under the authority of this Act, or any part thereof, in exoneration therefrom of the respective lessees or tenants of such lands, any or either of them, and to accept and reserve an additional or increased rent or rents in consideration thereof, and in any lease or leases, contract or contracts, to be made or entered into in pursuance of this Act, to enter into or cause to be inserted such covenants, stipulations, and agreements on the part of such University or College, or the lessee or lessees, his, her, or their heirs, executors, administrators, or assigns, with respect to the land tax and tithe rentcharges, or either

of them, to which the lands thereby leased or agreed to be leased are or may be respectively liable, or any part thereof, as upon a due consideration of all circumstances shall to such University or College seem advisable.

18. It shall be lawful for the said Universities and any College therein respectively, and the College* of Saint Mary of Winchester near Winchester and of King Henry the Sixth at Eton, to lay out and appropriate any part or parts of the lands authorized to be leased on building or repairing leases under the provisions of this Act, as and for a way or ways, streets, squares, approaches, avenues, roads, courts, passages, sewers, drains, yards, gardens, or pleasure grounds, or other easements or conveniences for the general improvement of the said lands, or for the accommodation or convenience of the tenants and occupiers thereof, in such manner and upon such terms, and either subject to or without being subject to any annual or other payments by such tenants or occupiers, as shall be mentioned or agreed upon in any lease to be made in pursuance of this Act, or in any general deed to be executed for that purpose under the common seal of such University or College and to be enrolled in one of Her Majesty's Courts of Record at Westminster, and also by such lease or by such general deed to give such privileges and other easements in or over the said lands or any part thereof as such University or College shall deem reasonable or convenient.

Power to appropriate any part of lands for streets, squares, &c.

* *So in orig.*

19. It shall be lawful for the said Universities and any College therein respectively, and the Colleges of Saint Mary of Winchester near Winchester and of King Henry the Sixth at Eton, from time to time after the passing of this Act, under such restrictions as are hereafter mentioned, by any deed to be executed under their common seal, to grant by way of lease unto any person or persons whomsoever any liberties, licences, powers, or authorities to have, use, or take, either in common with or to the exclusion of any other person or persons, all or any of the water flowing or which shall or may flow or be made to flow in, through, upon, or over any lands belonging to such University or College, or any part or parts thereof (except as herein-after is mentioned), and also all wayleaves or waterleaves, canals, watercourses,

Power to lease running waters and water leaves and wayleaves &c.

tramroads, railways, and other ways, paths, passages, either subterraneous or over the surface of any lands, yards, wharfs, or other like easements or privileges in, upon, out of, or over any part or parts of the lands belonging to such University or College (except as herein-after is mentioned), for any term or number of years not exceeding sixty years, to take effect in possession and not in reversion or by way of future interest; so as there be reserved on every such grant by way of lease as last aforesaid, payable half-yearly or oftener during the continuance of the term thereby granted, the best yearly rent or rents, either in the shape of a stated or fixed sum of money, or by way of toll or otherwise, that can be reasonably obtained for the same, without taking any fine, premium, or foregift, or anything in the nature of a fine, premium, or foregift, for the making thereof, (other than any provision or provisions which it may be deemed expedient to insert in any such grant, rendering it obligatory on the grantee or lessee, or grantees or lessees, to repair or contribute to the repair of any roads or ways, or to keep open or otherwise use in any specified manner any water or watercourse to be comprised in or affected by any such grant or lease;) and so as there be contained in every such grant by way of lease as last aforesaid a condition or power of re-entry, or a power to make void the same, in case the rent thereby reserved or made payable, or any part thereof, shall not be paid within some reasonable time to be therein specified in that behalf; and so as the respective grantees or lessees do execute counterparts of the respective grants or leases; and generally that in and by any such grant by way of lease as last aforesaid there shall or may be reserved and contained any other reservations, covenants, agreements, or stipulations whatsoever, not inconsistent with those hereby required to be reserved or contained, which it shall be deemed expedient to introduce therein.

Power to grant Mining Leases for a term not exceeding sixty years.

20. It shall be lawful for the said Universities and for any College therein respectively, and for the Colleges of Saint Mary of Winchester near Winchester and of King Henry the Sixth at Eton, from time to time after the passing of this Act, by indenture sealed with their common seal, to lease any mines, quarries, minerals, and substances in, under, or upon any lands belonging to such University or College, either

with or without any messuages, buildings, or lands convenient to be held or occupied with the same respectively, and either with or without the surface of any lands in or under which the same or any part thereof respectively shall lie, and whether the same have or have not been hitherto opened or worked, unto any person or persons, for any term or number of years not exceeding sixty years, to take effect in possession and not in reversion or by way of future interest, together with full liberty, power, and authority to search, bore, dig, sink for, work, and raise the said mines, quarries, minerals, and substances, and to work any adjacent mine by way of out-stroke or other underground communication, and for those purposes from time to time to do whatever shall be needful or requisite for, in, or about the winning, working, getting, cleansing, and smelting of the said minerals and substances and for the manufacturing and carrying away the same, or otherwise incident to mining operations; so as in every such lease there be reserved and made payable during the term thereby granted the best and most improved yearly or other rent or rents, whether certain or contingent, either in money or in tolls, duties, royalties, and reservations, by the acre, or by the ton, or otherwise, as can under the circumstances of the case be reasonably obtained for the same; and so as such lease be made without any fine, premium, or foregift for the same; and so as in every such lease there be contained on the part of the lessee a covenant for the due payment of the rent to be thereby reserved, and of all taxes, charges, rates, assessments, and impositions whatsoever affecting the lands therein comprised, and also a proviso or condition of re-entry for nonpayment of the rent thereby respectively reserved for some reasonable time to be therein specified, or for nonperformance or nonobservance of any of the covenants or agreements on the part of the lessee therein contained (except such, if any, of the same covenants and agreements, not being for the payment of rent, as such University or College shall think it reasonable to except); and so as there be not contained in such lease any clause or words authorizing the lessee to commit waste, or exempting him from punishment for committing waste, save so far as may be necessary for the purposes aforesaid; and so as the lessee do execute a counterpart of such

T

lease, and enter into such further or other covenants and agreements as such University or College granting such lease shall deem expedient, due regard being had in every case to the custom of the country or district within which such mines, quarries, minerals, or substances are situate or found.

Application of mineral rents, &c.

21. All the net rents, tolls, duties, royalties, and reservations which shall be received by the University or College for or in respect of any lease to be granted under the authority of the last foregoing section shall be applied and disposed of by such University or College in manner following; (that is to say,) one equal third part of such net rents, tolls, duties, royalties, and reservations shall be applicable and be applied by such University or College as part of their ordinary income, and the remaining two equal third parts thereof shall be applicable and be applied by such University or College in or upon any of the purposes following; (that is to say,) in the purchase of lands to be conveyed to the use or for the benefit of such University or College, or in the erection of new buildings, or in the addition to and enlargement of any existing buildings, or in the drainage or other permanent and lasting improvement of any lands belonging to such University or College, or in the purchase of any wayleaves or other easements in, over, or upon any lands adjoining or near to any such lands; and in the meantime, until such two equal third parts shall be applied in or upon any of the purposes aforesaid, the same shall be invested by such University or College in the purchase of Government Stocks, Funds, or Securities, and the interest, dividends, and annual proceeds thereof shall be received by such University or College, and be applicable as part of their ordinary income.

Powers to release, enter into new contracts, and accept surrenders of Leases, &c.

22. It shall be lawful for the said Universities and any College therein respectively, and the Colleges of Saint Mary of Winchester near Winchester and of King Henry the Sixth at Eton, at any time to release any person or persons with whom any contract or contracts may be entered into in pursuance of this Act, and his, her, or their executors, administrators, and assigns, from the performance of all or any part of the same contract or contracts respectively, and to enter into any new contract or contracts, according to the provisions of this Act, with the same or any other person or persons,

or his, her, or their executors, administrators, or assigns, in lieu of the contract or contracts or the part or parts of the contract or contracts in respect whereof such release shall have been made; and to enter into any new covenants and agreements with any person or persons with whom any contract or contracts may be entered into, by way of addition to or explanation or alteration of all or any part or parts of the covenants and agreements in any such contract or contracts respectively contained; and also to accept a surrender or surrenders of all or any part of the lands which may be comprised in any such contract or contracts, and of all or any part of the lands comprised in any lease to be granted under any of the powers herein-before contained, or which shall have been granted before the passing of this Act; and, upon any such surrender, to grant, according to the powers herein-before contained, either to the person surrendering or to any other person or persons, one or more new lease or leases of the lands so surrendered or any part thereof, either alone or together with any other lands, and with liberty, in regulating the terms upon which such new lease or leases shall be granted, to make such allowance or remuneration, either by way of annual charge upon the lands so surrendered or otherwise, to the person surrendering the same, or his or her executors, administrators, or assigns, for the value (if any) of the estate or interest which shall have been so surrendered, as to such University or College shall seem reasonable, but so that no such allowance or remuneration by way of annual charge shall continue for a longer term or period than the term or period at which the estate or interest which shall be surrendered would, if not surrendered, have determined by effluxion of time: provided always, that upon any such surrender as aforesaid it shall be lawful for the said University or College, if they shall think fit, to grant a new lease or new leases of the lands so surrendered, either to the person surrendering the same or to any other person, for any term or number of years not exceeding the then unexpired residue of the term granted by the surrendered lease, at a rent or several rents equivalent to the amount of the rent which was reserved by the surrendered lease in respect of the entirety of the lands so surrendered; and, in making such new lease or leases, either again to subject the whole of the lands so surrendered to a rent equivalent to the whole amount of the rent which was payable for the same lands under such surrendered lease, or so to apportion the amount of rent which was payable under such surrendered lease as that in the new lease or leases, so to be made as aforesaid, some specific part or parts only and not the whole of such lands shall be subject to the whole or some specific portion only of the amount of rent which was payable under such surrendered lease, and so that, if a rent or rents equivalent to the whole amount of the rent which was payable under such surrendered lease shall by any such new lease or leases be reserved or made payable in respect of a part or parts only of such lands, such University or College may grant a lease or leases of the residue of such lands at the yearly rent of a peppercorn: provided always, that a certificate in writing under the hand of the Solicitor, Steward, Chapter Clerk, or Agent for the time being of such University or College, that the entire rent mentioned in the surrendered lease has been duly reserved in pursuance of this enactment, shall, as regards the lessee or lessees under such new lease or leases, and all persons claiming under him or them, be sufficient and conclusive evidence of such reservation: provided also, that, when and as any such new lease shall be granted, under the powers herein contained, of any lands comprised in any such surrendered lease, the lease so surrendered shall form no part of the title to such new lease.

On recovery of possession of any lands under a condition of re-entry new Leases may be granted.

23. If the University or College shall at any time hereafter enter upon and resume or recover possession of any lands comprised in any lease or contract, to be granted or entered into under the powers of this Act, by virtue of any condition of re-entry therein contained, then and in every such case it shall be lawful for such University or College, if they shall think fit, to grant leases, or enter into contracts to grant leases and afterwards to grant leases, of the same lands and every or any part thereof, pursuant to the powers and subject to the restrictions herein contained: provided always, that in any such case as last aforesaid it shall be lawful for such University or College, if they shall think fit, to grant a lease, or to enter into a contract to grant a lease

and afterwards to grant a lease, of the lands comprised in any such forfeited lease or contract, for any term or number of years not exceeding the then unexpired residue of the term granted or agreed to be granted by such forfeited lease or contract, at a yearly rent or yearly rents which shall not be less in amount than the yearly rent reserved or agreed to be reserved by such forfeited lease or contract, but subject in all other respects to the restrictions herein contained.

24. If any lease or grant purporting to have been granted or made by virtue of this Act shall, by reason of any technical error or informality in exercising the powers of this Act, be void or voidable, then and in every such case it shall be lawful for the University or College, if they shall think fit, to confirm such lease or grant, or to make a new lease or grant of the lands therein comprised, pursuant to the powers and subject to the restrictions herein contained, in lieu of such void or voidable lease, for any term or number of years not exceeding the then residue of the term of years granted or purported to be granted by such void or voidable lease, and at and under a yearly rent or yearly rents which shall be not less in amount than the yearly rent reserved by such void or voidable lease. *Power to confirm Leases which may be void or voidable by reason of any technical error or informality.*

25. A memorandum in writing under the hand of the Steward, Chapter Clerk, Solicitor, or Agent of the University or College endorsed upon any lease to be granted under the powers of this Act, acknowledging that he has received such counterpart of the said lease as is hereby required to be executed, or a recital or statement in such lease to the effect that such counterpart has been duly executed, shall, in favour of the lessee and of all persons claiming under him, be conclusive evidence that such counterpart was duly made and executed pursuant to the provisions of this Act. *Receipts endorsed upon Leases,&c., to be evidence of execution of counterparts.*

26. Provided always, that this Act or anything herein contained shall not authorize the granting of any lease, or the laying out or appropriating for the purposes in this Act mentioned, of any house or building or lands forming part of or attached to or locally situate within the boundaries or precincts of any College, or of any offices, outbuildings, yards, and gardens to any such College adjoining or appertaining, and which may be necessary or convenient for actual *Particular property not to be leased.*

occupation by the members of any such College or any of them, or the grant or lease of any mines, minerals, quarries, ways, watercourses, or other easements the grant thereof* may be prejudicial to the convenient enjoyment of any such house or building or the offices or gardens thereto belonging.

* So in orig.

Powers to raise monies, with consent of Copyhold Commissioners, by Mortgage for certain purposes.

27. It shall be lawful for the said Universities and any College therein respectively, and for the Colleges of St. Mary of Winchester near Winchester and of King Henry the Sixth at Eton, from time to time and at any time hereafter, with the consent of the said Copyhold Commissioners (such consent to be evidenced by an order, to be issued under their hands and common seal, in the form or to the effect set forth in the said schedule hereto), to raise by mortgage of any lands belonging to such University or College, for any term of years (determinable as hereafter provided), such sum or sums of money (together with all reasonable costs and expenses incidental to such raising and the application thereof) as shall be certified by the surveyor of the University or College to be properly required, and shall be authorized by the said Commissioners, with interest thereon not exceeding the rate to be specified in such order, and to apply such sum or sums of money for all or any of the purposes following; (that is to say,) for or towards the restoration and improvement and (if need be) enlargement of any house or building forming part of or connected with or otherwise belonging to such University or College, or for or towards the erection of new or additional houses or buildings, or for the extension and improvement of any existing houses or buildings upon any lands belonging to such University or College, or for the drainage or other permanent and lasting improvement of any lands belonging to such University or College.

Provision for the discharge of the monies borrowed on Mortgages.

28. Where any mortgage is made by any University or College under either of the powers herein-before contained for that purpose, such University or College shall, out of the rents and profits of the lands comprised in any such mortgage, or out of the funds and revenues of such University or College, either repay the same monies by the grant of an annuity, upon such terms as shall be approved of by the said Commissioners, to the lender or other person to whom the same monies shall be due, or shall keep down all the

interest of such monies as the same shall become due, and annually thereafter reserve or raise out of the same rents and profits, or funds and revenues, and out of the income arising from any such sinking fund as shall have been created under the provisions following, one thirtieth part at least of the amount of the principal debt, and apply the same to the reduction thereof, either by direct payment to the lender or other person to whom the same shall be due, if he shall consent or be under engagements or otherwise required to receive the same, or by the creation of a sinking fund for that purpose in such manner as shall be approved of by the said Commissioners, to the end that the whole of every such principal debt may be discharged, with the mesne interest thereof, out of the said rents and profits, or funds and revenues and income, within or at the expiration of the period of thirty years from the borrowing thereof: provided also, that in every such mortgage there shall be contained a proviso, that, when the whole of such principal debt, interests, and costs shall be discharged and satisfied in manner aforesaid, the mortgage term thereby created shall absolutely cease and determine: provided always, that, where any such mortgage is made for raising money for the purchase of the estate or interest of a lessee of lands held under such University or College, provision shall be made for applying by some of the means aforesaid, so long as the lease but for such purchase would have continued (unless the monies secured by such mortgage be sooner discharged), towards the interest and discharge of the principal money, such yearly sum as shall be certified by the said Copyhold Commissioners to be equal to the clear yearly value of the lands comprised in such lease, after deducting the rent reserved to the University or College, and making other usual and proper landlord's deductions.

29. The powers and provisions of this Act in relation to any lands vested in the said Universities and in any College therein respectively, and in the Colleges of Saint Mary of Winchester near Winchester and of King Henry the Sixth at Eton, shall extend and be applicable not only to any lands so vested as the property or for the general purposes of the University or College, but also to any lands so vested which may be held upon any trusts or for any special

Act to extend to lands held in trust or for special endowments.

endowment or other purpose connected with the University or College.

Act not to restrain existing powers.

30. Nothing in this Act contained shall restrain the said Universities or any College therein respectively, or the Colleges of Saint Mary of Winchester near Winchester or of King Henry the Sixth at Eton, from exercising any powers of sale, enfranchisement, exchange, purchase, or borrowing monies, or from granting any leases or making any grants, whether by way of renewal or otherwise, which the said Universities or any such College as aforesaid might have exercised or granted under the provisions of any Public or Private Act of Parliament, or under any other authority, or in any other manner whatsoever, in case this Act had not been passed: provided, that upon any exchange being effected under the provisions of the Acts for Inclosure, Exchange, and Improvement of Land it shall be lawful for the Inclosure Commissioners for England and Wales to authorize any monies by way of equality of exchange to be received by any such University or College; and any monies to be so received shall be paid into the Bank of England to the account and in manner herein-before particularly mentioned; and until such payment as aforesaid no order of exchange shall be finally confirmed by the said last-named Commisssioners; and a recital of such payment in the order of exchange shall be conclusive evidence thereof: provided also, that, notwithstanding

18 Eliz. c. 6.

the provisions of the Act passed in the eighteenth year of the reign of Her Majesty Queen Elizabeth, chapter six, it shall not be necessary to reserve or make payable in corn any part of the rent to be reserved upon any lease to be granted under the powers of this Act.

Christ Church to be considered a College.

31. For the purposes of this Act the Cathedral or House of Christ Church in Oxford shall be considered to be to all intents and purposes a College of the University.

Interpretation of terms.

32. In the construction of this Act (unless there be something in the subject or context repugnant thereto) the word "person" or the word "persons" shall include corporations, whether aggregate or sole, authorized by law to take and hold lands; the word "lease" shall include grant by copy of court roll; the word "lands" shall include tenements and hereditaments, corporeal and incorporeal; and the word "lessee"

shall include any person or body corporate in whom any subsisting lease or grant, or the term or estate thereby granted in the whole or any part of the lands comprised in such lease, is, either by the original grant or demise, or by assignment, devise, or operation of law, for the time being vested.

33. It shall be sufficient for all purposes to cite this Act as Short "The Universities and College Estates Act, 1858."

The SCHEDULE referred to in the foregoing Act.

Form of Order authorizing Sale or Enfranchisement or Exchange.

COPYHOLD COMMISSION.

In the matter of " The Universities and College Estates Act, 1858." *Ex parte* Oxford [*or*   ] University [*or*   College in the University of   ].

WHEREAS a statement has been submitted to the Copyhold Commissioners on behalf of the said University [*or* College] containing a proposal for the sale or enfranchisement or exchange [*as the case may be*] of certain lands, &c., belonging to the said University [*or* College] [*state shortly the particulars of such lands, &c., the terms of such enfranchisement, and the consideration money or description of other lands to be given in exchange, with any other material circumstances*] : Now the said Commissioners, being of opinion, upon consideration of the circumstances, that the said proposed sale, [*or* enfranchisement, *or* exchange,] will be advantageous and for the interests of the said University [*or* College] and their successors, do authorize the said University [*or* College] to carry such proposed sale, [*or* enfranchisement, *or* exchange,] into effect upon the terms above stated.

Witness their hands and common seal, this   day of

Form of Order approving a Reinvestment in the Purchase of other Lands.

COPYHOLD COMMISSION.

In the matter of "The Universities and College Estates Act, 1858." *Ex parte* Oxford [*or*   ] University [*or*   College in the University of   ].

WHEREAS there is now standing in the books of the Governor and Company of the Bank of England, to the credit of the account of the Copyhold Commissioners *ex parte* [*here state the particular account*], the sum of £   [*insert amount of cash or stock*], being monies received from the sale [*or* enfranchisement, *or* for equality of exchange, *as the case may be*] of certain lands belonging to the said University [*or* College] by virtue of certain orders heretofore issued by the said Commissioners under the provisions of the said Act: and whereas it has been represented to the said Commissioners that the purchase of certain lands situate at   consisting of   [*state shortly the particulars of such lands, the purchase money, with any other material circumstances*] is a fit and proper purchase whereon to invest the said sum of £   [*or the sum of* £   , *part of the said aggregate sum of* £   ]: Now the said Commissioners, being of opinion, upon consideration of the above circumstances, that the said proposed purchase will be advantageous and for the interests of the said University [*or* College] and their successors, do hereby approve of the same on the terms above stated, and do direct that the same purchase shall forthwith be completed by such University [*or* College], and that upon the completion thereof the said sum of £   , now standing to the credit of the said account of the said Commissioners as aforesaid, [*or* the said sum of £   , to be paid or raised out of the said sum of £   now standing to the credit of the account of the Commissioners as aforesaid,] shall be applied in payment of the said purchase money.

Witness their hands and common seal, this   day of

Form of Order authorizing a Mortgage.

COPYHOLD COMMISSION.

In the matter of "The Universities and College Estates Act, 1858." *Ex parte* Oxford [*or*   ] University [*or*   College in the University of   ].

WHEREAS a statement has been submitted to the Copyhold Commissioners on behalf of the said University [*or* College], containing a proposal for the raising of the sum of £   by way of mortgage of [*name the lands proposed to be mortgaged, the purposes for which the sum is to be raised, with any other material circumstances*] : Now the said Commissioners, being of opinion, upon consideration of the circumstances, that the said proposed sum of £   may be advantageously raised and applied in the manner and for the purposes aforesaid, do authorize the said University [*or* College] to raise the same sum for the purposes aforesaid by mortgage of the said lands, for any term not exceeding   years with interest thereon in the meantime after the rate of £   per cent. per annum, payable half-yearly during the continuance of the said loan, or [*as the case may be*] by the grant of an annuity to be secured on such lands in manner provided by the twenty-seventh section of this Act.

Witness their hands and common seal, this   day of

An Act to regulate the qualifications of Practitioners in Medicine and Surgery.

3. A Council, which shall be styled "The General Council of Medical Education and Registration of the United Kingdom," herein-after referred to as the General Council, shall be established, and Branch Councils for England, Scotland, and Ireland respectively formed thereout as herein-after mentioned.

[By section 4 the Universities of Oxford and Cambridge are two of the Bodies each of which is to choose one person from time to time to be a Member of the General Council.

[Section 15 provides for the registration of persons possessing any one or more of the qualifications described in the Schedule (A.) annexed to the Act: and one of the items in Schedule (A.) is "Doctor, or Bachelor, or Licentiate of Medicine, or Master in Surgery, of any University of the United Kingdom."]

Council may require information as to course of study, &c., required for obtaining qualifications.

18. The several Colleges and Bodies in the United Kingdom mentioned in Schedule (A.) to this Act shall from time to time, when required by the General Council, furnish such Council with such information as they may require as to the courses of study and examinations to be gone through in order to obtain the respective qualifications mentioned in Schedule (A.) to this Act, and the ages at which such courses of study and examination are required to be gone through, and such qualifications are conferred, and generally as to the requisites for obtaining such qualifications; and any Member or Members of the General Council, or any person or persons deputed for this purpose by such Council, or by any Branch Council, may attend and be present at any such examinations.

Colleges may unite in conducting examinations.

19. Any two or more of the Colleges and Bodies in the United Kingdom mentioned in Schedule (A.) to this Act may, with the sanction and under the directions of the General Council, unite or co-operate in conducting the examinations required for qualifications to be registered under this Act.

Defects in the course of study or examinations may be represented by General Council to Privy Council.

20. In case it appear to the General Council that the course of study and examinations to be gone through in order to obtain any such qualification from any such College or Body are not such as to secure the possession by persons obtaining such qualification of the requisite knowledge and skill for the efficient practice of their profession, it shall be lawful for such General Council to represent the same to Her Majesty's Most Honourable Privy Council.

Privy Council may suspend the right of registration in respect of qualifications granted by College &c. in default.

21. It shall be lawful for the Privy Council, upon any such representation as aforesaid, if it see fit, to order that any qualification granted by such College or Body, after such time as may be mentioned in the order, shall not confer any right to be registered under this Act: provided always, that it shall be lawful for Her Majesty, with the advice of Her Privy Council, when it is made to appear to Her, upon further representation from the General Council or otherwise, that such College or Body has made effectual provision, to

the satisfaction of such General Council, for the improvement of such course of study or examinations or the mode of conducting such examinations, to revoke any such order.

28. If any of the said Colleges or the said Bodies at any time exercise any power they possess by law of striking off from the list of such College or Body the name of any one of their Members, such College or Body shall signify to the General Council the name of the Member so struck off; and the General Council may, if they see fit, direct the Registrar to erase forthwith from the Register the qualification derived from such College or Body in respect of which such Member was registered, and the Registrar shall note the same therein: provided always, that the name of no person shall be erased from the Register on the ground of his having adopted any theory of medicine or surgery.

^{marginal:} Names Member struck from li College &c. to signifie Genera Counci

21 & 22 Vict. c. 98.

An Act to amend the Public Health Act, 1848, and to make further provision for the Local Government of towns and populous districts.

82. Notwithstanding anything contained in this Act, the Oxford and Cambridge Commissioners described in the thirty-first section of the Public Health Act, 1848, shall be the Bodies authorized to adopt this Act for the districts respectively within their jurisdiction; and in the event of the adoption of this Act by the said Cambridge Commissioners, the said Commissioners shall be the Local Board for the District of Cambridge; and in the event of such adoption by the said Oxford Commissioners, the Local Board of the Oxford District shall consist of the Vice-Chancellor of the University of Oxford and the Mayor of Oxford for the time being, and of forty-five other Commissioners, fifteen to be elected by the University of Oxford, sixteen by the Town Council of Oxford, and fourteen by the Ratepayers of the Parishes situate within the jurisdiction of the Oxford Commissioners; and the election of such Commissioners by the Town Council and by the Ratepayers of the Parishes respectively shall be conducted at the same tmie, in the same way, and subject to the same

^{marginal:} Except of Oxfc and Ca bridge.

regulations in and subject to which Members constituting the Body of Oxford Commissioners are now respectively chosen by such Town Council and Parishes; and the fifteen Commissioners to be elected by the University shall be elected as follows; namely, four Commissioners shall be elected by the University in Convocation, and eleven Commissioners shall be elected by the Heads and Senior Bursars of the several Colleges and by the Heads of the several Halls; and the elections shall be conducted by the said University and by the Colleges and Halls respectively at the same time and in the same way and subject to the same regulations in and subject to which Guardians of the Poor for the University and for the Colleges and Halls are now chosen by them respectively, save that in the election of Commissioners the Heads and Bursars of all the Colleges and the Heads of all the Halls shall be summoned by the Vice-Chancellor for that purpose, and shall be entitled to vote; and differences between either of the Universities of Oxford and Cambridge and the Local Boards of Oxford and Cambridge respectively within the meaning of the one hundred and fifth section of the Public Health Act, 1848, shall be settled by arbitration in the manner provided by that Act.

22 & 23 Vict. c. 19.

An Act to repeal part of an Act passed in the thirteenth year of Elizabeth, chapter twenty-nine, concerning the several Incorporations of the Universities of Oxford and Cambridge, and the confirmation of the charters, liberties, and privileges granted to either of them.

WHEREAS in and by an Act passed in the thirteenth year of Her Majesty Queen Elizabeth, intituled An Act concerning the several Incorporations of the Universities of Oxford and Cambridge and the confirmation of the charters, liberties, and privileges granted to either of them, it is amongst other things enacted, that the Letters Patent of the Queen's Highness's father, King Henry the Eighth, made and granted to the Chancellor and Scholars of the said

13 Eliz. c. 29, s. 2.

University of Oxford, bearing date the first day of April in the fourteenth year of His reign, and the Letters Patents of the Queen's Majesty that then was, made and granted unto the Chancellor Masters and Scholars of the University of Cambridge, bearing date the sixth-and-twentieth day of April in the third year of Her Highness's most gracious reign, and also all other Letters Patents by any of the progenitors or predecessors of our said Sovereign Lady made to either of the said corporated bodies severally or to any of their predecessors of either of the said Universities, by whatsoever name or names the said Chancellor Masters and Scholars of either of the said Universities in any of the said Letters Patents had been theretofore named, should from thenceforth be good, effectual, and available in the law, to all intents, constructions, and purposes, to the foresaid then Chancellor Masters and Scholars of either of the said Universities and to their successors for evermore, after and according to the form, words, sentences, and true meaning of every of the same Letters Patents, as amply, fully, and largely as if the same Letters Patents had been recited verbatim in that present Act of Parliament, anything to the contrary in anywise notwithstanding; and it was further enacted, that all manner of instruments, inden- Ibid. s. 4. tures, obligations, writings obligatory, and recognizances made or acknowledged by any person or persons or body corporate to either of the said corporated bodies of either of the said Universities, by what name or names soever the said Chancellor Masters and Scholars of either of the said Universities had been theretofore called in any of the said instruments, indentures, obligations, writings obligatory, or recognizances, should be from thenceforth available, stand and continue of good, perfect, and full force and strength, to the then Chancellor Masters and Scholars of either of the said Universities and to their successors, to all intents, constructions, and purposes, although they or their predecessors or any of them in any of the said instruments, indentures, obligations, writings obligatory, or recognizances were named by any name contrary or diverse to the name of the then Chancellor Masters and Scholars of either of the said Universities; and it was also enacted, that as well the said Letters Patents of the Ibid. s. 5. Queen's Highness's said father, King Henry the Eighth, bearing date as was before expressed, made and granted to the said corporated body of the said University of Oxford, as the Letters Patents of the Queen's Majesty aforesaid granted to the Chancellor Masters and Scholars of the University of Cambridge, bearing date as aforesaid, and all other Letters Patents by any of the progenitors or predecessors of Her Highness, and all manner of liberties, franchises, immunities, quietances, and privileges, leets, law days, and other things whatsoever therein expressed, given or granted to the said Chancellor Masters and Scholars of either of the said Universities or to any of their predecessors of either of the said Universities, by whatsoever name the said Chancellor Masters and Scholars of either of the said Universities in any of the said Letters Patents be named, were and by virtue of that present Act should be from thenceforth ratified, stablished, and confirmed unto the said Chancellor Masters and Scholars of either of the said Universities and to their successors for ever, any statute, law, usage, custom, construction, or other thing to the contrary in anywise notwithstanding;

Ibid. s. 7. provided always, and it was enacted, that the said Act or anything therein contained should not extend to the prejudice or hurt of the liberties and privileges of right belonging to the Mayors Bailiffs and Burgesses of the Town of Cambridge and City of Oxford, but that they the said Mayors Bailiffs and Burgesses and every of them and their successors should be and continue free in such sort and degree, and enjoy such liberties, freedoms, and immunities, as they or any of them lawfully might have done before the making of that present Act, anything contained in the said Act to the contrary notwithstanding:

And whereas by Letters Patent, dated the twenty-ninth day of May in the thirty-second year of the reign of His late Majesty King Henry the Third, the said King did grant to the Scholars of the University of Oxford, amongst other things, that, so often and whensoever the Mayor and Bailiffs of Oxford should take the Oath of their Fealty in their Common Place, the Commonalty of the same Town should inform the Chancellor, in order that, if he wished, by himself or by some chosen persons, he might be present at the taking of the aforesaid Oath, which Oath indeed as to the

22 & 23 VICT. c. 19.   289

aforesaid Scholars should be of this sort, that is to say, that the Mayor and Bailiffs themselves should keep the liberties and customs of the aforesaid University, otherwise their Oath should be of no avail, but should be taken again according to the prescribed form; but if the Chancellor should not wish to be present, either by himself or by a Proctor, the Oath should nevertheless be taken:

And whereas provisions in relation to the observance of the same Oath, or an altered Oath in lieu thereof, have been made by subsequent Letters Patent granted by Kings and Queens of this realm to the Chancellor Masters and Scholars of the University of Oxford, and also by Orders of the Privy Council made in the reigns of Queen Elizabeth, King James the First, and King Charles the Second:

And whereas by the Statutes of the University of Oxford, which the Chancellor and Vice-Chancellor of the University have taken their respective oaths to observe and perform, it is enjoined on each of them that they do exact the said annual Oath of the Mayor and Burgesses of Oxford:

And whereas the Mayor Aldermen and Citizens of the City of Oxford desire to be relieved from the obligation of taking any such Oath, and the Chancellor Masters and Scholars of the University of Oxford are willing that the said Mayor Aldermen and Citizens should be so relieved, but they are advised that such relief can only be granted by the authority of Parliament:

Be it therefore enacted by the Queen's most excellent Majesty, by and with the advice and consent of the Lords spiritual and temporal and Commons in this present Parliament assembled, and by the authority of the same, as follows:

1. So much of the herein-before recited Act of Parliament, and of all Charters, Letters Patent, Orders in Council, Obligations, Deeds, or Instruments, as imposes upon the said Mayor Aldermen and Citizens, or any of them, or any Municipal Officer of the City of Oxford, the obligation of taking any Oath for the conservation of the liberties and privileges of the University of Oxford, or any such Oath as is herein-before referred to, shall be and the same is hereby repealed and annulled and made void. *Obligation of Mayor &c. of Oxford to take Oath to keep the liberties and privileges of the University annulled.*

2. The Mayor Aldermen and Citizens of Oxford shall not *Prohibition of any*

U

<small>requisition to Mayor &c. to take such Oath.</small> hereafter, nor shall any of them, nor shall any Municipal Officer of the City of Oxford, be required to take any Oath or to make any Declaration for the conservation of the liberties and privileges of the University of Oxford: provided always, that, notwithstanding anything herein contained, the Mayor Aldermen and Citizens of Oxford and all Officers of the same City shall observe and keep all manner of lawful liberties and customs which the Chancellor Masters and Scholars of the said University have reasonably used, without any gainsaying; saving nevertheless the fidelity of the said Mayor Aldermen Citizens and Officers to the Queen's Majesty, and saving also the liberties and privileges of right belonging to the said Mayor Aldermen and Citizens and to the Officers of the said City.

22 & 23 Vict. Cap. 56.

<small>5 & 6 Will. 4, c. 63.</small> *An Act to amend the Act of the fifth and sixth years of King William the Fourth, chapter sixty-three, relating to Weights and Measures.*

<small>Powers of Universities to remain in force.</small> 11. The powers heretofore lawfully belonging to the Universities of Oxford and Cambridge respectively shall continue in full force, anything in this Act contained notwithstanding.

23 & 24 Vict. Cap. 23.

An Act to provide for the consideration of an Ordinance which has been laid before Parliament in a Report of the Oxford University Commissioners[b].

[The Commission under 17 & 18 Vict. c. 81 having expired, and an Ordinance concerning St. John's College having been left unsettled, this Act provides for the consideration of the Ordinance, and for any modification of it which may seem necessary, by a Committee of the Privy Council, and for the bringing it ultimately into force.]

---

[b] This Act is published entire at page 489 of "Ordinances and Statutes framed or approved by the Oxford University Commissioners," printed at the Clarendon Press in 1863.

23 & 24 Vict. Cap. 27.

An Act for granting to Her Majesty certain Duties on Wine Licences and Refreshment Houses, and for regulating the licensing of Refreshment Houses and the granting of Wine Licences.

45. Nothing in this Act contained shall extend to alter or in any manner to affect any of the rights or privileges of the Universities of Oxford or Cambridge, or the powers of the Chancellors or Vice-Chancellors of the same, as by law possessed under the respective charters of the said Universities or otherwise.

<small>Not to affect the privileges of the two Universities.</small>

23 & 24 Vict. Cap. 59.

An Act to extend the provisions of the Universities and College Estates Act, 1858, and of the Copyhold Acts, and of the Act of the third and fourth years of the Reign of Her Majesty, chapter one hundred and thirteen, and of the seventeenth and eighteenth years of the same Reign, chapter eighty-four, so far as the same relate to Universities and Colleges.

WHEREAS it is expedient that the provisions of the Universities and College Estates Act, 1858, should be extended, and that power should be given to Universities and Colleges, with the consent hereafter required, to raise monies by mortgage, under proper restrictions, to provide compensation for the loss of fines on non-renewal of leases; be it enacted by the Queen's most excellent Majesty, by and with the advice and consent of the Lords spiritual and temporal and Commons in this present Parliament assembled, and by the authority of the same, as follows:

<small>21 & 22 Vict. c. 44.</small>

1. Whenever any lease of any lands belonging to the Universities of Oxford, Cambridge, or Durham respectively,

<small>Power to raise monies by</small>

mortgage by way of compensation for loss of Fines on non-renewal of Leases.

or any College therein respectively, or the Colleges of Saint Mary of Winchester near Winchester or of King Henry the Sixth at Eton, the leases of which have been customarily renewed on payment of a fine, shall from any cause whatever, (other than the refusal of the University or College entitled to the reversion of such lands to accept such a sum of money by way of fine as shall be deemed reasonable by the Copyhold Commissioners, and shall be tendered by the lessee at the first and each successive time of renewal after the commencement of this Act, or within three months of such time, for the renewal of any lease theretofore regularly renewed), remain unrenewed at any customary period of renewal, or whenever any loss of fines shall have been occasioned by the surrender of any lease upon any transaction by way of sale or exchange between the said Universities or Colleges and their lessees under the fourth section of the Universities and College Estates Act, 1858, it shall be lawful for the said Universities and Colleges respectively from time to time, with the consent of the Copyhold Commissioners (such consent to be evidenced by an Order to be issued under their hands and the common seal of their Board), to raise by mortgage of any lands belonging to such University or College for any term of years (determinable as herein-after provided) such sum or sums of money (together with all reasonable costs and expenses incidental to such raising) as shall be required, and be stated in such Order, with interest thereon not exceeding the rate to be specified in such Order, for the purpose of paying, by way of indemnity, to the then existing Members of such University or College the same amount of money which would have accrued to the said Members if any such lease as aforesaid had been renewed in manner theretofore accustomed: provided always, that the said power of raising monies by mortgage shall not be exercised for the purpose of providing for the loss of more than two fines in respect of the same lands, and that, upon the creation of any such mortgage, provision shall be made by such University or College, with the approval of the said Copyhold Commissioners, for the discharge of the borrowed monies by some or one of the modes prescribed by the twenty-eighth section of the Universities and College Estates Act, 1858, or otherwise, so and in such manner as that the principal money to be borrowed at each customary period of renewal in respect of the same lands may be discharged, with the mesne interest of such money, within or at the expiration of thirty years from the borrowing thereof; provided also, that in every such mortgage there shall be contained a proviso, that, when the whole of such principal monies, interest, and costs shall be discharged, the mortgage term thereby created shall absolutely cease: provided always, that, after any sum shall have been raised under the power herein-before contained in lieu of the fines payable in respect of any lease of any lands, no fine shall thenceforth be taken for the renewal or grant of any lease of the same lands.

2. The Order to be issued by the said Commissioners pursuant to the foregoing provisions shall be similar to the "Form of Order authorizing a Mortgage" contained in the Schedule to the said Universities and College Estates Act, 1858, with such variations only as the circumstances of the case shall necessarily require. *Form of Order to be issued by Copyhold Commissioners.*

3. Where any lands belonging to any such University or College as aforesaid shall at any time have been leased at the best and most improved yearly rent without fine, no fine, premium, or foregift, or anything in the nature thereof, shall thereafter be taken by such University or College for the grant or renewal of any lease of the same lands. *Lands once leased at rack rent not thereafter to be leased upon fine.*

4. And whereas it is expedient that certain provisions of the Copyhold Acts, so far as the same provisions relate to Universities and Colleges, should be amended and explained as hereafter provided: be it further enacted, that, where any manor belonging to any of the Universities of Oxford, Cambridge, and Durham respectively, or any College therein respectively, or the Colleges of Saint Mary of Winchester near Winchester or King Henry the Sixth at Eton, shall be held by any person or persons on lease for a life or lives, or for a term of years, granted by any such University or College, the University or College entitled to such manor in reversion expectant on such lease, and the lessee thereof as aforesaid, shall jointly constitute "the lord" of such manor within the meaning of the Copyhold Acts; and all consideration monies payable to the lord of any such manor under the *Amendment of certain provisions of the Copyhold Acts with respect to Universities and Colleges.*

same Acts shall be dealt with in the manner directed by the thirty-ninth section of the Copyhold Act, 1852, or the sixteenth section of the Copyhold Act, 1858, (due notice of any such dealing being previously given to the University or College entitled as aforesaid,) until the time when the reversionary interest of such University or College in the manorial rights of such manor would, if the same had not been extinguished, have come into possession, when the said consideration monies, or any securities in which the same may have been invested, shall, upon petition to the Court of Chancery or on application to the trustees in whom the same shall then be vested (as the case may be), be paid or transferred to the Copyhold Commissioners to the account of the University or College entitled thereto, in the same manner and to be applied for the same purposes as enfranchisement monies payable for the benefit of any University or College are directed to be paid and applied by the first section of the Universities and College Estates Act, 1858.

Power to transfer lands vested in individual Members of Universities or Colleges to the University or College in its corporate capacity upon like trusts.

5. When any lands shall be vested in any person or persons being a Member or Members of any of the said Universities or Colleges in trust or for the benefit of the University or College, or the Head or any other Member thereof, it shall be lawful for such person or persons (with the consent of the said Copyhold Commissioners to be signified by any writing under their hands and the common seal of their Board) to convey and transfer such lands in such manner as that the same may be vested in the University or College in its corporate capacity, upon the trusts nevertheless affecting the same lands respectively.

Two Copyhold Commissioners to form a Board for exercise of powers under 21 & 22 Vict. c. 44.

6. Any two of the Copyhold Commissioners shall form a Board for the exercise of the powers and authorities conferred on the said Commissioners by the Universities and College Estates Act, 1858, and this Act; and any order, power of attorney, or other instrument, issued or executed pursuant to the provisions of the said Acts, which shall have been or shall hereafter be signed by any two of the said Commissioners, and sealed with the common seal of their Board, shall be valid and sufficient for all purposes whatsoever.

Extension of certain provisions

7. And whereas it is expedient that the provisions of the Act of the third and fourth years of the Reign of Her Majesty

(chapter one hundred and thirteen), and also of the Act of the seventeenth and eighteenth years of the same Reign (chapter eighty-four), so far as the same relate to Universities and Colleges, should be extended and amended as hereafter provided: be it further enacted, that section sixty-nine of the said Act of the third and fourth years of Her Majesty shall be construed to extend to and shall include as well benefices with cure of souls as ecclesiastical rectories, prebends, and other preferments without cure of souls, advowsons, and rights of patronage, whether exclusive or alternate, impropriate rectories, and other lands and hereditaments annexed or belonging to, or held either wholly or partly by or in trust for, any of the Universities of Oxford, Cambridge, and Durham, or any College therein respectively, or either of the Colleges of Saint Mary of Winchester near Winchester and of King Henry the Sixth at Eton, or the Head or any other Member of any such College; and also to extend to and to include and to authorize sales by each of the same Universities, as well as each of the Colleges therein respectively, and the said Colleges of Saint Mary of Winchester near Winchester and of King Henry the Sixth at Eton; and shall also be construed to enable the said Universities or Colleges to sell advowsons of benefices, the patronage whereof shall be vested in any person or persons in trust for any of the said Universities or Colleges or for the benefit of the Head or any other Member thereof respectively; and also to authorize, under the authority herein-after mentioned, the annexation of the whole or any part of the lands or other hereditaments or endowments belonging to any such ecclesiastical rectory, prebend, or other preferment without cure of souls, impropriate rectories, and other lands and hereditaments aforesaid, or the application of the proceeds of any sale thereof, and also the application of the proceeds of any sale of advowsons and rights of patronage, or any part of the proceeds of any such sales, which may be made under the said section of the said last-mentioned Act, or the Universities and College Estates Act, 1858, or under any other authority, or of any monies, stocks, funds, or securities belonging to such University, College, Head, or Member, by way of endowment or augmentation of any benefice with cure of souls, the patronage

of 3 & 4 Vict. c. 113 with respect to Universities and Colleges.

whereof shall belong to or be held in trust for or for the benefit of such University or College or the Head or other Member thereof: provided nevertheless, that the powers conferred by this clause shall not be exercised to the prejudice of the existing interest of any such Head or other Member of a College without his consent; and in case of any diminution being occasioned in the income of any such Head or other Member of a College by any sale, annexation, purchase, or investment that may be made under the provisions of the said Acts, arrangements may be made under the like authority for giving to such Head or other Member adequate compensation for such diminution of his income out of the revenues of such College or out of the proceeds of any such sale or investment: and the said section of the said last-mentioned Act shall extend to authorize under the like authority the purchase, out of any of the corporate funds or revenues of any such University or College, of advowsons of benefices and also of any rights of perpetual presentation or nomination to benefices, whether such benefices be or be not annexed to or held by or in trust for any of the said Universities or any such College as aforesaid or the Head or other Member of any such College, to be added to those in the patronage of such University or College; and the words "Colleges" and "College" in the said section of the said last-mentioned Act shall include the Cathedral or House of Christ Church in Oxford; and the words "proper securities" in the same section shall be construed to extend to authorize and shall include the purchase of lands in fee simple, and also an investment on any of the parliamentary stocks or public funds of Great Britain; and all such securities, lands, and stocks or funds shall be settled, held, applied, or disposed of in such manner as by the University or College effecting such sale, purchase, or investment, and by the like authority, shall be arranged and determined in that behalf; and every endowment or augmentation which shall be made by any University or College of any benefice with cure of souls under the authority of this section, or by virtue of the provisions of the Act of the first and second years of His late Majesty King William the Fourth (chapter forty-five) or any other Act or Acts of Parliament, shall be valid, notwithstanding the clear annual value of such benefice shall at the time of such endowment or augmentation exceed or be thereby made to exceed the limits prescribed by the sixteenth section of the said Act of the first and second years of King William the Fourth or any other Act or Acts of Parliament: provided, that no such augmentation or endowment beyond the clear annual value of five hundred pounds shall be made under the said Act of the first and second years of King William the Fourth, except with the consent of the Ecclesiastical Commissioners for England (to be testified by writing under their common seal) in addition to such other consents as may be otherwise required thereto.

8. On the sale or annexation under the last preceding clause of any ecclesiastical rectory, prebend, or other preferment without cure of souls, or of any impropriate rectory, to which any right of patronage shall belong, and which is not intended to be included in such sale or to accompany such annexation, such right of patronage shall, immediately after such sale or annexation, be separated from and be no longer exercised by the holder of such ecclesiastical rectory, prebend, or other preferment without cure of souls, or impropriate rectory, but shall by force of this Act be absolutely transferred to and vested in the University or College, the former patrons or owners of such ecclesiastical rectory, prebend, or other preferment, or impropriate rectory. *Provision as to right of Patronage severed.*

9. The Lands Clauses Consolidation Act, 1845, (except such parts thereof as relate to the purchase of lands otherwise than by agreement, and to the recovery of forfeitures, penalties, and costs, and to the sale of superfluous lands,) shall be incorporated with and form part of the said section sixty-nine of the said Act of the third and fourth years of Her Majesty (chapter one hundred and thirteen) as extended by this Act, and as if the corporate name or denomination of the University or College in each particular case had been inserted therein instead of "the Promoters of the Undertaking:" provided, that the powers by the said Act vested in "the Promoters of the Undertaking" shall be exercised only by such University or College with the consent of the Ecclesiastical Commissioners for England testified as aforesaid. *8 & 9 Vict c. 18 incorporated with 3 & 4 Vict. c. 113 s. 69.*

10. The "Authority" herein-before and in the said Act *The Ecclesiastical*

of the third and fourth years of Her Majesty provided shall, so far as relates to Universities and Colleges, be and be deemed to be the Ecclesiastical Commissioners for England; and such authority shall be deemed to be sufficiently exercised and evidenced by any writing under their common seal.

Commissioners constituted the "Authority" referred to.

Power to substitute land or other permanent endowment in lieu of annual rents or other payments, in extension of certain provisions of 17 & 18 Vict. c. 84.

11. Where any rent or annual sum of money granted, reserved, or made payable, or to be granted, reserved, or made payable, under any of the powers of the said Act of the seventeenth and eighteenth years of Her Majesty (chapter eighty-four) or of the several Acts therein mentioned or otherwise, to the Incumbent of any Church or Chapel, by way of endowment or in augmentation of the endowment of any such Church or Chapel, is or shall be charged upon or made payable out of any rectory impropriate, tithes, annual revenues, lands, tenements, or other hereditaments belonging to any of the said Universities or Colleges respectively, it shall be lawful for the said Universities and Colleges respectively, with the consent of the Incumbent for the time being of the said Church or Chapel, and also with the consent of the Archbishop or Bishop of the Diocese within which the said Church or Chapel shall be situate, and also of the Patron or Patrons of the said Church or Chapel, (such consent to be signified by the said consenting parties respectively executing the deed or deeds herein-after mentioned,) and notwithstanding any statute or law to the contrary, by deed duly executed to appropriate and annex in perpetuity to such Church or Chapel any lands, tithes or portion of tithes, or other hereditaments belonging to any such University or College as aforesaid, to the intent that the same may be held and enjoyed by the Incumbent for the time being of such Church or Chapel in lieu of and substitution for such rent or annual sum of money as aforesaid; and it shall be lawful for the said Incumbent for the time being to accept to him and his successors such substituted endowment or augmentation, and thereupon by the same or any other deed duly executed by him, and with such consents and so signified as aforesaid, to release any impropriate rectory, tithes, annual revenues, lands, tenements, or other hereditaments theretofore charged with the said rent or annual sum of money; and the premises so

released shall be thenceforth wholly discharged from the said rent or sum of money and from all powers and remedies for the recovery thereof: provided always, that no consent of any Archbishop or Bishop shall be given to any such annexation and release respectively as aforesaid, unless such substituted endowment or augmentation shall be proved to the satisfaction of the said Archbishop or Bishop to produce an income which shall exceed or be fully equal to the rent or annual sum of money for which the same shall be substituted, and be expressed to be so proved in the deed by which such consent shall be signified: provided also, that, when any lands, tithes or portions of tithes, or other hereditaments, which shall be so annexed as aforesaid, shall be comprised in any subsisting lease or leases previously granted thereof, such annexation shall not prejudice or affect any such subsisting lease or leases; but in every such case any rent or rents reserved by any such lease or leases, or a proportionate part thereof (in case other hereditaments shall also be comprised in such lease or leases), shall during the continuance of the said lease or leases be payable to the Incumbent for the time being of the Church or Chapel to which the premises shall be annexed as aforesaid; and such Incumbent for the time being shall have all the same powers for the recovery of the said rent or rents, or of the proportionate part thereof, as aforesaid, as the University or College by whom the annexation shall have been made might have had in case the premises had not been so annexed.

12. This Act shall be read and construed according to the definitions and interpretations contained in the thirty-first and thirty-second sections of the Universities and College Estates Act, 1858; and the word "College" in the said Act of the third and fourth years of Her Majesty and in this Act shall be interpreted to include any "Hall" in the said Universities or either of them. *Interpretation of terms.*

13. It shall be sufficient for all purposes to cite this Act as "The Universities and College Estates Act Extension, 1860." *Short Title.*

23 & 24 Vict. Cap. 91.

An Act for removing doubts respecting the Craven Scholarships in the University of Oxford, and for enabling the University to retain the custody of certain Testamentary Documents.

WHEREAS it is expedient to remove certain doubts respecting the Craven Scholarships in the University of Oxford, and to enable the University to retain the custody of certain Testamentary Documents; be it enacted by the Queen's most excellent Majesty, by and with the advice and consent of the Lords spiritual and temporal and Commons in this present Parliament assembled, and by the authority of the same, as follows:

Removing doubts as to Scholarships founded by Will of Lord Craven, in regard to 17 & 18 Vict. c. 81.

1. Whereas doubts have arisen whether the Scholarships founded by the Will of John Lord Craven, and commonly called the Craven Scholarships, are included within the words " University or College Emolument" in the Act of the seventeenth and eighteenth years of the reign of Her Majesty: be it enacted, that the said Craven Scholarships shall be deemed to be University Emoluments within the meaning of the said Act, and that all Statutes or Regulations which heretofore and since the passing of the said Act have been made by the University and approved by Her Majesty in Council, conformably to the conditions and provisions of the said Act, in relation to the said Craven Scholarships, shall have the same force and effect as if the said Scholarships had been expressly named and included in the said Act as University Emoluments; and in elections to the said Scholarships no person shall be entitled to preference by reason of his being of the name or kindred of the Founder: provided, that nothing herein or in the said Act or in such Statutes or Regulations contained shall preclude the High Court of Chancery from augmenting from time to time the number of Scholars, whenever the increased income of the Foundation shall permit.

Recital of 20 & 21 Vict. c. 77, s. 89.

2. And whereas by an Act twenty and twenty-first Victoria, chapter seventy-seven, it was enacted, that the acting

Judge and Registrar of every Court and other person now having jurisdiction to grant Probate or Administration, and every person having the custody of the documents and papers of or belonging to such Court or person, shall, upon receiving a requisition for that purpose under the seal of the Court of Probate from a Registrar, and at the time and in the manner mentioned in such requisition, transmit to the Court of Probate, or to such other place as in such requisition shall be specified, all Records, Wills, Grants, Probates, Letters of Administration, Administration Bonds, Notes of Administration, Court Books, Calendars, Deeds, Processes, Acts, Proceedings, Writs, Documents, and every other Instrument relating exclusively or principally to matters or causes Testamentary, to be deposited and arranged in the Registry of each District, or in the principal Registry, as the case may require, so as to be easy of reference under the control and direction of the Court: and whereas in the case of the Court of the Chancellor of the University of Oxford it has been found inconvenient to separate the Testamentary Records, Instruments, and Papers of or belonging to the said Court from the other Records, Instruments, and Papers thereof: be it further enacted, that the Vice-Chancellor of the said University shall, as soon as conveniently may be, cause to be made an Index to such of the Records and other Instruments and Papers whatsoever of or belonging to the said Court as relate exclusively or principally to matters or causes Testamentary, which shall be as accurate as the nature of the said Records and other Instruments and Papers will permit, and shall transmit a copy of such Index to the Principal Registrar of Her Majesty's Court of Probate; and such transmission thereof shall be a sufficient compliance with the above-recited enactment of the said Act, so far as regards the Court of the Chancellor of the said University; and it shall thereafter be lawful for the said University, notwithstanding the said Act, to retain the custody of all the Records, Documents, and Papers to which such Index shall relate: provided, that all the said Records, Instruments, and Papers shall at all convenient times be liable to be inspected and to have extracts or copies taken therefrom by the authority of the Principal Registrar of Her Majesty's Court of Probate, or of the

University to retain the custody of certain Testamentary Documents and transmit an Index thereof to Court of Probate.

District Registrar of the same Court at Oxford, on payment of the same fees as would have been payable if such Records, Instruments, and Papers had been deposited in the principal Registry, or in the Registry of the Oxford District, as the case might have required; such fees to be paid to the same person or persons as would in that event have been entitled to receive the same; and that no officer of the said University, or of the said Court of the Chancellor thereof, shall be entitled to receive any fee from any person inspecting the said Records or taking extracts or copies therefrom by the authority aforesaid.

23 & 24 Vict. Cap. 127.

An Act to amend the laws relating to Attorneys, Solicitors, Proctors, and Certificated Conveyancers.

[The Preamble of this Act begins by reciting the Act, 6 & 7 Vict. c. 73, "for consolidating and amending several of the laws relating to Attorneys and Solicitors practising in England and Wales."]

Persons having taken Degrees at certain Universities may be admitted after three years' service.

2. Section seven of the first herein-before mentioned Act shall be repealed, and any person having taken the Degree of Bachelor of Arts or Bachelor of Laws in the University of Oxford, Cambridge, Dublin, Durham, or London, or in the Queen's University in Ireland, or the Degree of Bachelor of Arts, Master of Arts, Bachelor of Laws, or Doctor of Laws in any of the Universities of Scotland, none of such Degrees being honorary Degrees, and who at any time after having taken such Degree, and either before or after the passing of this Act, has been bound by and has duly served under Articles of Clerkship to a practising Attorney or Solicitor for the term of three years, and has been examined and sworn in manner directed by the first herein-before mentioned Act and by this Act, may be admitted and enrolled as an Attorney or Solicitor; and service for any part of the said term not exceeding one year with the London Agent of such Attorney or Solicitor in the business, practice, or employment of an

Attorney or Solicitor, either by virtue of any stipulation in such Articles, or with the permission of such Attorney or Solicitor, shall be and be deemed to have been good service under such Articles for such part of the said term[c].

5. The Lords Chief Justices of the Courts of Queen's Bench and Common Pleas, and the Lord Chief Baron of the Court of Exchequer, jointly with the Master of the Rolls, may, if they think fit, from time to time, by Regulations to be made by them, direct that any person having successfully passed any Examination now or hereafter to be established in any of the Universities herein-before mentioned, and to be specified in such Regulations, may be admitted and enrolled as an Attorney or Solicitor, after having been subsequently bound by, and having duly served under, Articles of Clerkship to a practising Attorney or Solicitor for the term of four years, and been examined and sworn as aforesaid; and the said Judges may from time to time revoke or alter such Regulations as they think fit, but not so as to allow a less term of service than four years[d]. *Judges may ma: Regulations for persons who hav passed c tain Exa minatior before Articles to be ad mitted after fou years' se vice.*

[c] Section 7 of the Act 6 & 7 Vict. c. 73, which is hereby repealed, allowed such Graduates of Oxford and Cambridge as are here described to be admitted Attorneys after three years' service, as this section does; but it set limits for the time of graduation and for the date of the Articles of Clerkship afterwards.

[d] By a Regulation made July 26, 1861, the Judges specified in this section ordered that "every person who, before entering into Articles of Clerkship, shall produce to the Registrar of Attorneys a certificate that he has successfully passed the First Public Examination before Moderators at Oxford or the Previous Examination at Cambridge .... shall be entitled to the benefit of the 5th section" of this Act.

By a second Regulation of the same date the same Judges, in virtue of the 8th section of this Act, prescribed a Special Examination in certain branches of general knowledge to be passed by every person proposing to enter into Articles of Clerkship, not having been called to the Bar, or not having taken a Degree, or not being entitled to the benefit of s. 5. But by a subsequent Regulation, made June 6, 1862, they ordered that such Special Examination shall not be requisite for any person "who shall, previously to being articled, produce to the Registrar of Attorneys a certificate that he has successfully passed one of the Local Examinations established by the University of Oxford or one of the Non-Gremial Examinations established by the University of Cambridge."

24 & 25 Vict. Cap. 9.

An Act to amend the law relating to the conveyance of land for Charitable Uses.

Act not to prejudice the two Universities &c.

* 9 Geo. 2, c. 36.

6. Nothing in this Act contained shall extend or be construed to extend .... to make void any dispositions made or to be made to or in trust for either of the two Universities, or any of the Colleges or Houses of Learning within either of such Universities, in the first recited Act* mentioned, or to or in trust for the Colleges of Eton, Winchester, or Westminster, or any or either of them, for the better support and maintenance of scholars only upon the foundation of the said Colleges of Eton, Winchester, and Westminster.

24 & 25 Vict. Cap. 53.

An Act to provide that Votes at Elections for the Universities may be recorded by means of Voting Papers.

WHEREAS it is expedient to afford greater facilities for voting to the electors at elections for Burgesses to serve in Parliament for the Universities of Oxford, Cambridge, and Dublin; be it enacted by the Queen's most Excellent Majesty, by and with the advice and consent of the Lords spiritual and temporal and Commons in this present Parliament assembled, and by the authority of the same, as follows:

Electors to vote by means of Voting Papers.

1. It shall be lawful for such electors, in lieu of attending to vote in person, to nominate any other elector or electors of the same University, competent to make the declaration herein-after mentioned, to deliver for them at the poll voting papers containing their votes, as by this Act provided. Every such voting paper shall bear date subsequently to notice given by the returning officer of the day for proceeding to election, and shall contain the name or names of the Candidate or Candidates thereby voted for, and the name or names of the elector or electors authorized on behalf of the voter to tender

such voting paper at the poll, and shall be according to the form or to the effect prescribed in the Schedule to this Act annexed. Such voting paper, the aforesaid date and names being previously filled in, shall, on any day subsequent to notice given by the returning officer of the day for proceeding to election, be signed by the voter in the presence of a Justice of the Peace for the county or borough in which such voter shall be then residing; and the said Justice shall certify and attest the fact of such voting paper having been so signed in his presence, by signing at the foot thereof a certificate or attestation in the form or to the effect prescribed in the said Schedule, with his name and address in full, and shall state his quality as a Justice of the Peace for such county or borough.

2. The voting paper, signed and certified as aforesaid, may be delivered to the Vice-Chancellor of the University for which the election is held or to any Pro-Vice-Chancellor appointed by him, or, in the case of the University of Dublin, to the Provost of Trinity College or to any person lawfully deputed to act for him, at any one of the appointed polling places, during the appointed hours of polling, by any one of the persons therein nominated in that behalf, who shall, on tendering such voting paper at the poll, read out the same; and the said Vice-Chancellor, Pro-Vice-Chancellor, Provost, or deputy shall receive the voting papers as the same shall be delivered, and shall cause the votes thereby given, or such of them as may not appear to be contrary to the provisions of this Act, to be recorded in the manner heretofore used, in all respects as if such votes had been given by the electors attending in person; and all votes so recorded shall have the same validity and effect as if they had been duly given by the voters in person: provided always, that no person shall be entitled to sign or vote by more than one voting paper at any election, and that no voting paper containing the names of more Candidates than there are Burgesses to be elected at such election shall be received or recorded: provided also, that no voting paper shall be received or recorded unless the person tendering the same shall make the following declaration, which he shall sign at the foot or back thereof: *Voting Papers to be read, and Votes recorded.*

'I solemnly declare, that I am personally acquainted with A. B. [the voter], and I verily believe that this is the paper by which he intends to vote pursuant to the provisions of the Universities Elections Act.'

provided also, that no voting paper shall be so received and recorded if the voter signing the same shall have already voted in person at the same election: provided also, that every such elector shall be entitled to vote in person, notwithstanding that he has duly signed and transmitted a voting paper to another elector, if such voting paper has not been already tendered at the poll.

Voting Papers may be inspected by any person now entitled to object to Votes.

3. It shall be lawful for any person now by law or custom authorized on behalf of any Candidate to object to votes to inspect any voting paper tendered at the poll before the same shall be received or recorded, and to object to it on one or more of the following grounds; 1. That the person on whose behalf the voting paper is tendered is not qualified to vote; 2. That the person tendering the voting paper is not duly qualified in that behalf; 3. That the person in whose behalf the voting paper is tendered has already voted at that election in person or by voting paper; 4. That the voting paper bears date anterior to notice given by the returning officer of the day for proceeding to election; 5. That the voting paper is forged or falsified; and the returning officer, his deputy or assessor, or any officer having by law or custom power to decide objections in respect of votes tendered by voters attending the poll in person, shall have power to put questions to the person tendering such voting paper, and to reject, receive, and record, or receive and record as objected to or protested against, any votes tendered by voting papers: provided, that in case the objection offered to any voting paper shall be that it is forged or falsified, such returning or other officer shall receive and record such voting paper, having previously written upon it, "Objected to as forged," or "Objected to as falsified," together with the name of the person making such objection.

Voting Papers to be filed.

4. All voting papers received and recorded at such election, as well as any voting papers rejected for informality or on any other ground, shall be filed and kept by the officer entrusted with the care of the poll books or other documents relating to the said election; and any person shall be allowed to examine such voting papers at all reasonable times, and to take copies thereof, upon payment of a fee of one shilling.

5. Any person falsely or fraudulently signing any voting paper in the name of any other person, either as a voter or as a witness, whether such other person shall be living or dead, and every person signing, subscribing, endorsing, attesting, certifying, tendering, or transmitting as genuine any false or falsified voting paper, knowing the same to be false or falsified, and any person falsely making any such declaration as aforesaid, or such declaration as is contained in the Schedule, or with fraudulent intent altering, defacing, destroying, withholding, or abstracting any voting paper, and any person wilfully making a false answer to any question put to him by the returning or other officer as herein-before provided, shall be guilty of a misdemeanour, and punishable by fine, or imprisonment for a term not exceeding one year.

Penalty for falsely signing Voting Papers.

6. No such voting paper as herein-before mentioned shall be liable to any stamp duty.

Voting Papers not liable to Stamp Duty.

SCHEDULE.

University Election, 18 .

I A. B. [*the Christian and surnames of the elector in full, his College or Hall, if any, and his degree or academical rank or office, if any, to be here inserted*], do hereby declare, that I have signed no other voting paper at this election, and do hereby give my vote at this election for

And I nominate   C. D.
                              E. F.
                              G. H.

or one of them, to deliver this voting paper at the poll.

Witness my hand this   day of   18 .

    (Signed)   A. B. of [*the elector's place of residence to be here inserted.*]

Signed in my presence by the said A. B., who is personally known to me, on the above-mentioned   day of 18 , the name [*or* names] of as the Candidate [*or* Candidates] voted for having been previously filled in.

    (Signed)   Z. M. of [*the witness's place of residence to be here inserted,*]

a Justice of the Peace for

25 & 26 VICT. Cap. XXVI.

An Act to extend the power of making Statutes possessed by the University of Oxford, and to make further provision for the Administration of Justice in the Court of the Chancellor of the said University.

WHEREAS it is expedient to extend the powers of making Statutes possessed by the University of Oxford, and to make further provision for the administration of justice in the Court of the Chancellor of the said University; be it therefore enacted by the Queen's most excellent Majesty, by and with the advice and consent of the Lords spiritual and temporal and Commons in this present Parliament assembled, and by the authority of the same, as follows:

Power of the University as to regulation of the Professorships named in Schedule.

1. The University of Oxford may make Statutes for the regulation of the Professorships specified in the Schedule annexed hereto in respect of the following matters; that is to say,

1. The functions and duties of each of the Professors holding the said Professorships;
2. The fees, if any, to be charged for admittance to the lectures of each Professor;
3. The determination of the periods during which each Professor is to reside in the University, the authority in whom a power of granting leave of absence is to be vested, and the mode of enforcing the required residence;
4. The appointment of a temporary substitute for each Professor in case of his illness or temporary absence with leave, and of a permanent substitute in case of his being permanently incapacitated by old age or infirmity;
5. The remuneration of any such temporary or permanent substitute out of the income of the Professor in whose place he is substituted;
6. The constitution of a court or other authority em-

powered to admonish and, if necessary, remove a Professor guilty of notable negligence or inefficiency in conducting the duties of his office or of immorality.

2. The University may by Statute determine in respect of each of the Professorships specified in the said Schedule (other than the Professorship of Political Economy and the Sherard Professorship of Botany) how and by whom, upon the occasion of the next or any subsequent avoidance of such Professorship, the Professor is to be elected; and in the case of the Sherard Professorship of Botany therein named the Professor shall be appointed by the President and Council for the time being of the Royal College of Physicians of London; and the said University may, with consent of the said President and Council of the College of Physicians, vary and define the qualifications of candidates for election to the said Sherard Professorship. *Power of the University as to elections to the Professorships named in Schedule.*

3. If at any time hereafter a new Professorship of Political Economy, Chemistry, Geology, or Mineralogy is established in the University of Oxford, it shall be lawful for the University by Statute to suppress the existing Professorship of that Science for which provision is made by a new Professorship; and, after the suppression of any Professorship authorized to be suppressed by this section, the annual sum now payable by the University as a salary to the Professor holding the suppressed Professorship shall be applied in promoting and assisting, by the purchase of materials or apparatus, by the support of assistant teachers, or by such other means as the University may by Statute determine, the study and cultivation in the University of the Science which forms the subject matter of the suppressed Professorship: provided, that if the Professorship of Mineralogy is suppressed the annual sum thereby rendered disposable may, if it be thought fit, be applied in manner aforesaid to the promotion of the study of Geology or any branch thereof, and if the Professorship of Geology be suppressed the annual sum may, if it be thought fit, be applied to the promotion of the study of Mineralogy or any branch thereof. *Power of suppressing certain Professorships.*

4. The power hereby given to the University of suppressing any of the said Professorships of Political Economy, Chemistry, Geology, or Mineralogy may be exercised although the new *Such power may be exercised although*

the substituted Professorship is attached to a College.

Professorship, substituted for any suppressed Professorship, is a Professorship attached to a College and established under a Statute of such College now in force, if the functions and duties of such new Professorship are subject to regulation by the University, and are not confined to the instruction of Members of the College.

Conditions may be annexed to certain Professorships.

5. The election or appointment of any person who may be hereafter elected or appointed to any of the said Professorships of Political Economy, Chemistry, Geology, and Mineralogy may, if it be thought fit, be declared by Statute of the University to be subject to the operation of any Statute for the suppression of the Professorship that may afterwards be made or come into operation.

Trusts of certain Scholarships &c. may be varied.

6. The University may vary by Statute the directions, trusts, or regulations relating to the Kennicott Scholarships, and to the Johnson Scholarships, and to the Denyer Theological Prizes, with a view of promoting the study of Theology, Hebrew, and Mathematics respectively, and may for that purpose, if it be deemed advisable, convert the Denyer Theological Prizes into a Theological Scholarship or Scholarships.

Statutes made under this Act require the approval of Her Majesty in Council.

7. Every Statute passed by the University by virtue of this Act shall with all convenient speed after the passing thereof be laid before Her Majesty in Council, and forthwith published in the London Gazette; and any person or body corporate affected thereby may within a month after the publication thereof petition Her Majesty in Council against the same or any part thereof; and every such petition shall be referred by Her Majesty by Order in Council for the consideration and advice of five Members of Her Privy Council, of whom two, not including the Lord President, shall be Members of the Judicial Committee; and such five Members may, if they think fit, admit any petitioner to be heard by counsel in support of his petition; and if, no such petition having been presented, or if, after any petition so presented has been referred and considered, such five Members of the Privy Council, or the major part thereof, shall report to Her Majesty their opinion that such Statute should be approved with or without modifications, the said Statute or modified Statute shall be forthwith laid before both Houses

of Parliament, if Parliament be then sitting, or, if not, then within three weeks after the commencement of the then next ensuing Session of Parliament; and unless an address be within forty days presented by one or other of the said Houses, praying Her Majesty to withhold her consent from such Statute or modified Statute or any part thereof, it shall be lawful for Her Majesty, if she think fit, to declare by order in Council her approbation of the Statute or modified Statute, and the same shall thereupon become a Statute of the University of Oxford, notwithstanding any Act of Parliament, decree or order, deed or instrument of foundation or endowment; and, if the Statute or any part thereof is not so approved by Her Majesty, the University may frame and pass another Statute in the matter, and so on from time to time as often as occasion requires.

8. Every Statute made by the University by virtue of this Act shall be subject to alteration or repeal by the University with the approval of Her Majesty in Council. *Statutes made under this Act,*

9. Every Statute of the University made in pursuance of the said Act of the seventeenth and eighteenth years of Her present Majesty Queen Victoria, chapter eighty-one, and intituled, An Act to make further provision for the good Government and Extension of the University of Oxford, of the Colleges therein, and of the College of Saint Mary, Winchester, which has been approved by Her Majesty in Council, shall from and after the passing of this Act be subject to alteration and repeal by the University with the approval of Her Majesty in Council. *or under 17 & 18 Vict. c. 81, may be altered or repealed with the approval of Her Majesty in Council.*

10. This Act shall not be construed to take away or affect any power of making Statutes or Regulations now possessed by the University or by any College therein, nor shall it prejudice or affect any interest vested in any Member of the University previously to the passing of this Act. *Saving of rights.*

11. In the construction of this Act the words "Professor" and "Professorship" respectively shall include Public Readers and Praelectors and their several offices. *Interpretation of terms.*

12. Section forty-five of the said Act of the Session of the seventeenth and eighteenth years of Her present Majesty shall be repealed; and in lieu thereof be it enacted, that the Vice-Chancellor of the said University may from time to *Repeal of 17 & 18 Vict. c. 81, s. 45. Power to make*

Rules for regulation of the Chancellor's Court. time, with the approval of any three of the Judges of Her Majesty's Superior Courts, make Rules for regulating the practice and forms of procedure in all proceedings within the jurisdiction of the Court of the Chancellor of the said University commonly called the Vice-Chancellor's Court, and may from time to time, with the like approval, annul, alter, or add to any such Rules.

Short Title. 13. This Act may be cited for all purposes as "The Oxford University Act, 1862."

SCHEDULE.

The Professorship of Political Economy.
The Readership in Experimental Philosophy.
The Sherard Professorship of Botany.
The Aldrich Professorship of Chemistry.
The Readership in Geology.
The Readership in Mineralogy.

27 & 28 Vict. Cap. LXVIII.

An Act to amend the Local Government Act of 1858 so far as it applies to Oxford.

[Section 1 appointed the first election of Members of the Oxford Local Board to take place within the first fortnight of November 1864. Section 2 made a similar appointment for every subsequent annual election: but this has been superseded by the provision made in 28 & 29 Vict. c. 108, s. 4.]

Qualification of University Members of Local Board. 3. Notwithstanding anything in the said Local Government Act contained, the Members of the Local Board to be elected by the said University and Heads and Bursars of Colleges and Heads of Halls respectively shall not be required to possess any qualification to act as Members of the said Board other than that they are of the Degree of Master of Arts, Bachelor of Civil Law, Bachelor in Medicine, or any superior Degree of the said University.

28 & 29 Vict. Cap. LV.

An Act to empower the University of Oxford to make Statutes as to the Vinerian Foundation in that University.

WHEREAS it is expedient to extend the powers of making Statutes possessed by the University of Oxford; be it enacted by the Queen's most Excellent Majesty, by and with the advice and consent of the Lords spiritual and temporal and Commons in this present Parliament assembled, and by the authority of the same, as follows:

1. That the said University may, with the view of better promoting the teaching and study of the Law in the said University, vary by Statute all or any of the directions, trusts, and regulations now in force relating to the Vinerian Professorship and the Vinerian Fellowship and Scholarships respectively, and to the application of the funds held in trust by the said University under the Will of Charles Viner, Esquire, deceased: provided, that part of the income of such funds shall always be applied to the teaching of Law, and the residue towards encouraging the study of the Law by means of Fellowships or Scholarships or both, and that the name of the said Charles Viner, or the title Vinerian, shall always be retained in connexion with the said Foundation: provided also, that the interests of the present Professor, Fellow, and Scholars respectively on the said Vinerian Foundation shall not, without their respective consents, be altered or affected by any such Statute; but every person who, after the passing of this Act, may be elected a Vinerian Professor, or Fellow, or Scholar, shall be subject to any Statute to be afterwards made by the University under the powers of this Act as fully as if he had been elected under such Statute. *Power to University to make Statutes as to the Vinerian Foundation.*

2. All the provisions of the Oxford University Act, 1862, as to Statutes of the University passed by virtue thereof, shall extend and apply to Statutes of the University made by virtue of this Act; and the Oxford University Act, 1862, and this Act, shall be construed together as one Act. *Provisions of 25 & 26 Vict. c. 26 to apply to Statutes under this Act.*

3. This Act may be cited for all purposes as the "Oxford University Vinerian Foundation Act, 1865." *Short Title.*

28 & 29 Vict. Cap. CVIII.

An Act to confirm certain Provisional Orders under the Local Government Act, 1858, relating to the Districts of Nottingham . . . . . and Oxford, and for other purposes relative to certain Districts under the said Act.

WHEREAS the Secretary of State for the Home Department, being one of Her Majesty's Principal Secretaries of State, has, under the provisions of the Local Government Act, 1858, duly made certain Provisional Orders which are contained in the Schedule to this Act annexed; and it is provided by the aforesaid Local Government Act that no such Orders shall be of any validity whatever until they shall have been confirmed by Parliament; and it is expedient that the said Orders should be so confirmed; be it therefore enacted by the Queen's most excellent Majesty, by and with the advice and consent of the Lords spiritual and temporal and Commons in this present Parliament assembled, and by the authority of the same, as follows:

Provisional Orders in Schedule confirmed.

1. The Provisional Orders contained in the Schedule hereunto annexed shall, from and after the passing of this Act, be absolute, and be as binding and of like force and effect as if the provisions of the same had been expressly enacted in this Act.

The Oxford Local Board to be elected between the 9th and 24th of November annually.

4. The yearly election of the Members of the Local Board for the District of Oxford under section eighty-two of the Local Government Act, 1858, shall take place on such day between the ninth and twenty-fourth days of November in every year, not being Sunday, as the Local Board from time to time at their ordinary meeting in the month of October in the respective year determine; and the Members of the Local Board already and from time to time hereafter elected shall continue in office until the commencement of the meeting of the Local Board next after the day of the then next yearly election of Members thereof, and thereupon the Members then elected shall come into office: provided,

that, if and whenever the Local Board do not so fix any other day for the yearly election, then it shall take place on the tenth day of November, or, if that day be Sunday, on the then next day.

5. The Members of the Oxford Local Board to be elected by the ratepayers of the Parishes within the District shall be elected one for every Parish by the ratepayers of the respective Parish, and, except as is by this Act otherwise provided, shall be so elected by the ratepayers in vestry assembled. *Ratepayers of each Parish in Oxford District to elect one Member in Vestry.*

6. It shall not be obligatory on any of the fifteen Members of the Local Board from time to time elected by the University of Oxford to make any declaration of qualification for the office of Member of the Local Board. *University Members not required to make declaration.*

7. The Oxford Local Board shall yearly, at their first meeting in November, appoint one of their number to be Chairman for one year at all meetings at which he is present; and in case the Chairman so appointed be absent from any meeting at the time appointed for holding the same, the Members present shall appoint one of their number to act as Chairman thereat; and in case the Chairman appointed for the year die, resign, or become incapable of acting, another Member shall be appointed to be Chairman for the period during which the person so dying, resigning, or becoming incapable would have been entitled to remain in office, and no longer; and the Chairman at any meeting shall have a second or casting vote in case of an equality of votes. *The Local Board shall appoint a Chairman.*

8. All public buildings of the University and City of Oxford, and any lands, tenements, and hereditaments within the Oxford District not now assessed or assessable to rates for the relief of the poor, except all such as belong to or are held by the county, and except churches and other public places of religious worship, shall be assessable on a fair valuation thereof by an equal pound rate to the General District Rates to be from time to time made and levied by the Local Board. *All public buildings (except churches &c.) shall be assessable to the General District Rates.*

[Sections 9–12 relate to the Parishes of Cowley, Binsey, and North Hincksey, directing, 1. that the number of members of the Oxford Local Board shall be increased by one, who "shall from time to time be elected by the owners and ratepayers within that part of the Parish of Cowley" which is added to the Oxford District; 2. that "the ratepayers of the Parish of Binsey shall form part of the vestry of the Parish of St. Thomas" for the election of one Member of the Board; 3. that "the ratepayers of that part of the Parish of North Hinksey" which is added to the Oxford District "shall form part of the vestry of the Parish of St. Aldate" for the election of one Member; and 4. that the overseers of those three Parishes shall exhibit their rate books to persons duly appointed from time to time by the Local Board.]

Provisional Order made applicable to the Oxford District &c.

13. The Provisional Order relating to the Oxford District set forth in the Schedule to this Act annexed shall, in accordance with the provisions of this section, apply to the Oxford District and the Local Board for the Oxford District as that District and that Local Board respectively are from time to time constituted.

Assessment Committee to be appointed by the Local Board.

14. The Oxford Local Board, within fourteen days after their yearly election, shall appoint for the current year a Committee of their own number to be the Assessment Committee, and shall determine their number, quorum, and procedure, and shall, when requisite, supply vacancies in their number;

(*a*.) All objections to the General District Rate shall be heard and considered by the Assessment Committee;

(*b*.) And if and when the assessment to the rate for the relief of the poor of all or any part of the property assessable to the General District Rate to be made and levied by the Local Board is in the judgment of the Local Board an unfit criterion for making a General District Rate, or there is no such assessment, the net annual value of the property shall be ascertained by the Assessment Committee.

The Mayor and Recorder of the City and the Vice-Chancellor of the University of Oxford to be a Court of Appeal

15. The Mayor and Recorder of the City of Oxford and the Vice-Chancellor of the University of Oxford, instead of the Court of Quarter Sessions, shall be the Court of Appeal for all purposes of appeals from assessments and rates of the Local Board:

(*a*.) Provided, that during the absence of the Recorder the Deputy Recorder, and during the absence of the Vice-Chancellor one of the Pro-Vice-Chancellors, to be appointed by the Vice-Chancellor by writing under his hand delivered to the Clerk to the Local Board, and during the absence of the Mayor the Deputy Mayor of the city, shall act in the place of and shall accordingly represent the Recorder, or, as the case shall be, the Vice-Chancellor or the Mayor. *for objections to Assessments.*

[Sections 16–18 direct how complaints against assessments are to be heard by the Assessment Committee, and appeals against decisions of that Committee by the Court of Appeal.]

19. The expenses of the Assessment Committee and of the Court of Appeal shall be paid by the Oxford Local Board, and the Clerk to the said Local Board shall be the Clerk to the Court of Appeal. *Expenses of Assessment Committee and of Court of Appeal.*

20. With respect to the General District Rate from time to time made and levied by the Oxford Local Board, *Who to be rated to the General District Rates of the Oxford Local Board.*

(a.) All rateable property belonging to the Chancellor Masters and Scholars of the University shall be rated in the name of the Vice-Chancellor of the University;

(b.) All rateable property belonging to the Mayor Aldermen and Citizens of Oxford shall be rated in the name of the Mayor of the City;

(c.) All rateable property belonging to the Dean and Chapter of Christ Church and to the other Colleges and the Halls in the University shall respectively be rated in the names of the Treasurer of Christ Church and of the Senior Bursar or Treasurer of the several other Colleges and of the Principals of the several Halls respectively;

(d.) All rateable property belonging to feoffees or trustees of charities or public buildings shall respectively be rated in the names of the feoffees and trustees respectively.

21. The General District Rate from time to time made by the Oxford Local Board, and payable by the University and Christ Church and the other Colleges and the Halls respectively, shall be collected and paid to the Local Board by the Vice-Chancellor: provided, that this arrangement may at any time be determined by notice in writing in that behalf given by the Vice-Chancellor to the Local Board, or by the Local Board to the Vice-Chancellor; and if notice be so given, and *Rates on the University and Colleges and Halls of Oxford to be collected and paid by the Vice-Chancellor. Power to*

<small>determine that arrangement.</small> be not withdrawn within twelve months after the service thereof, then from and after the expiration of that period the General District Rate payable by the University and Christ Church and the several other Colleges and the Halls respectively shall be collected by the Local Board.

[Section 22 directs that " the custody, care, and management of the Public Library in the City of Oxford shall be vested in the Local Board," and that all the expenses thereof shall from time to time be paid out of the General District Rate : " provided, that the amount expended by the Local Board in any one year for the purposes of the Public Library shall not exceed the amount which might be raised by them by a rate for the purpose made under" the Public Libraries Act, 1855.]

<small>Act incorporated with 21 & 22 Vict. c. 98.</small> 23. This Act shall be deemed to be incorporated with the Local Government Act, 1858, and shall be as if this Act and the said Local Government Act were one Act.

<small>Short Title.</small> 24. In citing this Act in any other Act of Parliament, or in any proceeding, instrument, or document whatever, it shall be sufficient to use the words and figures "The Local Government Supplemental Act, 1865 (No. 5)."

SCHEDULE of Provisional Orders referred to in the preceding Act.

1. NOTTINGHAM.—   *   *   *   *
11. OXFORD.—Repealing and altering parts of Local Acts in force within the District of the Oxford Local Board.
12. HINCKSEY (Oxford District).—Altering the boundaries of the District of Oxford, under the Local Government Act, 1858.
13. COWLEY (Oxford District).—Altering the boundaries of the District of Oxford, under the Local Government Act, 1858.

   *   *   *   *

OXFORD.

Provisional Order repealing and altering parts of Local Acts in force within the District of the Oxford Local Board.

Whereas the Local Government Act, 1858, has been duly adopted within the University and City of Oxford, the Suburbs thereof, and the adjoining Parish of St. Clement by the Oxford Commissioners mentioned and referred to in the 82nd section of the Local Government Act aforesaid; and the Local Board for the Oxford District have, in pursuance of the provisions of section 77 of the Local Government Act, 1858, presented a petition to me, as one of Her Majesty's Principal Secretaries of State, praying that the provisions of the Public Health Act, 1848, and the Local Government Act, 1858, respectively, with respect to the paving, pitching, repairing, lighting, and cleansing of the several public streets, lanes, ways, passages, and places within the District, should come into operation therein, and that the powers of the Commissioners with respect to Magdalen Bridge and the Mileways, and with respect to Gasworks and Gas supply, should be transferred to and vested in the said petitioners; that further provision should be made with respect to the election of Members of the Local Board; and that provision should be made for rendering the property in the University and the Colleges and Halls thereof liable to the General District Rates of such Local Board:

And whereas for such purposes the said petitioners prayed that such of the provisions of the Oxford Local Acts of 1771 and 1781 and 1812 and 1815 and 1848 respectively as do not relate to the Markets and to the Gasworks and the Gas supply respectively (which provisions do not confer powers or privileges upon corporations, companies, undertakers, or individuals for their own pecuniary benefit) should be in part repealed and in part amended, and other provisions enacted, and an order for the purpose under section 77 of the Local Government Act should accordingly be made:

And whereas, in pursuance of the said Local Government Act, inquiry has been directed in the said District in respect of the several matters mentioned in the said petition, and Mr. Robert Rawlinson, the Inspector appointed for the purpose, has reported to me thereon:

And whereas it appears expedient to issue a Provisional Order in relation to the said matters, but no such Order can be valid without confirmation by Parliament:

Now, therefore, in pursuance of the powers vested in me by the said Local Government Act, I, as one of Her Majesty's Principal Secretaries of State, do, by this Provisional Order under my hand, direct that, from and after the passing of any Act of Parliament confirming this Order,—

From what day this Order shall have effect.

1.—The following provisions shall have effect on and after the third Wednesday next after the day of the passing of the Act confirming this Order.

The Local Government Act, 1858, with certain exceptions, to come into operation in the Oxford District.

2.—The provisions of the Local Government Act, 1858, relating to the several purposes included in the five several Local Acts of the 11th year of George the 3rd, chap. 19, and the 21st year of George the 3rd, chap. 47, and the 52nd year of George the 3rd, chap. 72, and the Session of the 5th and 6th years of William the 4th, chap. 69, and the Session of the 11th and 12th years of Her present Majesty, chap. 37, which are respectively in force in the Oxford District (in this Order called the five Local Acts), with relation to any of the purposes of the Public Health Act, 1848, or the Local Government Act, 1858, which have not already come into operation within the District, shall (except only as in this Order is otherwise provided) come into and be in operation in all places within the District.

This Order subject to provisions of Local Acts as to Mileway Tolls &c., and as to Markets.

3.—Provided, that this Order shall be subject to the several powers and provisions of the five Local Acts respectively, so far as the same relate to the tolls to be demanded and taken in respect of Magdalen Bridge and the Mileways, and to the mortgages of the tolls and the rights and remedies of the mortgagees thereof, and to the Markets respectively.

Repeal of the five Local Acts, 11 Geo. 3, c. 19, 21 Geo. 3, c. 47, 52 Geo. 3, c. 72, 5 & 6 Will. 4, c. 69, 11 & 12 Vict. c. 37, save as to Mileway Tolls &c., Markets, and Gasworks.

4.—The five Local Acts respectively are by this Order repealed, save only the sections and provisions thereof following, so far as the same respectively are now in force; that is to say, the sections and provisions of the five Local Acts respectively relating to Magdalen Bridge and the Mileways, and the tolls to be demanded and taken in respect of the same, and the mortgages of the tolls, and the rights and remedies of the mortgagees thereof, and relating to the Markets, and relating to Gasworks and the supply of Gas, and relating to all matters incidental to those matters respectively.

5.—The sections and provisions of the five Local Acts respectively which are so saved (except the sections and provisions thereof relating to the Markets) shall, so far as the same respectively are now in force, apply not to the Commissioners but to the Local Board instead of the Commissioners, and shall be read and have effect as if wherever in those sections respectively the Commissioners are named or referred to the Local Board instead of the Commissioners were named or referred to.

Sections of Local Acts so saved, except such as relate to the Markets, to apply to the Local Board.

6.—All sewers, drains, and other works respectively made by and vested in the Commissioners, and all lands and interests in lands respectively acquired by and vested in the Commissioners for the widening Magdalen Bridge and its approaches and the streets, and all rights incidental to the same respectively, and the benefit and burden of all contracts entered into by or with the Commissioners with respect to the lighting of streets and other public places, and the supplying of paving stone and materials for paving and repairing streets and other public places, and the cartage thereof, and all rates duly assessed under the provisions of the said five Local Acts or any of them, and not collected at the time that this order shall begin to have effect as first herein-before mentioned, and all other property and effects, rights, and liabilities whatsoever of the Commissioners under the five Local Acts respectively with respect to any of the purposes thereof, other than the purposes thereof relating to the Markets, are by this Order transferred to and vested in the Local Board.

Property, Rights, and Liabilities of the Commissioners transferred to the Local Board.

7.—All the deeds, records, minutes, accounts, account books, minute books, and other documents, papers, and writings of the Commissioners with respect to any of the purposes of the five Local Acts respectively, other than the purposes thereof with respect to the Markets, shall be the property of the Local Board, and shall forthwith be delivered to them by the Commissioners accordingly, the Local Board giving to the Commissioners, if so required by them, a schedule of and a receipt in writing for the same; but the same shall at all seasonable times be open to the inspection

All Records &c. of the Commissioners to be delivered to the Local Board.

and transcription of the Commissioners and their agents in that behalf, and, if and when requisite for enforcing any claim or demand by or resisting any claim or demand against the Commissioners, shall, at their request and expense, be produced in any Court of law or equity or elsewhere.

The Local Board substituted for the Commissioners in 58 Geo. 3, c. 64.

8.—Wherever in the Act of the 58th year of George the 3rd, chap. 64, intituled an Act for lighting with gas the University and City of Oxford and the Suburbs of the same City, the Commissioners are named or referred to, the Local Board instead of the Commissioners shall be deemed to be named or referred to, and that Act shall be read and have effect accordingly.

The Local Board to act under Acts relating to Nuisances and to Common Lodging Houses.

9.—For the purposes of all Acts from time to time in force with respect to the removal or prevention of nuisances, and also with respect to the well ordering of common lodging houses, the Local Board instead of the Commissioners shall be the local authority with respect to the execution of those Acts within the District.

This Order not to affect any thing previously done under Local Acts.

10.—Notwithstanding the repeal of parts of the five Local Acts respectively, and the transfer by this Order to the Local Board of parts of the property, powers, rights, and liabilities of the Commissioners, and except only as is by this Order otherwise expressly provided, everything before the coming into effect of this Order done, suffered, and confirmed respectively under or by the five Local Acts respectively shall be as valid as if the repeal and transfer had not happened; and the repeal and transfer and the operation of this Order shall accordingly be subject and without prejudice to everything so done, suffered, and confirmed respectively, and to all rights, liabilities, claims, and demands, both present and future, which, if the repeal and transfer had not happened, would be incident to or consequent on everything so done, suffered, and confirmed respectively; and with respect to everything so done, suffered, and confirmed respectively, and to all those rights, liabilities, claims, and demands, the Local Board shall to all intents represent the Commissioners.

11.—The accounts of the Commissioners with respect to the several purposes of the five Local Acts respectively, other than the purposes thereof with respect to the Markets, shall forthwith be made up and stated and audited; and if the accounts show a balance in the hands of the Commissioners, then the amount of the balance shall thereupon be paid by them to the Local Board; or if the accounts show that the debts and liabilities of the Commissioners are not fully paid or discharged, then the lawful debts and liabilities of the Commissioners remaining unpaid or undischarged shall be paid or discharged by the Local Board. *Accounts of Commissioners to be made up.*

12.—Provided, that this Order shall not give to the mortgagees of the tolls to be demanded and taken in respect of Magdalen Bridge and the Mileways any security, right, or remedy in excess of the securities, rights, and remedies which they would have if this Order were not confirmed, and shall not relieve the parishes of Cowley, Iffley, and Saint Clement, or either of them, nor any person or persons, body or bodies politic or corporate, from any liability with respect to the repair of the Mileways or Magdalen Bridge, and shall not impose on the Local Board any liability with respect to the repair of Magdalen Bridge and the Mileways to which the Commissioners would not be subject if this Order were not confirmed. *This Order not to alter the rights of Mortgagees of Mileway Tolls, nor the liabilities of Parishes &c. to repair Mileways or Magdalen Bridge.*

13.—If any rates duly assessed under the provisions of the said five Local Acts shall not have been collected at the time that this Order shall begin and have effect as first herein-before mentioned, the Local Board shall have all the powers for the recovery of the said uncollected rates which were heretofore possessed by the said Commissioners, and the monies which shall be collected or recovered shall be applied by the Local Board for their general purposes as if they had been part of a General District Rate. *Power to recover Rates not yet collected.*

14.—The accounts of the Commissioners to be made up, stated, and audited, as by this Order provided, and the accounts of the Local Board, shall be audited by the Auditor of the accounts of the Guardians of the Poor *Audit of Accounts.*

within the City of **Oxford** under the Oxford Poor Rate Act, 1854; and there shall be paid to him by the Commissioners, and from time to time by the Local Board respectively, the like remuneration for his services in so auditing their respective accounts as is from time to time paid to him for his services in auditing the accounts of the Guardians.

<small>Local Board may cleanse the rivers Cherwell and Thames, &c.</small>

15.—The Local Board from time to time, if and when they think fit, may, within the District, cleanse any parts of the Rivers Cherwell and Thames or Isis respectively, and of the streams running into those rivers respectively, and may prevent or remove any encroachments on any of those rivers and streams respectively, and may convert any parts of any of those streams into which any sewer or drain is from time to time emptied into a covered sewer, and may do and execute all works and things which the Local Board shall think requisite for or incidental to any of those purposes.

<small>As to streams converted into covered sewers.</small>

16.—Where the Local Board shall so convert any part of any of those streams into a covered sewer, the arch or other covering over the same, and all works executed by them for the purpose of covering over the same and incidental thereto, shall be by this Order vested in the Local Board.

<small>Power to prevent the emptying of sewers &c. into rivers.</small>

17.—Except as regards any sewer or drain which now is lawfully emptied into any of those rivers and streams before mentioned, the Local Board may prevent the emptying of any sewer or drain into any of those rivers and streams, and may do and execute all works and things which they shall think requisite in such case.

<small>Power to divert sewers &c. in certain cases.</small>

18.—Where any present or future sewer of the Local Board is within 100 feet from any sewer or drain which now is lawfully emptied into any of those rivers and streams respectively, the Local Board may divert the sewer or drain so that it shall thenceforth be emptied into the sewer instead of into such river or stream, and may do and execute all works and things which they think requisite in such case; but the Local Board shall not so divert any sewer or drain without providing for it a proper and sufficient outfall into their own sewer.

19.—All properties whatsoever within the District which are or hereafter may be assessable to any rate for the relief of the poor shall be assessable to the General District Rates to be made and levied by the Local Board, in the same manner in all respects as is provided by section 55 of the Local Government Act, 1858; and all exemptions from rates heretofore allowed under any or either of the five Local Acts shall henceforth cease. *All property within the District assessable to Poor Rates to be assessable to General District Rates.*

20.—The several powers by this Order conferred on the Local Board shall be in addition to and not in any respect restrictive of their other powers. *This Order in no way to restrict Powers of Local Board.*

21.—Except only as is by this Order expressly provided, nothing in this Order shall take away, lessen, prejudice, alter, or affect any privilege or right whatsoever of the University, or of any of the magistrates, officers, ministers, or servants thereunto belonging, or any privilege or right whatsoever of the City, or of any of the magistrates or servants thereunto belonging, or any exercise of any such respective privilege or right. *Saving Rights of University and City.*

  Given under my hand this thirty-first day of May one thousand eight hundred and sixty-five.
      (Signed) G. GREY.

[The Provisional Order respecting North Hincksey, dated May 20, 1865, and signed by Sir George Grey, directs, " that, from and after the passing of any Act of Parliament confirming this Order, the District of Oxford aforesaid shall be extended by including within its boundaries all that detached portion of the Parish of North Hincksey in the County of Berks which adjoins the Liberty of Grandpont in the Parish of Saint Aldate in the said County, and is bounded by the Shirelake Ditch, and including the same on the north, Grandpont in the Parish of Saint Aldate on the east, the northern side of the towing-path adjoining the river Isis on the south (excluding such towing-path), and the river Isis on the southwest and west, including the said river." *Part of North Hincksey added to the Oxford District.*

[The Provisional Order respecting Cowley, similarly dated and signed, directs, " that, from and after the passing of any Act of Parliament confirming this Order, the District of Oxford

Part of Cowley added to the Oxford District.

aforesaid shall be extended by including within its boundaries the two meadows numbered 1 and 2 on the map annexed to the award, dated the twenty-eighth day of June one thousand eight hundred and fifty-three, of the valuer acting in the inclosure of the open fields of Cowley, the Marsh, Bullingdon Green, and Elder Stubbs, situate in the Parishes of Cowley, Iffley, and Saint Clement, in the County of Oxford, and which lie on the west side of Magdalen Bridge and between the branches of the river Cherwell there; and also all and so much of the said Parish of Cowley, including Church Cowley and Temple Cowley, as lies between and is bounded on the north, north-west, and west by the river Cherwell and the stream leading out of the same to the private road bounding the allotment numbered 3 on the said award, and bounded on the south by the said private road and on the east by the Henley Mileway; and also so much of the Parish of Cowley as lies between and is bounded by the Henley Mileway on the west, the Cowley Mileway on the east and north-east, and the road called Magdalen Road on the south or south-east; also the allotment numbered 40 on the said award, lying on the south side of the said Magdalen Road; also so much of the parish of Cowley as lies north or north-west of the Divinity Footway and east or north-east of the Cowley Mileway; also that part of the said Henley Mileway which extends from the Saint Clement's Turnpike to the first part of the same Mileway marked as belonging to Iffley, and tinted yellow on the map annexed to the said award; also the whole of the Magdalen Road, and so much of the Cowley Mileway as extends from the Divinity Footway to Saint Clement's Turnpike and is not in the Parish of Saint Clement; and also all other such parts, if any, of the Parish of Cowley as are not herein-before described and are in the Borough of Oxford."]

29 & 30 Vict. Cap. LIX.

An Act to appoint additional Commissioners for executing the Acts for granting a Land Tax and other Rates and Taxes[c].

[Among the Commissioners appointed by this Act are the following.]

For the University of Oxford.

The Registrar and the Keeper of the Archives for the time being.

29 & 30 Vict. Cap. LXXXIX.

An Act for vesting in the Conservators of the River Thames the conservancy of the Thames and Isis from Staines in the County of Middlesex to Cricklade in the County of Wilts, and for other purposes connected therewith.

[This Act increased the then "existing number of eighteen Conservators of the River Thames" by the addition of five, one to be appointed by the Board of Trade, the other four to be elected by the persons qualified as Commissioners under "the Upper Navigation Act of 1795," 35 Geo. III, c. 106. Among such Commissioners are "the Representatives in Parliament for the University of Oxford," "the Vice-Chancellor and Heads of Colleges and Halls in the University of Oxford," and "the Dean and Canons of Christ Church."]

---

[c] See the first note on 7 & 8 Geo. 4, c. 75.

30 & 31 Vict. Cap. LXXV.

An Act to remove certain religious disabilities affecting some of Her Majesty's subjects, and to amend the law relating to Oaths of Office.

<small>The Oath herein named shall be substituted in all cases for the Oaths now required to be taken by office-holders and others in lieu of the Oaths of Allegiance, Supremacy, and Abjuration.</small>

5. In all cases in which any Oath which has been substituted for the Oaths of Allegiance, Supremacy, and Abjuration is now required to be taken, or taken and subscribed, as a qualification for the exercise or enjoyment of any office, franchise, or civil right, the following Oath shall be taken, or taken and subscribed, as the case may be, in lieu and instead of such substituted Oath[f]:

I *A. B.* do swear, that I will be faithful and bear true allegiance to Her Majesty Queen Victoria; and I do faithfully promise to maintain and support the Succession to the Crown, as the same stands limited and settled by virtue of the Act passed in the reign of King William the Third, intituled An Act for the further limitation of the Crown and better securing the Rights and Liberties of the Subject, and of the subsequent Acts of Union with Scotland and Ireland.

So help me GOD.

<small>The name of the Sovereign for the time being shall be used in the Oath.</small>

6. Where in the Oath hereby appointed the name of Her present Majesty is expressed, the name of the Sovereign of this Kingdom for the time being, by virtue of the Act for the further limitation of the Crown and better securing the Rights and Liberties of the Subject, shall be substituted from time to time, with proper words of reference thereto.

---

[f] By 21 & 22 Vict. c. 48 one Oath was appointed to be taken and subscribed in every case in which the Oaths of Allegiance, Supremacy, and Abjuration were then by law required either simply to be taken or to be taken and subscribed, modifications being allowed for Jews and for Roman Catholics.

30 & 31 VICT. Cap. LXXVI.

An Act to repeal certain Ordinances made for the Cathedral or House of Christ Church in Oxford by the Commissioners appointed under the Oxford University Act, 1854, and to substitute a new Ordinance in lieu thereof.

[The preamble recites that, the two Ordinances[a] which were made in relation to Christ Church by the Commissioners appointed by 17 & 18 Vict. c. 81 having been found to be in various respects defective and insufficient, it had been referred, by agreement between the Dean, the Canons, and the Senior Students, to the Archbishop of Canterbury, the Right Honourable Sir John Taylor Coleridge, Sir William Page Wood, Sir Roundell Palmer, and the Honourable Edward Turner Boyd Twisleton, (the Archbishop, Sir John Coleridge, and Mr. Twisleton having been three of the Commissioners by whom the two Ordinances were made,) to take into consideration all questions relating to the Government of the House, the management and application of its Revenues, and the Elections to Studentships therein, and to frame such a scheme for the future Government of the House as they might deem most likely to conduce to its welfare and usefulness; and that the Referees have recommended certain alterations in and additions to the said Ordinances, " and have expressed their opinion that such alterations and additions may most conveniently be made by substituting for the said Ordinances the amended Ordinance or Body of Regulations in the Schedule to this Act set forth :"

[And then the Act repeals the two Ordinances of the Commissioners, and directs that " the Ordinance set forth in the Schedule to this Act," except clause 28 thereof, shall from

---

[a] Published at page 349 of " Ordinances and Statutes framed or approved by the Oxford University Commissioners," printed at the Clarendon Press in 1863.

and after the 11th of October 1867 take effect and have force in their stead, and that the Regulations therein contained shall thenceforth be "Statutes" of the House.

[The Schedule contains "the Ordinance or Statutes above referred to," consisting of twenty-nine clauses or sections.

The House or Collegiate Foundation.
[Clause 1 directs that "the House or Collegiate Foundation of the Cathedral Church of Christ in Oxford shall include the Dean, six Canons, twenty-eight Senior Students, and fifty-two Junior Students, beside Chaplains and other Ministers and Servants of the said Cathedral Church," and that "the six Canonries shall be those annexed respectively to the Regius Professorships of Divinity, Hebrew, Ecclesiastical History, and Pastoral Theology, the Lady Margaret's Professorship of Divinity and the Archdeaconry of Oxford;" but permits a future increase in the number of Studentships, both Senior and Junior.

The Governing Body: its Constitution and general Powers.
[By clause 2 "the Government of the Foundation and the disposal and management of its possessions and revenues" are "vested in the Dean, Canons, and Senior Students; and all powers and authorities whatsoever heretofore exercised by the Dean and Canons alone, or by the Dean and Canons conjointly with any other person or persons within the House," are henceforth to "be exercised by the Dean, Canons, and Senior Students, as the Governing Body of the House;" except only certain powers, having relation mainly to the Cathedral Church itself, which are expressly reserved to the Dean and Canons. Students of the old Foundation qualified as residents to vote in the Congregation of the University, or holding any office within the House, are also to be Members of the Governing Body.

Regius Professor of Greek's Fund.
[Clause 9 is as follows: "The Governing Body shall cause a yearly sum of £500 to be set apart and paid out of the revenues of the House to the Regius Professor of Greek within the University for the time being, in addition to the two yearly sums of £40 each now payable to the Regius Professor of Hebrew and the Regius Professor of Divinity."]

30 & 31 Vict. Cap. CII.

An Act further to amend the laws relating to the Representation of the People in England and Wales.

2. This Act shall not apply to Scotland or Ireland, nor in anywise affect the election of Members to serve in Parliament for the Universities of Oxford or Cambridge. Application of Act.

[Section 59 directs that "this Act, so far as is consistent with the tenor thereof, shall be construed as one with the enactments for the time being in force relating to the Representation of the People and with the Registration Acts."]

30 & 31 Vict. Cap. lxxvii.

An Act to change the name of the Cambridge Gas-light Company, to confer further powers on the Company, and for other purposes.

[Section 6 repeals 4 & 5 Will. IV, c. xxiv, by which the Cambridge Gas-light Company was incorporated; and section 7 enacts that, notwithstanding such repeal, the Company shall continue as a body corporate under the name of "The Cambridge University and Town Gas-light Company" with perpetual succession and a common seal.

[Sections 34-38 relate to the number, qualification, and election of Directors.]

39. And whereas the University of Cambridge is largely interested in the execution of the undertaking by this Act authorized, and it is expedient that the Heads of Colleges, Halls, and Houses, and the Bursars and resident Fellows of Colleges, Halls, and Houses in that University be empowered to participate in the management of the said undertaking, notwithstanding that they may be spiritual persons; therefore so much of any Act of Parliament as prohibits any spiritual Provision as to Spiritual Persons being Directors.

person holding any cathedral preferment, benefice, curacy, or lectureship, or who shall be licensed or allowed to perform the duties of any ecclesiastical office, from acting as a director or managing partner of any association or copartnership, or from carrying on any trade, or dealing in person, shall not (so far as regards the Directors named in this Act, or any Directors or Managing Partners of the Company who may hereafter be elected or appointed,) extend or apply to any Heads or Bursars or resident Fellows of Colleges, Halls, or Houses in the said University: provided always, that if any of the aforesaid spiritual persons, being a Director or Managing Partner of the Company, shall cease to be the Head or a resident Fellow of any such College, Hall, or House in the said University, he shall thereupon become disqualified and incompetent to act as a Director or Managing Partner, and shall cease to be a Director of the Company.

No works to be erected within 300 yards of Botanic Garden, or of any College or Hall, &c.

44. Provided always, that nothing in this Act contained shall authorize the Company to erect, make, or use any works for the manufacture or storage of Gas within three hundred yards of the Botanic Garden at Cambridge or any Public Building, Museum, Garden, Pleasure-ground, or Walks belonging to or held or occupied by the Chancellor Masters and Scholars of the University of Cambridge without first obtaining their consent in writing under their common seal, or within three hundred yards of any College or Hall in the said University or of the Precincts, Gardens, or Walks of any such College or Hall without first obtaining the consent in writing of such College or Hall under their common seal.

No pipe to be laid in any ground belonging to the University or any College &c. without consent.

45. Nothing in this Act contained shall authorize or empower the Company or any person acting on their behalf to carry or lay any pipe or pipes or other apparatus into or against any grounds, buildings, or premises belonging to the Chancellor Masters and Scholars of the said University, or belonging to any of the Colleges or Halls in the said University, without first obtaining the consent in writing of the Vice-Chancellor for the time being of the said University or his deputy under his hand, or, in case of a College or Hall, without first obtaining the consent in writing of the Master or Keeper or Bursar for the time being of the said College or Hall under his hand.

[Section 62 provides for the reparation of any injury or damage done by the Company or their agents to any of the pipes or apparatus "laid down by any waterworks owners, including in that term as well the Cambridge University and Town Waterworks Company, as every other Body Corporate Politic or Collegiate, Trustees, Commissioners, and person, owning or having the control of waterworks or water pipes used for supplying water within the limits of this Act;" and section 63 directs that notice shall be given to waterworks owners, " or their Secretary, Clerk, Bursar, or Solicitor," before any of their pipes are interfered with.

[Section 86 saves all rights of the said Waterworks Company; and section 87 saves all rights of the University and of the several Colleges and Halls and Corporations sole within it.]

31 & 32 Vict. Cap. LXV.

An Act to amend the law relating to the use of Voting Papers in Elections for the Universities.

WHEREAS by an Act passed in the Session holden in the twenty-fourth and twenty-fifth years of the reign of Her present Majesty, chapter fifty-three, intituled An Act to provide that Votes at Elections for the Universities may be recorded by means of Voting Papers, it is provided that at the elections for Burgesses to serve in Parliament for the Universities of Oxford, Cambridge, and Dublin votes may be given by means of voting papers; but it is by the said Act provided that no voting paper shall be received or recorded unless the person tendering the same shall make the following declaration, which he shall sign at the foot or back thereof: 24 & 25 Vict. c. 53.

' I solemnly declare that I am personally acquainted with *A. B.* [the voter], and I verily believe that this is the paper by which he intends to vote, pursuant to the provisions of the Universities Election Act.'

30 and 31 Vict. c. 102.

And whereas by virtue of the Representation of the People Act, 1867, the said first-mentioned Act applies to every election of a Member for the University of London:

And whereas it is expedient to amend the said first-mentioned Act so far as respects the said recited declaration:

Be it enacted by the Queen's most Excellent Majesty, by and with the advice and consent of the Lords spiritual and temporal and Commons in this present Parliament assembled, and by the authority of the same, as follows:

Repeal of Form of Declaration.

1. From and after the passing of this Act the said recited form of declaration shall not be required, and there shall be substituted in place thereof the form of declaration following; that is to say,

'I solemnly declare that I verily believe that this is the paper by which *A.B.* [the voter] intends to vote pursuant to the provisions of the "Universities Election Acts, 1861 and 1868."'

[Section 2 relates only to the University of London.]

Officers in whose presence Voting Papers may be signed in the Channel Islands.

3. A voting paper for the election of any Burgess or Member to serve in Parliament for any Universities or University, in respect of which the provisions of the said first-mentioned Act may for the time being be in force, may be signed by a voter being in one of the Channel Islands in the presence of the following officers; that is to say,

1. In Jersey and Guernsey, of the Bailiffs or any Lieutenant Bailiff, Jurat, or Juge d'Instruction.
2. In Alderney, of the Judge of Alderney or any Jurat.
3. In Sark, of the Seneschal or Deputy Seneschal.

And for the purpose of certifying and attesting the signature of such voting paper, each of the said officers shall have all the powers of a Justice of the Peace under the first-mentioned Act, and a statement of the official quality of such officer shall be a sufficient statement of quality in pursuance of the provisions of the said Act.

Short Title.

4. This Act may be cited for all purposes as "The Universities Elections Act, 1868," and the said first-mentioned Act and this Act may be cited together as "The Universities Election Acts, 1861 and 1868."

31 & 32 Vict. Cap. LXXII.

An Act to amend the law relating to Promissory Oaths.

[This Act, which may be cited as the " Promissory Oaths Act, 1868," prescribes a new form of the Oath of Allegiance, and requires certain persons, specified in the Schedule or described in the Saving Clause (s. 14), to take that Oath. It also prescribes a form of Official Oath to be taken by each of the persons specified in the First Part of the Schedule, and a form of Judicial Oath to be taken by each of the persons specified in the Second Part.]

8. The form of the Oath of Allegiance provided by this Act shall be deemed to be substituted in the case of the Clerical Subscription Act, 1865, for the Form of the Oath of Allegiance and Supremacy therein referred to; in the case of the Parliamentary Oaths Act, 1866, for the Form of the Oath thereby prescribed to be taken and subscribed by Members of Parliament on taking their seats; and in the case of the Office and Oaths Act, 1867, for the Form of the Oaths of Allegiance, Supremacy, and Abjuration therein referred to; and all the provisions of the said Acts shall apply to the Oath substituted by this Section in the same manner as if that Form of Oath were actually inserted in each of the said Acts in the place of the Oath for which it is substituted. *Form of Oath of Allegiance in this Act substituted for Form in certain other Acts.*

9. No person shall be required or authorized to take the Oaths of Allegiance, Supremacy, and Abjuration, or any of such Oaths, or any Oath substituted for such Oaths or any of them, or to make any Declaration to the like effect of such Oaths or any of them, except the persons required to take the Oath of Allegiance by this Act and the Clerical Subscription Act, 1865, and the Parliamentary Oaths Act, 1866, or one of such Acts, any Act of Parliament, charter, or custom to the contrary notwithstanding [h]. *Prohibition of Oath of Allegiance except in accordance with Act.*

[h] Although the Office and Oaths Act, 1867, (30 & 31 Vict. c. 75,) is mentioned in s. 8, it is not mentioned in s. 9, which prohibits the taking of the

Regulations as to substitution of Declarations for Oaths.

12. The following regulations shall be enacted with respect to the substitution of Declarations for Oaths; (that is to say,)

*   *   *   *

3. Where before the passing of this Act an Oath was required to be taken on or as a condition of admission to membership or fellowship or participation in the privileges of any guild, body corporate, society, or company, a Declaration to the like effect of such Oath shall be substituted:

4. Where in any case not otherwise provided for by this Act or included within the Saving Clauses thereof an Oath is required to be taken by any person on or as a condition of his accepting any employment or office, a Declaration shall be substituted for such Oath to the like effect in all respects as such Oath:

5. The making a Declaration in pursuance of this Section instead of Oath shall in all respects have the same effect as the taking the Oath for which such Declaration is substituted would have had if this Act had not passed.

Saving of powers of alteration hitherto exercised.

15. Where a Declaration has been substituted for an Oath under this Act, any person, guild, body corporate, or society, which before the passing of this Act had power to alter such Oath or to substitute another Oath in its place, may exercise a like power with regard to such Declaration.

Oath of Allegiance except as is required by this Act; and there is no part of this Act by which any person is required or authorised to take the Oath of Allegiance on admission to any degree or office in either of the Universities, or to any office, employment, or emolument in any College or Hall, or in any capacity whatever as a member of either University, unless the words "Justices of the Peace for Counties and Boroughs" in the Second Part of the Schedule can be construed to include the Vice-Chancellors. In that case the Vice-Chancellors must also take the Judicial Oath prescribed by s. 4 of this Act in the manner prescribed by s. 6.

Parts of 1 Eliz. c. 1, 7 Jac. I, c. 6, 1 Gul. & Mar. c. 8, 1 Geo. I, st. 2, c. 13, and 30 & 31 Vict. c. 75, relating to the Oaths of Supremacy and Allegiance, are printed in this collection.

31 & 32 Vict. Cap. LXXXIX.

An Act to alter certain provisions in the Acts for the Commutation of Tithes, the Copyhold Acts, and the Acts for the Inclosure, Exchange, and Improvement of Land; and to make provision towards defraying the expense of the Copyhold, Inclosure, and Tithe Office.

2. In all cases of exchanges, partitions, or divisions of intermixed lands proposed to be effected under the said Acts, the Commissioners shall not proceed to carry the same into effect unless the valuations required to be furnished to them shall be duly stamped with a stamp, as required by the Acts in force for the time being for levying stamp duties on appraisements; and all valuations attached to the reports of any University or College Surveyor, made for the purpose of transactions to which the consent of the Commissioners is required, under the Universities and College Estates Acts, shall in like manner be stamped before the Commissioners shall issue their Order authorizing such transaction. *(Valuations to be stamped.)*

31 & 32 Vict. Cap. CXIV.

An Act to amend the law relating to the Ecclesiastical Commissioners for England.

[Section 12 contains an amendment of the law relating to schemes for securing the better performance of clerical duties in ill-endowed parishes.]

14. * * * * Nothing in this Act contained, except Section Twelve, shall affect or apply to the Cathedral Church of Christ, Oxford.

31 & 32 Vict. Cap. CXVIII.

An Act to make further provision for the good government and extension of certain Public Schools in England.

[This Act, which may be cited as the "Public Schools Act, 1868," applies to the Schools of Eton, Winchester, Westminster, Charterhouse, Harrow, Rugby, and Shrewsbury.]

Governing Bodies of Schools to which this Act applies to make Statutes with respect to matters herein named.

6. Subject to the restrictions hereinafter mentioned, the new Governing Body of every School to which this Act applies may at any time before the first day of January One thousand eight hundred and seventy, or within such further time as may be determined by Her Majesty in Council as hereinafter mentioned, make statutes with respect to all or any of the following matters:

*   *   *   *

(4.) With respect to Scholarships, Exhibitions, or other emoluments, either tenable at the School, or tenable after quitting the School by boys educated thereat, to do all or any of the following things; that is to say,

a.   *   *'   *   *

b. To convert emoluments attached to any particular College at Oxford or Cambridge, but not payable out of funds held by such College, into emoluments tenable at any College or Hall at either University, or otherwise by any member of such University.

Restrictions on making Statutes as herein stated.

8. The following restrictions shall be imposed on any Governing Body of a School making statutes under this Act:

*   *   *   *

(2.) Where any statute proposed to be made by any Governing Body of a School affects any Scholarship, Exhibition, or emolument attached to any College in either of the Universities of Oxford and Cambridge, notice in writing of such intended statute shall be given to the Head of such College two months at least before such statute is submitted to the Special Commissioners as hereinafter mentioned.

[Another restriction, the fourth, is that no statute made by a Governing Body shall be of any validity until it has been approved by the Queen in Council.

[Section 9 directs that every statute made by a Governing Body shall be submitted to the Special Commissioners appointed by the Act; that, if approved by them, it shall be laid before the Queen in Council, and shall be forthwith published in the London Gazette; and that "it shall be lawful for the trustees of any Scholarship, Exhibition, or emolument to which such statute may relate, or for any person or body corporate directly affected thereby, within two months after such publication in the London Gazette, to petition Her Majesty in Council, praying Her Majesty to withhold her approval from the whole or any part of such statute."

[By section 19 all such powers of making statutes as are by this Act vested in any Governing Body of any School to which this Act applies shall, after a time to be limited, pass to and vest in the Special Commissioners appointed under this Act; and the Commissioners may then exercise such powers in respect of all matters in which any Governing Body may have failed to do so. In the case of a statute affecting any Scholarship, Exhibition, or emolument attached to any College in either of the Universities, the Commissioners are to give two months' notice to the Head of such College, and are to hear all objections which the College may be desirous of urging against the statute.]

31 & 32 Vict. Cap. lix.

An Act for the establishment of a united Constabulary Force in and for the University and City of Oxford.

WHEREAS the power of Watch and Ward within the University and City of Oxford has heretofore been customarily exercised during the night by the Chancellor Masters and Scholars of the University of Oxford, and during the day by the Mayor Aldermen and Citizens of the City of Oxford: and whereas such division of authority has been found very inconvenient and injurious to the efficiency of the Police within the said University and City: and whereas the said Chancellor Masters and Scholars and Mayor Aldermen and Citizens are respectively desirous to establish a united Police Force, and it is expedient that provision should be made for that purpose upon the terms and subject to the conditions hereinafter appearing: and whereas the object aforesaid cannot be carried into effect without the authority of Parliament: may it therefore please your Majesty that it be enacted, and be it enacted by the Queen's most excellent Majesty, by and with the advice and consent of the Lords spiritual and temporal and Commons in this present Parliament assembled, and by the authority of the same, as follows; (that is to say,)

Short Title.
1. This Act may be cited for all purposes as "The Oxford Police Act, 1868."

Interpretation of terms.
2. In the construction of this Act (if not inconsistent with the context) the words and expressions "University," "Chancellor Masters and Scholars," "Vice-Chancellor," "Proctors," "Pro-Proctors," "Registrar," and "Marshal" shall be respectively understood to refer to the University of Oxford; the words "City," "Mayor," "Town Clerk," and "Borough Fund" shall be understood to refer to the City of Oxford; the expression "the Convocation" shall mean the Chancellor Masters and Scholars of the University of

Oxford in Convocation; the word "College" shall include Christ Church; and the expression "the Council" shall mean the Mayor Aldermen and Citizens of the City of Oxford in Council; the expression "the Watch and Ward Committee" shall mean the Watch and Ward Committee appointed by the Council; the word "District" shall mean and include the District of the Oxford Local Board as defined by the Local Government Supplemental Act, 1865, and as from time to time extended; and the expression "the Local Board" shall mean the Oxford Local Board.

3. From and after the thirty-first day of December one thousand eight hundred and sixty-eight, the powers and duties of the Watch and Ward Committee shall cease, and the powers of Watch and Ward by day and night within the District shall be exercised as follows: there shall be one Constabulary Force for the whole of the District, and the determination of the number, the appointment, dismissal, and entire management and direction of the said Force shall be vested in a Police Committee which shall consist of the Vice-Chancellor and five Members of the Convocation (hereinafter called "University Members") annually appointed by the Convocation, and of the Mayor and eight Members of the Council (hereinafter called "City Members") annually appointed by the Council. *Establishment of a united Constabulary Force and Police Committee.*

4. The first appointment of Members of the Police Committee by the Convocation and the Council respectively shall be made on or before the fifteenth day of November one thousand eight hundred and sixty-eight, and subsequent appointments shall be made on or before the fifteenth day of November in each year; any University or City Member going out of office shall be capable of forthwith being re-elected; occasional vacancies in the Police Committee shall be filled up by the Convocation or the Council respectively as they may occur, and the persons appointed to supply such vacancies shall continue in office so long as the persons whose places they fill would have remained in office. *Appointment of Members of Police Committee.*

5. The Registrar shall from time to time with all convenient speed notify in writing to the Mayor all appointments of Members of the Police Committee made by the Convocation; and the Town Clerk shall in like manner notify in *Appointments by Convocation and Council respectively*

<small>to be notified.</small> writing to the Vice-Chancellor all appointments of Members of the Police Committee made by the Council.

<small>Power to Police Committee to appoint and pay Officers and to make Rules.</small> 6. The Police Committee may appoint a Clerk and a Treasurer, if necessary, and may pay them reasonable salaries, and may make such Rules as the Police Committee may think fit with respect to the meetings of that Committee and the transaction of its business: provided, that no business shall be transacted at any meeting unless at least five Members shall be present thereat, and all questions shall be decided by a majority of the votes of those present.

<small>As to appointment of Chairman and Vice-Chairman of Police Committee.</small> 7. The Police Committee shall yearly at their first meeting appoint a Chairman and Vice-Chairman for the year: if the Chairman so appointed be absent from any meeting at the time appointed for holding the same, then the Vice-Chairman shall act as Chairman; and if both be absent, then the Members present shall appoint one of their number to act as Chairman thereat: if the Chairman appointed as first aforesaid, or the Vice-Chairman, die, resign, or become incapable of acting, another Member shall be appointed to be Chairman or Vice-Chairman, as the case may require, for the period during which the person so dying, resigning, or becoming incapable would have been entitled to remain in office, and no longer: the Chairman at any meeting shall have a second or casting vote in case of an equality of votes.

<small>Powers of Watch and Ward Committee vested in Police Committee.</small> 8. The powers and duties now vested in the Watch and Ward Committee shall, from and after the said thirty-first day of December one thousand eight hundred and sixty-eight, be vested in the Police Committee; and any Act for which, if done by the Watch and Ward Committee, the consent or approbation of the Council would now be required, may be done by the Police Committee without such consent or approbation; and the Police Committee shall and may have, exercise, and fulfil within the District, or any part thereof, the same rights, powers, and duties in respect of Watch and Ward as are now possessed, exercised, and fulfilled by the Chancellor Masters and Scholars, except as hereinafter excepted by Sections Ten and Twenty-four of this Act.

<small>Police Committee to have Supervision of</small> 9. All the powers and authorities now vested in and exercised by the Chancellor Masters and Scholars, or their officers, or by the Council, with respect to the Supervision of

Weights and Measures within the District, or any part thereof, (including the appointment of an Inspector or Inspectors,) shall, from and after the said thirty-first day of December one thousand eight hundred and sixty-eight, cease to be exercised by them the said Chancellor Masters and Scholars and Council respectively, and shall be vested in and exercised by the Police Committee. *Weights and Measures.*

10. There shall be provided by the Police Committee a common Police Station within the District for the purposes of this Act, to which all persons apprehended shall be taken, and at which all charges or complaints shall be made and entered; but the establishment of such Police Station shall in no way prejudice or affect the respective jurisdictions of the Vice-Chancellor, and of the Mayor or other Justices of the Peace for the City, in respect of such charges or complaints, but such jurisdictions shall remain; and the Courts or places of meeting of the Vice-Chancellor, and Mayor or other Justices, shall, during the hearing of such charges or complaints, be respectively free and open to the public without let or hindrance. If the University shall desire at their own expense to retain a separate Station for the detention of persons apprehended by the Proctors, a list of all persons taken to such separate Station and not forthwith released by the Proctors, and of the charges entered against such persons respectively, shall be sent to the common Police Station aforesaid on the following morning, and there shall be written upon such list the time and place at which the Vice-Chancellor will sit for hearing the charges therein mentioned, such time not being earlier than one hour after the delivery of the list. *Police Station for the District.*

11. For the maintenance of the Constabulary Force there shall be a fund annually contributed by the Chancellor Masters and Scholars and Mayor Aldermen and Citizens in the following proportions; (that is to say,) two-fifths thereof by the Chancellor Masters and Scholars, and three-fifths thereof by the Mayor Aldermen and Citizens. *Providing a Police Fund.*

12. The Police Fund shall be at the disposal of the Police Committee, and shall be applicable to the following purposes: *Application of Police Fund.*

(1.) The maintenance of the Constabulary Force, and

the payment of all charges and expenses properly incurred by the Police Committee in relation thereto:

(2.) The payment of gaol expenses (including the salaries of the Chaplain and Surgeon, and other salaries, rent, repairs, alterations, rates, and taxes), and the expenses of all other buildings required for Police purposes:

(3.) The payment of the salaries of the Recorder, Clerk of the Peace, Clerk or Clerks to the Vice-Chancellor (as Justice of the Peace) and the Mayor or other Justices, and the officers from time to time appointed by the Police Committee, and the cost of prosecutions for offences, and other expenses connected with the administration of justice within the District:

(4.) The payment of all expenses properly incurred by the Police Committee in relation to the Supervision of Weights and Measures, including the salaries of Inspectors:

(5.) The payment of all expenses properly incurred by the Police Committee in carrying this Act into execution not herein expressly provided for.

Police Committee to prepare Estimate.
13. The Police Committee shall, between the fifteenth day of November and the twenty-fifth day of December in every year, make an estimate of the amount required for the purposes to which the Police Fund is hereby made applicable for the ensuing year, commencing on the first day of January, after taking into account all fees, payments, allowances, and other sums of money (other than sums paid by the Chancellor Masters and Scholars and the Mayor Aldermen and Citizens under this and the next following Section), received by the Police Committee during the year immediately preceding, and shall thereupon give notice in writing to the Vice-Chancellor and to the Mayor respectively, specifying in such notice the total amount of such estimate, and the sum (being such proportionate part of the said total amount as aforesaid) which is to be paid by the Chancellor Masters and Scholars and the Mayor Aldermen and Citizens respectively in four quarterly payments; and the Chancellor Masters and

Scholars and the Mayor Aldermen and Citizens shall respectively pay or cause to be paid the sums so charged on them respectively to the Police Committee, or their Treasurer, within twenty-one days after the several days mentioned in such notices respectively for each quarterly payment.

14. If, at any time after the delivery of the notices of the estimate for the then current year, the amount so estimated by the Police Committee prove insufficient to defray the expenses of the Police Committee actually and properly incurred by them during the preceding part of the year, or if the Police Committee have reason to anticipate that such amount will prove insufficient to meet the expenses which the Police Committee may be properly called upon to incur during the subsequent part of such year, the Police Committee may, by like notice in writing to the Vice-Chancellor and the Mayor, specify the sums necessary to be paid by them respectively in order to make good such deficiency; and the Chancellor Masters and Scholars and the Mayor Aldermen and Citizens respectively shall pay or cause to be paid the sums so charged on them respectively in so many payments as there are quarterly days in the unexpired portion of the year, the first payment being made on the first day after the delivery of the notice specifying the same on which any quarterly payment of the amount originally estimated becomes payable: provided, that any money which may be received by the Police Committee, under this or the last preceding Section, in excess of the amount which the Police Committee shall at the end of the year, in respect of which the same was received by them, have actually and properly expended in that year, shall be taken into account by the Police Committee in their estimate for the following year. *How insufficiency in Estimate to be made up.*

15. The proportionate part of the Police Fund to be contributed and paid by the Chancellor Masters and Scholars shall be paid by the Vice-Chancellor out of the corporate or general funds of the University; and if such funds, upon an estimate thereof made in such manner as the University may from time to time provide, shall appear to be insufficient for payment of the said proportionate part, the amount of the estimated deficiency shall, not less than fourteen days before *As to the payment of the University contribution to the Police Fund.*

the making of the then next General District Rate, be notified by the Vice-Chancellor in writing under his hand to the Clerk to the Local Board, who shall cause such amount, together with any actual or estimated expenses attending the raising thereof, to be laid before the Local Board under the title " University Police Expenses " at the same time as the estimate for such next General District Rate; and the same amount shall be assessed by an equal pound rate on all the rateable property belonging to the Chancellor Masters and Scholars and the several Colleges and Halls of the University, in exclusion of all other property in the District liable to such General District Rate; and the said amount having been so assessed shall be added to that portion of the said General District Rate which is leviable on the said properties of the Chancellor Masters and Scholars, Colleges, and Halls; and the same amount, together with the portion leviable as last aforesaid, shall be inserted in one sum in the columns of the Rate Book of the Local Board under the head of the General District Rate; and the aggregate sum so inserted shall be levied and recoverable as the General District Rate, and by the means provided for raising the same rate.

As to payment of the City contribution to the Police Fund.

16. The proportionate part of the Police Fund to be contributed and paid by the Mayor Aldermen and Citizens shall be paid by them out of the Borough Fund; and if upon an estimate of such fund, and of all other charges payable thereout, the Council shall be of opinion that it be insufficient (after satisfying such other charges) for payment of the said proportionate part, the amount of the estimated deficiency shall, not less than fourteen days before the making of the then next General District Rate, be notified by the Mayor in writing under his hand to the Clerk to the Local Board, who shall cause such amount, together with any actual or estimated expenses attending the raising thereof, to be laid before the Local Board under the title " City Police Expenses" at the same time as the estimate for such next General District Rate; and the same amount shall be assessed by an equal pound rate on all property (other than rateable property belonging to the Chancellor Masters and Scholars and the several Colleges and Halls of the University) in respect of which the General District Rate may from time to

time be leviable; and the said amount having been so assessed shall be added to that portion of the said General District Rate which is leviable on the said property (other than property belonging to the Chancellor Masters and Scholars, Colleges, and Halls); and the same amount, together with the portion leviable as last aforesaid, shall be inserted in one sum in the columns of the Rate Book of the Local Board under the head of the General District Rate; and the aggregate sum so inserted shall be levied and recoverable as the General District Rate, and by the means provided for raising the same rate.

17. All monies to be raised as aforesaid by the Local Board for University Police Expenses and City Police Expenses respectively shall, when and as collected, be paid by the Local Board to the Police Committee or their Clerk or Treasurer, and the receipt of the Clerk or Treasurer shall be a sufficient discharge to the Local Board and its officers; and no person liable to the payment of any sum for Police Expenses under this Act shall, during the continuance of such liability, be liable to any payment for like purposes leviable under any other authority. *Police Expenses to be paid to Police Committee.*

18. All fees, allowances, and other sums in reference to matters of Police, prosecutions, maintenance of prisoners, and the administration of justice generally, which may be payable in any year, (except such as are by any Act or Acts from time to time in force required to be paid into any Superannuation Fund for the benefit of the Police Force which may be established under the authority of such Acts,) and also all fees and payments in respect of Weights and Measures, shall be paid to the Police Committee, and carried by them to the credit of the Police Fund, and shall be taken into account by them in preparing their estimate for the next ensuing year. *Certain monies received by Police Committee to be carried to credit of Police Fund.*

19. For the purposes of the Sixteenth Section of the Act of the nineteenth and twentieth years of Her present Majesty, Chapter Sixty-nine, intituled An Act to render more effectual the Police in Counties and Boroughs in England and Wales, the Police Force established under the provisions of this Act shall be deemed to be the Police of a Borough, established under the provisions of the said Act of the nineteenth *Extending 16th sect. of 19 & 20 Vict. c. 69 to Police Force established under this Act.*

Police Committee to keep Accounts, and same to be audited.

20. The Police Committee shall keep true and accurate accounts of all their receipts and expenditure; and such accounts shall be audited and examined once a year in the month of January by two Auditors, of whom one shall be nominated by the Vice-Chancellor and Proctors, and approved by the Convocation, and is hereinafter called "the University Auditor," and the other shall be nominated by the Council, and is hereinafter called "the City Auditor;" and the Police Committee shall, after every such audit, cause a full abstract of such accounts to be printed, and copies thereof to be delivered to the Vice-Chancellor and to the Mayor respectively.

Regulating the appointment of Auditors.

21. The University Auditor and the City Auditor respectively shall be appointed between the fifteenth day of November in each year and the first day of January next ensuing (the latter day being reckoned inclusively), and shall hold office from the first day of January in every year until and including the first day of January in the ensuing year; and occasional vacancies in the office of University Auditor shall, as soon as may be after they occur, be filled up by the Vice-Chancellor and Proctors, with the approval of the Convocation; and occasional vacancies in the office of City Auditor shall, as soon as may be after they occur, be filled up by the Council; and the persons appointed to supply such vacancies shall continue in office until and including the first day of January succeeding their appointment. The Registrar shall from time to time notify in writing to the Town Clerk all appointments of University Auditors, and the Town Clerk shall in like manner notify to the Registrar all appointments of City Auditors, and no such Auditor shall enter upon his office until such notification has been made.

Claims for compensation to be paid out of Police Fund.

22. In case any claim shall be made on the inhabitants of the City under the Act of the seventh and eighth years of King George the Fourth, Chapter Thirty-one, or under any other Act or law heretofore made or hereafter to be made relating either to riots or malicious injuries, for compensation to any person or corporation by reason of damages sustained by such person or corporation in consequence of any riot or

malicious injury, the Police Fund shall be the fund from which such compensation shall be made.

23. No public exhibition or performance, whether strictly theatrical or not, other than performances in theatres which are regulated by the Act of the sixth and seventh years of Her present Majesty, Chapter Sixty-eight, shall take place within the District unless with the consent in writing of the Vice-Chancellor and the Mayor, or (during the academical vacations intervening between Trinity and Michaelmas Terms and between Michaelmas and Lent Terms respectively) with the consent in writing of the Mayor; and every person who shall offend against this enactment shall be liable to a penalty of not exceeding twenty pounds for every offence, recoverable in like manner as penalties imposed by the said Act. *Prohibiting public exhibitions.*

24. Nothing in this Act contained shall affect the jurisdiction of the University, or of the Chancellor or Vice-Chancellor thereof, as it now by law exists, nor the jurisdiction of the City, or of the Mayor, as it now by law exists, nor the powers of the University now exercised by the Proctors; and the Proctors, Pro-Proctors, and their servants, including the Marshal, shall not be deemed to be included within the Constabulary Force to be appointed under the provisions of this Act: provided, that the Chancellor or Vice-Chancellor shall not, during the continuance of this Act, appoint any persons as Constables under the provisions of the Act of the sixth year of King George the Fourth, Chapter Ninety-seven, other than Proctors' servants (including the Marshal) and Special Constables. *Saving Jurisdictions of the University and City.*

25. This Act shall continue in force until the first day of January one thousand eight hundred and eighty-two, and no longer, unless Parliament in the meantime otherwise provides. *Continuance of Act.*

26. All costs, charges, and expenses of and incident to the preparing for, obtaining, and passing of this Act, or otherwise in relation thereto, shall be paid in equal moieties by the Chancellor Masters and Scholars and the Mayor Aldermen and Citizens. *Expenses of Act.*

OMITTED IN THE PROPER ORDER.

31 Geo. III, Cap. XXXII.

An Act to relieve, upon conditions and under restrictions, the persons therein described from certain penalties and disabilities to which Papists, or persons professing the Popish Religion, are by law subject.

[Section 13 permits Roman Catholics, upon certain conditions, to act as tutors or schoolmasters.]

14. Provided always, that no person professing the Roman Catholick religion shall obtain or hold the mastership of any college or school of royal foundation or of any other endowed college or school for the education of youth, or shall keep a school in either of the Universities of Oxford and Cambridge.

INDEX.

The chief articles in this Index are

BENEFICES	COLLEGES	ESTATES	UNIVERSITIES
CAMBRIDGE	COLLEGES IN CAMBRIDGE	LEASES	UNIVERSITY OF CAMBRIDGE
CHRIST CHURCH	COLLEGES IN OXFORD	OXFORD	UNIVERSITY OF OXFORD.

ABJURATION, Oath of: *see* OATHS.

ADDENBROOKE, John, M.D., founder of Hospital at Cambridge; p. 76.

ADDERBURY turnpike road, Trustees of; 37 G. 3, c. 170.

ALEHOUSES: *see* UNIVERSITIES, tit. *Privileges;* UNIV. CAMBRIDGE.

ALLEGIANCE, Oath of: *see* OATHS.

ALMANACS: *see* UNIVERSITIES.

ANNE, Queen, annexed a Prebend at Gloucester to the Mastership of Pembroke College, Oxford, a Prebend at Rochester to the Provostship of Oriel College, and a Prebend at Norwich to the Mastership of St. Katharine's College; pp. 55-57.

ANNEXATION: *see* BENEFICES, tit. *Augmentation.*

APOTHECARIES: *see* UNIVERSITIES, tit. *Privileges.*

ARUNDEL, Thomas, Abp. of Canterbury, claimed the right of visiting the University of Oxford; p. 4.

ARUNDEL, Thomas, Earl of; p. 4.

ASSISE of bread, wine, and ale: *see* UNIV. OXFORD.

ATTORNEYS AND SOLICITORS:
graduates may be admitted after having served three years under articles of clerkship; 23 & 24 V. c. 127, s. 2.

persons having passed certain University Examinations may be admitted after four years' service; *ib.* s. 5, *note.*

ATTORNEYS AND SOLICITORS *continued:*
persons having passed University Local Examinations are exempted from the Special Examination requisite before entering into articles; p. 303, *note* d.

AUGMENTATION: *see* BENEFICES.

BACHELORS of Divinity: *see* BENEFICES.

BEDFORD Level, Navigation Commissioners of rivers in, 7 & 8 G. 4, c. xlvii.

BEER: *see* ALEHOUSES.

BENEFICES:
valued at or above £30 a year in the Queen's Books to be held by none except Bachelors of Divinity or Preachers allowed by some Bishop or by one of the Universities; 13 El. c. 12.

Augmentation.

any augmentation granted, reserved, or made payable, by any College (*University not mentioned*), out of any rectory impropriate or tithes, to the incumbent of any church or chapel within the place in which the rectory lies or the tithes arise, to be perpetual and never recalled; 1 & 2 W. 4, c. 45, s. 3.

any augmentation granted, reserved, or made payable, by any College (*University not mentioned*), out of any lands &c., to the incumbent of any church or chapel in the patronage (whether sole or alternate) of the College, to be perpetual in like manner; *ib.* ss. 4, 15.

BENEFICES *continued*:
such augmentation to be in the form of an annual rent; *ib.* s. 5.
See LEASES, tit. *Division of Lands*.
an augmentation may be granted, to take effect on the determination of a beneficial lease; 1 & 2 W. 4, c. 45, ss. 7, 8.
no augmentation allowed to raise the clear annual value of any benefice to a greater amount than £300; *ib.* s. 16: but the limit is enlarged to £500 by 23 & 24 V. c. 59, s. 7.
power to appropriate and annex lands, tithe rent charge, or other permanent endowment to any church or chapel in lieu of annual rents or other payments previously reserved or granted by way of augmentation or endowment, with consent of incumbent, diocesan, and patron; 23 & 24 V. c. 59, s. 11.
Colleges enabled to annex any rectory impropriate or tithes to any church or chapel within the place in which the rectory lies or the tithes arise, and to annex any lands &c. to any church or chapel in their own patronage (whether sole or alternate), yet not so as to raise the clear annual value to a greater amount than £300; 1 & 2 W. 4, c. 45, ss. 11–16: but the limit is enlarged to £500 by 23 & 24 V. c. 59, s. 7.
deed of annexation to be deposited in the registry of the diocese; 1 & 2 W. 4, c. 45, s. 26.
power to sell sinecure rectories &c., advowsons, impropriate rectories, lands &c., power also to endow or augment benefices in the patronage of the University or College selling &c., either from the proceeds of such sale or other moneys, or by annexation of impropriate rectories &c., up to the value of £500 a year, or even above that with consent of Ecclesiastical Commissioners; 23 & 24 V. c. 59, ss. 7–10.
Colleges may lend money without interest for the purpose of building, rebuilding, repairing, or purchasing residence houses on benefices in their patronage; 17 G. 3, c. 53; 1 & 2 V. c. 23; 1 & 2 V. c. 106, s. 73: also for the purpose of purchasing land to become glebe; 55 G. 3, c. 147.

Land Tax.
Colleges empowered to redeem Land Tax on livings in their patronage, and to become entitled to an equivalent rent charge; 42 G. 3, c. 116.

Patronage.
Papists disabled from presenting to benefices, and from nominating to schools,

BENEFICES *continued*:
hospitals, and donatives, and the right of presenting &c. given to the Universities; 3 J. 1, c. 5; 13 Anne, c. 13, s. 1; 10 G. 4, c. 7: *see* UNIV. CAMBRIDGE, UNIV. OXFORD.
the same disability extended to trustees of Papists; 1 W. & M. c. 26; 13 Anne, c. 13, s. 1.
any such trustee presenting without having given notice to the proper University within three months after the vacancy to forfeit £500; 1 W. & M. c. 26.
either University, or their presentees, may exhibit bills in any Court of Equity for the discovery of secret trusts of advowsons; 13 Anne, c. 13, s. 4.
the Court in which any Quare impedit is depending at the instance of either University, or of their clerk, may take proceedings for the discovery of secret trusts; *ib.* s. 5.
no lapse shall incur nor plenarty be a bar against either University till after a time limited, provided a bill of discovery be exhibited before lapse incurred; *ib.* s. 8.
either University may bring writ of Quare impedit either by the name of "Chancellor and Scholars" (see 3 J. 1, c. 5) or by the proper name of incorporation; *ib.* s. 9.
every grant of any advowson or right of presentation by any Papist or his trustee to be void unless made bona fide and for a full and valuable consideration to a Protestant purchaser, and every devise of the same made with intent to secure the benefit to the heirs or family of such Papist to be void; 11 G. 2, c. 17.
grantees and their presentees compellable to make discovery relating to grants, as directed by c. 13 of 13 Anne in the case of trustees; *ib.*

Plurality.
See HEADS OF COLLEGES.

Residence.
Heads of Colleges and Halls, Head Masters of Eton and Winchester, holding but one benefice with cure of souls, exempt from penalties for non-residence; 1 & 2 V. c. 106, s. 37.
Professors and Public Readers resident within the precincts of their University and reading lectures, Provost of Eton, and Warden of Winchester, may count time of requisite and actual residence there as residence on a benefice; *ib.* s. 38.
Canons of cathedral churches, Fellows of Eton and Winchester, statutably resi-

BENEFICES continued:
dent and performing duties there, may count such residence as residence on a benefice, but not for more than five months in a year; ib. s. 39.

BEQUESTS, Specific: see LEGACIES.

BODLEY, Sir Thomas: his agreement with the Stationers' Company for copies of published books; p. 187, n.

BOOKS: see COPY, COPYRIGHT, LEGACIES.

BOTANIC Gardens: see TOBACCO.

BOUNDARIES, unknown or disputed: see ESTATES.

BRENT, Benedict, Proctor of Oxford; p. 4.

BRICKENDEN, Colwell, D.D., Master of Pembroke College, Oxford; p. 55.

BURGHLEY, Sir William Cecil, Lord, Chancellor of Cambridge; p. 28.

BYRCH, John, Proctor of Oxford; p. 4.

CAM, River:
three of the Conservators to be nominated by the Chancellor or Vice-Chancellor of Cambridge and the Heads of Colleges; 14 & 15 V. c. xcii, ss. 14-16.
the Chancellor or Vice-Chancellor to be one of the auditors of the Conservators' accounts, and a Head of a College to be another auditor; ib. s. 22.
no boats &c. to remain or lie in any part of the river along the backs of the Colleges; ib. s. 23.
bargemen &c. damaging property or trespassing on premises of any College abutting on the river liable to a fine of £5; ib.
tolls to be made up, if necessary, by the London and Cambridge Junction Canal Company; 52 G. 3, c. cxli, s. 54.

CAMBRIDGE:
Local Acts; Award, 19 & 20 V. c. xvii.
Gas, 30 & 31 V. c. lxxvii.
Improvement, 28 G. 3, c. 64; 34 G. 3, c. 104.
Waterworks, 16 & 17 V. c. xxiii.
Addenbrooke's Hospital established; 7 G. 3, c. 99: entitled to certain fines which may be imposed on the Eastern Counties Railway Company; 7 & 8 V. c. lxii, s. 188.
Finance Committee to be appointed annually by the Council; 19 & 20 V. c. xvii, ss. 60, 61.
Hobson's Conduit protected; 52 G. 3, c. cxli.
Commissioners under the Improvement Acts to be the Local Board of Health

CAMBRIDGE continued:
for the Cambridge District; 11 & 12 V. c. 63, s. 31: seven Members of such Board to be a quorum; ib. s. 34: the Board may supply water to Colleges and Halls and to University premises on special terms; ib. s. 93.
Mayor and Bailiffs not required to promise to observe the privileges of the University; 19 & 20 V. c. xvii, s. 4: Oaths of Aldermen &c. required by Henry III abolished; ib. s. 5.
Watch Committee, constitution of, ib. ss. 51-54: such Committee to have entire control of the Constabulary Force; ib. s. 55.
Watercourse supplying the Town protected; 47 G. 3, sess. 2, c. lx.
See also COLLEGES, tit. Rooms; COLLEGES IN CAMBRIDGE, tit. Improvement Acts; UNIV. CAMBRIDGE.

CANONRIES: no person to hold one, until he has been six years in Priest's Orders, unless it be a Canonry annexed to a Professorship or to a Headship of a College; 3 & 4 V. c. 113, s. 27.

CANTERBURY, Archbishop of: see UNIVERSITIES, tit. Visitation.

CANTERBURY, [Dr. Longley] Archbishop of, a referee in the matter of Christ Church; p. 329.

CARTER, George, D.D., Provost of Oriel College; p. 56.

CATHEDRAL preferment: see HEADS OF COLLEGES.

CHAPLAINS: see COMMON PRAYER.

CHARLES I in Council adjudged to the Archbishop of Canterbury the right of visiting the Universities jure metropolitico; p. 7, n.

CHARTERS: see LETTERS PATENT.

CHRIST CHURCH:
affected by the Universities and College Estates Acts; 21 & 22 V. c. 44, s. 31; 23 & 24 V. c. 59, s. 7.
affected only by ss. 5 and 6 of the Cathedral Act, 3 & 4 V. c. 113; and only by s. 12 of the Ecclesiastical Commission Act of 1868, 31 & 32 V. c. 114.
annexed to the Oxford Incorporation for the relief of the Poor; p. 220, n.
entitled to a rent charge of 4d. for part of the site of Hertford College; p. 132.
premises protected against vicinity of gasometer &c., and against disturbance by the Gas Company; 58 G. 3, c. lxiv, ss. 11, 48.

Canons.
trustees of Adderbury turnpike road; 37 G. 3, c. 170: also electors of four Con-

CHRIST CHURCH *continued*:
servators of the Thames; 29 & 30 V. c. 89.
a Canonry annexed to the Regius Professorship of Divinity without any form of admission; 10 Anne, c. 45.
a Canonry annexed to the Margaret Professorship of Divinity; 3 & 4 V. c. 113, s. 5.
a Canonry subject to provisions (contained in the Act) respecting the endowment of Archdeaconries; *ib.*
two Canonries annexed to two new Professorships about to be founded by the Queen; *ib.* s. 6.
a Canonry stated to be annexed to the Regius Professorship of Hebrew; p. 330: see also 3 & 4 V. c. 113, s. 5.
a Member of any other College or Hall in Oxford accepting any Professorship with a Canonry annexed ceases thereby to be a Member of such College or Hall; 3 & 4 V. c. 113, s. 6.
New Ordinance.
sanctioned by 30 & 31 V. c. 76.
of whom the House or Collegiate Foundation to consist; *ib.* cl. 1.
Governing Body thereof; *ib.* cl. 2.
£500 to be paid yearly to the Regius Professor of Greek; *ib.* cl. 9.
£40 apiece payable yearly to the Regius Professors of Divinity and Hebrew; *ib.*

CHRIST'S COLLEGE, Cambridge, specially interested in Hobson's Conduit; p. 125.

CLERKS, Articled; *see* ATTORNEYS.

COLERIDGE, Rt. Hon. Sir John Taylor, a reference in the matter of Christ Church; p. 329.

COLLEGES:
not affected by the following Acts; against misemployment of charitable gifts, 43 El. c. 4; restraining the gift of land for charitable uses, 9 G. 2, c. 36 (*see* 24 & 25 V. c. 9); for registering charitable gifts, 52 G. 3, c. 102; for improving Grammar Schools, 3 & 4 V. c. 77; for the better administration of charitable trusts, 16 & 17 V. c. 137.
College Premises.
no lease to be granted of College premises &c.; 21 & 22 V. c. 14, s. 26.
allowances, in respect of Property Tax, to be granted for repairs of chapels, of the public buildings and offices, and of the gardens, walks, and grounds for recreation, maintained by Colleges or Halls; 5 & 6 V. c. 35.
power to borrow money, from the Commissioners under the Acts for the issuing of Exchequer Bills for Public Works, for the building, rebuilding, enlarging, improving, or fitting up additional or

COLLEGES *continued*:
existing rooms, buildings, and offices, for the purpose of increasing the accommodation of students; 5 G. 4, c. 36.
Common Prayer.
to use the Book of Common Prayer in their Chapels; 14 C. 2, c. 4, ss. 1, 13.
may use Common Prayer (except Holy Communion) in Greek, Latin, or Hebrew, in their Chapels; 2 & 3 E. 6, c. 1: may use the whole in Latin; 14 C. 2, c. 4, s 14.
Elections of Fellows &c.
taking any reward for voting in favour of any person to make the offender's place vacant; 31 El. c. 6, s. 1.
taking any reward for resigning any place, how to be punished; *ib.* s. 2.
this Act, and the College Statutes, to be publicly read at every election; *ib.* s. 3.
First Fruits.
discharged from payment of first fruits and tenths; 27 H. 8, c. 42; 1 El. c. 4: but benefices in their gift are not discharged; 27 H. 8, c. 42, s 6.
Land Tax.
sites exempt from Land Tax; 38 G. 3, c. 5: also all Headships, Fellowships, &c., from duty of four shillings in the pound imposed on offices &c. by the Land Tax Acts; *ib.*
See also BENEFICES.
Public Lecturer.
to maintain in each University a Public Lecturer in such science or language as the King shall appoint; 27 H. 8, c. 42, s 4.
Rooms.
occupation of College rooms, &c., not to entitle any person to vote in elections of Members of Parliament for Oxford or Cambridge; 2 & 3 W. 4, c. 45: nor to be enrolled a citizen of Oxford or a burgess of Cambridge; 5 & 6 W. 4, c. 76, s. 137.
separate apartments in Colleges and Halls to be charged with House Tax as entire houses; 14 & 15 V. c. 36.
Sale of Advowsons.
power to sell, or to purchase, advowsons of benefices now annexed to Headships; 3 & 4 V. c. 113, s. 69; see 23 & 24 V. c. 59, s. 10.
Scholarships.
Scholarships &c. now tenable only at particular Colleges by persons educated at certain Public Schools may be made tenable by such persons free from that restriction; 31 & 32 V. c. 118.
See also
BENEFICES, tit. *Augmentation*; ESTATES; LEASES; MORTMAIN; TUTORS.

COLLEGES IN CAMBRIDGE:
Footways.
footways in front of Colleges and Halls, when to be swept; 34 G. 3, c. 104, s. 20.
Gas.
premises protected against vicinity of gasometer, gas-pipes, &c.; 30 & 31 V. c. lxxvii, ss. 44, 45.
Heads of Houses &c.
Heads of Colleges and Halls trustees of several turnpike roads; 12 G. 3, c. 90; 37 G. 3, c. 179; 55 G. 3, c. xlix: also Commissioners under the Improvement Acts; 34 G. 3, c. 104, ss. 3, 5: also Commissioners for Navigation of the river Ouse; 35 G. 3 c. 77: also interested in the Borough Fund; 19 & 20 V. c. xvii, s. 62.
Heads of Houses, Bursars, and resident Fellows, though in Holy Orders, may be Directors or Managing Partners of the Cambridge Waterworks Company; 16 & 17 V. c. xxiii; also of the Cambridge Gas Company; 30 & 31 V. c. lxxvii, s. 39.
Improvement Acts.
Colleges empowered (jointly with the University) to borrow money, not exceeding £6000 in the whole, for the purposes of the Improvement Acts; 28 G. 3, c. 64, ss. 111, 112; 34 G. 3, c. 104, ss. 1, 2.
Commissioners, how to be elected by the several Colleges and Halls; 34 G. 3. c. 104. ss. 3–5.
quotas of payments under these Acts, how to be assessed and paid; 28 G. 3, c. 64, ss. 113, 114.
lessees of Colleges or Halls deemed landlords and owners for the purposes of these Acts; *ib.* ss. 26, 34.
College Courts &c. exempt from operation of these Acts; *ib.* s. 60.
Colleges empowered to sell houses &c. in Cambridge; *ib.* s. 87; 34 G. 3, c. 104, s. 25.
Lamp Breaking.
any member of a College or Hall wilfully damaging any lamp in the Town to pay the full amount of damages; if he refuse, his Tutor answerable; 28 G. 3, c. 64, s. 74; 34 G. 3, c. 104, s. 21.
Oaths &c.
no declaration of religious belief and no oath to be required of Undergraduates obtaining Scholarships or other College emoluments; 19 & 20 V. c. 88, s. 46.
Poor Rates &c.
in what parishes respectively College property to be rated; 19 & 20 V. c. xvii, s. 22.
in what name to be assessed; *ib.* s. 24.
Chapels and Libraries exempt; *ib.* s. 23.
See also
CAM; CAMBRIDGE; CHRIST'S COLLEGE; COLLEGES, tit. *Rooms;* EASTERN COUN-

COLLEGES IN CAMBRIDGE *continued:*
TIES RAILWAY; EMANUEL COLLEGE; OATHS; ST. KATHARINE'S COLLEGE; TRINITY HALL.

COLLEGES IN OXFORD:
were enabled by 11 G. 3, c. 19, ss. 74, 75, to sell tenements or hereditaments in Oxford or its suburbs; p. 78.
Gas.
premises protected against vicinity of gasometer &c., and against disturbance by the Gas Company; 58 G. 3 c. lxiv, ss. 11, 48.
Heads of Houses.
Heads of Colleges and Halls trustees of Adderbury turnpike road; 37 G. 3, c. 170: also electors of four Conservators of the Thames; 29 & 30 V. c. 89.
Living Funds.
Colleges empowered, with consent of Visitor, to apply Living Funds to the augmentation of livings in their patronage, or to the building of residence houses, or to the augmentation or foundation of Scholarships or Exhibitions, or to other purposes for the advancement of religion, learning, and education; but not when the Living Fund belongs to any particular foundation; 20 & 21 V. c. 25, s. 3.
Local Board.
Heads and Bursars of Colleges and Halls to elect eleven Members of the Local Board; 21 & 22 V. c. 98: such elected persons qualified sufficiently by their degree; 27 & 28 V. c. 68; 28 & 29 V. c. 108, s. 6.
who to be rated to rates made by the Local Board on College property; 28 & 29 V. c. 108, s. 10.
See OXFORD.
Poor Rates.
certain Colleges and Halls made liable to Poor Rates: *see* UNIV. OXFORD. Heads and Bursars of those Colleges and Halls to elect Guardians of the Poor; 17 & 18 V. c. ccxix, ss. 2, 3.
See also
COLLEGES, tit. *Rooms;* GREAT WESTERN RAILWAY; MAGDALEN COLLEGE; OATHS; ORIEL COLLEGE; PEMBROKE COLLEGE; QUEEN'S COLLEGE; ST. JOHN'S COLLEGE; WADHAM COLLEGE.

COMMON PRAYER:
Declaration of conformity to the Liturgy of the Church of England to be subscribed before the Vice-Chancellor of either University by every Head, Fellow, Chaplain, and Tutor of any College or Hall, and by every public Professor and Reader, on pain of forfeiting Headship &c.; 14 C 2, c. 4, s. 6.

COMMON PRAYER *continued*:
every Head of a College or Hall to declare his assent to the Thirty-nine Articles and to the Book of Common Prayer publicly in the presence of the Fellows and Scholars within one month after his admission on pain of being suspended by the Visitor for six months and of forfeiture afterwards; *ib.* ss. 2, 13.
also, if in Holy Orders, to read publicly the Morning Prayer in his Chapel once at least in every quarter of a year on the same penalty; *ib.* s. 13.
See also COLLEGES, SERMONS.

CONFORMITY: *see* COMMON PRAYER.

CONSTABLES: *see* UNIVERSITIES.

COPY of every book, and of any second or subsequent edition of every book containing additions or alterations, together with all maps and prints belonging thereto, to be delivered (on demand in writing made within twelve months after the publication) to an officer of the Stationers' Company for the Bodleian Library at Oxford and for the Public Library at Cambridge; 5 & 6 V. c. 45.

COPYHOLD COMMISSIONERS, consent of, requisite to various transactions under the Universities and College Estates Acts, 21 & 22 V. c. 44; 23 & 24 V. c. 59.

COPYHOLD LANDS: provisions respecting consideration moneys for enfranchisement, in the case of a manor under lease; 23 & 24 V. c. 59, s. 4.

COPYRIGHT of all books given or bequeathed for the advancement of learning and other beneficial purposes of education secured in perpetuity to the two Universities and the Colleges within them (as well as to the four Universities of Scotland and the Colleges of Eton, Westminster, and Winchester), provided such books are printed only at their own printing presses and for their sole benefit, and that the title to the copyright is entered in the register of the Stationers' Company within two months after the gift or bequest is known; 15 G. 3, c. 53; 5 & 6 V. c. 45, s. 27.

CORN Rents: *see* LEASES.

CORN Returns: *see* INSPECTORS.

COURTENAY, Richard, Chancellor of Oxford, resisted the claim of Archbishop Arundel to visit the University; p. 4.

COWLEY, part of, added to the Oxford District under the Local Government Act; p. 325.

CRACHERODE, Rev. C. M., a benefactor to the British Museum; p. 112.

CRAVEN Scholarships: *see* UNIV. OXFORD, tit. *Scholarships*.

DAMASK, to, a verb; p. 85, l. 28.

DEANERIES: *see* HEADS OF COLLEGES.

DECLARATIONS: *see* OATHS.

DECLARATIONS of Assent and of Conformity: *see* COMMON PRAYER.

DEGREES: *see* OATHS, STAMP DUTY, and tit. *Oaths* in UNIV. CAMBRIDGE and UNIV. OXFORD.

DENYER Theological Prizes at Oxford, power to vary trusts of; 25 & 26 V. c. 26, s. 6.

DISCOMMUNING: *see* UNIV. CAMBRIDGE.

EASTERN COUNTIES RAILWAY COMPANY:
to give to certain Officers of the University of Cambridge and to the Heads of Colleges and Halls free access to all stations &c., and to furnish information on demand with reference to passengers supposed to be Members of the University; 7 & 8 V. c. lxii, s. 184.
to refuse, after notice duly given, to convey Members of the University below a certain standing; *ib.* s. 185.
not to take up or set down Members of the University below a certain standing anywhere except at regular stations; *ib.* s. 186.
not to take up or set down passengers at the Cambridge station or within three miles thereof between 10 a.m. and 5 p.m. on Sundays, under penalty of a fine to the use of Addenbrooke's Hospital or some other county charity selected by the University; *ib.* s. 188.
to pay £1000 yearly to the Commissioners under the Cambridge Improvement Acts in lieu of tolls; p. 96, *n.*; p. 196, *n.*
See also 9 & 10 V. c. clxxii.

ECCLESIASTICAL COMMISSIONERS empowered to authorise sales of advowsons &c. and augmentations of benefices in the patronage of the Universities or Colleges; 3 & 4 V. c. 113, s. 69; 23 & 24 V. c. 59, ss. 7, 10.

ELECTIONS to Fellowships &c.: *see* COLLEGES.

ELECTIONS to Parliament: *see* COLLEGES, tit. *Rooms*; UNIVERSITIES.

INDEX. 357

ELY, two Canonries at, annexed to the Regius Professorships of Hebrew and Greek at Cambridge; 3 & 4 V. c. 113, s. 12.

EMANUEL COLLEGE, Cambridge, specially interested in Hobson's Conduit; p. 125.

ESTATES:

houses not to be aliened without equivalent in lands; 14 El. c. 11, s. 7.

power, by means of agreements with lessees &c. or with owners of adjoining lands &c., to get unknown or disputed boundaries of estates ascertained and settled; 2 & 3 W. 4, c. 80.

power to sell, enfranchise, and exchange lands in possession or with only 7 years of lease still to run, with consent of Copyhold Commissioners and under certain conditions; 21 & 22 V. c. 44, ss. 1–3.

power to accept surrenders from lessees in consideration of annual payments during residue of term in order to sell to such lessees; *ib.* s. 4.

power to purchase the interest of lessees either by a gross sum or for annual payments during residue of term, and to raise money by mortgage in order to such purchases; *ib.* ss. 6–9.

power to sell the liberty or privilege of digging gravel or sand or brick earth; *ib.* ss. 15, 21.

this Act not to restrain powers of sale &c. previously existing; *ib.* s. 30.

in exchanges effected under the Acts for inclosure, exchange, and improvement of lands, money may be received by way of equality of exchange; *ib.*

power to transfer lands vested in individual Members of Universities or Colleges to the University or College interested, but upon the like trusts; 23 & 24 V. c. 59, s. 5.

power to raise money upon mortgage, with consent of Copyhold Commissioners, for restoring &c. University or College buildings, for improving farm buildings, for draining or otherwise permanently improving lands; 21 & 22 V. c. 44, ss. 27, 28.

valuations under the Universities and College Estates Acts to be stamped; 31 & 32 V. c. 89.

See also LEASES.

ETON COLLEGE:

discharged from first fruits and tenths; 27 H. 8, c. 42 : 1 El. c. 4.

exempt from Land Tax for its site; 38 G. 3, c. 5.

affected by the following Acts; for augmentation of Vicarages &c., 1 & 2 W. 4, c. 45; for ascertaining boundaries &c.

ETON COLLEGE *continued*:

of lands, 2 & 3 W. 4, c. 80; granting perpetual copyright, 15 G. 3, c. 53; requiring corn rents, 18 El. c. 6; 39 & 40 G. 3, c. 41, s. 7; for redemption of Land Tax, 42 G. 3, c. 116; Uniformity, 14 C. 2, c. 4; Universities and College Estates, 21 & 22 V. c. 44; 23 & 24 V. c. 59.

not affected by the following Acts; against misemployment of charitable gifts, 43 El. c. 4; restraining the gift of land for charitable uses, 9 G. 2, c. 36 (see 24 & 25 V. c. 9); for registering charitable gifts, 52 G. 3, c. 102; for improving Grammar Schools, 3 & 4 V. c. 77.

no Deanery tenable with Provostship; 13 & 14 V. c. 98, s. 5.

See also BENEFICES, tit. *Residence*.

EWELME in Oxfordshire, Rectory of, annexed to the Regius Professorship of Divinity at Oxford, without presentation, institution, or induction, but not discharged from first fruits, tenths, and other dues, nor from canonical obedience; 10 Anne, c. 45.

EXETER College, Oxford: rent charge of 1*l.* 13*s.* 4*d.* for part of the site of Hertford College (now made over to Magdalen Hall) to be paid by Magdalen College; 56 G. 3, c. 136, ss. 7–9.

FELLOWS of Colleges: *see* COLLEGES, titt. *Elections, Land Tax;* COMMON PRAYER.

FINES: *see* LEASES.

FIRST FRUITS and TENTHS: *see* COLLEGES, UNIVERSITIES.

FYFIELD in Berkshire, Manor of, belonging to St. John's College, Oxford; pp. 35, 36.

GARDENS, PHYSIC: *see* TOBACCO.

GLOUCESTER, Prebend at, annexed to the Mastership of Pembroke College, Oxford; 13 Anne, c. 6; 3 & 4 V. c. 113, s. 15.

GREAT WESTERN RAILWAY COMPANY:

to give to certain Officers of the University of Oxford and to the Heads of Colleges and Halls free access to all stations &c., and to furnish information on demand with reference to passengers supposed to be Members of the University; 6 & 7 V. c. x, s. 304.

to refuse, after notice duly given, to convey Members of the University below a certain standing; *ib.* s. 305.

GREAT WESTERN RAILWAY COMPANY continued:
not to take up or set down Members of the University below a certain standing anywhere except at regular stations; *ib.* s. 306.

HALLS: most of the enactments concerning COLLEGES apply, as far as possible, to Halls likewise.
HALLS, Private: *see* UNIV. OXFORD.
HEADS OF COLLEGES AND HALLS:
no Deanery (except Christ Church) tenable with any Headship; 13 & 14 V. c. 98, s. 5.
no Head holding any benefice to hold therewith any Cathedral preferment or any other benefice, and no Head holding any Cathedral preferment to hold therewith any benefice, except benefices and preferment annexed to Headship; *ib.* s. 6.
See also BENEFICES, tit. *Residence*; CANONRIES; COLLEGES, tit. *Sale of Advowsons*; COMMON PRAYER; JUSTICES.
HENRY III: his Letters Patent requiring the Mayor and Bailiffs of Oxford to swear to observe the liberties and customs of the University; p. 288.
HENRY IV adjudged to the Archbishop of Canterbury the right of visiting the University of Oxford; p. 5.
HENRY VIII: his Public Lecture at each University; 27 H. 8, c. 42, s. 4: his Professorships; p. 17, *n.*: masses were to be kept for him; 27 H. 8, c. 42, s. 5.
HERTFORD COLLEGE, dissolved, site of, and certain lands at North Moreton in Berkshire, to be made over to the University of Oxford in trust for the Principal and Members of Magdalen Hall for the purpose of their removing to that site; 56 G. 3, c. 136.
HINCKSEY, North, part of, added to the Oxford District under the Local Government Act; p. 325.
HOUSES not to be aliened without equivalent in lands; 14 El. c. 11, s. 7.

INCOME TAX, Commissioners of; p. 144, *note* m.
INCORPOREAL hereditaments: *see* LEASES.
INSPECTORS of Corn Returns for Oxford and Cambridge to be appointed and removed (when necessary) by the University of the place; 5 & 6 V. c. 14.

JAMES I annexed a Prebend at Salisbury to the Regius Professorship of Civil Law at Oxford; p. 47: also a Canonry in Christ Church and the Rectory of Ewelme to the Regius Professorship of Divinity at Oxford, the Rectory of Somersham to the Regius Professorship of Divinity at Cambridge, and the Rectory of Terington to the Margaret Professorship of Divinity at Cambridge; p. 52.
JOHNSON Scholarships at Oxford, power to vary trusts of; 25 & 26 V. c. 26, s. 6.
JURISDICTION: *see* UNIVERSITIES, tit. *Privileges*.
JUSTICES of the Peace: property qualification not required for Heads of Colleges or Halls, or for the Vice-Chancellor, in either University; 18 G. 2, c. 20.

KENNICOTT Scholarships at Oxford, power to vary trusts of; 25 & 26 V. c. 26, s. 6.

LANDS intermixed, boundaries of, how to be determined; p. 163, *n.*
LAND TAX:
begun in the time of the Commonwealth; p. 111, *note* c.
See COLLEGES, UNIVERSITIES.
Commissioners for either University; 7 & 8 G. 4, c. 75; 29 & 30 V. c. 59.
LAUD, Archbishop, claimed the right to visit the Universities jure metropolitico; p. 7, *n.*
LEASES:
granted by consent of a majority of a College or other corporation are good and effectual; 33 H. 8, c. 27.
no lease to be granted of College premises &c.; 21 & 22 V. c. 44 s. 26.
receipt endorsed on a lease to be conclusive evidence of the execution of the counterpart; *ib.* s. 25.
Concurrent Leases.
not to be made concurrent with any former lease for any longer period than three years; 18 El. c. 11.
Corn Rents.
in leases of lands one third part at least of the old rent to be reserved in corn, to be delivered or the value paid, at the option of the lessees, according to the market price at Cambridge or Oxford, or at Winchester for Winchester College, or at Windsor for Eton College; 18 El. c. 6: but not in

LEASES continued:
leases granted under the Universities and College Estates Act, 1858 ; 21 & 22 V. c. 44, s. 30.

Division of Lands.
lands &c. heretofore comprised in one lease may be divided and demised by several leases, or part may be demised and part retained, provided the aggregate of the rents reserved be not less than the ancient rent, and the right proportion be reserved in corn according to 18 El. c. 6 ; 39 & 40 G. 3, c. 41, ss. 1–7.
payments to Vicars &c. accustomably reserved in any lease shall, in case of division into several leases, be reserved on lands of not less annual value than three times the amount of such payments ; *ib.* ss. 8, 9: see 1 & 2 W. 4, c. 45, s. 9. *See* BENEFICES, tit. *Augmentation.*

Fines.
power to raise money upon mortgage, with consent of the Copyhold Commissioners, for the purpose of indemnifying present Members of a Society for loss of fines, except when they have refused to renew a lease on reasonable terms ; but such power not to extend beyond two fines for the same lands, and no fine to be ever again taken for a lease of such lands ; 23 & 24 V. c. 59, ss. 1, 2.
no fine to be ever again taken on lands once leased at rack rent ; *ib.* s. 3.

Improvement of Estates.
power to make arrangements with lessees for lighting, paving, draining, cleansing, or general improvement of lands demised, or for payment of land tax or tithe rent charge ; 21 & 22 V. c. 44, ss. 16, 17.
also, in building or repairing leases, to appropriate part of lands for streets, squares, roads, gardens, &c. ; *ib.* s. 18.

Incorporeal Hereditaments.
power to grant leases of incorporeal hereditaments for three lives or for 21 years, subject to limitations of College Statutes ; 5 G. 3, c. 17.

Informal Leases.
power to confirm leases which may be void or voidable by reason of any technical error or informality ; 21 & 22 V. c. 44, s. 24.

Insurance.
power to insure houses and buildings demised, and to charge the lessees with the premiums ; *ib.* s. 14.

New Leases.
power to release persons from contracts for leases, to make new contracts, to accept surrenders of leases, and to grant new leases with reasonable allowance for such surrenders and with the rent specifically apportioned ; *ib.* s. 22.
power to grant new leases of lands resumed under any condition of re-entry ; *ib.* s. 23.

Rent.
leases in which no annual rent is reserved not valid ; 39 & 40 G. 3, c. 41, s. 6 ; also leases made at less than the accustomed rent ; 13 El. c. 10, s. 2.
power to grant leases for a term of 21 years at rack rent under certain conditions ; 21 & 22 V. c. 44, s. 10.
mineral rents &c. under ss. 15 and 20, how to be applied or invested ; *ib.* s. 21.
See tit. *Corn Rents.*

Term.
leases made for a longer term than 21 years or three lives, or at less than the accustomed rent, to be void ; 13 El. c. 10, s. 2.
not to be made for a longer term than is limited by College Statutes ; *ib.* s. 3.
houses with ground belonging to them (but not above the quantity of ten acres), situate in any city or town, may be demised for a term of 40 years, but not for any longer term, nor in reversion, nor at less than the accustomed rent, nor without charging the lessee with the repairs ; 14 El. c. 11.
power to grant building and repairing leases for a term of 99 years under certain conditions ; 21 & 22 V. c. 44, ss. 11–13.
also to grant by lease for a term of 60 years use of running water, water-leaves, wayleaves, &c., under certain conditions ; *ib.* s. 19.
also to grant mining leases for a term of 60 years ; *ib.* s. 20.
See also ESTATES.

LECTURE, King Henry the Eighth's, at each University ; 27 H. 8, c. 42, s. 4.
LECTURES in the Universities may be delivered in places not licensed ; 39 G. 3, c. 79, s. 22.
not affected by the Act for preventing publication without consent ; 5 & 6 W. 4, c. 65.
LEGACIES of books, prints, pictures, statues, gems, coins, medals, specimens of natural history, or other specific articles, bequeathed to or in trust for any body corporate, whether aggregate or sole, in order to be kept and preserved, and not for the purposes of sale, exempt from Legacy Duty ; 39 G. 3, c. 73.

INDEX.

LEICESTER, Robert, Earl of, Chancellor of Oxford; p. 27.
LETTERS PATENT heretofore granted to either University confirmed; 13 El. c. 29, ss. 2, 5.
LIBRARIES, University: *see* COPY &c.
LITURGY: *see* COMMON PRAYER.
LOANS of Public Money: *see* COLLEGES, tit. *College Premises*.
LOCAL Examinations: *see* ATTORNEYS.
LOLLARDS; p. 2.

MAGDALEN COLLEGE, Oxford, enabled to do all necessary acts for the removal of Magdalen Hall to the site of Hertford College, and charged with payment of a rent charge due to Exeter College for part of the site; 56 G. 3, c. 136.
MAGDALEN HALL, Oxford, removal of the Principal and Members of, from their ancient site next Magdalen College to the site of Hertford College now dissolved; *ib.*
MANORS under lease: *see* COPYHOLD LANDS.
MATRICULATION: *see* STAMP DUTY, and tit. *Oaths* in UNIV. CAMBRIDGE and UNIV. OXFORD.
MEASURES: *see* WEIGHTS AND MEASURES.
MEDICINE:
graduates may practise without examination by the College of Physicians; 14 & 15 H. 8, c. 5.
General Council of Medical Education &c. established; 21 & 22 V. c. 90, s. 3.
Universities of Oxford and Cambridge each send one member to such Council; *ib.* s. 4.
graduates in Medicine entitled to be registered by the Council; *ib.* s. 15.
Council empowered to require from Universities information as to course of study &c., and to send deputies to be present at examinations; *ib.* s. 18.
Council may report to Privy Council any insufficient course of study or examinations, and the Privy Council may then withdraw or suspend title to registration; *ib.* ss. 20, 21.
MILITIA, resident Members of either University not liable to serve in; 42 G. 3, c. 90.
MINISTER: this word erroneously changed into "Master" in the Land Tax Act; p. 111, *note* b.

MORTMAIN:
the Act empowering the King to grant licences to alien and to hold in mortmain was passed with the special object of furthering the founding and augmenting of Colleges and Schools for encouragement of learning; 7 & 8 W. 3, c. 37, s. 1.
the Act directing that no lands, nor any money to be laid out in lands, shall be given for any charitable uses, unless by indenture made 12 months before the death of the donor &c. &c., does not apply to the Universities or Colleges; 9 G. 2, c. 36; 24 & 25 V. c. 9.

NIGHT Walkers; *see* PROSTITUTES.
NORWICH, Prebend at, annexed to the Mastership of St. Katharine's College; 13 Anne, c. 6; 3 & 4 V. c. 113, s. 15.

OATHS:
Oath of Abjuration to be taken by persons admitted into civil offices, by Foundation Members of Colleges, &c., within six months after admission, at the Quarter Sessions; 1 G. 1, st. 2, c. 13.
Oath of Allegiance to be taken on graduation and by Fellows and Scholars of Colleges; 7 J. 1, c. 6; 1 W. & M. c. 8: also with the Oath of Abjuration, as above.
Oath of Supremacy to be taken on graduation; 1 El. c. 1; 1 W. & M. c. 8: also with the Oath of Abjuration, as above.
Oath substituted for the Oaths of Allegiance, Supremacy, and Abjuration, as a qualification for holding offices, remaining on Foundation of Colleges, &c.; 30 & 31 V. c. 75.
all the above Oaths abolished so far as regards academical persons; 31 & 32 V. c. 72, s. 9.
Oaths of secrecy &c. in Colleges at Oxford made illegal; 17 & 18 V. c. 81, s. 24: also at Cambridge; 19 & 20 V. c. 88, s. 22.
power to substitute Declarations for Oaths; 5 & 6 W. 4, c. 62.
Declarations to be substituted; 31 & 32 V. c. 72, ss. 12, 15.
See also CAMBRIDGE, OXFORD; and tit. *Oaths* in COLLEGES IN CAMBRIDGE, COLLEGES IN OXFORD, UNIV. CAMBRIDGE, and UNIV. OXFORD.

OBSERVATORY at Oxford: *see* RADCLIFFE INFIRMARY.

ORIEL COLLEGE, Oxford, Provost of, incorporated; 13 Anne, c. 6: *see* ROCHESTER.

OUSE, Commissioners for Navigation of; 35 G. 3, c. 77.

OXFORD:

Local Acts.

Gas; 58 G. 3, c. lxiv.

Local Government; 28 & 29 V. c. 108.

Paving, Lighting, &c.; 11 G. 3, c. 19; 21 G. 3, c. 47; 52 G. 3, c. lxxii; 5 & 6 W. 4, c. lxix: see 28 & 29 V. c. 108.

Police, to continue in force until Jan. 1, 1882; 31 & 32 V. c. lix, s. 25.

Poor Rates; 17 & 18 V. c. ccxix.

Gas.

annual account from the Gas Company to be laid before the Vice-Chancellor and the Mayor; 58 G. 3, c. lxiv, s. 33.

clear profits of the Gas Company above ten per cent. on an average of three years to be paid to the Local Board in aid of rates; *ib.*

Local Board.

composition of the Local Board of Health for the Oxford District; 21 & 22 V. c. 98.

annual election to take place on some day, between Nov. 9 and 24, fixed by the Board in October; 28 & 29 V. c. 108, s. 4.

Board to appoint a Chairman for the year; *ib.* s. 7.

seven Members of the Board to be a quorum; 11 & 12 V. c. 63, s. 34.

the Board may supply water to Colleges and Halls and to University premises on special terms; *ib.* s. 93.

Market.

Market for the sale of meat, fish, poultry, and garden stuff to be established on ground between High Street and Jesus College Lane; 11 G. 3, c. 19, ss. 77, 78; also for the sale of butter, eggs, and English fruit; 21 G. 3, c. 47, s. 26.

no person may hold any other market in Oxford or its suburbs (except the present markets for corn, pigs, and butter) or expose to sale any meat, fish, poultry, or garden stuff anywhere out of the new Market under penalty of £5, except fishmongers and poulterers, who may sell in their own shops or houses as heretofore; 11 G. 3, c. 19, ss. 80, 81: the like prohibition as to butter, eggs, and English fruit, except fruit raised in Oxford, or purchased in the Market; 21 G. 3, c. 47, ss. 26, 27.

Committee of Management of the Market to consist of six resident Members of Convocation and six resident Members of the Council of the City; 11 G. 3, c. 19, s. 83.

OXFORD *continued.*

rents and profits of the Market to be for the use and benefit of the University and the City, equally, share and share alike; *ib.* s. 95.

the Market protected against vicinity of gasometer &c. and against disturbance by the Gas Company; 58 G. 3, c. lxiv, ss. 11. 44.

power to enlarge the Market Place, and to establish a second Market; 5 & 6 W. 4, c. lxix.

Mayor's Oath.

Mayor and others relieved from obligation to swear to keep the liberties and privileges of the University; 22 & 23 V. c. 19.

Police.

one Constabulary Force to be appointed for the District of the Local Board under the control of a Police Committee; 31 & 32 V. c. lix, s. 3.

constitution and appointment of Police Committee; *ib.* ss. 3–5.

officers, quorum, Chairman, and Vice-Chairman of Committee; *ib.* ss. 6, 7.

power of Watch and Ward vested in the Committee; *ib.* s. 8.

also supervision of Weights and Measures; *ib.* s. 9.

a Police Fund, contributed two fifths by the University and three fifths by the City, to be at the disposal of the Police Committee for Police purposes; *ib.* ss. 11, 12.

amount of Police Fund how to be estimated and paid; *ib.* ss. 13–18.

accounts of Police Committee to be audited annually in January; *ib.* s. 20.

a common Police Station to be provided for the District, the University being at liberty to retain a separate Station for persons apprehended by the Proctors; *ib.* s. 10.

See also

COLLEGES, tit. *Rooms;* COLLEGES IN OXFORD; UNIV. OXFORD.

PALMER, Sir Roundell, a referee in the matter of Christ Church; p. 329.

PARSONAGES impropriate, grants of, to either University or to any College or Hall confirmed; 1 El. c. 4.

PATRONAGE: *see* BENEFICES.

PATTESON, Rt. Hon. Sir John, arbitrator between the University and Borough of Cambridge in 1855; p. 241.

PEMBROKE COLLEGE, Oxford, Master of, incorporated; 13 Anne, c. 6: *see* GLOUCESTER.

PHYSIC Gardens: *see* TOBACCO.
PICTURES: *see* LEGACIES.
POLE, Archbishop, visited Oxford and Cambridge as legate; p. 7, *n*.
POLICE: *see* CONSTABLES, OXFORD, UNIV. CAMBRIDGE, UNIV. OXFORD.
POOR RATES: *see* COLLEGES IN CAMBRIDGE, UNIV. CAMBRIDGE, UNIV. OXFORD.
PRAYER: *see* COMMON PRAYER.
PREACHERS allowed by one of the Universities: *see* BENEFICES.
PREBENDS now annexed to Professorships &c. secured to them; 3 & 4 V. c. 113, s. 51.
PRESSES, Printing, of the Universities need not be registered; 39 G. 3, c. 79, s. 24: books and papers printed at them need not bear the printer's name; 2 & 3 V. c. 12, s. 3. *See also* COPYRIGHT.
PRINTING, Decree of Court of Star Chamber concerning; p. 187, *n*.
PRIVILEGES: *see* UNIVERSITIES.
PROFESSORS or Public Lecturers: *see* BENEFICES, tit. *Residence;* CANONRIES; COMMON PRAYER; PREBENDS; UNIV. CAMBRIDGE; UNIV. OXFORD.
PROSTITUTES, Common, found wandering in any public walk &c. within the precincts of the University of Oxford, to be dealt with as idle and disorderly persons; 6 G. 4, c. 97, s. 3.
PUBLIC SCHOOLS, Scholarships &c. from: *see* COLLEGES.

QUARE impedit, Writ of: *see* BENEFICES, tit. *Patronage.*
QUEEN'S College in Oxford called "la Quenhalle"; p. 8.

RADCLIFFE Infirmary at Oxford exempt from the Act for registering charitable gifts, 52 G. 3, c. 102.
protected, jointly with the Observatory, against vicinity of gasometer &c.; 58 G. 3, c. lxiv, s. 11.
RAWLINSON, Robert; p. 319.
READERS, Public: *see* PROFESSORS.
RENT: *see* LEASES.
RESIDENCE on Benefices: *see* BENEFICES.
RESIDENTS in Oxford, who to be deemed; 17 & 18 V. c. 81, s. 48.
RICHARD II adjudged to the Archbishop of Canterbury the right of visiting the University of Oxford; p. 3.

ROCHESTER, Prebend at, annexed to Provostship of Oriel College; 13 Anne, c. 6; 3 & 4 V. c. 113, s. 15.
ROMAN Catholics not to keep school in either University; 31 G. 3, c. 32, *at page* 350; 10 G. 4, c. 7.
not enabled by the Roman Catholic Relief Act to hold office or place in the Universities or Colleges; 10 G. 4, c. 7.
See also BENEFICES, tit. *Patronage.*
RONHALE, Richard; p. 3.
ROOMS in College, Occupation of: *see* COLLEGES.

ST. JOHN'S COLLEGE, Oxford, empowered to grant special leases of the manor of Fyfield in Berkshire; 18 El. c. 6, and c. 11, s. 4.
Ordinance concerning this College referred to a Committee of the Privy Council; 23 & 24 V. c. 23.
ST. KATHARINE'S COLLEGE, Cambridge, Master of, incorporated; 13 Anne, c. 6: *see* NORWICH.
SALISBURY, Prebend of Shipton at, tenable by the Regius Professor of Civil Law at Oxford notwithstanding any requirement of the Act of Uniformity; 14 C. 2, c. 4, s. 25.
SCHOLARSHIPS: *see* COLLEGES; COLLEGES IN OXFORD, tit. *Living Funds;* UNIV. OXFORD.
SERMONS before either University in the University Church may be preached apart from Common Prayer; 14 C. 2, c. 4, s. 19.
SHERLOCK, Thomas, D.D., Master or Warden of St. Katharine's College or Hall; p. 56.
SOLICITORS: *see* ATTORNEYS.
SOMERSHAM in Huntingdonshire, Rectory of, annexed to the Regius Professorship of Divinity at Cambridge, without presentation, institution, or induction, but not discharged from first fruits, tenths, and other dues, nor from canonical obedience; 10 Anne, c. 45.
SPECIMENS of Natural History: *see* LEGACIES.
STAMP Duty on certificate of admission to degrees; 55 G. 3, c. 184.
Duty on matriculations and on admission to degrees abolished in consideration of certain payments henceforward to be made from the University Chest to Professors at Oxford; 17 & 18 V. c. 81, s. 46; 18 & 19 V. c. 36: also at Cambridge; 19 & 20 V. c. 88, s. 47; 21 & 22 V. c. 11.

STATIONERS' Company, an officer of, to receive books for transmission to University Libraries ; 5 & 6 V. c. 45. *See also* BODLEY, COPYRIGHT.

SUNDAY : elections &c. of officers now required to be held on a Sunday, to be held on the day before or the day after ; 3 & 4 W. 4, c. 31.

SUPREMACY, Oath of : *see* OATHS.

TENTHS : *see* FIRST FRUITS.

TERINGTON in Norfolk, Rectory of, annexed to the Margaret Professorship of Divinity at Cambridge, without presentation, institution, or induction, but not discharged from first fruits, tenths, and other dues, nor from canonical obedience ; 10 Anne, c. 45.

TESTAMENTARY Documents : *see* UNIV. OXFORD, tit. *Wills*.

THAMES, Conservancy of ; 29 & 30 V. c. 89.

THEATRES : no licence to be granted for the performance of stage plays within the precincts of either University, or within 14 miles of Oxford or Cambridge, without consent of the Chancellor or Vice-Chancellor ; 6 & 7 V. c. 68, s. 10.

rules for management of licensed theatres within the said limits to be subject to the approval of the Chancellor or Vice-Chancellor ; *ib.*

penalty on persons performing for hire in unlicensed places ; *ib.* ss. 11, 16, 17.

See also UNIV. CAMBRIDGE, UNIV. OXFORD.

THE TURL, in Oxford ; p. 89, *n.*

TOBACCO may be planted in any Physic Garden of either University in quantity not exceeding half a pole ; 12 C. 2, c. 34.

TRINITY HALL, Cambridge : exchange of lands in order to the removal of the Botanic Garden of the University to a better site ; 1 W. 4, c. 5.

TUTORS of Colleges, after five years' service, specially eligible to benefices in chapter patronage ; 3 & 4 V. c. 113, s. 44.

TWISLETON, Hon. Edward T. B., a referee in the matter of Christ Church ; p. 329.

UNIVERSITIES :

not affected by the following Acts ; restraining the gift of land for charitable uses, 9 G. 2, c. 36 (see 24 & 25 V. c. 9) ;

UNIVERSITIES *continued* :

prohibiting the delivery of lectures for money in places not licensed, and requiring the registration of printing presses, 39 G. 3, c. 79 ; for registering charitable gifts, 52 G. 3, c. 102 ; for improving Grammar Schools, 3 & 4 V. c. 77 ; for better administration of charitable trusts, 16 & 17 V. c. 137.

Almanacs.

allowance of £500 yearly to each University in compensation for the lost privilege of printing Almanacs, to be paid by the Receiver General of Stamp Duties to the Vice-Chancellor or some person duly authorised by him ; 21 G. 3, c. 56.

Constables.

Chancellor or Vice-Chancellor of either University empowered to appoint any number of constables to act within the precincts and four miles therefrom either permanently or for a time ; 6 G. 4, c. 97.

Elections to Parliament.

elections not affected by the Representation of the People Acts ; 2 & 3 W. 4, c. 45 ; 30 & 31 V. c. 102.

writs for elections to be directed to the Vice-Chancellor, who is to proceed to election within six days after receipt of the writ, giving three clear days' notice at least of the day of election, exclusive of the day of proclamation and the day of election ; 16 & 17 V. c. 68, ss. 1, 3.

polling not to continue for more than five days, excluding Sunday, Christmas Day, Good Friday, and Ascension Day ; *ib.* s. 4.

Vice-Chancellor empowered to appoint three polling places in addition to the Convocation House or Senate House, and to direct at which place Members of the several Colleges shall vote ; also to appoint any number of Pro-Vice-Chancellors to receive votes and decide questions in his absence, and any number of Poll Clerks ; *ib.* s. 5.

votes may be given by voting papers delivered at the poll by other voters named for the purpose in the papers ; 24 & 25 V. c. 53, s. 1.

voting papers when and how to be signed and attested ; *ib.* ; 31 & 32 V. c. 65, s. 3.

— how to be tendered, received, and recorded ; 24 & 25 V. c. 53, s. 2.

declaration to be made by person tendering a voting paper ; 31 & 32 V. c. 65, s. 1.

persons acting on behalf of Candidates entitled to inspect voting papers when

UNIVERSITIES *continued*:
tendered, and to object to them on certain grounds; 24 & 25 V. c. 53, s. 3.
voting papers to be filed; *ib.* s. 4.

First Fruits.
Universities discharged from payment of first fruits and tenths; 27 H. 8, c. 42; 1 El. c. 4.

Incorporation.
each incorporated by the name of "the Chancellor Masters and Scholars of the University of Oxford" *or* "Cambridge," with confirmation of all Letters Patent heretofore granted, and of all possessions now belonging, to either; 13 El. c. 29: see 13 Anne, c. 13, s. 9.

Inspectors of Weights and Measures.
Chancellor or Vice-Chancellor authorised to appoint Inspectors of Weights and Measures; 5 & 6 W. 4, c. 63; 22 & 23 V. c. 56.

Land Tax &c.
all offices in both Universities exempt from duty of four shillings in the pound imposed on offices &c. by the Land Tax Acts; 38 G. 3, c. 5: they are also exempt from the duty of one shilling in the pound imposed in 31 G. 2; 32 G. 2, c. 33.

Libraries.
See COPY &c.

Municipal Offices.
no resident Member to be compelled to take any municipal office in Oxford or Cambridge; 5 & 6 W. 4, c. 76, s. 137.

Privileges Reserved.
all, in the Municipal Reform Act; *ib.*
in respect of Apothecaries; 55 G. 3, c. 194.
in respect of jurisdiction of Chancellors' Courts, in the County Courts Act; 9 & 10 V. c. 95.
in respect of licensing Ale-houses &c.; 9 G. 4, c. 61; 11 G. 4 & 1 W. 4, c. 64.
in respect of Weights and Measures; 5 & 6 W. 4, c. 63; 22 & 23 V. c. 56.
in respect of Wine Licences; 23 & 24 V. c. 27.

Visitation.
the Universities subject to visitation by Archbishop of Canterbury jure metropolitico; 13 H. 4.

See also
ATTORNEYS, BENEFICES, COLLEGES, COPYRIGHT, ESTATES, INSPECTORS, LEASES, LECTURES, MEDICINE, MILITIA, MORTMAIN, OATHS, PRESSES, ROMAN CATHOLICS, SERMONS, STAMP DUTY, THEATRES.

UNIVERSITY OF CAMBRIDGE:
Addenbrooke's Hospital.
the Chancellor, the Representatives in Parliament, the Vice-Chancellor, to be Governors of Addenbrooke's Hospital; 7 G. 3, c. 99.

Alehouse Licences.
Vice Chancellor not to grant alehouse licenses except as Justice of the Peace; 19 & 20 V. c. xvii, s. 8.
alehouse licences may be revoked by Justices of the Peace on complaint of the Vice-Chancellor; *ib.* s. 9.

Borough.
Members of the University not to become electors or burgesses of the Borough, nor to be forced to serve any municipal or parochial office or on any jury &c., by reason of any rate on University or College property; *ib.* s. 35.
Senate to appoint three auditors to join in auditing the accounts of the Borough Fund; *ib.* ss. 56–59.
such auditors authorised to attend meetings of Finance Committee of the Council of the Borough; *ib.* ss. 60, 61.
Vice-Chancellor and Heads of Colleges to be deemed persons interested in the Borough Fund; *ib.* s. 62.
See also titt. *Police, Weights and Measures.*

Botanic Garden.
no Improvement Rate to be paid for the Botanic Garden; 28 G. 3, c. 64, s. 23.
removal of the Garden to a better site; 1 W. 4, c. 5.

Buildings &c.
public buildings, Botanic Garden, and other premises, protected against vicinity of gasometer, gaspipes, &c.; 30 & 31 V. c. lxxvii, ss. 44, 45.
footpath before Senate House and Senate House Walk, when to be swept; 34 G. 3, c. 104, s. 20.
facilities given, by means of the Land Clauses Consolidation Act, for the purchase of land in Cambridge in order to the extension of University or College buildings; 19 & 20 V. c. 88, s. 51.
See also tit. *Poor Rates.*

Conusance.
right to claim conusance of pleas when one party is not a Member of the University abolished; 19 & 20 V. c. xvii, s. 18.

Council of the Senate.
Council of the Senate established in lieu of the Caput Senatus; 19 & 20 V. c. 88, s. 5.
composition of the Council; *ib.* ss. 6, 14.
by whom to be elected, and how; *ib.* ss. 6, 12.
seats in the Council to be vacated periodically; *ib.* ss. 9–11: and for nonattendance; s. 13.

INDEX. 365

UNIVERSITY OF CAMBRIDGE *continued:*
who to be president of the Council; *ib.* s. 19.
five members to be a quorum; *ib.* s. 20.
questions in the Council how to be decided; *ib.*
the Council to nominate for offices for which the Heads of Colleges have heretofore nominated; *ib.* 21.
Discommuning.
power of discommuning continued, but with certain limitations; 19 & 20 V. c. xvii, s. 17.
Election of Chancellor.
power to provide by Statute for voting by proxy at any election of a Chancellor; 19 & 20 V. c. 88, s. 32
Electoral Roll.
Electoral Roll, who to be on; *ib.* ss. 7, 8.
Hostels.
power to establish Hostels under licensed Principals; *ib.* ss. 23-25.
Improvement Acts.
the University empowered (jointly with the Colleges) to borrow money, not exceeding £6000 in the whole, for the purposes of the Improvement Acts; 28 G. 3, c. 64, ss. 111, 112; 34 G. 3, c. 104, ss. 1, 2.
certain Officers of the University appointed Commissioners; 34 G. 3, c. 104, ss. 3, 5.
quota of payments under the Acts (see 28 G. 3, c. 64, ss. 113, 114) reduced from two fifths of the whole to one fourth; 19 & 20 V. c. xvii, s. 50.
lessees of the University deemed owners for the purposes of the Acts; 2 & G. 3, c. 64, s. 34.
Land Tax.
Commissioners of Land Tax; 7 & 8 G. 4, c. 75.
Oaths.
Oaths and Declarations on matriculation, and on taking any degree in Arts, Law, Medicine, or Music, abolished; but such degree not to qualify for the Senate, nor for offices hitherto held by Members of the Church of England, without a declaration of bona fide membership of the Church; 19 & 20 V. c. 88, s. 45.
Patronage.
the University to have the presentation and nomination to all Benefices &c. in the patronage of Papists, within the counties of Anglesey, Bedfordshire, Cambridgeshire, Carnarvonshire, Cheshire, Cumberland, Denbighshire, Derbyshire, Durham, Essex, Flintshire, Glamorganshire, Hertfordshire, Huntingdonshire, Lancashire, Leicestershire, Lincolnshire, Merionethshire, Norfolk, North-

UNIVERSITY OF CAMBRIDGE *continued:*
umberland, Nottinghamshire, Radnorshire, Rutlandshire, Shropshire, Suffolk, Westmoreland, Yorkshire; but not to present a beneficed person to any such Benefice; 3 J. 1, c. 5. *See* BENEFICES.
Police.
appointments of University Constables to be notified to the Town Clerk by the Vice-Chancellor; 19 & 20 V. c. xvii, s. 20.
convictions of Members of the University by Justices of the Peace to be notified to the Vice-Chancellor, and copies of depositions to be furnished to him on application; *ib.* s. 19.
Proctors, Pro-Proctors, and their men not included in the "Constabulary Force" of the Borough; *ib.* s. 3: exempt from summary jurisdiction of Justices of the Peace; *ib.* s. 7.
Senate to appoint five members of the Watch Committee of the Borough; *ib.* ss. 51-54.
Poor Rates.
public buildings and property of the University, in what parishes to be rated; *ib.* s. 21.
certain buildings exempt from rates; *ib.* s. 23.
property to be valued for assessment; *ib.* ss. 25, 28, 29.
valuers to determine parochial boundaries in the case of property situate in more than one parish; *ib.* s. 26.
provision for fresh valuation after three years, if required; *ib.* s. 27.
costs of valuations, how to be paid; *ib.* s. 30.
property acquired after valuation made, how to be rated; *ib.* s. 31.
payments under agreement of 1650 to cease; *ib.* s. 33.
who to be deemed agents of the University and of Colleges at vestry meetings; *ib.* s. 34.
Privileges.
privileges not affected by the Acts for building a new Gaol; 7 & 8 G. 4, c. cxi: 2 & 3 V. c. ix: nor by 13 & 14 V. c. xxxvii.
privilege to grant wine licences retained, but no money to be taken for them; 19 & 20 V. c. xvii, ss. 11, 12.
privileges with respect to markets and fairs abolished; *ib.* s. 15.
Proctors.
See tit. *Police.*
Professors.
power to sell the advowsons of the benefices annexed to the Regius Professorship of Divinity; 3 & 4 V. c. 113, s. 70.
Professors of Anatomy, Chemistry, Civil

UNIVERSITY OF CAMBRIDGE continued:
Law, Mineralogy, and the Jacksonian, each to receive yearly from the University Chest £100,—of Botany £182, —of Modern History £371 ; 21 & 22 V. c. 11.
See also ELY, SOMERSHAM, TERINGTON.
Statutes.
Statutes of Queen Elizabeth repealed ; 19 & 20 V. c. 88, s. 41.
doubts as to meaning of new Statutes to be settled by the Chancellor; *ib.* s. 42.
Theatrical performances.
no occasional public exhibition or performance, whether strictly theatrical or not, to take place within the Borough without consent of the Vice-Chancellor and the Mayor, except during Midsummer Fair and in the Long Vacation ; 19 & 20 V. c. xvii, s. 16.
See also THEATRES.
Vice-Chancellor.
the Vice-Chancellor one of the Navigation Commissioners of rivers in the Bedford Level ; 7 & 8 G. 4, c. xlvii.
always to be a Head of a College ; 19 & 20 V. c. 88, s. 21.
may be appointed a Justice of the Peace for the Borough ; 6 & 7 W. 4, c. 105.
not to grant alehouse licences except as Justice of the Peace ; 19 & 20 V. c. xvii, s. 8.
See also titt. Addenbrooke's Hospital, Borough, Police.
Voting by proxy.
See tit. Election of Chancellor.
Weights and Measures.
supervision of Weights and Measures transferred from the University to the Justices of the Peace for the Borough ; 19 & 20 V. c. xvii, ss. 13, 14.
Wine Licences.
no person to sell wine by retail within the precincts of the University without licence from the University, under penalty of £5 recoverable in the Chancellor's Court ; 17 G. 2, c. 40; 19 & 20 V. c. xvii, ss. 11, 12 ; 23 & 24 V. c. 27.
See tit. Privileges.
See also
CAM, CAMBRIDGE, COLLEGES IN CAMBRIDGE, EASTERN COUNTIES RAILWAY.

UNIVERSITY OF OXFORD :
Assise of Bread &c.
remission of fee farm rent of 100s. for the assise of bread, wine, and ale, confirmed ; 12 & 13 E. 4.
Buildings &c.
buildings &c. protected against vicinity of gasometer &c, and against disturbance by the Gas Company ; 58 G. 3, c. lxiv, ss. 11, 48.

UNIVERSITY OF OXFORD continued:
facilities given, by means of the Land Clauses Consolidation Act, for the purchase of land in Oxford in order to the extension of University or College buildings &c. ; 20 & 21 V. c. 25, s. 4.
See tit. Local Board.
Chancellor's Court &c.
the Vice-Chancellor empowered to make rules from time to time, with approval of three of the Judges of the Queen's Superior Courts, for regulating the proceedings in the Chancellor's Court ; 25 & 26 V. c. 26, s. 12.
jurisdiction of the University, and of the Chancellor or Vice-Chancellor, not affected by the Gas Company's Act ; 58 G. 3, c. lxiv, s. 69 : nor by the Police Act ; 31 & 32 V. c. lix, ss. 10, 24.
Clerks of the Market.
See tit. Market.
Congregation of the University.
composition of the Congregation ; 17 & 18 V. c. 81, s. 16.
Register of Members of Congregation to be made and published annually ; *ib.* ss. 14, 15.
on promulgation of any proposed Statute Members of Congregation may speak in English ; *ib.* s. 20.
all provisions of this Act respecting the Hebdomadal Council, and respecting the Congregation, subject to repeal and alteration by the University with the approval of the Queen in Council ; *ib.* s. 40.
Conservators of the Thames.
Representatives in Parliament, and Vice-Chancellor, electors of four Conservators of the Thames ; 29 & 30 V. c. 89.
Craven Scholarships.
See tit. Scholarships.
Denyer Prizes.
See tit. Scholarships.
Election of Chancellor.
power to provide by Statute for voting by proxy at any election of a Chancellor ; 17 & 18 V. c. 81, s. 23.
Halls.
See titt. Magdalen Hall, Private Halls.
Hebdomadal Council.
Hebdomadal Council established in lieu of the Hebdomadal Board ; 17 & 18 V. c. 81, s. 5.
composition of the Council ; *ib.* s. 6.
seats in the Council to be vacated periodically ; *ib.* ss. 8, 10 ; and in default of required residence ; *ib.* s. 13.
by whom to be elected, and how ; *ib.* ss. 14, 21.
a Vice-Chancellor leaving office to continue in the Council until the next

UNIVERSITY OF OXFORD *continued:*
triennial election, or for one year if such election comes sooner; *ib.* s. 11.
See tit. *Congregation of the University. Johnson* and *Kennicott Scholarships.*
See tit. *Scholarships.*
Jurisdiction.
See tit. *Chancellor's Court &c.*
Land Tax.
Commissioners of Land Tax: 7 & 8 G. 4, c. 75; 29 & 30 V. c. 59.
Local Board.
the Vice-Chancellor and four persons elected by Convocation to be Members of the Local Board; 21 & 22 V. c. 98: such elected persons sufficiently qualified by their degree; 27 & 28 V. c. 68; 28 & 29 V. c. 108, s. 6.
public buildings assessable to rates levied by the Board; 28 & 29 V. c. 108, s. 8.
the Vice Chancellor a member of the court of appeal in case of assessments and rates made by the Board; *ib.* s. 15.
— to be rated for University property; *ib.* s. 20.
— to collect and pay to the Local Board rates made on University and College property, but empowered to transfer this task to the Board on twelve months' notice; *ib.* s. 21.
Magdalen Hall.
the University empowered to co-operate in effecting the removal of Magdalen Hall to the site of Hertford College; 56 G. 3, c. 136, ss. 6, 11-17.
Market.
right to appoint Clerks of the Market reserved to the University; 11 G. 3, c. 19, s. 79; 5 & 6 W. 4, c. lxix, s. 59: also the right to govern and regulate the Market; *ib.*
Oaths &c.
Oaths and Declarations on matriculation and on taking the degrees of B.A., B.C.L., B.M., and B.Mus. abolished; but such degrees not to qualify for offices hitherto held by Members of the Church of England, unless the requisite declarations are made either at the time of graduation or subsequently; 17 & 18 V. c. 81, ss. 43, 44.
Patronage.
the University to have the presentation and nomination to all Benefices &c. in the patronage of Papists, within the counties of Berkshire, Brecknockshire, Buckinghamshire, Cardiganshire, Carmarthenshire, Cornwall, Devonshire, Dorsetshire, Gloucestershire, Hampshire, Herefordshire, Kent, Middlesex including the City of London, Monmouthshire, Montgomeryshire, Northamptonshire, Oxfordshire, Pembroke-

UNIVERSITY OF OXFORD *continued:*
shire, Somersetshire, Staffordshire, Surrey, Sussex, Warwickshire, Wiltshire, Worcestershire; but not to present a beneficed person to any such Benefice; 3 J. 1, c. 5. See BENEFICES.
Police.
the Vice-Chancellor and five Members of Convocation to be Members of the Police Committee for the Oxford District; 31 & 3 V. c. lix, ss. 3-5.
two-fifths of the Police Fund to be contributed by the University; *ib.* ss. 11, 15.
one Auditor of Police Accounts to be appointed yearly by the Vice-Chancellor and Proctors with approval of Convocation; *ib.* ss. 20, 21.
Proctors, Pro-Proctors, and their servants not reckoned within the Constabulary Force under this Act; *ib.* s. 24.
constables, other than Proctors' servants and special constables, not to be appointed by the Vice-Chancellor under 6 G. 4, c. 97, during continuance of this Act; *ib.*
the University at liberty to retain a separate Police Station for persons apprehended by the Proctors; *ib.* s. 10.
charges before the Vice-Chancellor to be heard in public; *ib.*
See also OXFORD.
Poor Rates.
property of the University and of the Colleges and Halls within the united parishes made liable to Poor Rates; 17 & 18 V. c. ccxix.
the Vice-Chancellor and two Graduates to be Guardians for the University, and eight Graduates to be Guardians for the rated Colleges and Halls; *ib.* s. 2.
Guardians, how to be elected, and when; *ib.* ss. 3, 4.
no elector of Guardians for Colleges to vote at election of parochial Guardians; *ib.* s. 6
valuation of rateable property, how to be made; *ib.* 29.
the like valuation to be made from time to time at the end of every ten years on the requisition of either the University or the City; *ib.*
claim of the University and Colleges for exemption of certain premises from rates, how decided; *ib.* s. 31.
rates on University and College property to be made by the Vice-Chancellor; *ib.* s. 33.
rates to be paid by Bursars of Colleges and Principals of Halls to the Vice-Chancellor or to the University Bailiff or other authorised receiver; *ib.*
rates how to be recovered in default of payment within appointed time; *ib.*

UNIVERSITY OF OXFORD *continued:*
who to be rated in respect of the several portions of University and College property; *ib.* s. 34.
assessments to be deposited with the Registrar, and open to inspection; *ib.* s. 35.
appeals against rates, how to be made; *ib.* s. 36: "Delegates of Appeals in cases of Poor Rates" to be nominated annually by the Proctors; *ib.* s. 37.

Private Halls.
power to establish Private Halls under licensed Masters; 17 & 18 V. c. 81, ss. 25-27.

Proctors.
trustees of Adderbury turnpike road; 37 G. 3, c. 170.
See also titt. *Police, Poor Rates.*

Professors.
trustees of Adderbury turnpike road; 37 G. 3, c. 170.
Professors of Chemistry, Experimental Philosophy, Geology, and Mineralogy, each to receive yearly from the University Chest £100,—of Botany £182,—of Modern History £371; 18 & 19 V. c. 36.
power to make Statutes, subject to approval of the Queen in Council, for regulation of Professorships of Botany, Chemistry, Experimental Philosophy, Geology, Mineralogy, Political Economy; 25 & 26 V. c. 26, ss. 1, 7, 8.
also respecting election to the Chairs of Experimental Philosophy, Geology, and Mineralogy, and the qualifications of candidates for the Chair of Botany; *ib.* s. 2.
also, in case of a new Professorship of Chemistry, Geology, Mineralogy, or Political Economy being founded, to suppress the existing Professorship, and apply the salary to other means for promoting the study of the Science; *ib.* ss. 3-5.
Professor of Botany to be appointed by the President and Council of the College of Physicians of London; *ib.* s. 2.
See *also* CHRIST CHURCH, EWELME, SALISBURY, WORCESTER.

Residents.
who to be deemed Residents; 17 & 18 V. c. 81, s. 48.

Scholarships.
power to deal with Craven Scholarships as University emoluments under 17 & 18 V. c. 81; 23 & 24 V. c. 91, s. 1.
claim of founder's kin to those Scholarships abolished; *ib.*
right of Court of Chancery to augment the number from time to time retained; *ib.*
power to vary the trusts &c. of the Kenni-

UNIVERSITY OF OXFORD *continued:*
cott and Johnson Scholarships and the Denyer Prizes; 25 & 26 V. c. 26, s. 6.

Statutes.
course of legislation in making Statutes; *ib.* ss. 17-20.
on promulgation of any proposed Statute Members of Congregation may speak in English; *ib.* s. 20.
Statutes made under this Act subject to repeal or alteration in the usual way; 17 & 18 V. c. 81, s. 39.
Statutes made under 17 & 18 V. c. 81 may be altered or repealed with approval of the Queen in Council; 25 & 26 V. c. 26, s. 9.

Theatrical Performances.
no public exhibition or performance, whether strictly theatrical or not, to take place within the Oxford District unless with the consent of the Vice-Chancellor and the Mayor, or (during the Christmas Vacation and the Long Vacation) with the consent of the Mayor; 31 & 32 V. c. lix, s. 23.
See also THEATRES.

Trusts.
power to alter by Statute (made during the continuance of the Commission) the trusts of any gift or endowment held by the University which has taken effect for more than fifty years; 17 & 18 V. c 81, s. 30.

Vice-Chancellor.
See titt. *Chancellor's Court &c., Conservators of the Thames, Hebdomadal Council, Local Board, Police, Poor Rates, Theatrical Performances, Wine Licences.*

Vinerian Foundation.
power to vary the trusts &c. of the Vinerian Foundation; 28 & 29 V. c. 55.

Voting by proxy.
See tit. *Election of Chancellor.*

Watch and Ward.
See OXFORD, tit. *Police.*

Weights and Measures Supervision of.
See OXFORD, tit. *Police.*

Wills.
power to retain custody of Wills and other Testamentary Documents belonging to the Chancellor's Court instead of transmitting them to the Queen's Court of Probate; 23 & 24 V. c. 91, s. 2.

Wine Licences.
no person to sell wine by retail within the precincts of the University without licence from the Chancellor or Vice-Chancellor, under penalty of £5 recoverable in the Chancellor's Court; 17 G. 2, c. 40; 23 & 24 V. c. 27.
See also
COLLEGES IN OXFORD, GREAT WESTERN RAILWAY, OXFORD.

INDEX.

VICARS, payments reserved to: *see* BENEFICES, tit. *Augmentation;* LEASES, tit. *Division of Lands.*

VINER, Charles, Esq.: power to vary the trusts &c. of his foundation at Oxford; 28 & 29 V. c. 55.

VISITATION: *see* UNIVERSITIES.

WADHAM COLLEGE, Oxford: so much of the College Statutes as requires the Warden to be unmarried declared null and void; 46 G. 3, c. clxvii.

WALKER, Richard, D.D., Vice-Master of Trinity College, founder of the Botanic Garden at Cambridge; p. 147.

WEIGHTS and Measures: *see* OXFORD, tit. *Police;* UNIV. CAMBRIDGE.

WHITE, Sir Thomas, founder of St. John's College, Oxford; pp. 35, 36.

WILLS and Testamentary Documents: *see* UNIV. OXFORD.

WINCHESTER COLLEGE:
discharged from first fruits and tenths; 27 H. 8, c. 42; 1 El c. 4.
exempt from Land Tax for its site; 38 G. 3. c. 5.
affected by the following Acts; for aug-

WINCHESTER COLLEGE *continued:*
mentation of Vicarages &c., 1 & 2 W. 4, c. 45; for ascertaining boundaries &c. of lands, 2 & 3 W. 4, c. 80; granting perpetual copyright, 15 G. 3, c. 53; requiring corn rents, 18 El. c. 6; 39 & 40 G. 3, c. 41, s. 7; for redemption of Land Tax, 42 G. 3. c. 116; Uniformity, 14 C. 2, c. 4; Universities and College Estates, 21 & 22 V. c. 44; 23 & 24 V. c. 59.

not affected by the following Acts; against misemployment of charitable gifts, 43 El. c. 4; restraining the gift of land for charitable uses, 9 G. 2, c. 36 (see 24 & 25 V. c. 9); for registering charitable gifts, 52 G. 3, c. 102; for improving Grammar Schools, 3 & 4 V. c. 77.

no Deanery tenable with Wardenship; 13 & 14 V. c. 98, s. 5.
See also BENEFICES, tit. *Residence.*

WINE, licence to sell, by retail: *see* UNIV. CAMBRIDGE, UNIV. OXFORD.

WOOD, Sir William Page, a referee in the matter of Christ Church; p. 329.

WORCESTER, Canonry at, detached from the Margaret Professorship of Divinity at Oxford; 3 & 4 V. c. 113, s. 5.

November, 1868.

BOOKS

PRINTED AT

THE CLARENDON PRESS, OXFORD,

AND PUBLISHED FOR THE UNIVERSITY BY

MACMILLAN AND CO.,

16, BEDFORD STREET, COVENT GARDEN,

LONDON.

LEXICONS, LANGUAGE, &c.

A **Greek-English Lexicon**, by Henry George Liddell, D.D., and Robert Scott, D.D. *Fifth Edition.* 1861. crown 4to. *cloth*, 1*l*. 11*s*. 6*d*.

A **Greek-English Lexicon, abridged** from the above, chiefly for the use of Schools. *Twelfth Edition.* 1867. square 12mo. *cloth*, 7*s*. 6*d*.

Graecae Grammaticae Rudimenta in usum Scholarum, a Carolo Wordsworth, A.M. *Sixteenth Edition.* 1867. 12mo. *bound*, 4*s*.

Etymologicon Magnum. Ad Codd. MSS. recensuit et notis variorum instruxit Thomas Gaisford, S.T.P. 1848. fol. *cloth*, 1*l*. 12*s*.

Suidae Lexicon. Ad Codd. MSS. recensuit Thomas Gaisford, S.T.P. Tomi III. 1834. fol. *cloth*, 3*l*. 12*s*.

A **Practical Introduction to Greek Accentuation**, by H. W. Chandler, M.A. 1862. 8vo. *cloth*, 10*s*. 6*d*.

Scheller's Lexicon Linguae Latinae, with the German explanations translated into English by J. E. Riddle, M.A. 1835. fol. *cloth*, 1*l*. 1*s*.

Thesaurus Syriacus; collegerunt Quatremère, Bernstein, Lorsbach, Arnoldi, Field. Edidit R. Payne Smith, S.T.P.R. Fasciculus I. 1868. sm. fol. 1*l*. 1*s*.

———— Fasciculus II. *In the Press.*

Lexicon Aegyptiaco-Latinum ex veteribus Linguae Aegyptiacae Monumentis, etc., cum Indice Vocum Latinarum ab H. Tattam, A.M. 1835. 8vo. *cloth*, 1*l*. 10*s*. 6*d*.

A **Practical Grammar of the Sanskrit Language,** arranged with reference to the Classical Languages of Europe, for the use of English Students, by Monier Williams, M.A. *Third Edition.* 1864. 8vo. *cloth*, 15*s*.

Nalopákhyánam. Story of Nala, an Episode of the Mahá-Bhárata: the Sanskrit text, with a copious Vocabulary, Grammatical Analysis, and Introduction, by Monier Williams, M.A. The Metrical Translation by the Very Rev. H. H. Milman, D.D. 1860. 8vo. *cloth*, 15s.

A Sanskrit-English Dictionary, by Monier Williams, M.A., Boden Professor of Sanskrit. *In the Press.*

A Handbook of the Chinese Language. Parts I and II, Grammar and Chrestomathy. By James Summers. 1863. 8vo. *half bound*, 1l. 8s.

GREEK AND LATIN CLASSICS.

Æschylus; Tragœdiæ et Fragmenta, ex recensione Guil. Dindorfii. *Second Edition*, 1851. 8vo. *cloth*, 5s. 6d.

——— Annotationes Guil. Dindorfii. Partes II. 1841. 8vo. *cloth*, 10s.

——— Scholia Græca, ex Codicibus aucta et emendata a Guil. Dindorfio. 1851. 8vo. *cloth*, 5s.

Sophocles; Tragœdiæ et Fragmenta, ex recensione et cum commentariis Guil. Dindorfii. *Third Edition*. 1860. 2 vols. fcap. 8vo. *cloth*, 1l. 1s.

Each Play is sold separately, 2s. 6d.

The Text alone, printed on writing paper, with large margin. Royal 16mo. *cloth*, 8s. Square 16mo. *cloth*, 3s. 6d. Each Play separately, 6d.

——— Tragœdiæ et Fragmenta cum Annotatt. Guil. Dindorfii. Tomi II. 1849. 8vo. *cloth*, 10s.

The Text, Vol. I. 5s. 6d. The Notes, Vol. II. 4s. 6d.

——— Scholia Græca. Vol. I. ed. P. Elmsley, A.M. 1825. 8vo. *cloth*, 4s. 6d. Vol. II. ed. Guil. Dindorfius. 1852. 8vo. *cloth*, 4s. 6d.

Euripides; Tragœdiæ et Fragmenta, ex recensione Guil. Dindorfii. Tomi II. 1834. 8vo. *cloth*, 10s.

——— Annotationes Guil. Dindorfii. Partes II. 1840. *cloth*, 10s.

——— Scholia Græca, ex Codicibus aucta et emendata a Guil. Dindorfio. Tomi IV. 1863. 8vo. *cloth*, 1l. 16s.

Aristophanes; Comœdiæ et Fragmenta, ex recensione Guil. Dindorfii. Tomi II. 1835. 8vo. *cloth*, 11s.

——— Annotationes Guil. Dindorfii. Partes II. 1837. 8vo. *cloth*, 11s.

——— Scholia Græca, ex Codicibus aucta et emendata a Guil. Dindorfio. Partes III. 1839. 8vo. *cloth*, 1l.

Metra Æschyli Sophoclis Euripidis et Aristophanis descripta a Guil. Dindorfio. Accedit Chronologia Scenica. 1842. 8vo. *cloth*, 5s.

Aristoteles; ex recensione Immanuelis Bekkeri. Accedunt Indices Sylburgiani. Tomi XI. 1837. 8vo. *cloth*, 2l. 10s.

Each volume separately, 5s. 6d.

Catulli Veronensis Liber; recognovit, apparatum criticum prolegomena appendices addidit, Robinson Ellis, A.M. 1867. 8vo. *cloth*, 16s.

Demosthenes; ex recensione Guil. Dindorfii. Tomi IV. 1846. 8vo. cloth, 2l. 2s.

——— Tomi V. VI. VII. Annotationes Interpretum. 1849. 8vo. cloth, 1l. 16s.

——— Tomi VIII. IX. Scholia. 1851. 8vo. cloth, 15s.

Homerus; Ilias, ex recensione Guil. Dindorfii. 1856. 8vo. cloth, 5s. 6d.

——— **Odyssea,** ex recensione Guil. Dindorfii. 1855. 8vo. cloth, 5s. 6d.

——— Scholia Græca in Odysseam. Tomi II. 1855. 8vo. cloth, 15s. 6d.

Plato; Philebus, with a revised Text and English Notes, by Edward Poste, M.A. 1860. 8vo. cloth, 7s. 6d.

——— Theætetus, with a revised Text and English Notes, by L. Campbell, M.A. 1861. 8vo. cloth, 9s.

——— Sophistes and Politicus, with a revised Text and English Notes, by L. Campbell, M.A. 1866. 8vo. cloth, 18s.

——— The Apology, with a revised Text and English Notes, and a Digest of Platonic Idioms, by James Riddell, M.A. 1867. 8vo. cloth, 8s. 6d.

——— The Dialogues, translated into English, with Introductions, by B. Jowett, M.A., Fellow of Balliol College and Regius Professor of Greek. In four volumes; Vols. 1 to 3 will be published in the course of the ensuing year.

——— The Republic, with a revised Text and English Notes, by B. Jowett, M.A., Fellow of Balliol College and Regius Professor of Greek. Demy 8vo.

Xenophon; Historia Græca, ex recensione et cum annotationibus L. Dindorfii. *Second Edition.* 1852. 8vo. cloth, 10s. 6d.

——— Expeditio Cyri, ex rec. et cum annotatt. L. Dindorfii. *Second Edition.* 1855. 8vo. cloth, 10s. 6d.

——— Institutio Cyri, ex rec. et cum annotatt. L. Dindorfii. 1857. 8vo. cloth, 10s. 6d.

——— Memorabilia Socratis, ex rec. et cum annotatt. L. Dindorfii. 1862. 8vo. cloth, 7s. 6d.

——— Opuscula Politica Equestria et Venatica cum Arriani Libello de Venatione, ex rec. et cum annotatt. L. Dindorfii. 1866. 8vo. cloth, 10s. 6d.

THE HOLY SCRIPTURES, &c.

The Holy Bible in the earliest English Versions, made from the Latin Vulgate by John Wycliffe and his followers: edited by the Rev. J. Forshall and Sir F. Madden. 1850. 4 vols. royal 4to. cloth, 5l. 15s. 6d.

The Holy Bible, an exact reprint, page for page, of the Authorized Version published in the year 1611. Demy 4to. *half bound,* 1l. 1s.

Vetus Testamentum Græce secundum exemplar Vaticanum Romæ editum. Accedit potior varietas Codicis Alexandrini. Tomi III. 1848. 12mo. cloth, 14s.

Origenis Hexaplorum quæ supersunt; sive, Veterum Interpretum Græcorum in totum Vetus Testamentum Fragmenta. Edidit Fridericus Field, A.M.

    Tom. II. Fasc. I. 1867. 4to. *1l.*   Tom. II. Fasc. II. 1868. 4to. 16*s.*

Novum Testamentum Græce. Antiquissimorum Codicum Textus in ordine parallelo dispositi. Accedit collatio Codicis Sinaitici. Edidit E. H. Hansell, S.T.B. Tomi III. 1864. 8vo. *half morocco,* 2*l.* 12*s.* 6*d.*

Novum Testamentum Græce. Accedunt parallela S. Scripturæ loca, necnon vetus capitulorum notatio et canones Eusebii. Edidit Carolus Lloyd, S.T.P.R., nuper Episcopus Oxoniensis. 1863. 18mo. *cloth,* 3*s.*

    Also an edition on writing paper, with large margin, small 4to. *cloth,* 10*s.* 6*d.*

Novum Testamentum Græce juxta Exemplar Millianum. 1868. 12mo. *cloth,* 2*s.* 6*d.*

    Also an edition on writing paper, with large margin, small 4to. *cloth,* 6*s.* 6*d.*

The New Testament in Greek and English, on opposite pages, arranged and edited by E. Cardwell, D.D. 1837. 2 vols. crown 8vo. *cloth,* 6*s.*

Diatessaron: sive Historia Jesu Christi ex ipsis Evangelistarum verbis apte dispositis confecta. Ed. J. White. 1856. 12mo. *cloth,* 3*s.* 6*d.*

Harmonia Evangelica. Edidit Edvardus Greswell, S.T.B. *Editio quinta.* 1856. 8vo. *cloth,* 9*s.* 6*d.*

Canon Muratorianus. The earliest Catalogue of the Books of the New Testament. Edited with Notes and a Facsimile of the MS. in the Ambrosian Library at Milan, by S. P. Tregelles, LL.D. 1868. 4to. *cloth,* 10*s.* 6*d.*

FATHERS OF THE CHURCH, &c.

Patrum Apostolicorum, S. Clementis Romani, S. Ignatii, S. Polycarpi, quæ supersunt. Edidit Guil. Jacobson, S.T.P.R. Tomi II. *Fourth Edition.* 1863. 8vo. *cloth,* 1*l.* 1*s.*

Clementis Alexandrini Opera, ex recensione Guil. Dindorfii. Tomi IV. 8vo. (*Nearly ready.*)

Cyrilli Archiepiscopi Alexandrini in XII Prophetas. Edidit P. E. Pusey, A.M. Tomi II. 1868. 8vo. *cloth,* 2*l.* 2*s.*

Cyrilli Commentarii in Lucæ Evangelium quæ supersunt Syriace. E MSS. apud Mus. Britan. edidit R. Payne Smith, A.M. 1858. 4to. *cloth,* 1*l.* 2*s.*

The same, translated by R. Payne Smith, M.A. 1859. 2 vols. 8vo. *cloth,* 14*s.*

Ephraemi Syri, Rabulæ Episcopi Edesseni, Balæi, Aliorumque, Opera Selecta. E Codd. Syriacis MSS. in Museo Britannico et Bibliotheca Bodleiana asservatis primus edidit J. J. Overbeck. 1865. 8vo. *cloth,* 1*l.* 1*s.*

A Latin translation of the above, by the same Editor. *Preparing.*

Reliquiæ Sacræ secundi tertiique sæculi. Recensuit M. J. Routh, S.T.P. Tomi V. *Second Edition.* 1846—1848. 8vo. *cloth*, 2*l.* 11*s.*

Scriptorum Ecclesiasticorum Opuscula. Recensuit M. J. Routh, S.T.P. Tomi II. *Third Edition.* 1858. 8vo. *cloth*, 1*l.*

Catenæ Græcorum Patrum in Novum Testamentum. Edidit J. A. Cramer, S.T.P. Tomi VIII. 1838—1844. 8vo. *cloth*, 2*l.* 4*s.*

Eusebii Pamphili Historia Ecclesiastica. Edidit E. Burton, S.T.P.R. 1856. 8vo. *cloth*, 8*s.* 6*d.*

Socratis Scholastici Historia Ecclesiastica. Gr. et Lat. Edidit R. Hussey, S.T.B. Tomi III. 1853. 8vo. *cloth*, 1*l.* 11*s.* 6*d.*

Sozomeni Historia Ecclesiastica. Edidit R. Hussey, S.T.B. Tomi III. 1859. 8vo. *cloth*, 1*l.* 6*s.* 6*d.*

Theodoreti Ecclesiasticæ Historiæ Libri V. Recensuit T. Gaisford, S.T.P. 1854. 8vo. *cloth*, 7*s.* 6*d.*

Dowling (J. G.) Notitia Scriptorum SS. Patrum aliorumque vet. Eccles. Mon. quæ in Collectionibus Anecdotorum post annum Christi MDCC. in lucem editis continentur. 1839. 8vo. *cloth*, 4*s.* 6*d.*

ECCLESIASTICAL HISTORY.

Bedæ Historia Ecclesiastica. Cura R. Hussey, S.T.B. 1846. 8vo. *cloth*, 7*s.* 6*d.*

Bingham's Antiquities of the Christian Church, and other Works. 1855. 10 vols. 8vo. *cloth*, 3*l.* 5*s.*

Burnet's History of the Reformation of the Church of England. *A new Edition.* Carefully revised, and the Records collated with the originals, by N. Pocock, M.A. With a Preface by the Editor. 1865. 7 vols. 8vo. *cloth*, 4*l.* 4*s.*

Fuller's Church History of Britain, edited by J. S. Brewer, M.A. 1845. 6 vols. 8vo. *cloth*, 1*l.* 19*s.*

Hussey's Rise of the Papal Power traced in three Lectures. *Second Edition.* 1863. fcap. 8vo. *cloth*, 4*s.* 6*d.*

Inett's Origines Anglicanæ (in continuation of Stillingfleet), edited by J. Griffiths, M.A. 1855. 3 vols. 8vo. *cloth*, 1*l.* 11*s.* 6*d.*

John, Bishop of Ephesus, The Third Part of the Ecclesiastical History of. [In Syriac.] Now first edited by William Cureton, M.A. 1853. 4to. *cloth*, 1*l.* 12*s.*

The same, translated by R. Payne Smith, M.A. 1860. 8vo. *cloth*, 10*s.*

Le Neve's Fasti Ecclesiæ Anglicanæ, *corrected and continued from* 1715 *to* 1853 by T. Duffus Hardy. 1854. 3 vols. 8vo. *cloth*, 1*l.* 17*s.* 6*d.*

Prideaux's Connection of Sacred and Profane History. 1851. 2 vols. 8vo. *cloth*, 10s.

Shuckford's Sacred and Profane History connected (in continuation of Prideaux). 1848. 2 vols. 8vo. *cloth*, 10s.

Shirley (W. W.) Some Account of the Church in the Apostolic Age. 1867. fcap. 8vo. *cloth*, 3s. 6d.

Stillingfleet's Origines Britannicæ, with Lloyd's Historical Account of Church Government, edited by T. P. Pantin, M.A. 1842. 2 vols. 8vo. *cloth*, 13s.

Stubbs' (W.) Registrum Sacrum Anglicanum. An attempt to exhibit the course of Episcopal Succession in England. 1858. small 4to. *cloth*, 8s. 6d.

ENGLISH THEOLOGY.

Beveridge's Discourse upon the XXXIX Articles. *The third complete Edition.* 1847. 8vo. *cloth*, 8s.

Bull's (Bp.) Works, with Nelson's Life, by E. Burton, D.D. *A new Edition.* 1846. 8 vols. 8vo. *cloth*, 2l. 9s.

Burnet's Exposition of the XXXIX Articles. 1846. 8vo. *cloth*, 7s.

Butler's Works, with an Index to the Analogy. 1849. 2 vols. 8vo. *cloth*, 11s.

Butler's Analogy of Religion. 1833. 12mo. *cloth*, 2s. 6d.

Cranmer's Works, collected and arranged by H. Jenkyns, M.A., Fellow of Oriel College. 1834. 4 vols. 8vo. *cloth*, 1l. 10s.

Clergyman's Instructor. *Sixth Edition.* 1855. 8vo. *cloth*, 6s. 6d.

Enchiridion Theologicum Anti-Romanum.

> Vol. I. Jeremy Taylor's Dissuasive from Popery, and Treatise on the Real Presence. 1852. 8vo. *cloth*, 8s.
>
> Vol. II. Barrow on the Supremacy of the Pope, with his Discourse on the Unity of the Church. 1852. 8vo. *cloth*, 7s. 6d.
>
> Vol. III. Tracts selected from Wake, Patrick, Stillingfleet, Clagett, and others. 1837. 8vo. *cloth*, 11s.

Fell's Paraphrase and Annotations on the Epistles of St. Paul. 1852. 8vo. *cloth*, 7s.

Hall's (Bp.) Works. *A new Edition*, by Philip Wynter, D.D. 1863. 10 vols. 8vo. *cloth*, 5l. 5s.

Hammond's Paraphrase and Annotations on the New Testament. 1845. 4 vols. 8vo. *cloth*, 1l. 10s.

Hammond's Paraphrase on the Book of Psalms. 1850. 2 vols. 8vo. *cloth*, 1l. 1s.

Heurtley's Collection of Creeds. 1858. 8vo. *cloth, 6s. 6d.*

Hooker's Works, with his Life by Walton, arranged by John Keble, M.A. *Fifth Edition.* 1865. 3 vols. 8vo. *cloth, 1l. 11s. 6d.*

Hooker's Works, without Keble's Notes. 1865. 2 vols. 8vo. *cloth,* 11s.

Homilies appointed to be read in Churches. Edited by J. Griffiths, M.A. 1859. 8vo. *cloth,* 10s. 6d.

Leslie's (Charles) Theological Works. 1832. 7 vols. 8vo. *cloth, 2l.*

Patrick's (Bp.) Theological Works. 1859. 9 vols. 8vo. *cloth, 3l. 14s. 6d.*

Pearson's Exposition of the Creed. Revised and corrected by E. Burton, D.D. *Fifth Edition.* 1864. 8vo. *cloth,* 10s. 6d.

Pearson's Minor Theological Works, now first collected, with a Memoir of the Author, Notes, and Index, by Edward Churton, M.A. 1844. 2 vols. 8vo. *cloth,* 14s.

Sanderson's Works, edited by W. Jacobson, D.D. 1854. 6 vols. 8vo. *cloth, 1l. 19s.*

South's Sermons. 1842. 5 vols. 8vo. *cloth, 2l. 10s. 6d.*

Stanhope's Paraphrase and Comment upon the Epistles and Gospels. *A new Edition.* 1851. 2 vols. 8vo. *cloth,* 18s.

Wall's History of Infant Baptism, with Gale's Reflections, and Wall's Defence. *A new Edition,* by Henry Cotton, D.C.L. 1862. 2 vols. 8vo. *cloth, 1l. 1s.*

Waterland's Works, with Life, by Bp. Van Mildert. *A new Edition,* with copious Indexes. 1857. 6 vols. 8vo. *cloth, 2l. 11s.*

Waterland's Review of the Doctrine of the Eucharist, with a Preface by the Bishop of Lincoln. 1868. crown 8vo. *cloth, 6s. 6d.*

Wheatly's Illustration of the Book of Common Prayer. *A new Edition.* 1846. 8vo. *cloth,* 5s.

HISTORY OF ENGLAND.

Two of the Saxon Chronicles parallel, with Supplementary Extracts from the Others. Edited, with Introduction, Notes, and a Glossarial Index, by J. Earle, M.A. 1865. 8vo. *cloth,* 16s.

Magna Carta, a careful Reprint. Edited by W. Stubbs, M.A., Regius Professor of Modern History. 1868. 4to. *stitched,* 1s.

Britton, a Treatise upon the Common Law of England, composed by order of King Edward I. The French Text carefully revised, with an English Translation, Introduction, and Notes, by F. M. Nichols, M.A. 1865. 2 vols. royal 8vo. *cloth, 1l. 16s.*

Burnet's History of His Own Time, with the suppressed Passages and Notes. 1833. 6 vols. 8vo. *cloth*, 2*l*. 10*s*.

Burnet's History of James II, with additional Notes. 1852. 8vo. *cloth*, 9*s*. 6*d*.

Burnet's Lives of James and William Dukes of Hamilton. 1852. 8vo. *cloth*, 7*s*. 6*d*.

Carte's Life of James Duke of Ormond. *A new Edition*, carefully compared with the original MSS. 1851. 6 vols. 8vo. *cloth*, 2*l*. 6*s*.

Clarendon's (Edw. Earl of) History of the Rebellion and Civil Wars in England, carefully printed from the original MS. in the Bodleian Library. To which are subjoined the Notes of Bishop Warburton. 1849. 7 vols. medium 8vo. *cloth*, 2*l*. 10*s*.

Clarendon's (Edw. Earl of) History of the Rebellion and Civil Wars in England. 1839. 7 vols. 18mo. *cloth*, 1*l*. 1*s*.

Clarendon's (Edw. Earl of) History of the Rebellion and Civil Wars in England. Also His Life, written by Himself, in which is included a Continuation of his History of the Grand Rebellion. With copious Indexes. 1842. In one volume, royal 8vo. *cloth*, 1*l*. 2*s*.

Clarendon's (Edw. Earl of) Life, including a Continuation of his History, carefully printed from the original MS. in the Bodleian Library. 1857. 2 vols. medium 8vo. *cloth*, 1*l*. 2*s*.

Freeman's (E. A.) History of the Norman Conquest of England: its Causes and Results. Vols. I. and II. 8vo. *cloth*, each 18*s*.

Luttrell's (Narcissus) Diary. A Brief Historical Relation of State Affairs, 1678–1714. 1857. 6 vols. 8vo. *cloth*, 3*l*. 3*s*.

May's History of the Long Parliament. 1854. 8vo. *cloth*, 6*s*. 6*d*.

Rogers' History of Agriculture and Prices in England, A.D. 1259–1400. 2 vols. 8vo. *cloth*, 2*l*. 2*s*.

Sprigg's England's Recovery; being the History of the Army under Sir Thomas Fairfax. *A new Edition*. 1854. 8vo. *cloth*, 6*s*.

Whitelock's Memorials of English Affairs from 1625 to 1660. 1853. 4 vols. 8vo. *cloth*, 1*l*. 10*s*.

Ordinances and Statutes [for Colleges and Halls] framed or approved by the Oxford University Commissioners. 1863. 8vo. *cloth*, 12*s*.

MATHEMATICS, PHYSICAL SCIENCE, &c.

Archimedis quæ supersunt omnia cum Eutocii commentariis ex recensione Josephi Torelli, cum novâ versione Latinâ. 1792. folio. *cloth*, 1*l*. 5*s*.

Bacon's Novum Organum, edited, with English notes, by G. W. Kitchin, M.A. 1855. 8vo. *cloth*, 9*s*. 6*d*.

Bacon's Novum Organum, translated by G. W. Kitchin, M.A. 1855. 8vo. *cloth*, 9*s*. 6*d*.

The Works of George Berkeley, D.D., formerly Bishop of Cloyne. Collected and edited, from published and unpublished sources, with Prefaces, Notes, Dissertations, and an Account of his Life and Philosophy. By Alexander Campbell Fraser, M.A., Professor of Logic and Metaphysics in the University of Edinburgh. *In the Press.*

Bradley's Miscellaneous Works and Correspondence. With an Account of Harriot's Astronomical Papers. 1832. 4to. *cloth*, 17s.

Reduction of Bradley's Observations by Dr. Busch. 1838. 4to. *cloth*, 3s.

Enunciations of the Propositions of Euclid. 1862. fcap. 8vo. *limp cloth*, 1s.

Treatise on Infinitesimal Calculus. By Bartholomew Price, M.A., F.R.S., Professor of Natural Philosophy, Oxford.

    Vol. I. Differential Calculus. *Second Edition.* 1858. 8vo. *cloth*, 14s. 6d.

    Vol. II. Integral Calculus, Calculus of Variations, and Differential Equations. *Second Edition.* 1865. 8vo. *cloth*, 18s.

    Vol. III. Statics, including Attractions; Dynamics of a Material Particle. 1856. 8vo. *cloth*, 14s. 6d.

    Vol. IV. Dynamics of Material Systems; together with a Chapter on Theoretical Dynamics, by W. F. Donkin, M.A., F.R.S. 1862. 8vo. *cloth*, 16s.

An Account of Vesuvius and its Eruptions, by John Phillips, M.A., F.R.S., Professor of Geology, Oxford. *In the Press.*

Thesaurus Entomologicus Hopeianus, or a Description, with Plates, of the rarest Insects in the Collection given to the University by the Rev. William Hope. By J. O. Westwood, M.A., Hope Professor of Zoology. *Preparing.*

The Delegates of the Clarendon Press have also undertaken the publication of a series of works, chiefly educational, and entitled the 𝕮𝖑𝖆𝖗𝖊𝖓𝖉𝖔𝖓 𝕻𝖗𝖊𝖘𝖘 𝕾𝖊𝖗𝖎𝖊𝖘, in which the following are either published or in course of preparation.

I. CLASSICS, &c.

Cicero's Philippic Orations. With English Notes, by J. R. King, M.A., formerly Fellow and Tutor of Merton College, Oxford. Demy 8vo. *cloth*, 10s. 6d.

Cornelius Nepos. With English Notes, by Oscar Browning, M.A., Fellow of King's College, Cambridge, and Assistant Master at Eton College. Ext. fcap. 8vo. *cloth*, 2s. 6d.

Ovid. Selections for the use of Schools. With Introductions and Notes, and an Appendix on the Roman Calendar. By W. Ramsay, M.A., Author of "Manual of Roman Antiquities," &c. Edited by G. G. Ramsay, M.A. Ext. fcap. 8vo. *cloth*, 5s. 6d.

Passages for Translation into Latin. For the use of Passmen and others. Selected by J. Y. Sargent, M.A., Tutor, and formerly Fellow of Magdalen College, Oxford. *Second Edition.* Ext. fcap. 8vo. *cloth*, 2s. 6d.

Greek Verbs, Irregular and Defective; their forms, meaning, and quantity; embracing all the Tenses used by Greek writers, with references to the passages in which they are found. By W. Veitch. *New and revised Edition.* Ext. fcap. 8vo. *cloth*, 616 pp., 8s. 6d.

Sophocles. Œdipus Rex, Dindorf's Text, with English Notes by the Ven. Archdeacon Basil Jones, M.A., formerly Fellow of University College, Oxford. Ext. fcap. 8vo. *limp cloth*, 1s. 6d.

The Golden Treasury of Ancient Greek Poetry; being a Collection of the finest passages in the Greek Classic Poets, with Introductory Notices and Notes. By R. S. Wright, M.A., Fellow of Oriel College, Oxford. Ext. fcap. 8vo. *cloth*, 8s. 6d.

The Elements of Greek Accentuation (for Schools): abridged from his larger work by H. W. Chandler, M.A., Waynflete Professor of Moral and Metaphysical Philosophy, Oxford. Ext. fcap. 8vo. *cloth*, 2s. 6d.

Selections from the less known Latin Poets. By North Pinder, M.A., formerly Fellow of Trinity College, Oxford. *In the Press.*

Livy, Books I-X. By J. R. Seeley, M.A., Fellow of Christ's College, Cambridge; Professor of Latin, University College, London. *In the Press.*
Also a small edition for Schools.

Theocritus (for Schools). With English Notes, by H. Snow, M.A., Fellow of King's College, Cambridge, and Assistant Master at Eton College.

Sophocles. By Lewis Campbell, M.A., Professor of Greek at St. Andrews, formerly Fellow of Queen's College, Oxford.

Homer, Iliad. By D. B. Monro, M.A., Fellow and Tutor of Oriel College, Oxford.

Homer, Odyssey, Books I-XII. By W. W. Merry, Fellow and Lecturer of Lincoln College, Oxford; and the late James Riddell, M.A., Fellow of Balliol College, Oxford.

Homer, Odyssey, Books XIII-XXIV. By Robinson Ellis, M.A., Fellow of Trinity College, Oxford.

A Golden Treasury of Greek Prose, being a collection of the finest passages in the principal Greek Prose Writers, with Introductory Notices and Notes. By R. S. Wright, M.A., Fellow of Oriel College, Oxford, and J. E. L. Shadwell, B.A., Student of Christ Church.

Horace. With English Notes and Introduction. By Edward C. Wickham, M.A., Fellow and Tutor of New College, Oxford.
Also a small edition for Schools.

Cicero. Select Letters. By Albert Watson, M.A., Fellow and Tutor of Brasenose College, Oxford.

Aristotle's Politics. By W. L. Newman, M.A., Fellow and Lecturer of Balliol College, and Reader in Ancient History, Oxford.

Selections from Xenophon (for Schools). With English Notes and Maps, by J. S. Phillpotts, B.C.L., Fellow of New College, Oxford, and Assistant Master in Rugby School.

Caesar. The Commentaries (for Schools). Part I. The Gallic War, with English Notes, &c., by Charles E. Moberly, M.A., Assistant Master in Rugby School; formerly Scholar of Balliol College, Oxford.

Also, to follow: Part II. The Civil War: by the same Editor.

Select Epistles of Cicero and Pliny (for Schools). With English Notes, by C. E. Prichard, M.A., formerly Fellow of Balliol College, Oxford.

Selections from Plato (for Schools). With English Notes, by B. Jowett, M.A., Regius Professor of Greek, and J. Purves, M.A., Fellow and Lecturer of Balliol College, Oxford.

II. MENTAL AND MORAL PHILOSOPHY.

The Elements of Deductive Logic, designed mainly for the use of Junior Students in the Universities. By T. Fowler, M.A., Fellow and Tutor of Lincoln College, Oxford. *Second Edition*, with a Collection of Examination Papers on the subject. Ext. fcap. 8vo. *cloth*, 3s. 6d.

A Manual of Political Economy, for the use of Schools. By J. E. Thorold Rogers, M.A., formerly Professor of Political Economy, Oxford. Ext. fcap. 8vo. *cloth*, 4s. 6d.

III. MATHEMATICS.

Quaternions, An Elementary Treatise on. By P. G. Tait, M.A., Professor of Natural Philosophy in the University of Edinburgh; formerly Fellow of St. Peter's College, Cambridge. Demy 8vo. *cloth*, 12s. 6d.

Book-keeping. By R. G. C. Hamilton, Accountant to the Education Committee of the Privy Council, and John Ball (of the Firm of Messrs. Quilter, Ball, & Co.), Examiners in Book-keeping for the Society of Arts' Examination. Ext. fcap. 8vo. *limp cloth*, 1s. 6d.

Pure Geometry, A Course of Lectures on. By H. J. Stephen Smith, M.A., F.R.S., Fellow of Balliol College, and Savilian Professor of Geometry in the University of Oxford.

A Treatise on Electricity and Magnetism. By J. Clerk Maxwell, M.A., F.R.S., formerly Professor of Natural Philosophy, King's College, London.

A Series of Elementary Works is being arranged, and will shortly be announced.

IV. HISTORY.

A History of Germany and of the Empire, down to the close of the Middle Ages. By J. Bryce, M.A., Fellow of Oriel College, Oxford.

A History of British India. By S. Owen, M.A., Lee's Reader in Law and History, Christ Church; and Reader in Indian Law in the University of Oxford.

A History of Greece. By E. A. Freeman, M.A., formerly Fellow of Trinity College, Oxford.

A Constitutional History of England. By W. Stubbs, M.A., formerly Fellow of Trinity College, Oxford, and Regius Professor of Modern History in the University of Oxford.

A History of Germany, from the Reformation. By Adolphus W. Ward, M.A., Fellow of St. Peter's College, Cambridge; Professor of History, Owen's College, Manchester.

V. LAW.

Roman Law, Commentaries on; from the original and the best modern sources. By H. J. Roby, M.A., formerly Fellow of St. John's College, Cambridge; Professor of Law at University College, London. 2 vols. Demy 8vo.

VI. PHYSICAL SCIENCE.

Natural Philosophy. In four Volumes. By Sir W. Thomson, LL.D., D.C.L., F.R.S., Professor of Natural Philosophy, Glasgow, and P. G. Tait, M.A., Professor of Natural Philosophy, Edinburgh; formerly Fellows of St. Peter's College, Cambridge. Vol. I. *now ready*, 8vo. *cloth*, 1*l*. 5*s*.

By the same Authors, a smaller Work on the same subject, forming a complete Introduction to it, so far as it can be carried out with Elementary Geometry and Algebra. *In the Press.*

Descriptive Astronomy. A Handbook for the General Reader, and also for practical Observatory work. With 224 illustrations and numerous tables. By G. F. Chambers, F.R.A.S., Barrister-at-Law. Demy 8vo. 856 pp., *cloth*, 1*l*. 1*s*.

Chemistry for Students. By A. W. Williamson, Phil. Doc., F.R.S., Professor of Chemistry, University College, London. Ext. fcap. 8vo. *cloth*, 8*s*. 6*d*. A new, enlarged, and revised Edition. *Just published.*

Heat, Treatise on, with numerous Woodcuts and Diagrams. By Balfour Stewart, LL.D., F.R.S., Director of the Observatory at Kew. Ext. fcap. 8vo. *cloth*, 7*s*. 6*d*.

Forms of Animal Life. By G. Rolleston, D.M., F.R.S., Linacre Professor of Physiology, Oxford. Illustrated by Descriptions and Drawings of Dissections. *In the Press.*

On Laboratory Practice. By A. Vernon Harcourt, M.A., F.R.S., Lee's Reader in Chemistry at Christ Church, and H. G. Madan, M.A., Fellow of Queen's College, Oxford. *In the Press.*

Geology. By J. Phillips, M.A., F.R.S., Professor of Geology, Oxford.

Mechanics. By Bartholomew Price, M.A., F.R.S., Sedleian Professor of Natural Philosophy, Oxford.

Acoustics. By W. F. Donkin, M.A., F.R.S., Savilian Professor of Astronomy, Oxford.

Optics. By R. B. Clifton, M.A., F.R.S., Professor of Experimental Philosophy, Oxford; formerly Fellow of St. John's College, Cambridge.

Electricity. By W. Esson, M.A., Fellow and Mathematical Lecturer of Merton College, Oxford.

Crystallography. By M. H. N. Story-Maskelyne, M.A., Professor of Mineralogy, Oxford; and Deputy Keeper, British Museum.

Mineralogy. By the same Author.

Physiological Physics. By G. Griffith, M.A., Assistant Secretary to the British Association, and Natural Science Master at Harrow School.

Magnetism.

VII.—ENGLISH LANGUAGE AND LITERATURE.

On the Principles of Grammar. By E. Thring, M.A., Head Master of Uppingham School. Ext. fcap. 8vo. *cloth*, 4s. 6d.

Grammatical Analysis, designed to serve as an Exercise and Composition Book in the English Language. By E. Thring, M.A., Head Master of Uppingham School. Ext. fcap. 8vo. *cloth*, 3s. 6d.

Specimens of Early English; being a Series of Extracts from the most important English Authors, Chronologically arranged, illustrative of the progress of the English Language and its Dialectic varieties, from A.D. 1250 to A.D. 1400. With Grammatical Introduction, Notes, and Glossary. By R. Morris, Editor of "The Story of Genesis and Exodus," &c. Ext. fcap. 8vo. *cloth*, 7s. 6d.

The Philology of the English Tongue. By J. Earle, M.A., formerly Fellow of Oriel College, Oxford, and Professor of Anglo-Saxon.

Typical Selections from the best English Authors from the Sixteenth to the Nineteenth Century, (to serve as a higher Reading Book,) with Introductory Notices and Notes, being a Contribution towards a History of English Literature.

Specimens of the Scottish Language; being a Series of Annotated Extracts illustrative of the Literature and Philology of the Lowland Tongue from the Fourteenth to the Nineteenth Century. With Introduction and Glossary. By A. H. Burgess, M.A.

VIII. FRENCH LANGUAGE AND LITERATURE.

Corneille's Cinna, and **Molière's** Les Femmes Savantes. Edited, with Introduction and Notes, by Gustave Masson. Ext. fcap. 8vo. *cloth*, 2s. 6d.

Selections from the Correspondence of **Madame de Sévigné** and her chief Contemporaries. Intended more especially for Girls' Schools. By the same Editor. Ext. fcap. 8vo. *cloth*, 3s.

Voyage autour de ma Chambre, by **Xavier de Maistre**; Ourika, by **Madame de Duras**; La Dot de Suzette, by **Fiévée**; Les Jumeaux de l'Hôtel Corneille, by **Edmond About**; Mésaventures d'un Écolier, by **Rodolphe Töpffer**. By the same Editor. Ext. fcap. 8vo. *cloth*, 2s. 6d.

Racine's Athalie, and **Corneille's** Le Menteur. With Louis Racine's Life of his Father. By the same Editor.

Molière's Les Fourberies de Scapin, and **Racine's** Andromaque. With Voltaire's Life of Molière. By the same Editor.

A French Grammar. A complete Theory of the French Language, with the rules in French and English, and numerous Examples to serve as first Exercises in the Language. By Jules Bué, Honorary M.A. of Oxford; Taylorian Teacher of French, Oxford; Examiner in the Oxford Local Examinations from 1858.

A French Grammar Test. A Book of Exercises on French Grammar; each Exercise being preceded by Grammatical Questions. By the same Author.

Exercises in Translation No. 1, from French into English, with general rules on Translation; and containing Notes, Hints, and Cautions, founded on a comparison of the Grammar and Genius of the two Languages. By the same Author.

Exercises in Translation No. 2, from English into French, on the same plan as the preceding book. By the same Author.

IX. GERMAN LANGUAGE AND LITERATURE.

Schiller's Wilhelm Tell. With a Life of Schiller; an historical and critical Introduction, Arguments, and a complete Commentary. By Dr. Buchheim, Professor of the German Language and Literature in King's College, London; and Examiner in German to the University of London. *In the Press.*

Goethe's Egmont. With a Life of Goethe, &c. By the same Editor. *In the Press.*

Lessing's Minna von Barnhelm. A Comedy. With a Life of Lessing, Critical Commentary, &c. By the same Editor.

X. ART, &c.

A Handbook of Pictorial Art. By R. St. J. Tyrwhitt, M.A., formerly Student and Tutor of Christ Church, Oxford. With coloured Illustrations, Photographs, and a chapter on Perspective by A. Macdonald. 8vo. *half morocco*, 18s.

A Treatise on Harmony. By Sir F. A. Gore Ouseley, Bart., M.A., Mus. Doc., Professor of Music in the University of Oxford. 4to. *cloth*, 10s.

A Treatise on Counterpoint, Canon, and Fugue, based upon that of Cherubini. By the same Author. *In the Press.*

A System of Physical Education: Theoretical and Practical. By Archibald Maclaren, The Gymnasium, Oxford. *In the Press.*

XI. ENGLISH CLASSICS.

Designed to meet the wants of Students in English Literature: under the superintendence of the Rev. J. S. BREWER, M.A., *of Queen's College, Oxford, and Professor of English Literature at King's College, London.*

A General Introduction to the Series. By Professor Brewer, M.A.

Chaucer. The Prologue to the Canterbury Tales; The Knightes Tale; The Nonne Prest his Tale. Edited by R. Morris, Editor for the Early English Text Society, &c., &c. Ext. fcap. 8vo. *cloth*, 2s. 6d.

Spenser's Faery Queene. Books I and II. Designed chiefly for the use of Schools. With Introduction, Notes, and Glossary. By G. W. Kitchin, M.A., formerly Censor of Christ Church. Ext. fcap. 8vo. *cloth*, 2s. 6d. each.

Hooker. Ecclesiastical Polity, Book I. Edited by R. W. Church, M.A., Rector of Whatley; formerly Fellow of Oriel College. Ext. fcap. 8vo. *cloth*, 2s.

Shakespeare. Select Plays. Edited by W. G. Clark, M.A., Fellow of Trinity College, Cambridge, and Public Orator; and W. Aldis Wright, M.A., Librarian of Trinity College, Cambridge.

    I. The Merchant of Venice. Ext. fcap. 8vo. *limp cloth*, 1s. *Just published.*

    II. Richard the Second. *In the Press.*

Bacon. Advancement of Learning. Edited by W. Aldis Wright, M.A. *In the Press.*

Milton. Allegro and Penseroso; Comus; Lycidas; Paradise Lost; Samson Agonistes. Edited by R. C. Browne, M.A., King's College, Cambridge.

Dryden. Stanzas on the Death of Oliver Cromwell; Astræa Redux; Annus Mirabilis; Absalom and Achitophel; Religio Laici; The Hind and Panther.

Bunyan. Grace Abounding; The Pilgrim's Progress. Edited by E. Venables, M.A., Precentor of Lincoln.

Pope. Essay on Man, with the Epistles and Satires. Edited by M. Pattison, B.D., Rector of Lincoln College, Oxford.

Johnson. Rasselas; Lives of Pope and Dryden. Edited by C. H. O. Daniel, M.A., Fellow and Tutor of Worcester College, Oxford.

Burke. Thoughts on the Present Discontents; the two Speeches on America; Reflections on the French Revolution. Edited by Goldwin Smith, M.A., Fellow of University College, Oxford; formerly Regius Professor of Modern History.

Cowper. The Task, and some of his minor Poems. Edited by J. C. Shairp, M.A., Professor of Humanity, St. Andrew's.

www.ingramcontent.com/pod-product-compliance
Lightning Source LLC
Chambersburg PA
CBHW030424300426
44112CB00009B/835